The System of Doctrines, contained in Divine Relation, Explained and Defended
Volume I
By Samuel Hopkins D. D. (1721-1803)
Edited by Anthony Uyl

Woodstock, Ontario, 2017

The System of Doctrines, contained in Divine Relation, Explained and Defended Volume I

The System of Doctrines, contained in Divine Relation, Explained and Defended

Shewing Their Consistence and Connexion with Each Other.

Volume I

To Which is Added, A Treatise on the Millenium

In Two Volumes

By Samuel Hopkins D. D. (1721-1803)

Late Pastor of the 1st Congregational Church in Newport

Edited by Anthony Uyl

Originally Published by:
Boston: Printed and Published by Lincoln & Edmands, No. 53 Cornhill. 1811.
Published according to Act of Congress.

The text of The System of Doctrines, contained in Divine Relation, Explained and Defended Volume I is all in the Public Domain. The cover and layout is Copyright ©2017 Devoted Publishing. This edition is published by Devoted Publishing a division of 2165467 Ontario Inc.

**What kind of philosophies do you have?
Let us know!**

Contact us at: devotedpub@hotmail.com
Visit our shop on Facebook: @DevotedPublishing

Published in Woodstock, Ontario, Canada 2017

For bulk educational rates, please contact us at the above email address.

ISBN: 978-1-77356-073-1

Table of Contents

PREFACE 4
PART I 6
   CHAPTER I - CONCERNING DIVINE REVELATION 6
      Footnotes: 17
   CHAPTER II - CONCERNING THE BEING AND PERFECTIONS OF GOD 19
      Footnotes: 33
   CHAPTER III - CONCERNING THE UNITY OF GOD; AND THE TRINITY 34
      Footnotes: 37
   CHAPTER IV - ON THE DECREES OF GOD 38
      Footnotes: 75
   CHAPTER V - CONCERNING THE CREATION OF THE WORLD, PARTICULARLY OF MAN 80
      Footnotes: 86
   CHAPTER VI - CONCERNING DIVINE PROVIDENCE IN GENERAL 87
      Footnotes: 89
   CHAPTER VII - ON THE PROVIDENCE OF GOD, AS IT RESPECTS MORAL AGENTS, ANGELS AND MEN 90
      Footnotes: 107
   CHAPTER VIII - ON THE APOSTASY OF MAN, AND THE EVIL CONSEQUENCE TO HIM 108
      Footnotes: 126
PART II 128
   CHAPTER I - CONCERNING THE REDEMPTION OF FALLEN, LOST MAN, BY JESUS CHRIST 128
      Footnotes: 136
   CHAPTER II - CONCERNING THE PERSON AND CHARACTER OF THE REDEEMER 138
      Footnotes: 162
   CHAPTER III - CONCERNING THE DESIGN AND WORK OF THE REDEEMER 166
      Footnotes: 185
   CHAPTER IV - ON THE APPLICATION OF REDEMPTION 188
      Footnotes: 214

PREFACE

SYSTEMATIC Divinity is considered and treated, by many, with slight and contempt. And if a book be written in this form, and published under the title of a System or Body of Divinity, this is a sufficient reason, with them, to neglect it, as not worthy their attention. But can this be supported by any good reason? Is not a System of Divinity as proper and important, as a System of Jurisprudence, Physic, or natural Philosophy?

If the Bible be a revelation from heaven, it contains a System of consistent important Doctrines; which are so connected, and implied in each other, that one cannot be so well understood, if detached from all the rest, and considered by itself; and some must be first known, before others can be seen in a proper and true light. When all these are stated, and explained, according to Scripture, and in their true order, connection and dependence, a System of Doctrines is formed. This every person must do in some measure and degree, who understands the Bible. And he who would assist others in doing this, and set the Doctrines of Christianity in a clear light, and to the best advantage to be understood, will, of course, form a System of Truths. And so far as he falls short of this, or deviates from it, he must be defective and confused.

If the following System do indeed contain the chief and most important doctrines of Christianity; and they be, in any good measure, explained and vindicated, shewing their consistence and connection with each other, the reader, it is hoped, will get some advantage by it. If it should be thought by any that it contains great errors and inconsistencies, it is to be wished, for their sake, and for the sake of truth, that they would not confidently rest in their conclusion, or drop the subject, till they are able to fix on a system of truths more consistent, and which can be better supported by the scripture, and are more agreeable to sound reason.

It is presumed, the author will not be suspected of going through the labour of composing the following work with a view of rendering himself popular, and obtaining the general applause; or that he has sought to "please men." The most that can be reasonably expected, is, that it may serve to confirm the friends of truth in the doctrines contained in the scripture; and enlighten some of those who have been in the dark respecting some truths, and have been inconsistent with themselves in the doctrines they have espoused: And that it may assist the honest inquirers to see what are the leading and most important doctrines of divine revelation; particularly those who are candidates for the evangelical ministry.

It is not pretended that every doctrine of Christianity is expressly mentioned in this System; but that the most important and essential truths are brought into view: And of these some are treated more concisely; and others are more particularly examined and vindicated, as was judged most convenient and useful. Nor was it thought necessary, or expedient, to mention all the objections which have been made to the doctrines here advanced, as they are sufficiently obviated, by establishing the truth, from scripture and reason; and as this would have enlarged the work to an undesirable length: Those only are mentioned, by an answer to which, the truth is more explained and established.

The same sentiments are brought into view, and repeated, in a number of instances; which could not well be avoided, in such a work: And it is hoped, that such repetitions will not be inconvenient or tedious to the reader.

To the most correct and elegant style, the author makes no pretension; as this is not his talent. If the words and expressions be not ambiguous, but are suited to convey the ideas, designed to be communicated to the mind of the reader, with ease and clearness, the chief and most important end of language is answered: And it is hoped, that they who are, with proper attention and concern, inquiring after the truth, will exercise so much candour, as not to be offended, or slight it, though it be not expressed in words and a style, more agreeable to their nice and critical taste; and they may observe a number of inaccuracies.

This work has been undertaken and prosecuted, under a conviction, that a performance of this kind is much wanted; and, if well executed, would be very useful, and greatly serve the cause of truth and religion. It is to be wished there were a more able hand, disposed to execute it: But as none appeared to do it, the author has done his best. Yet he doubts not that there are many defects; and is not confident that he has made no mistakes in less important points; while he has not the least doubt that the chief and leading doctrines here advanced are contained in the Bible, and are important and everlasting truths: And that all those sentiments, and schemes of doctrine and religion, which are wholly inconsistent with these, and contrary to them, are not consistent with the Bible, or with one another; and, if followed in their just consequences, will lead to universal scepticism, and, which is the same indeed, to the horrible darkness of atheism itself.

The truth is great, and has omnipotence to support it; and therefore will prevail: And all erroneous doctrines, and false religion, will be utterly abolished. And there is no reason to doubt, that light wall so increase in the church, and men will be raised up, who will make such advances in opening the scripture, and in the knowledge of divine truth; that what is now done and written, will be so far superseded, as to appear imperfect and inconsiderable, compared with that superior light, with which the church will then be blessed. Nevertheless, if publishing that to which we have now attained, may be a mean of making such advances, and a proper and necessary step to it, the labour and expense of doing it, will be abundantly compensated.

Newport, August 20, 1792.

PART I

CHAPTER I - CONCERNING DIVINE REVELATION

IT is evident from reason, fact and experience, that mankind stand in need of a revelation from God, in order to know what God is--what is their own true state and moral character--whether he be reconcileable to them, who have rebelled against him--and if he be, what is the method he has appointed, in which he will be reconciled; and what man must be and do, in order to find acceptance in his sight: Wherein true happiness consists--whether there be another state--what are the favours he will grant in a future state, to those who serve and please him in this life--what are his grand designs in creating and governing the world, &c. The ignorance and uncertainty, with respect to these most important points, in which all men have been and still are, who have enjoyed no such revelation, is a constant, striking evidence of this.

There are, indeed, those who refuse to admit this evidence; and insist that human reason alone, unassisted by any revelation, except what is made in the works of creation and providence, is sufficient to investigate every necessary and important truth; and therefore think themselves authorized to reject and despise every other revelation that pretends to come from God, as the contrivance and production of designing, or weak, deluded men. But while they entertain so high an opinion of human reason, and especially their own, in the face of the glaring evidence from fact and experiment, just now mentioned, they have produced an incontestible evidence of their own sad mistake; for upon examination, the writings of the deists are found to contain numerous contradictions to each other, on points of the highest moment; and most of them have embraced for truth, many tenets most unreasonable and absurd. Thus, when they have renounced revelation, and boasted of their own reason, and relied upon that, as a sufficient and infallible guide, they have all, or most of them, run into darkness and delusion. And at the same time, there is abundant evidence, that all the real light and knowledge they appear to have in divine things, which they attribute to the unassisted exercise of their own reason, and which is more than the benighted heathen have, originated from that very revelation, which they discard and despise. With great propriety therefore they have been compared to a man who is in a room, illuminated by the bright shining of a candle, and thereby is assisted to behold the objects around him distinctly: But being ignorant of the assistance which he has from the candle, imagines he discerns those objects by the strength of his own sight; and therefore despises and endeavours to extinguish that light, which, if withdrawn, would leave him wholly in the dark. [1] Besides, there is this farther evidence against them, and in favour of the revelation which they renounce, viz. It does not appear, that by all their writings and attempts, they have made any reformation in the morals of men, or that so much as one man has been reclaimed from a vicious course of life, and become sober, humble, benevolent, pious and devout, by being made a convert to them: But, on the contrary, most, if not all their disciples, are of a character directly the reverse of this; and they are most admired by men of vicious character, or who at least are evidently without those virtues which are essential to constitute a truly religious man.

Moreover, if the revelation they discard represents men to be in such a state of depravity and vicious blindness, as to be disposed to shut their eyes against the clearest light, and to treat it as these men in fact do treat the Bible; and foretells this same treatment and conduct of theirs, as it certainly does; while they are thus slighting and rejecting it, they are really giving a strong evidence of its divine original.

But, to return: The usefulness and necessity of such a revelation is abundantly evident from fact, and has been implicitly or expressly acknowledged by many of the most wise and inquisitive among the heathen. [2] Hence we may conclude, that God has given one to men: And when we find ourselves in possession of a book which has all the marks and evidence that we can reasonably expect or desire, that it is indeed from God, and suited to answer all the ends of a divine revelation, we shall be very criminal, if we do not receive it with gratitude, and improve it to promote all the important purposes for which it is given.

Such a revelation we find to be contained in the book called the Bible, or the holy scriptures. For while all other pretended revelations from God, which have been, or now are found among men, are without all proper evidence of their being such, and carry evident marks of imposture, which has been abundantly demonstrated, by those who have examined them: This has stood the test of the severest scrutiny both of its friends and enemies, and the more it has been examined, the more clearly does it appear, that all the objections which have been made against it are futile and groundless; and that there is sufficient and abundant evidence, that it is from God, suited to give satisfaction and a well grounded assurance of its divine original, to every impartial, honest mind.

The first part of this book was written by Moses, after he had given abundant evidence, by a series of astonishing miracles, done in the sight of the Egyptians, and all Israel, that he spake and acted, under the influence and direction of the supreme Ruler of the universe, and had sufficiently established his character, as a prophet divinely inspired. Moses said he was sent by Jehovah, the only true God, the God of Israel, to demand of Pharaoh, the king of Egypt, to let his people go out from under his oppressive hand; and foretold that if he refused to do it, God would slay his first born son. Pharaoh said he knew not who Jehovah was, and bid defiance to him, declaring he would pay no regard to his demand. This gave opportunity for an open trial and decision, whether Jehovah, the God of Israel, was the true God, or the gods of Pharaoh and the Egyptians. The priests and the magicians of Egypt were collected, and entered the dispute with Moses. They wrought several miracles, in imitation of those which Moses did in the name of the God of Israel; but there was an evident, decided superiority in those wrought by Jehovah. And the contest went on, till at length they were not able to stand before Moses, and confessed publicly that Jehovah was God, and superior to theirs. Moses went on doing wonders, in the sight of all Egypt, and inflicting various successive judgments on Pharaoh, and on the Egyptians; at the same time particularly foretelling the miraculous chastisement which Jehovah had revealed to him he would inflict. At length, Moses informed Pharaoh, that if he should still persist in refusing to let Israel go out of Egypt, Jehovah had said to him, that he would slay all the first born in Egypt; and this was foretold to all Israel; which accordingly came to pass: And the Egyptians were made to fear and tremble before the God of Israel, and entreated his people to pray to him for them, acknowledging he was the supreme God. Thus Israel went out of Egypt, as Jehovah had promised they should, and were led through the Red Sea, the waters dividing to make them a way, at the direction and command of their God; while Pharaoh and the Egyptians, who were so hardy as to follow them, were all drowned in the waters. Thus Jehovah publicly triumphed over all the gods of Egypt, and executed judgment upon them; and by the fullest and most incontestible evidence established his character as the only true God. The people of Israel felt, and solemnly acknowledged this, at the Red Sea; and they were led on by the hand of Moses, attended with a constant course of miracles, unto Mount Sinai. On that Mount, God appeared in a manner suited to manifest his presence and awful glorious majesty, and excite their utmost attention, fear and reverence; and then, from the top of the mountain, out of the fire, with a voice that could be distinctly heard by all that vast multitude, consisting of at least three millions of people, he spake the ten commandments, and added no more. They were after wards written on two tables of stone, by the finger of God; which was most probably the first writing by letters in this world: [3] And Moses, being taught of God to read it, and so how to write, was directed and inspired by God to write the history of the creation of the world, and the events which had taken place since; and of mankind, so far as was necessary these things should be recorded and known; and, more particularly, the history of the origin of the Hebrews, and the events of divine providence respecting them. As this is the first, and oldest, so it is the only authentic history of the creation of the world, and of mankind, from the beginning to that time, which is an era of about two thousand five hundred years. Moses also wrote a code of laws for that people, which he said were dictated to him by God, containing many promises and threatenings, together with a number of typical institutions, which were shadows of things to come. And there are many predictions in his writings, which have already come to pass; especially that God would raise up unto them that great prophet, the Messiah, of whom he himself was a type; and if they would not hear him, they should be destroyed.

God having thus established his character, as the only true God, by abundant and most clear evidence; and magnified Moses in the sight of the Egyptians and all Israel, as his servant and prophet, directed and inspired by him both to do, and to say, all that he did and said, in the name of Jehovah; he forbid them to hearken to a prophet, or any other person, who should arise and do wonders and miracles, not in the name of Jehovah, but of some other god, with a view to draw them away from obedience to the God of Israel, to worship and serve other gods. And every one who will attentively consider the subject, must at once see both the reasonableness of this injunction, and the wisdom and goodness of God in laying a proper foundation for it, and then giving it by Moses to Israel. For Jehovah having given all the evidence that could be reasonably expected or desired, by a

The System of Doctrines, contained in Divine Relation, Explained and Defended Volume I
series of public incontestible miracles, appearances, words and works, that he was the only true God; which all Israel had, under the fullest and most rational conviction, acknowledged, over and over again, and under this conviction, solemnly given themselves up to him, as their God; and promised to renounce all other gods, and cleave to, and obey Jehovah alone, as their God: It became them never from that time to call in question what had been made so abundantly evident, but with the greatest assurance, and the most sincere abhorrence, reject every thing which was evidently contrary to the light and revelation they had received; and not pay the least regard to any wonders and miracles, pretended to be done, or really wrought, to prove that Jehovah was not the only true God, and in favour of other gods.

These things have been observed, to show with what abundant evidence and assurance the church of Israel received the writings of Moses, as divine oracles, the infallible dictates of Heaven, which he was inspired to reveal and communicate; while it is at the same time acknowledged there are many other things which have not been here brought into view, which serve to strengthen this evidence, and show that to make any other supposition, and not to admit these writings as the oracles of Heaven, is most absurd, shutting the eyes against the most glaring light, and doing violence to every principle of reason.

After Moses, other prophets and inspired men were raised up to write the history of that nation; to declare the will of God, in reproving, directing and exhorting; and adding threatenings and promises, to deter them from rebellion against Jehovah, and excite them to obey him. Whose writings also contain innumerable predictions of things to come, many of which are already come to pass; those in particular which foretold the coming of the Messiah, his incarnation, death, resurrection, exaltation and reign: and the events that should attend his coming with regard both to Jews and Gentiles, &c. &c. And in these writings there is a constant reference to the things contained in the writings of Moses, the wonders wrought by his hand, when they were delivered from a state of bondage in Egypt, &c. and to the institutions and laws, which by him were given to Israel: And at the same time there is a perfect consistence and harmony, between these writings and those of Moses.

The last prophet, whose writings we have, lived about four hundred years before Christ; so that the sacred writings which were given to the church of Israel, and which they received as divine oracles, and have carefully kept and preserved, not only to the time of the incarnation of Christ, but even down to this day, were written at different times, by different men, through the space of above a thousand years, from Moses the first, to Malachi, the last writer. And yet they all agree; and the latter constantly refer to the writings of Moses, and what is contained in them; and therefore they mutually strengthen the evidence, that they all wrote by inspiration, as most of them declared they did. And Malachi concludes with foretelling the coming of Christ, and directing the church of Israel to attend to the laws and institutions of Moses, and obey them, until Christ should come; and to expect no more divine revelation, till that time; plainly intimating, that then some further revelations from God should be given to the church. [4] Thus the standing, written revelation, given to the Jewish church, was finished; and they were commanded not to attempt to make, or expect any addition to it, till the days of the Messiah.

Should it be said, that perhaps all these writings were forged by some wicked, designing man, or set of men, and that the facts and miracles therein related never did take place, nor was Moses, or any other man, inspired of God to write these things; but they were imposed upon that nation, and they were made to believe that which never had any reality: Such a supposition will appear most unreasonable, and even impossible, on the least reflection. When, and how, could this be done? How could that nation, even all of them, old and young, learned and unlearned, at any time be made to believe that all these things related in the writings of Moses, concerned them, and which he said took place publicly, and that they were seen and acknowledged by the whole nation; and that all those rites and laws had been received in a miraculous way from Jehovah, by their ancestors, and handed down, and practised from generation to generation, if there was no truth in all this; but they were all novo invented, and they never had any existence, or were heard of before, by any of them? This is perfectly incredible, and absolutely impossible. And it is equally incredible, that a whole nation should at any time receive such writings, and pretend they were all genuine and true, and handed down from their fathers, when at the same time they knew there was no truth in it, but was real imposture and delusion. Who can believe, that any nation or people under heaven, could ever be brought to do this; and receive and practise all those burdensome rites and ceremonies, and hand them down to their children as the institutions of Heaven, when they knew it was all a cheat? And this will appear yet more incredible, if possible, when we observe, that these writings give no agreeable, flattering idea of that nation, as a wise, excellent, and honourable people; but contrary to this, they are represented as a very stupid, ungrateful, rebellious people, always disposed to abuse and revolt from their God, and violate the most sacred obligations and solemn vows, by which they were constantly incurring the displeasure of Jehovah; and were severely punished, from time to time, for their horrid impiety, and most stupid idolatry, and their obstinate perseverance in shameful unrighteousness and cruelty towards each other. If a people could forge and receive a history of themselves as a nation, in which there was no truth; or if it were contrived and formed by any set of men, or by any one man among them, with a design to impose it on the nation, to be received by them as genuine; we may be sure it would be written in favour of that nation, and so as to flatter their selfishness, pride, and vanity, instead of representing them, as these writings do that nation, in a disagreeable, shameful, odious light.

Besides, these writings have no marks, not the least appearance of imposture and forgery, when most critically examined; but all appearance that can be desired, that they are genuine, and were written at the different times, and in the different circumstances, in which they are said to have been written, and by those different men: Whereas, if they were a forgery, and not written by inspiration, it cannot be supposed possible, they should carry all those marks of genuineness, and none of the contrary.

Moreover, they contain a system of truths, and point out and enjoin commands and duties to God and our neighbour, which bespeak their divine original, and are worthy to be revealed by God; and which no ungodly, selfish, designing impostor, and such these writers must be, if they wrote not by inspiration, would ever think of, and much less be disposed to publish and enjoin.

The promised Messiah at length made his appearance in the world, even at the very time in which it was foretold he should come! the way for his coming having been prepared by his harbinger, as was particularly predicted by Isaiah; and by Malachi, in the last words of the Old Testament.

It having been abundantly proved, as has been ob» served and shown, that Jehovah, the God of Israel, was the only true God, and that the writings in their hands were given by divine inspiration, in which the coming of the Messiah and his future kingdom were foretold, and particularly described; all that was now necessary, in order to his being on good ground received as king of the church, was to give proper evidence that he was the very person, the promised Saviour of the world. This was done not only by his appearing at the time, and in the character and circumstances, which were foretold by the prophets; but by working a series of miracles, done in a public manner: And by his predicting many things, which soon came to pass, especially his own death, and the particular circumstances of it; and that he would rise again on the third day. He was accordingly put to death, which his enemies as well as friends confess; and if he did rise again, as he said he would, the evidence that he was the Messiah, the same Jehovah who was the God of Israel, would be complete, and none could reasonably desire more.

That he did rise on the third day; and when he had continued on earth above forty days, conversing with his disciples and friends, and giving them instructions and commands, left the world and ascended to heaven, there were a competent number of chosen witnesses, who declared they were eye and ear witnesses of this; and that they had the most satisfactory, full and abundant evidence of it. And farther, to prove the truth of it, they had power to work innumerable miracles in the name of Jesus of Nazareth, as a testimony that he was alive, and consequently the Son of God, and Saviour of the world. And they gave up all their worldly interest in this cause; and subjected themselves to poverty, hatred and reproach of men; and to various hardships and cruel sufferings, and even to death, in bearing witness to this truth, and those that are implied in it, and preaching the gospel; which was attended by an invisible mighty power, purifying and renewing the hearts of multitudes, and leading them to renounce their former delusions and wicked ways, and to believe in Christ, and obey him; who became so many witnesses of the truth and power of Christianity.

A history of these things was written by those who had the most certain knowledge of them, and intimate acquaintance with them, giving an account of the birth, life, death and resurrection of Christ; and of the doctrines which he taught, and the instructions and commands he gave, and the miracles which were wrought by him, &c. &c. Also, a history was written of what took place for a number of years after the ascension of Christ to heaven; the promised gift of his Spirit to the apostles and others, whereby they were enabled to speak different languages, and to work miracles: Their bearing testimony for Christ, and preaching with great success, not only to the Jews, but to the Gentile nations, and erecting churches in many parts of the world, Sec. This history of Christ and his apostles is written in a manner remarkably different from that of any other history written by men not inspired. It is simple, plain and concise, consisting only in the most intelligible narration of facts, of what was said and done, without justifying or condemning any person; not giving the least encomium, or bestowing any praise on Christ himself, or any of his friends, nor saying a word in their favour; not reproaching or condemning their enemies, or any person, or speaking against them: but confining themselves to a plain history of simple facts, without any comments of their own, against any one, or in favour of him. This, by the way, is a striking evidence, among others innumerable, that these writings, "came not by the will of man;" but were composed under the direction and superintendency of the Holy Ghost, the authors being inspired

The System of Doctrines, contained in Divine Relation, Explained and Defended Volume I
and moved by him.⁵

We have also the writings of several of the apostles of Christ, containing a number of letters, which they wrote to churches, and to some particular persons, in which the doctrines and duties of Christianity, and the institutions and laws of Christ, are more particularly explained and inculcated. And last of all, there is a book, called "The revelation of Jesus Christ, which he sent and signified by his angel unto his servant John." This the apostle John wrote in his advanced age, after the destruction of Jerusalem by the Romans, when he was suffering for the cause of Christ, being banished to a desolate island, after his character had been long established as an apostle of Christ, by miracles, and a holy life. He says, he received this revelation from Christ, and was by him directed to write it, just as he here has done. It contains, among other things, a representation of the state of the church, and the great events that should take place respecting it, from that time to the end of the world, and of its perfect and glorious state from that period forever and ever; and of the endless punishment of all her implacable enemies. And many of the predictions in this book have been already accomplished: others are daily fulfilling before our eyes, which is a constant miracle, of the most indisputable kind, evidencing the divine original of this prophecy; and that the things therein foretold, which are not yet come to pass, will all be accomplished in their season.

And as the divine inspired writings, given to the Jewish church, conclude with an intimation that they should have nothing more of this kind, till the promised Messiah did come, and a command carefully to keep and observe what they had received; so this book concludes with a declaration, that there should be no addition to divinely inspired writings, given to the christian church; and therefore mankind must look for no more; but are commanded carefully to observe and obey what was then revealed, without adding any thing to it, or taking from it, until Christ shall come to judgment.

God having thus completed a revelation containing every thing he saw necessary and proper, to make it a sufficient, perfect, and unerring rule for his church to the end of the world; and every way adapted to answer all the desired ends of a divine revelation; attended with all the evidence that can be reasonably desired, that it is from God, and the whole that he ever will give; the use and end of miracles has of course ceased; and therefore the church is to expect no more, or any more prophets inspired to foretel things to come, not already foretold in the holy scriptures. And whatever pretences any may make of working miracles, and whatever miracles may be really wrought, in support of any pretended truths or institutions, or system of religion, the church of Christ has no liberty to pay the least regard to them; but ought to renounce all such pretences with abhorrence; and to hearken to them, and regard them in the least, is to renounce the Bible, and the God who has given it to his church. Nor have we any warrant to pay the least regard to any who pretend to a spirit of prophecy; even though the things they foretel, come to pass; but, on the contrary, ought wholly to disregard and renounce such pretences, being certain from divine revelation, that they are not from God, and cannot in the least strengthen the evidence of the divine authority of the Bible, or of any truth contained in it: but have a contrary tendency: And to pay any regard to them is really to slight the Bible, and may give Satan an advantage, and opportunity to introduce the most gross and fatal delusions.⁶

This general view of the holy scriptures, and the observations that have been made, are designed to exhibit no inconsiderable part of the evidence we have, that they do indeed contain a revelation from God, and may with the greatest safety be relied upon as such. But there are many other evidences of this, some of which ought to be brought into view, when this subject is considered. And it may be proper now to mention a number of arguments to prove that the writings contained in the Bible are a revelation from God, in which several things that have been already hinted will be included.

I. The series of miracles which have been wrought, as a testimony that this revelation is from God, is a standing, undeniable proof of it. These have been in some measure brought into view, in the observations above; from which the propriety and importance of these miracles, and the end for which they were wrought, appear. That these miracles were really wrought, we have as great evidence as the nature of the case will admit; and not the least ground of suspicion and doubt; especially when we consider the times and circumstances of them, and their apparent design, and the nature and contents of the revelation, the credit of which they are designed to establish. These things have been particularly and largely considered by many, and therefore are only mentioned here, except the last, which will be attended to in the sequel.

II. The numerous prophecies which are contained in the Bible, with their exact accomplishment, are a standing, clear evidence, that it is a revelation from God. The certain independent foreknowledge of future events, or of any thing to come, all will grant, belongs to the true God alone. Therefore we find Jehovah challenging this as his own prerogative; and his declaring what will be, and bringing it to pass accordingly, is asserted to be a demonstration that it is the true God who speaks. And he says, that he who can do this, does prove himself to be God.

"Produce your cause, saith the Lord; bring forth your strong reasons, saith the king of Jacob. Let them bring them forth, and shew what shall happen.--Shew the things that are to come hereafter, that we may know that ye are gods." "I, even I am the Lord, and beside me there is no Saviour. I have declared, and have saved, and I have shewed, when there was no strange god among you: Therefore, ye are my witnesses, saith the Lord, that I am God." When Jehovah brought Israel out of Egypt, he demonstrated that he was the only true God, and they renounced all other gods; then he foretold what would befall them, both in promises and threatenings, and a great number of predictions, which had actually come to pass in their sight: Therefore they were his witnesses, as they were witnesses of this fact, which was sufficient to support his character, as the only true God, in opposition to all other pretended gods. Jehovah tells them that one end of his thus foretelling events, and then bringing them to pass, was to give them an undeniable proof that he was the true God, who spoke to them by Moses, &c. and leave them inexcusable, if they should acknowledge any other God. "I have declared the former things from the beginning; and they went forth out of my mouth, and I shewed them; I did them suddenly, and they came to pass. Because I knew that thou art obstinate, and thy neck is an iron sinew, and thy brow brass; I have even from the beginning declared it to thee: Before it came to pass, I shewed it thee, lest thou shouldest say mine idol hath done them, and my graven image, and my molten image, hath commanded them." [7]

Though they had in many other ways good evidence that he was the true God, in whose name Moses spake and acted; yet God, knowing their evil disposition, and how prone they were to unbelief, and to turn away from him to other gods, in his great condescension and goodness, took care to give and heap up more abundant standing evidence that they had indeed the oracles of the true God, who was the God of Israel, by foretelling innumerable events, and then bringing them to pass before their eyes. When Moses wrought the numerous signs and wonders in Egypt, he foretold these events before they took place: And so most of the miracles wrought by the hand of Moses at the Red Sea, and in the wilderness, were foretold immediately before they took place: And also many things of which we have an account in the books of Joshua, Judges, and the two books of Samuel, &c. To such predictions as these, which were brought to pass immediately, the above cited words seem to have particular reference: God says, "They went forth out of my mouth, and I shewed them; I did them suddenly, and they came to pass." In this way they had not only the evidence which the miracles themselves gave of the truth, in favour of which they were wrought; but the prediction and the immediate accomplishment, was a yet farther evidence that he who wrought the miracle spoke and acted under the influence, and according to the dictates of the omniscient God. In this way were most of the miracles wrought by Christ and his apostles.

But there are almost innumerable prophecies in the Bible which foretel things to come, that were not to take place immediately; but a long time, and numbers of them many ages after the predictions were published. Many predictions of this kind are contained in the writings of Moses, which foretel a multitude of events respecting that nation, which have been exactly fulfilled. And indeed great part of the religious institutions and worship enjoined in the Mosaic ritual, are so many prophecies of what should take place in the person, character, and kingdom of Christ, as they are appointed types and shadows of these things, and have been exactly fulfilled in them. This is particularly attended to and illustrated in the Epistle to the Hebrews. This is a strong argument that these institutions and laws, were made by the only true God, who knows what is to come, even all his own designs, and works that are future.

A great part of the writings of Moses and the prophets are prophecies that respect Christ, his incarnation, his sufferings, and the glory that should follow in the salvation of men, and his kingdom. Jn these writings it is foretold that he should l3e the seed of Abraham by Isaac, that he should be of the tribe of Judah, and the family of David: Should be born of a virgin, in the town of Bethlehem; that he should be poor and despised, rejected, hated and put to death by the Jews and Gentiles, joining together to perpetrate this horrid deed. The particular time of his appearance and death is pointed out; and a great number of particulars relating to his life, death and resurrection are foretold; all which have been exactly fulfilled. They also foretel the rejection of the Jews, and calling of the Gentiles to be the people of God, and share in the blessings of Christ's kingdom; and speak much of the extent and glory of his kingdom, and particularly foretel that it should rise, prevail, and fill the world after the ruin of the Roman monarchy, and shall continue forever. Christ and his apostles did constantly appeal to these prophecies, as most plainly, and with die greatest exactness predicting what took place in Jesus of Nazareth. Christ himself, after his death .aid resurrection, addresses those who were wholly at a loss what to think of these things, in the following words; "O, fools, and slow of heart, to believe all that the prophets have spoken! Ought not Christ to have suffered these things, and to enter into his glory? And beginning at Moses and all the prophets, he expounded unto them, in all the scriptures, the things concerning himself." The apostle Peter publicly appeals to them, and says, "God hath spoken of these things by the mouth of all the prophets, since the world began. For Moses truly said unto the fathers, a prophet shall the

The System of Doctrines, contained in Divine Relation, Explained and Defended Volume I

Lord your God raise up unto you, of your brethren, like unto me. And it shall come to pass, that every soul which will not hear that prophet, shall be destroyed from among the people. Yea, and all the prophets from Samuel, and those that follow after, as many as have spoken, have likewise foretold of these days." And St. Paul declares, that in bearing testimony to the truth of Christianity, and preaching the gospel, he asserted "no other things than those which the prophets and Moses did say should come." And with this argument, taken from the fulfilment of prophecies in Jesus of Nazareth, the first preachers of the gospel often put to silence, and confounded the opposing Jews, and convinced many, that Jesus was the Christ.

The writings of the New Testament contain many predictions. Christ particularly foretold his death, and his resurrection on the third day after--Who should betray him, and who should deny him--The gift of the Spirit to the apostles in his miraculous powers--What treatment they should receive from the Jews--What support they should have; and what should be their success. He in a very particular manner foretold the calamities that should come on the nation of the Jews, and the destruction of Jerusalem and the temple; and said this should come to pass before all that generation did go off the stage of life. And though to human appearance, these events were not merely improbable, but even impossible; yet they all came to pass exactly agreeable to the prediction.

But passing over many other instances of prophecy, both of Christ and his apostles, and others in the primitive church, and the particular fulfilment of their predictions, that remarkable one of St. Paul, [8] of the grand apostasy in the christian church, by the rise and reign of one whom he calls the man of sin and wicked one; by which the Pope and the false church of Rome are exactly described, together with his final overthrow and destruction, is worthy of particular attention. This was then the most incredible and unlikely to come to pass of almost any event whatsoever: That the Emperor of Rome should be taken out of the way, to give opportunity for this apostasy, and the exaltation of this man of sin in the church of Christ, &c. But this is all come to pass. And this apostasy in the church, with all its circumstances and attendants, together with the general state of the church, and of the world down to the day of judgment, are yet more particularly and fully foretold in the revelation which Jesus Christ gave to the apostle John after his ascension. In this prophecy many things are foretold, which were then future, and which have already come to pass; and others are daily fulfilling in the sight of all who have wisdom to observe and discern; from which there is a standing, and increasing, public evidence of the truth of the christian religion, sufficient to silence and convince all the opposers of Christianity, would they honestly attend to the voice of reason.

From the view we have now taken of the prophecies, contained in the Bible, and their fulfilment, the following particulars may be observed.

1. Those predictions which have been exactly fulfilled are numerous, and made at different times, and by different persons; and most of them were made publicly; and the events foretold are many of them of a public nature, and lie open to the examination of all. Therefore if they were not given by the omniscient God, it cannot be supposed the events would in so many instances answer to the predictions so exactly, and not fail in one, among so many: For this may well be considered as impossible.

2. There is all the evidence that can be desired that many of these predictions were given long before the events took place, and while there was not the least ground from any thing that then appeared, to expect they would ever come to pass. Thus, all the prophecies in the Old Testament, which have been fulfilled in the days of Christ's appearance on earth, and of the apostles, and since, were certainly written and published, and in the hands of the Jewish church, long before the events took place. And prophecies of those things relating to the Pope and the church of Rome, and the kings of the earth who commit fornication with her, and join to support her, which have come to pass, and are now taking place in the world, were published, long before any of these things took place, or there was any appearance or probability that they ever would come to pass. And in many instances, all appearances, to human view, were against it.

3. Those prophecies are such, and the times and manner in which they are given such, as become an almighty, omniscient, infinitely wise and good Being. They are given in an orderly manner, with an apparent good design, and suited to answer important ends.--To establish the character of those who spake and wrote in his name, as men inspired by God, and prove that he was the omniscient God who spoke, and so to be a clear standing evidence that it is a divine revelation, most evidently distinguished from all possible deception and imposture--To confirm the faith of the friends of God, and direct, support and comfort them, under all dark appearances and afflictions, Sec. Sec.

Surely they who would honestly attend to these things and carefully consider and examine the prophecies contained in the Bible, with the exact fulfilment of so many of them, must be sensible that they afford clear and abundant evidence that the writings in this book are from God, as the prophecies found in it could not come by the will and contrivance of man; but these holy men of God evidently spake as they were moved by the Holy Ghost.

III. The writings in the Old Testament, and those in the New, reflect light and evidence on each other, that they are from God.

This appears from what has been observed on the preceding argument from prophecy: For the exact fulfilment of so many of the types and express predictions in the Old Testament, by the events and things of which we have a history in the New, does abundantly establish the credit of those writings as given by divine inspiration. And, at the same time, they prove the divine original of Christianity; and therefore that the writings in the New Testament are from God. And the perfect consistence and harmony between the writings of the Old Testament, and those of the New, does also afford a striking argument of the divine original of each of them. Moreover, Christ and his apostles constantly appeal to the writings of Moses and the prophets, the scriptures, as of divine authority, and the oracles of God. This establishes the credit of all those writings as given by inspiration of God, so far as the authority and testimony of Christ and the apostles is of any weight, and worthy of regard; so that if the writings in the New Testament be from God, the Old Testament is from him also, and is handed down to us uncorrupted, unless it has been corrupted since that time, which is many ways impossible, as might be easily shewn, were there need of it. At the same time, the prophecies contained in the Old Testament, of those very events which are recorded in the New, prove the latter to be from God, as has been shewn. In a word, the writings in the Old Testament are all established as the oracles of God, by those in the New: And that the writings in the New Testament are by divine inspiration, there is much and clear evidence from the writings of the Old. So that there could not be so much, so great evidence of the divine authority of either of them, if we had only one, without the other.

The Jews did not indeed acknowledge that their scriptures were fulfilled in Jesus Christ, and continue as a body to reject the gospel, as not from God. But this is so far from being any evidence against the divinity of the writings of the New Testament, that it is a great confirmation of it. For it was foretold by the prophets, whose writings they acknowledge to be from God, chat they should thus reject Christ and the gospel, and for this be cast off by God, and the church be called by another name: So that their unbelief and opposition to the gospel, is a clear and standing evidence of the truth of it.

IV. The great care taken by Jews and christians to receive no writings as divinely inspired, but those of which they had proper evidence that they were such; and to preserve those which they did receive as such from being corrupted or altered, is a further evidence that these writings are from God. If God has given a standing revelation to men, which is committed to writing, he will doubtless take care in his providence that it shall be received on good evidence and preserved uncorrupt; and that it shall be handed down to posterity in such manner and circumstances, as that all future generations shall have good evidence, that it was with proper care and caution received at first, and not without good evidence, that it was of divine authority; and that it has been handed down to them uncorrupt. And when we find the writings of the Bible be received and handed down to us in this manner, it carries an evidence that it is from God, which otherwise we could not have. That the writings of the Old and New Testaments have been thus received, and carefully preserved uncorrupt, has been abundantly proved by those who have written on the subject. It would swell this chapter beyond its designed brevity to produce this evidence at large. It may suffice only to observe here, that Jews and christians have been a guard with respect to each other, so as to render it impossible there should be any alteration made in the writings of the Old Testament, in favour of, or against either, without being detected by the other. And among christians, the different sects and opposite parties, which early sprung up in the church, made it impossible that they should agree to alter and corrupt those writings, which were received as divine oracles by them all; and if one sect or party had attempted it, they must have been detected by others.

V. The consistence and harmony found in the scriptures, is another argument of their divine original The agreement between the writings of the Old Testament and those of the New has been already mentioned; but the agreement of every particular part with the whole, and of every sentiment and sentence with each other, is the fact now intended. A divine revelation must be perfectly consistent and harmonious throughout, though it consists of many parts, and be made by many different men, and at different times and ages distant from each other. Therefore if any real, material contradictions or inconsistencies can be found in this book, it will be a sufficient reason for rejecting it, as not from God. There may be seeming contradictions, at first view, and to a superficial reader, and to one who does not attend to it with honesty and candour; but with prejudice and disaffection. This we know to be the case with respect to human writings, in many instances, when the fault lies wholly in the ignorance or prejudice of the objector, and the upright and judicious know them to be perfectly consistent. How much more may we expect it will be so with respect to those writings which come from God, and treat of the sublime things respecting his being, character, kingdom, designs, laws, works, &c. and which must be really contrary to every wrong propensity and lust of man.

The System of Doctrines, contained in Divine Relation, Explained and Defended Volume I

This indeed we find to be verified: Many have thought they have found numerous contradictions in the Bible; and its enemies have eagerly searched to find them, and have used all their art and plausible colouring to make them appear to be real contradictions; and urged them with all their powers against revelation. But this has turned to the advantage of the holy scriptures, and been the occasion of making their consistence and harmony more evident and certain, than if no such accusation had been brought against them. For the objections of this kind have been critically examined, and found to be entirely groundless. And since all the wit and art of men of the best abilities, and under the greatest advantages to try, cannot find any real contradictions in them; and those which have been most plausibly urged, or have had the greatest appearance of inconsistencies, at first view, appear, upon careful and thorough examination, to be perfectly consistent, this has cast new light on the subject, and made it more abundantly evident and certain that there is indeed no inconsistency to be found in them.

This is a very powerful argument that they are given by divine inspiration. For if those writings were only the contrivance of men, it appears impossible that so many men, who lived in different ages, of different natural tempers, and in such different and various circumstances and connections, writing on such a variety of subjects, with such difference of manner, style and expression, should so perfectly agree; and that even in those passages which at first view, and to a cursory, inattentive observer, may seem to contradict each other. There can be no parallel instance produced under heaven, of any number of writers thus agreeing, though they lived in the same age: and it is difficult to find any one author, not inspired, consistent with himself throughout. Therefore this consistence and harmony running through the writings of such a number of men, who lived in different ages, and which took up the space of fifteen hundred years to complete them, after they were begun, proves they must have been inspired by the all seeing, unchangeable God.

VI. The contents of the Bible, or the truths therein revealed and the duties enjoined, are the greatest and crowning evidence that these writings are given by divine inspiration, and serve to strengthen and confirm all the other arguments which have been mentioned.

This argument will of course be particularly illustrated in the proposed following work, in which the scriptures are to be examined, in order to find what are the truths and duties therein revealed and inculcated; what system of religion is there taught. It may be proper, however, to observe here in general, that we find in the Bible an orderly, intelligible, concise and well connected history of all those events which are most important and necessary to be known by the church, from the beginning of the world, down to the time in which this book was completed. The being, character, designs and works of God, are represented to be such as reason must approve, and pronounce harmonious, and becoming the true God. The state and character of man, and God's designs and works respecting him, are set in a clear light. What God requires of man, as his duty, and the way in which he may find acceptance with God, and be happy, are particularly stated with great plainness. A judgment to come, and a future state of rewards and punishments, are revealed. Promises to those who believe and obey the truth, and threatenings to the disobedient and impenitent, run through all those writings; and the best and strongest conceivable motives are set before men, to deter them from sin, and excite them to fear and obey God.

Here two things may be observed,--

1. What is revealed in the scriptures concerning the perfections and works of God, his laws as the rule of duty, the nature and evil tendency of sin, and the description given of true virtue and religion, and their happy tendency and end, appears so reasonable and evident to every attentive person, when revealed, that this, with the other evidences that have been mentioned, is sufficient to convince the reason and judgment of every one, that this is a revelation from God, though their hearts be ever so corrupt and vicious; and has generally proved sufficient, unless where peculiar prejudices by education or otherwise, have taken place.

2. The honest, virtuous mind only, which does discern and relish the beauty and excellence of truth and virtue, will see and feel the full force of this argument for the divinity of the holy scriptures. Such have true discerning to see the wonderful, excellent, glorious things revealed in the holy scriptures, which in themselves carry a most satisfying and infallible evidence of their truth and divinity. They see the divine stamp which this system of truth carries on it, and believe and are sure that this is the true God, and that here is eternal life . They therefore no longer need any other evidence but this which they find in the contents of the holy scriptures; in this they rest satisfied, and are assured that the writings contained in the Bible are the word of God.

Thus the holy scriptures are attended with the highest possible evidence that they came from God; they carry that external and internal evidence of their divinity, to the reason and conscience of men, which is sufficient to convince them, however corrupt their hearts may be: But the highest internal evidence is fully discerned only by the humble honest mind, which is disposed to relish, love and receive the truth. To such the true light shines from the holy scriptures with irresistible evidence, and their hearts are established in the truth. They believe from evidence they have within

Samuel Hopkins

themselves; from what they see and find in the Bible. And as all might have this evidence and certainty that the contents of the Bible are from God, did they not exercise and indulge those unreasonable lusts, which blind their eyes to the beauty and excellence of divine truth, unbelief is in every instance and degree of it wholly inexcusable and very criminal.

Having considered the abundant evidence there is that the writings contained in the Bible are given by divine inspiration, the following observations may be made concerning this sacred book.

1. This is a complete, unerring and perfect rule of faith and practice, and the only rule. This being understood and believed, is sufficient to make men wise unto salvation; and we have no warrant to believe any religious truth, unless it be revealed, or can be supported by the holy scriptures; and this is the only rule of our duty. We may be certain, if God has given us a revelation, it is in all respects complete, and in the best manner suited to answer the end: And must be the only standard of truth and duty.

2. Whatever may be justly and clearly inferred as a certain consequence from what is expressly revealed in the scriptures, must be considered as contained in divine revelation, as really as that which is expressed. For instance, if from any two or more truths, expressly revealed, another certainty follows, that other truth, by the supposition, is really contained in those expressly revealed, and therefore is in fact revealed or made known, in the revelation of them.

3. The holy scriptures are not to be understood without a constant, laborious attention to them, and a careful examination and search of them, in order to know the mind and will of God therein revealed. This is no evidence that the scriptures are not plain and easy to be understood; as plain and intelligible, as in the nature of things they can be, and adapted, in the best manner, to give instruction in those things about which they treat: For they cannot be instructed by the best possible means of instruction, who will not attend and take pains. They only who "incline their ear unto wisdom, and apply their heart to understanding; who cry after knowledge, and lift up their voice for understanding; who seek her as silver, and search for her as for hid treasures," will understand the sacred writings.

4. The holy scriptures were never designed to be understood, especially in those things that are most important and excellent, by persons of corrupt minds, whose hearts have no relish for these things: but do wholly oppose and hate them, and are determined in a course of disobedience to them. It is impossible indeed, that such should understand the sublime holy truths that relate to the infinitely holy God, his holy law, gospel and kingdom. Therefore their not being understood by such is no argument that they are not sufficiently plain. It is no evidence that the sun does not shine clear and bright, because they who have no eyes, or if they have, refuse to open them, do not see the light, and discern the objects it plainly discovers. It is abundantly declared in scripture, that wicked, evil men, will not understand the things there revealed. "The wicked know not, neither will they understand: They walk on in darkness." [9] "Evil men understand not judgment." [10] "The natural man (that is, the man of a corrupt, carnal mind) receiveth not the things of the Spirit of God; for they are foolish unto him: Neither can he know them, because they are spiritually discerned." [11] Christ says to the Jews, "How can ye believe, which receive honour one of another, and seek not the honour that cometh from God only!" [12] And again, "If any man will do his will, (that is, has an obedient heart ready to comply with the will of God, when it is made known to him) he shall know the doctrine, whether it be of God, or whether I speak of myself." [13] This implies that they who are of a contrary disposition do not understand and know, which is expressly asserted in the following words, "Every one that doth evil hateth the light, neither cometh to the light, lest his deeds should be reproved. But he that doth truth cometh to the light." [14] Therefore, if the scriptures be dark and unintelligible to any, especially in the most important matters there revealed, it is not owing to any defect or darkness in them; but the fault is wholly in the persons themselves, and they are altogether inexcusable and criminal, in not seeing what is revealed with sufficient clearness.

5. It can therefore be easily accounted for, that these sacred writings should be so little understood by multitudes, and so greatly misunderstood by many; and that there should be so many different and opposite opinions respecting the doctrines and duties inculcated in the Bible, among those who enjoy this revelation, and profess to make it their rule. This is not the least evidence of any defect in the scriptures, or that they are not sufficiently plain, and in the best manner suited to give instruction; but is wholly owing to the criminal blindness, corrupt propensities and unreasonable prejudices of men; who do not attend to the Bible with an honest heart. It is impossible that a revelation should be given, that cannot be misunderstood, and perverted to the worst purposes and to support the greatest errors and delusions, by the prejudices, wicked blindness, and perverse inclinations of artful men. Nothing has taken place, with respect to this, but what might justly be expected, if mankind are naturally as depraved and rebellious, as the scriptures represent them to be; and is perfectly consistent with the perfection of divine revelation. And when men shall in general become honest and virtuous to a proper degree, and their hearts shall be turned to the Lord, and to his word, willing and ready to receive the dictates of heaven, the vail of darkness

and error will vanish, and the true light which has so long shined in darkness, and so has not been seen and comprehended, shall shine in their hearts, and they, receiving the truth in the love of it, will be "perfectly joined together, in the same mind and in the same judgment."

This brings another observation into view.

6. The chief and greatest end of divine revelation is not yet answered. The Bible has been greatly neglected and abused, and not understood; and perverted to evil purposes by most of those who have enjoyed it. This light has hitherto shined, in a great measure, in vain, in the criminal darkness of this world, which has not comprehended, but abused and rejected it. And those few who have in some measure understood and received and practised the truth, have done it in a very imperfect degree; and the Bible has not been yet fully understood by any: But this same revelation informs us that it shall not always be so; but the time is coming, and is now just at hand, when God will destroy the face of the covering cast over all people, and the vail that is spread over all nations, by causing the gospel to be preached to them all, and giving them a heart to discern and understand the truth. Then "the light of the moon shall be as the light of the sun, and the light of the sun shall be seven fold, as the light of seven days." And the eyes of them that see shall not be dim, and the ears of them that hear, shall hearken. The heart also of the rash or inconsiderate foolish, shall understand knowledge, and the tongue of the stammerers shall be ready to speak plainly, and the earth shall be filled with the knowledge of the glory of the Lord, as the waters cover the sea." In that time the Bible shall be understood, and all the institutions and ordinances of the gospel shall have their proper, greatest and most happy effect, in the illumination and salvation of multitudes. All that precedes this time is but preparatory in order to introduce this day of salvation, in the reign of Christ on earth. The word of God shall then have free course and be glorified, as it never was before, and shall fully answer the end for which it was given. [15]

REFLECTIONS

I. WHAT gratitude do we owe to God for giving such a complete revelation to men, every way suited to give instruction in every necessary and most important truth: and without which mankind must have remained in the grossest darkness! What gratitude do we owe to God, who has distinguished us from so great a part of mankind, in giving us to enjoy this inestimable privilege, while they are left to grope in the dark!

The enemies to divine revelation have made this an objection against it, and said, if it were from God, it would have been given equally to all mankind, and not confined to so small a part, as this revelation has been. Such a partial revelation, say they, which was not completed or even began till after many ages and generations were passed and gone; and which when it is given is confined to so small a part of mankind, cannot be from God, who has no respect of persons, and would not conceal what is necessary to be known, from the greatest part of men, while a few only are indulged with this favour, if it be one. Among other things which might be and have been said in answer to this objection, it may be sufficient only to observe the following.

1. God was under no obligation to enter on those designs of good and salvation, and do those things in favour of man, which are now made known: And therefore could not be obliged to make this revelation. And if he is obliged to none, he may for good reasons, known to him, though we should not see them, order things so that but few shall enjoy it, as a distinguishing sovereign favour, while others are left in that state of darkness, in which all might have justly been left.

2. It is wholly owing to the fault of man that this revelation has been so long, and still is confined to such narrow bounds, and is known to so small a part of mankind. The most essential things in this revelation were made known to the first parents of mankind. Had they been faithful, and all their posterity wise, and disposed to make a good improvement of the light, it would have continued and increased, and every one of them would have enjoyed it. And after this light was abused and rejected, and almost wholly put out, by the wickedness of man, before the flood, it was again restored to the new world in the family of Noah; and was soon corrupted and extinguished by men, when they multiplied into nations, because they loved darkness, and hated this light. And when this revelation was renewed and enlarged, committed to writing and completed, had mankind been as desirous of knowing the truth, and as inquisitive after it, as they ought to have been; and had they, who enjoyed it, been as ready and as much engaged to understand and practise it, and spread and communicate it to others, as was most reasonable, and their duty, all nations would have enjoyed it fully, soon after it was published. It is not therefore owing to divine revelation that it is so confined, and not universal; but the fault is wholly in man. And it is to be wholly ascribed to God's merciful, irresistible interposition and care, that it has not been wholly lost and destroyed by men, long before this time. Therefore the scriptures being preserved as they have been, and handed down to this day, and put into our hands by God's merciful, wise, sovereign interposition and direction, is both an argument that they are from God, and of our great obligations to gratitude to him for this unspeakably distinguishing favour.

3. It may be observed, that they who do not enjoy this revelation, do not live up to the light they have, but misimprove and abuse it: And therefore have no reason to complain, that they have not greater light and advantages; but are most righteously given up to their chosen blindness and darkness. There cannot be a person that lives, or ever has lived in the heathen world, produced, who has fully improved, and lived up to the light he has had, or might have had, were it not his own fault. Divine revelation warrants this assertion. "The invisible things of God, from the creation of the world, are clearly seen, being understood by the things that are made, even his eternal power and divinity; so that they are without excuse; because that when they knew God, they glorified him not as God, neither were thankful, but became vain in their imaginations, and their foolish heart was darkened."

Oh! Let us not be unthankful, who enjoy so much greater light, which will render our ingratitude proportionably more criminal, and dreadful in its consequences. This leads to another reflection.

II. How very criminal and wretched are they who neglect or abuse this inestimable privilege of a revelation from God!--Many not only disregard it in practice, but reject and despise it, and speak evil of it. How much will the deists, who have been, and now are in the christian world, have to answer for! What they call foolishness, is the wisdom of God; and the wisdom of which they boast, is the height of folly and madness. Would to God there were none who abused and despised the holy scriptures, but professed deists! Multitudes, who profess to believe the Bible is a revelation from heaven, hold this truth in unrighteousness: They pay no proper regard to it, and constantly abuse it innumerable ways; and all the advantages they have by it, and concerns with it, will only serve to render their damnation greater, and unspeakably more dreadful. How much lower will they sink in eternal misery, who by their folly and impenitence perish from the countries enjoying divine revelation, than they who perish from heathen lands! This truth, though so obvious, solemn, and awakening, is too little thought of, by those who enjoy, and yet disregard and abuse the holy scriptures.

III. What obligations are we under to attend to this revelation, and make the best improvement of it; surely we ought to study it with great diligence and care, and meditate therein day and night, looking to God, the Father of lights, with sincerity, earnestness and constancy, that he would prevent our misunderstanding, and perverting it, and direct and lead us to discern all the truths he has revealed, and give us a heart to conform to them in practice. We ought to pay a conscientious and sacred regard to all the directions and commands in the Bible; to turn our feet unto these testimonies, and to improve the words of God, as to make it a constant light to our feet, and lamp to our path. Blessed are they who thus watch daily at wisdom's gates, and wait at the posts of her doors; for they shall be wise unto salvation, obtain favour of the Lord, and find eternal life.

Footnotes:

1. See Leland's View of the Deistical Writers. And Clarke on revealed religion. Proposition vii.

2. See Dr. Clarke on the truth and certainty of the christian revelation. Proposition vii.

3. See Dr Winder's history of the rise, progress, declension and revival of knowledge, chiefly religious.

4. Mal. iv. 4, 5.

5. "It is remarkable, that through the whole of their histories, the evangelists have not passed one encomium upon Jesus, or upon any of his friends: nor thrown out one reflection against his enemies; though much of both kinds might have been, and no doubt would have been done by them, had they been governed either by a spirit of imposture, or enthusiasm. Christ's life is not praised in the gospels; his death is not lamented; his friends are not commended; his enemies are not reproached, nor even blamed; but every thing is told, naked and unadorned, just as it took place; and all who read are left to judge, and make reflections for themselves. A manner of writing which the historians never would have fallen into, had not their minds been under the guidance of the most sober reason, and deeply impressed with the dignity, importance and truth of their subject."--Macknight's Harmony of the Gospels.

6. The church of Rome claim it as the mark of a true church, to be able to work miracles, and assert that this is essential to the true church of Christ, and pretend to have this evidence that they are the only true catholic church, viz. that a multitude of miracles have been, and still are wrought by them . But this is so far from being an evidence of a true church, that their pretending to such a power is an infallible mark and evidence that it is a false church; and this is warrant sufficient to condemn and renounce it as such, without being at the pains of examining all their pretended miracles, to see if they be real miracles or not. If that church could be supported and proved to be right, by the holy scriptures, we ought to own it as a true church; but if not, a thousand miracles will not prove any thing in its favour; but even their pretending to work miracles, and appealing to

The System of Doctrines, contained in Divine Relation, Explained and Defended Volume I
these, is a demonstration that it is not a true church, as this is a slight and rejection of the word of God.

    7. Isaiah xlviii. 3, 4, 5.
    8. 2 Thes. chap. ii.
    9. Psalm xxviii. 5.
    10. Prov. xviii. 5.
    11. 1 Cor. ii. 14.
    12. John V. 44.
    13. John vii. 17.
    14. John iii. 20, 21.
    15. See Treatise on the Millennium, at the end of this System.

CHAPTER II - CONCERNING THE BEING AND PERFECTIONS OF GOD

THOUGH the evidence of the existence of God be as clear and certain as that of our own, or of any thing else whatever, and it is one of the first dictates of reason, when offered to consideration, and attended to; and has by general consent been acknowledged by mankind in all ages, as most demonstrable and certain; yet it is most probable that even the knowledge, and general acknowledgment of this truth depends greatly, if not wholly on divine revelation. Mankind are so "alienated from the life of God, through the ignorance that is in them, because of the blindness of their hearts;" and so disposed by their depravity and wickedness to sink down into brutish ignorance and stupidity with regard to every thing invisible, that if they were not first told that there is a God, they would most probably grow up without believing, or ever thinking of this truth. The general acknowledgment of the being of God, is no evidence that it does not originate from divine revelation; for there are many things generally believed and practised in the heathen world, in their religion, which evidently depend on tradition; and though in many respects corrupted, had their original in divine revelation, handed down from Noah and his sons, or taken from the Jews, and the revelation given to them. But one instance shall be mentioned, viz. the practice of sacrificing beasts, or some animals, to appease the gods, or ingratiate themselves with them, which has so generally obtained in the heathen world; and which most certainly never would have been thought of by men, had not God first instituted it by revelation; and from that it was handed down, and the practice kept up among all nations, even long after they had lost, or corrupted, the original intent and design of such sacrifices. So the belief of the being of a God may derive from the same origin, and be handed down from generation to generation the same way. The following facts seem to favour this supposition, if they do not clearly prove it.

1. The absurd and ridiculous notions respecting God, or a plurality of gods, which have generally taken place in the heathen world: Such as the following, viz. That there are many gods both male and female--that they are embodied, like men and women--have carnal affections and lusts, and commit adulteries, rapes, &c.--have cruel hatred and contentions with one another--are taking advantage of each other by deceit and cunning, or by power to accomplish their own selfish, unreasonable inclinations and designs, &c. &c. All this can be well accounted for; on supposition their belief of the being of God depends chiefly on tradition; for this truth, being thus handed down by tradition, would naturally and easily be corrupted, and blended with endless absurd notions, according to the foolish and wicked humours and inclinations of man; which has been the case of all religious truths among the heathen, which originated from revelation. But if we suppose all nations ill the heathen world believe the existence of God by reasoning themselves into it, and attending to the clear and abundant evidence there is of this; how can it be accounted for, that they should make no use of their reason in forming their notions of Deity and determining what kind of a being a God must be; but contrary to all the dictates of reason, and the clearest evidence, embrace the greatest absurdities? If their belief, in the first instance, be founded on the dictates of reason and evidence, why is reason wholly laid aside, in the latter; and as soon as they have reasoned themselves into the being of a God, make no further use of their reason; but most unreasonably believe there are many gods, and embrace the greatest absurdities respecting Deity?

2. Those people and nations who are most out of the reach of the instruction and influence of divine revelation, and of the traditions which originated from it, have the most faint belief, and make the least acknowledgment of the being of a God. And historians and travellers tell us that there are people, and even whole nations, among whom there is not any acknowledgment of a Deity, or the least appearance of the belief of any. [16] These are nations, which by their situation and circumstances, are most out of the way of receiving any advantage by revelation, and by being long unconnected, and without any intercourse with other nations, have by degrees lost all tradition relating to every thing invisible. This seems to be a proof that if mankind were without all the light and advantages of a revelation, and traditions which originate from it, they would not pay any regard to an invisible supreme Being, or entertain any belief or notion of such a being; but would, in every sense, "live without God in the world." And, by the way, this may serve to shew what need mankind stand in, of a divine revelation, and that all religious light and knowledge originates

The System of Doctrines, contained in Divine Relation, Explained and Defended Volume I
wholly from this source.

3. There have been instances of persons who have been deaf from their birth, and consequently dumb; and after they have arrived to adult or middle age, have been able to hear and speak: And though before this, they attended public worship with others, and appeared very devout; and often made those signs which those with whom they conversed in this way, thought were expressions of their belief of the being of God, and of their piety: Yet, when they came to hear and speak, they declared, that +hey never had a thought that there was a God, until they could hear, and were by that means informed. And there never has been an instance known, of any such person's declaring that he had any belief or thought of the existence of a God, before he could hear and speak. [17]

Are not these facts an evidence that though the being, of God is so clearly manifested in the works of creation and providence, yet mankind, in their present fallen, corrupt state, would not discern and acknowledge this truth, had it not been otherwise revealed?

And since the nature of all sin, so far as it has dominion in the heart, is real Atheism, and a denial of the God who is above; and therefore the fool, the wicked man, always says in his heart, "There is no God:" and the tendency of it is to darken and stupify the mind, or rather is itself blindness and stupidity, with regard to the being of God, and every thing invisible, and naturally shuts all these things out of the mind; it can be easily accounted for, that without a revelation, the reason of man, who is totally corrupt and sinful, will never suggest to him the being of a God, however evident and demonstrable this is to reason, when once suggested and revealed, and men can be excited and persuaded to attend to the evidence, and exercise their reason on the subject.

We will now take a short and summary view of the evidence there is of this great and fundamental truth of all morality and religion; and mention some of the arguments which offer themselves to our reason, when we attend to the subject. These are not long and intricate; but when the truth is once suggested to us, it becomes an object of intuition, in a sense, so that though there be reasoning in the case, it is so short and easy, that it strikes the mind at once, and it is hardly conscious of any reasoning upon it, and of the medium by which the evidence comes to the mind. Hence it is probable, that some have thought, doubtless without any good reason for it, that the existence of God is, what they call an innate idea, which is essential to the mind of man, and impressed on it, independent of all reasoning on the subject.

I. It is certain there is a God from our own existence, and the things we behold around us. There must be some cause of the existence of these things. They could not cause their own existence, or make themselves; because this is a contradiction. There must therefore be some invisible cause which existed before them, and was able to give them existence, and to uphold them when they were made. And this first cause, maker and preserver of all things, is God.

It is natural for the inquisitive mind, when it is necessarily led thus far, to inquire, how came God to exist? Or, what is the cause of his existence? If he be the first cause, he must be the cause of his own existence, which implies a contradiction, or he must exist without any cause, and without beginning, which is perfectly inconceivable; and we may as well suppose the world exists without a cause, and go no farther back for a cause; and then we find no evidence of the existence of God.

Answer, The first cause of all things we behold, must certainly exist without beginning, and so without any cause, that is antecedent to his existence, or that is without himself. Yet there may be a reason or cause of his existence within himself, viz. The necessity of his existence, so that he exists necessarily, there being no other possible way or supposition, or it being infinitely impossible it should be otherwise; universal non existence, being the greatest contradiction in nature.

If it should be said, this runs all into darkness; for we can no more conceive of God's existing necessarily, and without beginning to exist, than we can of the world's existing without a cause; and therefore gives no relief to the mind: An easy, and it is hoped, a satisfactory answer, is at hand. It is a plain contradiction to say, that the world and all things in it exist without a cause, or a reason why they exist, rather than not: But necessary existence, and existence without beginning, implies no contradiction or impossibility. It is granted, that each of them is to us incomprehensible; but this is so far from being any argument against the truth and reality of them, that it is rather an evidence in favour of them; for if there be a God, he must be incomprehensible, as he is an infinite being, and exists in a manner infinitely above us; therefore must be infinitely above and beyond the comprehension of finite minds. It is very unreasonable to object that against the being of a God, which certainly must be true if God exists.

II. The being of God is evident from the manner of our own existence, and of all things visible, viz. the design, contrivance and wisdom that appear in them. It would fill volumes fully to illustrate this argument from the works of creation and providence, as this design and wisdom appear in them all; and the more particularly they are considered, the more clear the wisdom appears and shines. Volumes have been written on the subject, and many more might be written, and yet the subject not be exhausted. But it is not consistent with the design of this work, to enter particularly into this subject. Every one must have observed so much of this, as to see the propriety and force of this argument, at first view, unless he be very criminally inattentive. The innumerable creatures and things which come under our observation appear to be contrived and formed to answer some end; and the numerous ranks of different animals are all furnished with provision for their own support and defence, and have members and organs suited to their situation, and to obtain, receive and use what is necessary for the support of their lives, &c. If we attend only to our own bodies, we shall find them so admirably contrived, and so curiously formed; and though of so many parts, each one is suited to the rest, and all so contrived as to form one harmonious system of animal life, without any defect or any thing superfluous; is it possible, if we make any proper use of our reason, that we should find ourselves inhabiting such bodies, without discerning the contrivance and wisdom of our make, and seeing and acknowledging the hand and skill of the wise Author of this frame, so curious in all its parts and movements? As well may we behold a most beautiful, well contrived palace, furnished with every thing convenient and comfortable to dwell in, having nothing useless, nothing wanting; and not have one thought of a wise skilful architect, who contrived and built it; or imagine this building might exist without the exertion of any design or wisdom and have no author and maker.

Surely we cannot survey ourselves and the world in which we are, and see the design and contrivance apparently running through the whole, and not be convinced that there must be a wise contriver and author who has made them. Not to think of and acknowledge this, is to be more like beasts, than rational creatures. The language of the Psalmist is most rational and natural, when contemplating the works of creation and providence. "O Lord, how manifold are thy works! in wisdom hast thou made them all."

III. The being of God is made evident by the holy scriptures. Not merely by being there abundantly asserted; but by the existence of such a book as the Bible. It is as much impossible there should be such a book, were there no God, as that there should be such a world as we see, without an invisible cause. For it is as much beyond the power and skill of man, or any number of men, to form such a book, as it is to make the world. It is impossible that such a number of men, who lived in ages at such a distance from each other, should write so much, and not contradict themselves, nor each other; but agree and harmonize in every thing, were there no invisible, unerring, omniscient Being to direct and guide them: As impossible as it was that every stone and piece of timber in Solomon's temple, should come together, and be exactly fitted to its place, so as to make one complete, harmonious building, without any design, or contrivance; but by mere accident or chance. The character of God there given is far above and beside the thought of man, and could no more be drawn by man, were there no such God, than the world can be made by him. And the law of God there given, and at last summed up and comprehended in one sentence, "Thou shalt love the Lord with all thy heart, and thy neighbour as thyself," could no more be thought of and contrived by man, than the heavens and the earth could be planned and produced by him. The series of miracles wrought by those who said there was a God, and that Jehovah was the only true God; that he spake to them, and they did these wonders in his name, and by his power, are a standing proof of the existence of God.

But above all, the predictions contained in the Bible, with their exact and certain accomplishment, is a striking proof and demonstration of the existence of an omniscient, omnipotent Being. For it is as much beyond the art and power of men to foretel so many thousand events, so precisely answering the prediction, as it is for him to make the sun, moon and stars.

All these have been urged as proofs of the divinity of the scriptures, and they are equal proofs of the being of God. Therefore, though invisible things of God are clearly seen in the works of creation and providence, even his eternal power and godhead; so that all the nations who have not the Bible are left without excuse, which if they do not believe in, love and worship the true God: yet they who enjoy this book have more clear evidence of the being of God, as well as unspeakably greater advantages to know his true character; and consequently are far more inexcusable than the heathen, if they do not believe.

Upon the evidence of the existence of God, two things may be observed.

1. Though this be as evident a truth as any whatsoever, and men may have a full rational conviction of it, while their hearts are opposite to it, and receive no impressions answerable to this truth, and the whole system of their affections and exercises of heart, are just as if this were not true, or directly contrary to it; yet do really say in their hearts, there is no God. Therefore we find this asserted in the scriptures, "The fool, (that is, the wicked man whose heart is wholly corrupt, as it is there explained) says in his heart there is no God." Hence it is, that this conviction and profession, that there is a God, in multitudes of instances, has little or no effect on the heart and practice; but while they profess to know there is a God, in their hearts and in their works they deny him. In this case, the heart governs the man, and forms his true moral character, and not his speculative conviction and judgment, which is so weak and ineffectual that it flies, or vanishes, into

nothing, before the strong fixed propensities of the ungodly heart, as a bubble is blown away by the strong blast of a furious wind.

2. Where the heart is upright and honest, and men have a proper taste and relish for moral truth, the evidence of the being of God is discerned in a true light. The being and true character of God appear to be a pleasing reality; they have a genuine and powerful impression on the heart, and its leading affections and exercises are answerable to the truth. Therefore the scriptures represent such only, as knowing God and believing in him; and others are spoken of as not knowing God, and saying in their hearts there is no God, and in their works denying him. The latter are in darkness, and walk in darkness which blindeth their eyes. The god of this world hath blinded their minds, so that they believe not, and the light of the glorious gospel of Christ, who is the image of God, doth not shine unto them. But the light shines into the hearts of the former, and gives them the light of the knowledge of the glory of God, ill the face of Jesus Christ. For where the being of God is truly discerned, his whole revealed character, or his glory, is in some good measure seen; and they who have not discerning and relish of this glory, which is true of all wicked men, have not that belief of the being of God which good men have, as their faith consists in mere speculation; which is not the true light. This is so plain, that a heathen has said, "The mind destitute of virtue, cannot see the beauty of truth." [18]

This leads us to consider the character and perfections of God; or what God is. This is the must important subject in the whole compass of divinity, as right conceptions of God lay the best and only foundation for religious knowledge and right sentiments in general: And it is no doubt true, that all who agree in their sentiments respecting the divine character, will also agree in the same system of religious truth: And the origin of the difference and opposition of opinion that have taken place among professing christians, respecting the doctrines of Christianity, is their different and opposite notions of the character and perfections of God. Therefore the true knowledge of God is often mentioned in scripture as the sum of all knowledge, and comprehending all religious knowledge. This affords a good reason for our attending to this awful subject with great care and caution; with solemnity of mind, reverence and devotion, searching the holy scriptures, and praying that we may be saved from wrong and dishonourable conceptions of God; and obtain the true knowledge of him.

What are called the natural perfections of God, as distinguished from his moral perfections, are first to be considered. There is a general agreement respecting these, among those who enjoy divine revelation, as men are not so prone to prejudice and error on this head, as they are concerning the other. It will therefore be needless to enlarge here.

We are warranted by the scriptures, and it appears reasonable, to exclude every thing that implies any imperfection, when we consider what God is; and ascribe to him nothing that is not absolutely perfect in the highest degree. Therefore we must conceive God to be a pure spirit, which the scriptures assert: And hence we are certain that nothing corporeal, or that has any shape, figure or limits, is to be ascribed to him. Hence it is unreasonable and very dishonourable to God, to attempt to make any image or likeness of him, by any thing that has figure or shape, or to form or entertain any such notion in our minds. Moses gave a particular caution on this head to the people of Israel. "The Lord spake unto you out of the midst of the fire: ye heard the voice of the words, but saw no similitude, only ye heard a voice. Take ye therefore good heed unto yourselves, lest ye corrupt yourselves, and make you a graven image, the similitude of any figure; for ye saw no manner of similitude on the day that the Lord spake unto you in Horeb, out of the midst of the fire." And this is expressly prohibited in the second command, "Thou shalt not make unto thee any graven image, or any likeness of any thing that is in heaven above, or that is in the earth beneath, or that is in the water under the earth." Therefore when God is spoken of in the scriptures as if he had bodily parts and members, hands, eyes, ears, mouth, &c.--these expressions are to be taken in a figurative sense, and mean no more than that God does see and hear, &c. which we perform by those members and organs; and not that he has eyes of flesh, or sees as man does: Such language being used as better suited to convey knowledge to our minds, in conformity to man's way of speaking and conceiving.

In the scriptures God is represented as an infinite being, that he is, in every respect, without limits or bounds. His existence is infinite, or in him is an infinite degree of existence, so that all created existence is nothing when compared with him; and indeed is comprehended in him, and is really no addition to existence, it being only an emanation from him, the fountain and sum of all existence. And all his attributes and perfections are infinite, according to the scriptures. "His understanding is infinite," and consequently every thing that can be attributed to him.

And reason teaches that God must be infinite. He who exists without any cause, that is, without himself, or who exists of and from himself, from the necessity of his own nature; or, in other words, exists necessarily, must be infinite or cannot have any bounds or limits, in any respect; and that for these two plain reasons,

1. He can be limited or bounded by no thing, because there can be nothing to limit him; no possible cause or reason of any kind of limitation; and therefore there can be none.

2. Necessary existence must be infinite; for as there can be nothing to bound this necessity, it must take place with respect to every possible degree of existence, and is as much a reason of infinite existence, as of any existence at all. If any existence be necessary, infinite existence is necessary; so that it is a plain contradiction to suppose that God exists of himself, or necessarily; and yet has but a limited degree of existence, or is not infinite.

Hence it appears that God exists without beginning, or end; or is eternal, as he is represented in the scriptures: For he who has no limits, but is infinite, can have neither beginning or end, or must be infinite in duration. And necessary existence must be eternal, because this same necessity cannot be limited as to time or duration; but is always the same. It is a contradiction to say that self existence, or which is the same, necessary existence, does not exist, or can cease to exist.

For the same reason God is unchangeable in all respects; which the holy scriptures abundantly assert. He who exists necessarily, and is infinite, must exist unchangeably in the most perfect manner and degree. Change, or alteration in any respect, necessarily supposes limitation and imperfection. And as God is eternal and immutable, he must be without any succession; for this supposes change, and an advance in years and increase of duration. God does not grow older; there is nothing first or last, no beginning or end, past or to come, with respect to him; he has no change or succession of ideas; but he inhabits or possesses eternity, without the least variation or shadow of turning.

God is perfect and infinite in understanding and knowledge. He is omnipresent, which is necessarily implied in his infinite, unlimited existence.

God is almighty. He can do what he pleases, and nothing is impossible with him. And he must be absolutely and infinitely independent and all sufficient. All this is asserted in the scriptures, and it is easy to see they are essential to the character of God, who made and governs the world, and is to be trusted in all cases, and worshipped.

God is invisible. Invisibility is ascribed to him in the scriptures, as essential and peculiar to him: And the meaning is not merely, that he is invisible as all pure spirits are, not to be seen by our bodily eyes; but he is not to be seen by any created mind, by direct, immediate intuition; nor can he ever be seen thus to all eternity; but only as he reveals and manifests himself, ad extra, by his works, or some other medium, or exhibition. This seems to be asserted in the following words, "No man hath seen God at any time; the only begotten Son, which is in the bosom of the Father, he hath declared him." It is to be observed, that the word man, is not in the original; but it is none, or no one hath seen God; and the assertion may be considered as extending to angels as well as men. St. Paul says, No man hath seen, nor can see God.

God is incomprehensible, by all finite minds. This is as evident and certain, as it is that what is finite cannot reach unto and comprehend infinity. But a little portion can be known of God, compared with the whole of his existence: And none, among men or angels, can by searching find out God to perfection; though under the best possible advantages, and possessed of the greatest abilities to search; and though they exert all their powers and strength to the utmost, and wisely improve every advantage to get knowledge, without intermission, and without end. Though they should make the swiftest progress imaginable in the knowledge of God, they would still fall infinitely short of fully comprehending all that is in God, or even any one thing. For however great and extensive this knowledge may be, in itself considered; yet it is but finite, and therefore is infinitely less than the perfect, adequate knowledge of an infinite being. Creatures may have the true knowledge of God; they may know something of him, and what they know may be agreeable to the truth; but this is infinitely short of comprehending his being, or any of his attributes and perfections. This plain truth may well be improved to teach us modesty in our inquiries about God; and shew us the arrogancy and folly of those who refuse to believe any thing respecting the existence, character or works of God, which cannot be comprehended. Such, while they are valuing themselves, for their own reasoning abilities, are acting a most unreasonable part. How unreasonable are they who doubt of the being or any of the perfections of God, only because they cannot fully understand and comprehend how they can be. For if there be a God clothed with infinite perfection, he must be incomprehensible. They who will not believe in a God whose being and manner of existence are beyond their comprehension, must certainly have no true God; for what they reject, is essential to the true God; and were there nothing incomprehensible, it is certain there could be no God.

The moral perfections of God are next to be considered; or what the scriptures say of his moral character. As this is of the greatest importance to be known, we may be sure it is very clearly discovered, and precisely stated in divine revelation, whatever mistakes men may make about it, and however they may differ in their sentiments concerning those divine attributes. We have therefore the greatest reason and encouragement to search the scriptures with attention and care,

The System of Doctrines, contained in Divine Relation, Explained and Defended Volume I
and upright and honest hearts, that we may find the knowledge of God, in this part of his character.

The following general observations may be made concerning the moral perfections of God, before they are considered more particularly.

1. The infinite excellence, beauty and glory of God, consist wholly in his moral perfections and character. Infinite greatness, understanding and power, without any rectitude, wisdom and goodness of heart, if this were possible, would not be desirable and amiable; but worse than nothing, and infinitely dreadful. Therefore they who do not understand the true moral character of God, and discern the excellence and glory of it, have not the knowledge of God; his real amiableness and glory are hid from them. And this being true of all whose moral character is wholly evil, and who have hearts altogether opposed to the moral perfections of God, they are represented in the scriptures as not knowing God. "He that saith, I know him, and keepeth not his commandments, is a liar, and the truth is not in him." [19] "He that loveth not, knoweth not God; for God is love." [20]

2. The moral character and perfection of God consists in his holiness. Holiness comprehends all that belongs to his moral character, and does not consist in any particular attribute, distinct from any other moral perfection. The holiness of God is his goodness, wisdom, justice, truth and faithfulness, &:c. It consists in these, and cannot be distinguished from them. Therefore they who have considered holiness as a distinct attribute of God, and have attempted to describe it as distinguished from goodness, wisdom, Sec. do not appear to have any distinct, clear ideas, and to be able to give any satisfactory or intelligible definition of it. It does not appear that the scriptures warrant any such distinction; but there the holiness of God means the goodness of his moral character in general. And we find that when it is applied to men, it denotes a virtuous moral character and conduct, and comprehends every thing morally good, even every branch of moral excellence. And should any one attempt to define the holiness of a man, as distinct from goodness, his love to God and his neighbour, his humility, righteousness and temperance, he not only would have no scripture warrant for it; but must run himself into the dark, and be altogether unintelligible to himself and others.

3. The whole of true holiness, or the moral excellence and perfection of God, is comprehended in love, or goodness, by whatever names it may be called. Where there is no love or goodness of heart, there is nothing morally good; and where this love or goodness is, there is every moral virtue and excellence, as necessarily involved and implied in it. Therefore infinite goodness is infinite moral perfection, and forms an absolutely perfect and infinitely excellent moral character. By this love and goodness is meant good will, with every affection necessarily implied in it; that universal benevolence which consists in a disposition to seek and promote the greatest possible general good and happiness, and all those affections and exercises, and that conduct in which this is expressed and acted out. What absolutely perfect and infinite benevolence and goodness implies, and contains in the nature of it; and that nothing can be added to it to form an infinitely excellent moral character, will be more particularly considered and evinced hereafter. But it is proper first to consider what evidence we have from the scriptures, that the divine, moral character, or the holiness of God, consists wholly in this.

1. The holy law of God, which is not only the standard of holiness, or of moral excellence and perfection in the creature, but an expression and transcript of divine holiness, requires nothing but love or goodness; so that he who loveth, as the law of God requires, is perfectly conformed to the law, which is the same with being perfectly holy: And this is perfect conformity or likeness to God in his moral character; for holiness in the creature is the moral image of God: Therefore God. says to men, "Be ye holy; for I am holy."

Jesus Christ has taught us that the holy law of God requires nothing but love, in the following remarkable words, "Thou shalt love the Lord thy God with all thy heart, and with all thy soul, and with all thy mind. This is the first and great commandment. And the second is like unto it. Thou shalt love thy neighbour as thyself. On these two commandments hang all the law and the prophets." Agreeable to this St. Paul says, "Love is the fulfilling of the law." Nothing can be more expressly asserted than this, viz. that love, exercised to a proper degree, and expressed and acted out in all proper ways, forms a perfect moral character; and therefore that the divine moral character consists wholly in this.

2. The apostle John says repeatedly that God is love, and he that dwelleth in love dwelleth in God, and God in him. Here all the moral perfections of God are comprehended in love, and by this the whole of his moral character is expressed. If we know what love is, we know what God is; for God is love. And if we dwell in love, we are conformed to God, and he dwelleth in us, his moral image is formed in us by love.

3. When Moses besought God to shew him his glory; in answer to this petition, God said, "I will make all my goodness pass before thee." And when he granted this petition, it is said, "The Lord descended in the cloud, and stood with him there, and proclaimed the name of the Lord. And

the Lord passed by before him, and proclaimed, The Lord, the Lord God, merciful and gracious, long suffering, and abundant in goodness and truth." The glory of God consists in his moral perfection and character: But when he proposes to shew this his glory to Moses, he mentions his goodness, and nothing else, "I will make all my goodness to pass before thee." q.d. I have no glory to show but my goodness; this is the whole of my moral beauty and excellence. And when it is said, "he proclaimed the name of the Lord;" it means that he proclaimed his character, and declared that in which his moral perfection and glory did consist. And here is nothing but goodness or love mentioned. Love in the highest, most resplendent and glorious exercises and manifestations of it, in the pardon and salvation of sinners. Truth is indeed mentioned here; but not as any thing distinct from goodness or benevolence; but as that which is necessarily included in it. But this leads to a more particular consideration of the moral perfections of God, which are included in love or goodness.

    1. Infinite wisdom is a moral perfection of God. Wisdom consists in discerning, and proposing the highest and best end, and fixing on, and pursuing the most proper and best way and means, in order to accomplish it. Infinite wisdom does this with infinite ease, and without any possibility of the least error and mistake. It is certain that this wisdom is a moral excellence, and belongs to the heart, and therefore does not consist in mere speculation, or that knowledge or understanding, which may be without any rectitude or goodness of disposition or heart. Satan, who has no moral goodness, has no wisdom. He does not discern and propose any good end, but the contrary; and is devising and pursuing methods to accomplish his evil designs. Therefore, however clear and right his speculations may be in some instances, and though he may be very subtil and cunning, he has no wisdom, and no true discerning in things of a moral nature; but all his proposals, designs and pursuits, are directly the reverse of wisdom. They are consummate folly and madness. Therefore the scriptures speak of wisdom, as a moral excellence; yea, as including all moral rectitude; and perfectly opposed to all folly or moral evil; and a wise and understanding heart, in the scriptures, means a moral excellence depending on the disposition of the heart, and not consisting in any knowledge and speculations which are consistent with a corrupt and evil heart. Of this every one who has attended to the Bible, must be sensible; it is therefore needless to produce passages here to prove it. This true wisdom is called light, in the scriptures; in which sense God is said to be light, and to dwell in light. "God is light, and in him is no darkness at all."

    Wisdom and goodness, or benevolence, are not to be considered as distinct, and the former as independent of the latter. Where there is no benevolence there is no wisdom; for where benevolence or goodness is not, there no good end is proposed and pursued, or discerned. It is benevolence alone that seeks the highest general good, and proposes and pursues the best end; and where this is not, the true good is not discerned, and therefore the best end is not proposed, sought, or perceived. This therefore gives or contains all the light and discerning there is in true wisdom. If we have a just idea of benevolence or goodness of heart, and know what that is, we have an idea of true wisdom, the latter being necessarily included in the former. This will be evident to every one who considers and understands what benevolence is, and what is true wisdom; so that no farther proof of this point will be needed. This is agreeable to what is said in the scriptures of benevolence and wisdom. There love or benevolence is represented as being or containing all that light and knowledge which is in true wisdom; and that where this love is not, there is not any degree of this light and discerning. "Every one that loveth, knoweth God. He that loveth not, knoweth not God. He that saith he is in the light, and hateth his brother, is in darkness even until now. He that loveth his brother, abideth in the light: But he that hateth his brother, is in darkness, and walketh in darkness." Here love is said to be, or imply, all that light and discerning which is of a moral nature, in which true wisdom consists; therefore love is wisdom. Love is true light and discerning, and this is true wisdom. Love is the true knowledge of God, or implies it, and is essential to it. And in the knowledge of God true wisdom consists. "If thou incline thine ear unto wisdom, and apply thine heart to understanding-- thou shalt then understand the fear of the Lord, and find the knowledge of God: For the Lord giveth wisdom." [21]

    Moreover, the scriptures teach us that wisdom, considered as proposing and pursuing a good end by the best means, consists in love. There it is said, "The fear of the Lord is the beginning of wisdom. The fear of the Lord is the beginning of knowledge: But fools despise wisdom and instruction." And unto man he said, "The fear of the Lord, that is wisdom, and to depart from evil, is understanding." By the fear of the Lord, is evidently meant, true piety, or obedience to God, in keeping his commandments; which consists wholly in love, love to God and our neighbour. This, it is said, is true wisdom, and is the beginning of wisdom. There is no wisdom where there is no love to God, and wisdom begins in this, and this is wisdom itself. Therefore, according to the scriptures, love is wisdom and understanding. Agreeable to this, all true virtue and moral rectitude, which consists in love, is called wisdom, in the Proverbs of Solomon, and through the Bible; and the contrary is called folly: And the former is called understanding and knowledge, the latter darkness

The System of Doctrines, contained in Divine Relation, Explained and Defended Volume I
and ignorance.

Hence it appears, not only that wisdom is moral rectitude and excellence, and a moral perfection of God; but also that it is nothing more than benevolence or goodness, and is included in it; so that when it is said God is love, his wisdom is asserted, as well as his goodness; because love or goodness, is wisdom itself.

2. Justice or righteousness belongs to the moral character of God. This denotes in general the perfect and infinite rectitude of his will, in opposition to all injustice or unrighteousness. The scriptures constantly ascribe this to God, as essential to the perfection and glory of his character, as every one must be sensible who is acquainted with the Bible. "He is the rock, his work is perfect: For all his ways are judgment: A God of truth, and without iniquity, just and right is he." "The Lord is righteous in all his ways."

Righteousness often has a very extensive meaning in the scriptures, and seems frequently to be used to express the whole of the moral character and glory of God, or his moral rectitude in general; as it is also often used to express the moral character of a man who is conformed to God, or true holiness. "Put on the new man, which after God is created in righteousness and true holiness." Here righteousness and true holiness seem to mean the same thing, and the latter, true holiness, is put as exegetical of the former; because righteousness, expresses the whole of moral rectitude, both in God and the creature. "Blessed are they who hunger and thirst after righteousness," that is, true holiness. But the instances of righteousness being used in the scriptures in this extensive sense, as including all moral goodness, are too many to be particularly mentioned here. Every one who has read the Bible knows that the words just and righteous are commonly used to denote that moral character, rectitude and holiness, by which good or holy men are distinguished from others. To be righteous, is to be right according to the rule, the holy law of God, the standard of all moral rectitude; and therefore must include universal holiness.

But righteousness and justice are sometimes used in the scriptures in a more limited sense, both when applied to God and to men; and to be just or righteous, is to be disposed to do no wrong to any, and actually to do none; but to give to every one, every thing to which he has a right, and may justly claim as his due, and is therefore opposed to doing wrong or injuring any being, by withholding or taking from him that to which he hath a right, which is called injustice, or unrighteousness. Justice and righteousness of a judge, and when ascribed to God, as such also denote, judging according to truth between opposing and contending parties, justifying the innocent and injured, espousing, vindicating and maintaining his cause; and condemning and punishing the guilty and injurious, according to his desert; especially when this is necessary to vindicate the character and cause of the injured in the best manner, and to make proper restitution for the injury done. Not to do this would be to pervert justice and judgment.

This justice, righteousness or uprightness, is essential to a perfect moral character, and therefore must be included in infinite moral perfection. It is needless to him, who reads the Bible with attention, to say that justice, in this sense, is there constantly ascribed to God; and that he who overlooks this, or has wrong notions of it, must be ignorant of the moral character of God.

It is important to observe here, that God, in the exercise of justice, or righteousness, has a proper regard to himself, and is disposed to maintain the rights of Deity, and properly to resent all injuries done to him. Therefore he requires his rational creatures to love him with all their hearts, because this is his due; and has annexed to his law a threatening of a punishment, which is the just desert of the transgression of it, or of any injury done to him. This regard to himself, and disposition to assert and maintain his rights and character, is expressed, when he styles himself a jealous God, who is jealous for his holy name; [22] and will not give his glory to another, neither his praise to graven images: [23] "For my name's sake will I defer my anger, and for my praise will I refrain for thee, that I cut thee not off. For mine own sake, even for mine own sake will I do it; for how should my name be polluted? And I will not give my glory to another." [24] "God is jealous, and the Lord revengeth, the Lord will take vengeance on his adversaries, and he reserveth wrath for his enemies." [25]

It belongs to God to vindicate his own rights, his name and character, and see that justice is done to himself; for there is no other being who can have the care of this, or can do it, or see that it is done. But he who is most upright, infinitely righteous, and can do no wrong, and sees what is right in all cases, without any possibility of mistake, is every way qualified to judge, decide and act in this matter, and it becomes him to do it; and not to regard his own rights, and do justice to himself, would be infinitely unjust and wrong. As God is infinitely the greatest, and the sum and perfection of all being, and his character, interest and rights, are of infinitely the greatest worth and importance; to disregard his rights, and injure him, is infinitely the highest instance of injustice that can be; and the exercise of justice and righteousness, in the first place, and chiefly, respects him; and were it possible for God to disregard his own character, and not vindicate and maintain his own rights, he would be infinitely far from being just and righteous; and this would be a greater instance of injustice, than every possible injury to all creatures, can be. Therefore when God is said to be just, it necessarily includes his being just to himself, so that he will do himself no wrong, but will regard and maintain his own rights, and claim and secure the honour due to his name: and if he be injured by any, he will see that complete restitution is made, whatever it may cost him who does the injury. And at the same time he is infinitely engaged to administer justice through all his dominions, and not to injure any one of his creatures in the least degree. "The Judge of all the earth will do right."

Before we leave this head, it must be particularly observed, that justice or righteousness, whether taken in a more extensive, or in a confined sense, is nothing really distinct from love or goodness; but is included in it, and essential to it, though it has been thus distinctly considered. For injustice is directly opposed to good will; and goodness will not injure any one. He therefore, who is perfectly good, must be perfectly just; and goodness always is, and always will be justice. And infinite benevolence or love disposes to maintain and vindicate the rights of all; to administer justice and judgment in all cases; to condemn and punish the injurious so far as is necessary to make compensation to the injured. For as universal goodness seeks the greatest general good, it can do no wrong; and is therefore opposed to all ill will, and every thing that is contrary to the rights of any being, and to the highest general good. Love, therefore, still appears to comprehend all moral rectitude and excellence; and justice or righteousness in the divine Being, is nothing but universal, infinite benevolence, considered with relation to particular objects, and as acted out in particular circumstances.

3. Perfect truth and faithfulness are essential to the moral character of God, and included in his holiness. His declarations are all perfectly agreeable to the truth: and none can be deceived by believing what he says. Whatever he promises may be relied upon with the greatest safety; and all his predictions, promises and threatenings he punctually and completely accomplishes.

And here again, it must be observed, that truth and faithfulness are not to be distinguished from goodness, as though there were any thing in them different from it, and not contained in it, and essential to it; for there is no foundation for this, and it would be contrary to the truth. He who is infinitely benevolent must be perfect and unchangeable in truth and faithfulness; for love or goodness is itself truth and faithfulness, acted out in that particular manner, and towards those particular objects in which it obtains this denomination. There can be no truth and fidelity, where there is no goodness; and where the latter is, there, in the same degree, is the former.

We have new had some view of the moral character of God, or his holiness; and find it to consist in love or goodness, wisdom, righteousness or justice, truth and faithfulness. And that all is comprehended in love or benevolence, there being not only nothing contrary to this; but nothing really distinct from it, and that is not essential to it: The whole being nothing but infinite goodness, in different views of it, and as it respects different objects; and on this account, and that we may better understand it, the scriptures speak of it by parts, and call the parts of this whole, by different names.

But this very important and interesting subject requires yet further consideration; and it is hoped the following observations will not be useless; but tend to cast more light upon it.

I. When it is said that the moral character of God, or his holiness, consists in love, in which sense "God is love," universal, infinite benevolence or good will is meant by love, and all that which this necessarily implies. This has been supposed, and taken for granted, in all that has been already said on this subject; but needs to be more particularly explained, and made evident. When God is said to be love, it is evident that the love of benevolence, or the goodness of God, is here meant from the context, where the meaning of the apostle is explained. When it is said, "God is love," the words immediately following are these, "In this was manifested the love of God towards us, because that God sent his only begotten Son into the world , that we might live through him. Herein is love: Not that we loved God, but that he loved us, and sent his Son to be the propitiation for our sins." Here the love of benevolence or good will only, is mentioned as that in which the love of God was manifested and acted out: Therefore this is the love here intended, when it is said, "God is love." It is love of good will to enemies, to men in a state of rebellion against God; and therefore the most disinterested, generous love and goodness. This is the love and goodness spoken of by Christ, when he says, "God so loved the world, that he gave his only begotten Son, that whosoever believeth in him should not perish, but have everlasting life." This is by the angels, called good will to men. This is the highest instance of the most pure disinterested benevolence or goodness; in which God has made the clearest discovery of his infinite goodness, and so of all his moral perfections, that creatures have ever beheld. This benevolence has the highest good of being in general for its object: Being capable of life and happiness. It discerns what is the supreme, greatest good, and this it seeks and pursues with unerring wisdom; and being attended with omnipotence, all the infinite good, the proper object of infinite benevolence, which is discerned, willed and sought, must take place in the highest possible degree, without the least defect. This is universal

The System of Doctrines, contained in Divine Relation, Explained and Defended Volume I
benevolence; disinterested, unlimited, infinite goodness, which has the highest possible good of being in general for its object, that is, infinite good; which must infallibly take place, and be enjoyed forever.

II. This love of benevolence does not exclude, but necessarily includes, that which is called love of complacence; for he who is good, benevolent and friendly, must delight in goodness. He will not only take pleasure in the exercise of goodness; but will be pleased with benevolence wherever it exists. Therefore a complacency and delight in holiness, or moral excellence, is always implied in holiness. God is therefore represented in the scriptures as delighting and taking pleasure in the upright, in them that fear him, and are truly holy, and delighting in the exercise of loving kindness, judgment and righteousness. But it ought to be remembered that love of complacency is not the primary or chief part of holy love; for holiness must exist as the object of complacency, in order to the existence of the latter. And what can this holiness be, which is the object ox complacency and the spring of holy delight, but the love of benevolence or goodness? This is the primary and most essential part; yea, the sum of holy love, which implies the love of complacency in its nature; the latter being a branch and emanation from the former. Therefore when we think and speak of holy love, benevolence should be the primary and chief idea in our minds, as being the sum of all, and implying the whole: For holy complacency, is complacency in benevolence and a benevolent complacency. And if we leave benevolence out of our idea of the love of complacency, we have no idea of true holiness; nor understand the scriptures where they speak of holy love in God or creatures.

It is true indeed, that moral excellence, or the love of benevolence and complacency, may be the object of benevolence as well as complacency, for the more excellent any being is. the greater is his importance and worth, and his interest so much more valuable; and indeed, the more existence he has; for excellence is real existence: Therefore there will not only be more complacence and delight in such a being; but he is more the object of benevolence, in wishing him well, prosperous and happy, and doing him good if he stands in need, and there is opportunity; and in being friendly to his existence, prosperity and happiness, and rejoicing in the same. But this is not the primary object of benevolence, but what may be called the secondary object, which appears from what has been said; for benevolence is good will to being, and seeks the greatest good of the whole; and therefore loves those who have no excellence, and wishes well even to enemies; but is exercised in a stronger degree, and a peculiar manner, towards those beings who are themselves benevolent, and friends to the general good; while at the same time they are the only objects of complacence and delight.

III. Divine love or goodness is perfectly disinterested, in opposition to all self love, or selfishness. This is expressed by uprightness, or righteousness, and consists in it. Uprightness is ascribed to God in the scriptures, as essential to his character; yea, he is called "the most upright." [26] That is, perfectly, infinitely, and unchangeably so. This is opposed to partiality, which consists in self love, and is selfishness itself. True goodness, or love, is in its own nature uprightness, or disinterested, in opposition to this self love, which is in its nature partiality and unrighteousness, and contains in it the essence and sum of all that which is opposed to true holiness, that is, all sin. Therefore we must exclude from the love in which the divine holiness consists, all that can be properly called self-love, all selfish, partial, interested affection; and consider the holiness of God as infinitely opposed to all this.

IV. God himself is the object of his own love and goodness. Or, in the exercise of his love he has respect and regard to Deity as well as to creatures. This is necessarily implied in perfect, universal, infinite benevolence, which includes impartial uprightness and righteousness; for it would be infinitely otherwise, and the most partial, unrighteous affection, if there were no regard paid to the infinite fountain and sum of all being and perfection. That which is friendly to the greatest universal good of existence, and is most pleased and delighted with the highest moral perfection, must regard the interest of the supreme Head of the universe, and delight in the most perfect beauty and excellence. And it hence follows that God is the chief and supreme object of his own love and regard; and he loves and regards himself infinitely more than the whole creation, and makes himself his highest and last end of all: and therefore has made all things for himself, as the scriptures assert. This has nothing of the nature of what is called self-love in creatures; but is directly and perfectly opposed to it. There is not the least partiality and selfishness in it; but the contrary, and is uprightness and righteousness itself, as has been shown; for if God did not love and regard himself, his rights and interest, according to his own existence, importance and excellence, he would not be just, impartial and upright. Impartial, disinterested benevolence and affection must pay the greatest regard to the greatest and best being; and therefore to suppose this is partiality and selfishness is most unreasonable, and a direct contradiction.

This evident truth, which may be so easily demonstrated, ought to be impressed on our minds, and never forgotten; for if it be out of view, and wholly disregarded, we cannot have right conceptions of God, or understand the holy scriptures: and must be in darkness with respect to the most important doctrines of Christianity, and not know wherein true religion consists. Many, by making a mistake here, and considering the love of God as having no respect to himself, but wholly exercised towards his creatures, in seeking their good and happiness only, have conceived of him as an almighty tool or servant, existing only for the sake of his creatures, and seeking nothing but their happiness; and hence have gone into a scheme of doctrines and religion, which is wholly selfish, and as contrary to the holy scriptures, as darkness is to light.

Let it then be fixed and remembered, that God is love. He is infinite benevolence and goodness itself; and that he himself is the first, chief and last object of this love; so that he regards himself supremely and ultimately in all his works, and does every thing for himself, for his own sake: And that his wisdom and righteousness consist chiefly in this, as he would be neither just, faithful, nor wise, should he forget himself, and have no regard to his own rights and character, in any one thing that he does through all his dominions; and therefore to suppose he does, is to entertain the most dishonourable thought of him, which in the highest degree tarnishes and ruins his moral character. In the light of this truth, rightly understood, and cordially embraced, we shall have great assistance in finding the meaning of the holy scriptures; and determining what are the important doctrines there revealed, and see their consistence and beauty.

V. Infinite benevolence or goodness, which seeks and promotes the greatest good of the whole, is infinitely opposed to all malevolence or ill will, which opposes all the good of being, and tends to universal evil; and must be infinitely displeased with it. This is just as evident and certain, as it is that he who loves and is friendly to any particular character, or desirable object, is displeased with the contrary, and hates it, to as great a degree as he loves and is pleased with the other. And this displeasure and hatred is implied in his love to the opposite object and pleasure in it; and is really the same affection acting towards opposite objects.

He who is a friend to the greatest good, and therefore is pleased with such friendship, must be equally an enemy to all who oppose this good, and proportionally displeased and angry with them. And this displeasure, hatred and anger, in a perfectly benevolent being, is nothing in nature different from benevolence. It is nothing but goodness opposing its contrary; which it must do, or else cease to be love and goodness.

Agreeable to this, the scriptures represent God, who is infinite love and goodness, to be in a proportionable degree displeased with all sin, which is in its nature opposition to benevolence, and to the general good. This is represented as the object of his implacable hatred; and as exciting his anger, indignation, wrath and fury. This is so far from leading us to conceive of any thing in God contrary to infinite love and goodness, or really distinct from it, that it is nothing more than benevolence acting according to its own nature towards objects that oppose it. For love of good is itself opposition to evil, and hatred of it, and benevolence must be displeased with ill will, and hate and oppose the same. Nor are these opposite or different affections; but the same affection, love, acting towards different objects.

This displeasure, anger and wrath of God against sin, and the sinner, may therefore with propriety be called a just, benevolent, kind displeasure; which is the same with holy displeasure; all proceeding from love, and implied in it. Therefore, when we read in the scriptures of the divine displeasure, anger, wrath, &c. we must not form the same idea of this, as we do of those passions, as they exist in man; for this would be to conceive of God as exercising affections and passions, contrary to love; and as very imperfect, changeable and miserable. We must exclude, in our minds, every thing that implies imperfection or change, and that is inconsistent with infinite benevolence and felicity; and understand those expressions in the scriptures, as meaning perfect, unchangeable opposition of God to everything in moral agents that is contrary to infinite benevolence or goodness; for which they are wholly blameable and answerable, and deserve to be punished. And these words are doubtless the best chosen, and most fit to convey to us this idea of infinite love, considered as opposed, injured and affronted by selfish creatures, and acting accordingly.

VI. The infinite love and goodness of God, which has been described above, which is opposed to every thing in creatures that is contrary to itself, and with which it is displeased, must be disposed to manifest this displeasure and opposition to sin, in all proper ways, and to punish the sinner according to his desert whenever this is necessary in order to show his displeasure, to assert and vindicate his own character, and secure and promote the greatest good of the whole. It is proper and desirable that infinite benevolence and goodness should be manifested and acted out, in all instances, where there is opportunity for it; and therefore in its opposition to sin. For if it does not appear how opposite the moral character of God is to all sin, it cannot be set in the most clear and advantageous light; but this cannot be done, if opposition to this character be not punished in any instance or way, according to its desert. Besides, when thus to punish is necessary, in order to support the character of God, and secure the general good; not to do it would be injustice to himself and the creation: Therefore to punish, in this case, is the proper and necessary exercise of justice and righteousness, which has been shewn is included in goodness, and is an exercise of the same. It is therefore evident, that God's manifesting his displeasure and anger with the creature who is an enemy to his goodness, is not only consistent with infinite benevolence, but an expression and exercise of love and goodness itself; and it would be contrary to the nature and dictates of the most perfect goodness not to punish. And it may be added, such punishment is not the least evidence of want of benevolence to the creature who is punished. When a judge orders a criminal who is guilty of treason against his king and country, to be put to death, he does nothing contrary to perfect benevolence and goodness, but this very conduct is an expression of it, and dictated by goodness itself; for he herein acts as a friend to his king and country; and not to inflict this punishment would be unfriendly, and contrary to true goodness. Nor does he manifest any want of benevolence to the criminal, or of a proper regard for his life and welfare, by punishing him according to his deserts, when the public and general good requires it.

The disposition of the Most High to inflict punishment, and his actually inflicting evil on his creatures, as a testimony of his displeasure at sin, and to vindicate his own character, is often called vengeance in the scriptures; and is represented by his taking or executing vengeance, and being avenged on his enemies. And in this view he is frequently called. The mighty and terrible God, with whom is terrible majesty, &c. If God were not disposed to punish his creatures for their rebellion against him, and never did inflict evil on any for their sin, vengeance or vindictive justice could not he ascribed to him, nor would there be any thing terrible in his character; which would be an imperfection, and inconsistent with infinite benevolence or goodness, as has been shown. Therefore they who form notions of a love and goodness, in which there is no wrath and vengeance to punish enemies, nor any terrible majesty; and ascribe such love to God, have conceptions of his moral character which are essentially wrong, and very dishonourable to him.

VII. It appears from what has been said, and from reason, as well as scripture, that the moral perfection of God, or the divine holiness, consists in one most simple, pure, uncompounded, unchangeable act; though to accommodate it to our imperfect way of conceiving, it be divided into parts, and a number of attributes, and called by different names, as it is exercised in different views and towards various and opposite objects.

Benevolence or goodness is mercy, grace, compassion, patience, long suffering, &c. And the same benevolence is wisdom, justice, truth, faithfulness, complacence, displeasure, anger and wrath, in different views, and as it respects different objects.

VIII. Absolute, uncontrollable sovereignty may be considered as included in the moral character of God. This is the same with omnipotent love or goodness; benevolence doing whatever it pleases, infinitely above any control or obligation to any other being. Omnipotence is indeed a natural perfection; but benevolence, clothed with omnipotence, or doing what it pleases, is the essence of God's moral perfection, and if we leave out the idea of this sovereignty, we shall have not only an imperfect, but a wrong view of divine benevolence. Indeed, if we should conceive of divine sovereignty, as some seem to have done, as consisting in God's doing what he will, merely because he will, and without any possible reason why he wills thus, rather than the contrary, this would be so far from a moral perfection, that it would be no perfection; but infinitely undesirable and unbecoming the Most High, representing him rather as an almighty despot and tyrant, than an infinitely wise and good being. Though God does what he pleases, and is infinitely above all obligation or control by creatures; yet he has a good reason for all his determinations, and always wills that which is most wise, and the dictate of infinite rectitude and goodness. It is most agreeable, desirable, and of infinite importance, that infinite goodness and wisdom should be sovereign goodness, that is, above all possible control, or obligation to creatures, which is inconsistent with its doing what it pleases, or with God's "fulfilling all the good pleasure of his goodness." All the friends of God who can confide in his goodness, wisdom and righteousness, must be pleased with this sovereignty, and rejoice that he is above all control, doing whatever he pleases, through all his dominions, and "working all things according to the council of his own will:" And the idea and acknowledgment of the sovereignty of God attends all their views and pleasing sense of his moral character. This is the same with rejoicing that the Lord God omnipotent reigneth, which all good beings are represented to do; for to be under the least control, or involuntary obligation, is inconsistent with reigning, which consists in doing whatsoever he pleases. When it is said, however, that God reigns above all obligation to any, which is inconsistent with his doing what he pleases, it is not meant that he can in no instance be under obligation to his creatures. He may enter into voluntary obligation, by promise and covenant; for it may be truly said, that what God has promised he will do, he is obliged to fulfil. But all must be sensible that this is not in the least inconsistent with the most perfect sovereignty, as it has been now described.

IX. God is independently, infinitely and unchangeably happy. And this may be considered as included in his moral perfection and character, and depending upon it; for his happiness is not properly a natural, but a moral good, and consists hi moral exercises and enjoyment. If God were not benevolence or love, he would not be happy; but his infinite greatness, understanding, &c. would render him infinitely miserable; therefore his moral character is essential to his felicity, and he is blessed forever, because he is unchangeably holy: And his happiness is a holy happiness. This attribute of God is essential to complete his infinitely glorious character; and is most pleasing and delightful to all his true friends; and their benevolence or good will to God is gratified and expressed in seeing and rejoicing in his infinite, unchangeable, independent felicity and blessedness; and adding their hearty amen to it, as St. Paul did when he spoke of it. "Who is over all, God blessed forever, Amen."

Here it must however be observed, that when it is said God is independently happy, it is not meant that he takes no pleasure in his works of creation and providence, or delight in the holiness and happiness of his creatures; so that he would be as completely happy, were there no holy and happy creatures and no creation; for this is contrary to the scriptures, which represent God as pleased with his own works, and creating all things for his own pleasure; and as delighting in his holy creatures, and in exercising loving kindness, judgment and righteousness in the earth. So that it is not strictly true, that creatures add nothing to the enjoyment or happiness of God, even his essential happiness; and that he would have been as completely blessed forever, as he really is, had there been no creatures, which has been too often asserted, even in solemn addresses to God. Though the creation, with all its attendants and eternal consequences, be essential to the infinite happiness of God, and he could not have been so happy without it, this does not suppose him in the least dependent on creatures for his happiness, or for any thing else; for the creation is absolutely, perfectly, and in all respects, dependent on him; being only an emanation from his infinite fulness; and he is as independent of his creatures, as if they never had existed, and he took no pleasure in them. Nor is this inconsistent with the eternal, unchangeable happiness of God; for he from eternity perfectly enjoyed the creation, and every event that will take place to all eternity, without any change or succession of past, present and future, with respect to himself.

The scriptures, indeed, speak of God as repenting that he had made man, and being grieved at his heart, which, when spoken of man, denote uneasiness and pain; but these expressions concerning God cannot reasonably be understood as meaning any such thing; and only denote that the great wickedness and misery of man are so contrary and displeasing to the holiness and goodness of God, that were he a man, or his goodness as limited and imperfect as that of man, it would be very grievous to him, and make him repent that man ever existed. And these words are doubtless wisely chosen, as best suited to convey this idea to us, and gives us a proper sense of the exceeding wickedness and misery of man in the sight of God; even so as to render his existence infinitely worse than nothing, should things take their natural course, and not be checked and overruled by infinite power and wisdom. If God speak to men, he must speak after the manner of men.

REFLECTIONS

From the view we have now taken of the evidence of the existence of God, and his character and perfection, we may infer the following things.

1. What is meant by seeing God, or a true sensibility of his being and character. God is infinite power, knowledge, goodness, wisdom, justice and righteousness, unchangeable, eternal, every where present. To see God, is to have some proper discerning and sense of all these: and so as to make suitable impressions on the mind. And as the human mind is infinitely unequal to an adequate, comprehensive view of God; and cannot, at once, see all that it is capable of seeing, we view this infinite whole, by parts, and may sometimes attend to infinite power, more particularly, or to wisdom or goodness, and have a more affecting, pleasing sense of those, than of other perfections, though not excluding them. A discerning sensibility of any thing in God, is seeing him.

II. We hence learn what a foundation and source there is in the being and perfections of God, for the complete and eternal happiness of those who know and love him. In God there is every thing that is agreeable and desirable to an infinite degree, and no possible blemish or defect; nothing that can be in the least disagreeable, to a mind of a right taste and disposition. His whole character is superlatively beautiful, bright and excellent, and it is impossible it should be properly discerned and understood, without giving the most noble and highest kind of enjoyment! And perfect discerning and love of this infinitely excellent and glorious being, accompanied with an assurance of his love and favour, must be the most perfect and highest kind of happiness of which we are capable, or can have any conception. In this view, the truth and propriety of our Saviour's words appear in a striking light. "And this is life eternal, that they might know thee the only true God, and Jesus Christ, whom thou hast sent." And as this infinitely excellent and glorious object is unchangeable, eternal and infinite, he whose happiness consists in the knowledge and enjoyment of him, must have not only a perfect and unfailing, but also an increasing happiness; for as the object of his knowledge and love is infinite, there is a foundation for an endless progression or increase of

The System of Doctrines, contained in Divine Relation, Explained and Defended Volume I
knowledge and love, which is the same with an endless increase of enjoyment and happiness.

III. We hence learn the amazing folly, wickedness and misery of those who are displeased with the divine character and real enemies to it. This is true of all those who dislike the laws of God, and are unwilling to be under his government, and obey him; for the government and laws of God are all like himself, and an expression of his own character.

There can be no greater crime, than direct opposition to God, and hatred of him, disaffection to his existence and character; for this must be criminal in proportion to the greatness of God, his importance to being in general, and the excellence of his character, and his authority over us, and his goodness exercised towards us. But he is infinitely great, and therefore his existence is of infinite worth and importance, and he is as excellent as he is great, is infinite love and friendship to being in general; and his authority over us is great in proportion to his greatness and perfection, our inferiority to him, and dependence upon him. And what is the just and certain consequence from this? If it be not that disaffection and opposition to him is infinitely criminal, that is, a crime of unlimited infinite magnitude; then it cannot be proved to be any crime at all. This is certain, if no reason can be given, or argument offered to prove that opposition to God, and rebellion against him, is wrong and criminal, which does not equally prove that the crime is infinitely great. Any one will doubtless be convinced of this, if he will attend to the point so much as to make a trial.

The misery of such must be great. If infinite perfection and excellence give them no pleasure, but uneasiness and pain, they are of course shut out of all true happiness, and they have no object that can afford them any enjoyment, suited to their natural capacity and strong desires; and therefore must, in all their pursuits of happiness, meet with continual, vexatious disappointment, which must constantly render them very unhappy. And if they persist in this disaffection to God, and opposition to him, and so fall under the just and proper manifestations of his displeasure, and are punished in suffering evil answerable to their crimes, they must necessarily be miserable beyond all conception, and without any end!

The folly of this is beyond all expression, and the greatest that can be. To turn away from the fountain of all good and perfection, and renounce the only object of true enjoyment and happiness, and seek it in a way in which it is not to be found, but issues in complete and endless misery: what instance of folly can be great like this! No wonder the scriptures call such fools, in an emphatical sense, as if this was the sum of all folly, and there were no fools but these. These, in the highest sense, and in the most striking manner, "call evil good, and good evil; put darkness for light, and light for darkness; bitter for sweet, and sweet for bitter." The scriptures speak of such in the following language. "Be astonished, O ye heavens, at this, and be ye horribly afraid: For my people have committed two evils: They have forsaken me, the fountain of living waters, and hewed them out cisterns, broken cisterns, that can hold no water. For my people are foolish, they have not known me, they are sottish children, and have no understanding: They are wise to do evil; but to do good they have no knowledge."

IV. This subject leads us to reflect upon the very criminal blindness and great delusion of those who say in their hearts, "There is no God." The scriptures teach us there are such; and surely we must see the justice and propriety of calling them fools. "The fool hath said in his heart, there is no God." That there should be any such of the human race, is very shocking and deplorable; but it is more so to have it asserted by God, that this is true of all mankind in their natural state! That all are here declared to be such fools naturally, is certain from the context, which is quoted by St. Paul, and applied to all men. [27] What awful darkness and delusion must that be, in which they are, who, in the midst of the clearest light shining around them, do shut their eyes so as not to see the most evident and important truth, and to be quite blind to the most excellent, charming, glorious character! And that the heart of man should be thus stupid and blind, even when there is a rational conviction, and acknowledgment of the truth, is yet more shocking. This is the blindness of the heart, spoken of by St. Paul. [28] "Having the understanding darkened, being alienated from the life of God, through the ignorance that is in them, because of the blindness of their heart." When the light that is in men is, through the moral disorders of the mind, turned into such darkness, how great is that darkness!

And this blindness and delusion must be criminal in proportion to the clear and abundant evidence of the truth, and the infinite importance and excellence of the object, which this darkness hides from the mind; for it is the blindness of the heart, and therefore a moral, voluntary blindness, and cannot be distinguished from disaffection and real opposition of the heart to the being and character of God; and consequently the whole of it is nothing but sin. In this light, therefore, the scriptures every where represent this sort of blindness and delusion, which originates from the heart, and consists essentially in the moral disorders and depravity of the mind. All sin is indeed moral darkness and delusion, it is opposed to all moral truth, and is in its own nature a sort of Atheism, as it does in all the exercises of it deny the God that is above. It is therefore so far from being unaccountable that the scriptures should assert, that they whose hearts are wholly under the dominion of sin, say in their hearts there is no God, that the reason of it may be easily seen; and it is most evident and certain, that it cannot be otherwise, and to assert the contrary is a very gross and palpable contradiction. When all the feelings and exercises of the heart are as if there were no pod, or are opposed to his being and moral character, then the heart says, there is no God: Therefore they who have no true virtue, no love to God, are in the scriptures said not to know God; but to be alienated from the life of God, and without God in the world. [29]

Footnotes:

16. See Locke on the Human Understanding, Book I. Chap. IV. and the authors there quoted by him. Also Dr. Robertson's History of South America.

17. See President Clap's Essay on the Nature and Foundation of Moral Virtue. Page 42, &c. The following is transcribed from him, page 45. "I was well acquainted with a Negro, who was a man of superior natural powers, and made a profession of religion; who told me that he was born in the island of Madagascar, and lived there till he was above thirty years old: And in all that time he never had a thought of the being of a God, a Creator or Governor of the world, or of a future state after death." "Dr. Williots, in his sermon on the Light of Nature, relates a story of a man in France, who was born deaf and dumb; yet was very knowing, active and faithful in the common affairs of life: And upon a solemn trial before the bishop, by the help of those who could converse with him, was judged to be a knowing and devout christian, and admitted to the Sacrament of the Lord's Supper, which he attended for many years, with all the signs of high devotion, such as elevation of hands, eyes, &c. At length a large quantity of hard wax was taken out of his ears; upon which he could hear; and, after a while, could speak and read. He then declared, that while he was deaf, he had no idea of a God, or maker of the world, or of a future state; and that all he then did, in matters of religion, was purely in imitation of others."

18. Hierocles.
19. 1 John ii. 4.
20. Chap. iv. 8.
21. Prov. ii. 2, 5, 6.
22. Ezekiel xxxix. 25.
23. Isaiah xliii. 8.
24. Isaiah xlviii. 9, 11.
25. Nahum i. 3.
26. Isaiah xxvi. 7.
27. Ps. xiv. 3.--Rom. iii. 9, 12.
28. Eph. iv. 18.
29. Eph. ii. 12.--iv. 18.

CHAPTER III - CONCERNING THE UNITY OF GOD; AND THE TRINITY

THAT there is but one God, the scriptures every where assert; and this is agreeable to reason, and the works of creation and providence, which we behold. And the contrary supposition is most absurd, and undesirable, and really involves in it infinite evil. God must be a self existent being; which is the same with existing necessarily: But necessary existence must be infinite, as has been shewn. Therefore there can be but one first cause, who exists necessarily, and without beginning, for there can be but one infinite being. To suppose another, or a second, necessarily excludes the first, and to suppose the first, necessarily excludes the second, and any other infinite being. The same is evident from the consideration of the divine perfections: God is infinite power, infinite wisdom: But there cannot be two or more infinite wisdoms, &c. because this is a contradiction. Infinite power is all the power there is, or can be, and is clearly inconsistent with another power distinct from that, which is also infinite. Moreover, if we make the impossible supposition that there are two or more infinite beings, they must be perfectly alike in all respects, or not. If not perfectly alike and without any difference in any respect, then one or the other must be imperfect; for absolutely infinite perfection admits of no variation, or difference: so that if any two beings differ in any respect, they cannot both be absolutely perfect; therefore cannot both be God. But if they are perfectly alike in every respect and every thing, then they are perfectly one and the same; and the supposition destroys itself, being a direct contradiction. And there can be no possible need of more than one God; and therefore were this possible, it is not desirable. There can really be no more existence than one infinite being, or any addition to infinite perfection and excellence; therefore no more can be desired; and nothing can be effected or done, more than he can do. In a word, he is all-sufficient, and no addition can be made to this, or even conceived.

Yea, it is so far from being desirable, that there should be more gods than one, were it possible, that it is most undesirable, and would be the greatest evil. Such a supposition would only tend to perplex the pious mind, not knowing which of the gods he did worship, or what god to love and adore, or in which to put his trust. There have been those in the christian world, who have supposed two gods, a good and an evil one. The former the author of all good, the latter of all evil. Were it so, there must be infinite variance and opposition between these beings, and it is impossible that the votaries of either should be happy. Such a belief, as the acknowledgment of more gods than one, is even worse than atheism itself; or rather is the worst sort of atheism; for such are really without any God.

The scriptures teach us that there are three in this one God. Not three Gods; for this would be a contradiction; but that this infinite being exists in such a manner, as to be three distinct subsistencies or persons, and yet but one God. The most express declaration of this is by the apostle John. He says, "There are three that bear record in heaven, the Father, the Word, and the Holy Ghost: And these are One." [30] This is also clearly asserted by Christ himself, when he directs his disciples to baptize all the proselytes to Christianity, "In the name of the Father, and of the Son, and of the Holy Ghost." [31] Baptism being a covenant transaction between God and the creature, and a solemn act of worship, it would be idolatry to administer it in any other name but that of the only true God. Therefore these words warrant us to believe that the Father, the Son, and the holy Ghost, are God, and but one God, agreeable to what is said by the apostle John in the above cited passage, the Word and the Son meaning the same. This is also expressed by the apostle Paul, in his benediction or prayer, with which he concludes his second epistle to the Corinthians. "The grace of our Lord Jesus Christ, and the love of God, and the communion of the Holy Ghost, be with you all. Amen." [32] Hereby God must be meant, the Father, mentioned in the above cited passages; and this is therefore parallel to them. And divinity is ascribed to each of these; by his blessing in each of these names, and making them the object of prayer.

There are many passages in the Old Testament, which are agreeable to those in the New Testament, which have been mentioned, and represent a plurality or Trinity, as comprehended in the One true God: The following are some of them. It is remarkable that the Hebrew word, which is generally used for God, and is so translated, is commonly put in the plural, and not in the singular number. There is an instance of it the first time it is used in the Bible. "In the beginning God created the heaven and the earth." And agreeable to this it is said, "Remember thy Creators." [33] It is translated Creator, but the Hebrew word is plural. And the reason and propriety of it is discovered and best explained, by observing that a plurality, or Trinity, is included in the Creator of all things: for it is expressly and repeatedly asserted, that Jesus Christ created the world and all things in it. "In the beginning was the Word, and the Word was with God, and the Word was God. All things were made by him; and without him was not any thing made, that was made." [34] "For by him (the Son of God) were all things created, that are in heaven, and that are in earth." [35] And creation is also ascribed to the Holy Spirit. "And the Spirit of God moved upon the face of the waters." [36] "By his Spirit he hath garnished the heavens. The Spirit of God hath made me." [37]

Agreeable to this, God uses words in the plural number, when he is about to create man, and speaks as if there were a plurality of persons to do it. "And God said. Let us make man, in our image, after our likeness." [38] And this form of speech is repeatedly used. "And the Lord God said. Behold, the man is become like one of us. And the Lord said--Let us go down, and there confound their language." [39]

There is a remarkable passage in the prophecy of Isaiah, which represents a plurality, or three in Jehovah, or the Lord of Hosts. The Seraphims "cried one unto another, and said, Holy, holy, holy, is the Lord of Hosts. Also I heard the voice of the Lord, saying, Whom shall I send, and who will go for us?" [40] The plurality is here expressed by the plural pronoun, us. "Who will go for us?" And the Trinity is expressed by using the word holy three times successively; of which there is no instance of the kind in the Bible, when a single person, which is in no sense plural, is addressed. There is an instance of the same, indeed, when the same Being is addressed by the living creatures which John saw and heard. "And they rest not day and night, saying, Holy, holy, holy Lord God Almighty, which was, and is, and is to come." [41] But that a plurality and a Trinity, comprehended in Jehovah, is designed to be expressed here by these words, is confirmed and made certain, by the reference which is made to this passage, in the New Testament. All will grant that he who is called the Father, in the New Testament, when joined with the Son or Word, and the Holy Ghost, is intended or included in the word Jehovah, or the Lord of Hosts, in this passage in Isaiah. And the apostle John, referring to it, says, "These things said Isaiah, when he saw his glory, and spake of him." That is, of Jesus Christ. [42] The apostle Paul, when he quotes some of the words of this same passage in Isaiah, says, "Well spake the Holy Ghost, by Isaiah the Prophet, unto our fathers."[43] So that the glory of Jehovah was the glory of the Son, or Jesus Christ; and what was spoken of the Lord of Hosts, was spoken of Christ the Son of God. And what the Lord of Hosts said by Isaiah, the Holy Ghost said. It is hence certain, that these three, the Father, the Son, or the Word, and the Holy Ghost, into whose name christians are baptized, and in whose name the Apostles blessed, and who bear record in heaven, were included in the vision which Isaiah had of the Lord of Hosts. And who that attends to this scriptural view of the case, can doubt when it is said. Who will go for us? the plurality of the Father, Son and Holy Ghost is intended; and that when the Seraphim adored the Lord of Hosts, and cried, saying, Holy, holy, holy, there is reference to those three.

From the passages of scripture which have been now mentioned, to prove there is a plurality or Trinity in the one true God, it is also proved that the Word, the Son of God, the Lord Jesus Christ, is God, and as really, and as much included in the Deity, in Jehovah, as is the Father: And that this is equally true of the Holy Ghost. But the evidence of the real divinity of Jesus Christ, will appear yet more clear and strong, by examining the scripture more particularly on this point. But as this will be done in a more proper place in a following section, it is omitted here. And the divinity of the Holy Ghost will now be more particularly considered.

In addition to the evidence of this, from the scriptures, which have been produced above, a number of other passages of scripture will now be mentioned, from which it appears, that the Holy Ghost is God, and included in the Godhead.

Christ says, "Except a man be born of the Spirit, he cannot see the kingdom of God. What is born of the Spirit, is spirit." [44] And the apostle Paul says, "christians are saved by the washing of regeneration, and renewing of the Holy Ghost." [45] The apostle John speaks often of the same change, and renovation, common to all christians, as being born of God. [46] The inference is, that the Holy Spirit is God; since to be born of the Spirit, and to be born of God, is precisely the same thing. This renovation, by which men are born of God, and born of the Spirit, is called in scripture the new creature, or new creation. And it is indeed a greater work than the creation of the world; therefore the Spirit who thus renews men must be God.

"Why hath Satan filled thine heart to lie to the Holy Ghost? Thou hast not lied unto men, but unto God." [47] Here God and the Holy Ghost are synonymous, and mean the same thing; as much as if it had been said, thou hast lied unto God the Holy Ghost. "The things of God knoweth no man. But the natural man receiveth not the things of the Spirit of God, neither can he know them." [48] From these two sentences compared, it appears that the things of God, and the things of the Spirit of God, express the same thing. But if the things of the Spirit of God are the things of God, does it not

The System of Doctrines, contained in Divine Relation, Explained and Defended Volume I
follow that the Spirit of God is God? "All scripture is given by inspiration of God. Holy men spake as they were moved by the Holy Ghost." [49] To be inspired by God, and moved by the Holy Ghost, is the same; therefore the Holy Ghost is God. [50]

These three are spoken of, or addressed, in the scriptures, in such terms as are used to denote a distinct personality, such as I, thou, he, or him. Thus the Father speaks of himself, and the Son; and thus the Son speaks to the Father, and of him, and of the Holy Spirit; of which there are many instances, which must have been observed by those who read the Bible.

It is thought that the use of the above mentioned personal epithets, is a sufficient warrant to distinguish the three in the divine Trinity, by the word person. But it must be carefully observed, that when this word is applied to the Father, Son, and Holy Ghost, as three distinct persons, it does not import the same distinction which is expressed by it when applied to men. It means nothing inconsistent with the highest perfection, or with these three being really and most perfectly one God. Nor is it pretended that this word, when used in this instance, can be so defined as to give any clear and adequate idea of a subject so mysterious and infinitely incomprehensible. They who object to the word person, and will not use it because not applicable to the three who are one, may doubtless, with equal reason, object to any word which can be used, even the word Trinity, or three, which the apostle John uses, and to the personal words so often mentioned in scripture. However, if they who object to the word person, will allow that, according to the scripture, the one only true God does subsist in such a manner, and so infinitely above our comprehension, that there are three, viz. Father, Son, and Holy Ghost, in this one jehovah; and that this distinction and manner of existence is peculiar and essential to the infinite eternal Being as the most perfect, happy and glorious mode of existence, independent of any divine operations ad extra, and the proper foundation of these: If they will grant this, it is presumed none will contend with them about the word person.

It is acknowledged, that this is incomprehensible by us, we not being able to form any precise or adequate idea of three persons in one God, but as there is no inconsistence or contradiction in this, our not being able to comprehend it, is no reason why we should not believe it, when it is revealed; for if we will not believe any thing respecting God, which we cannot comprehend and is therefore above our reason, we shall not believe there is a God. If there be a God, he does exist without beginning or succession; but this is as much above our comprehension, as that he subsists in three persons; and we cannot have a more clear understanding of the former, than of the latter. God, who is infinitely great; and infinitely above us, exists in a manner infinitely above our conception: And if we will not believe what God has revealed of himself, because it is above our reason, and incomprehensible by us, we shall act a most unreasonable part; for reason teaches us, that God is incomprehensible in more respects than one; and in how many we know not. God has been pleased, for wise reasons, to reveal one instance of this, which we otherwise could not have known; and there can be no reason against believing it: and therefore to reject it, is most unreasonable and absurd.

There may be innumerable truths respecting this infinitely incomprehensible Being, which would be as much above the reach of our understanding and reason, as this is, were they revealed; for but a very small portion is yet known of him. This truth, respecting a Trinity of persons in the one God, is revealed, because it was necessary to be known and believed, in order to understand the gospel, revealing a way for the salvation of sinners, in which each of those Three are concerned, in different respects and views, and distinct from each other: For had there not been this distinction of persons in God, there would have been no foundation or sufficiency in him for the exercise of mercy, in the recovery of apostate man. In this view, the doctrine of the Trinity, one God subsisting in three persons, appears to be an important and essential doctrine of christianity.

There have been many attempts to explain this doctrine, and shew the particular manner of the distinct subsistence of the three persons in the divine Trinity; but these have often been so far from giving any light and satisfaction on the subject, that they have only darkened counsel, by words without knowledge; and rather given advantage to the opposers of the doctrine, and increased their prejudices. Therefore nothing of this kind will be attempted here. It may however be observed, that this manner of subsistence in three persons, though incomprehensible to us, may be essential to the infinitely perfect Being, and that otherwise he would not be absolutely perfect, all-sufficient, and infinitely blessed. Have we not reason to conclude that this distinction of three in one, is that in which the most perfect and happy society consists, in which love and friendship is exercised to the highest perfection, and with infinite enjoyment, and felicity? And that the most perfect and happy society of creatures, united together forever, in the kingdom of God, in the strongest, sweetest love and friendship, is an emanation from this infinite three one, as the fountain and pattern of all happy society and friendship; and the highest possible resemblance and imitation of it? This idea seems to be suggested, if not necessarily implied, in what Christ says in his prayer to the Father. "That they all may be one. as thou, Father, art in me, and I in thee; that they also may be one in us. That they may be one, even as we are one. I in them, and thou in me, that they may be made perfect in one. That the love wherewith thou hast loved me, may be in them, and I in them."

Footnotes:

30. 1 John v. 7.
31. Matthew xxviii. 19.
32. 2 Corinthians xiii. 14.
33. Eccles. xii. i. 2.
34. John i. 1, 3.
35. Col. i. 16.
36. Gen. i. 2.
37. Job xxvi. 13.--xxxiii. 4.
38. Gen. i. 26.
39. Gen.iii.22.--xi. 6, 7.
40. Chap. vi. 3, 8.
41. Rev. iv. 8.
42. John xii. 41.
43. Acts xxviii. 25.
44. John iii. 5, 6.
45. Titus iii. 5.
46. John i. 13--1 John iii. 9. iv. 7. v. 1, 4, 18.
47. Acts v. 3, 4.
48. 1 Cor. ii. 11, 4.
49. 2 Tim. iii. 16--1 Pet. i. 21.
50. Many more passages of scripture, of the same tenor, might be mentioned, were it needful. They may be seen in a small book entitled, "The Catholic Doctrine of a Trinity." By William Jones.

CHAPTER IV - ON THE DECREES OF GOD

HAVING considered what God is, the next inquiry will be concerning the divine operations and works. And in these are included the decrees, which are first to be considered; as they are the foundation and origin of all his exertions and works, ad extra, in creation and providence: For God worketh all things after the council of his own will. Indeed, every thing which is properly an effect, has its foundation in the purpose or decree of God, as its original cause, without which it could not have taken place. And every such effect is fixed and made sure of existence by the divine decree, and infallibly connected with it.

The assembly of Divines, in their shorter catechism, have given a concise definition of the decrees of God, which is both rational and agreeable to the holy scriptures, viz. "The decrees of God are his eternal purpose, according to the council of his own will, whereby for his own glory he hath foreordained whatsoever comes to pass." And in their confession of faith, in words a little different, "God from all eternity did, by the most wise and holy council of his own will, freely and unchangeably ordain whatsoever comes to pass."

The decrees of God must be from eternity, and not in time. He who exists without beginning, absolutely independent, omnipotent, infinite in understanding and wisdom, must know what is wisest and best, or what is most agreeable to him with respect to all possible effects or events; and therefore must determine what should actually take place, and what should not. Such determination or decree is, in such a sense, essential to the divine existence, that the former must be coeval with the latter, and is necessarily implied in it. Besides, if any of the purposes or decrees of God be in time, or later than his existence, he must be changeable, by having new determinations, new views and designs, which he had not before; which is inconsistent with his necessary existence, his infinity, and absolute perfection, all which are essential to God, as has been proved.

Therefore in scripture the purpose or decrees of God are said to be eternal, "Known unto God are all his works, from the beginning of the world," or from eternity, as it should have been rendered. If God's knowing all his works from eternity does not mean his purpose concerning them, it necessarily implies this; for how could he know what he would do, if he had no will or purpose to do? "According to the eternal purpose, which he purposed in Christ Jesus our Lord." [51]

Though God be sovereign in his decrees, and all his operations; that is, he has determined every thing and every event just as he pleased, being infinitely above all control by the will or power of any one; and under no obligation to any other being; yet they are not arbitrary, that is, determined and fixed without any reason why he should purpose and decree as he has done, rather than the contrary, or otherwise: But they are all infinitely wise and good, or the dictates of the most perfect wisdom. For if God decree or act, he must decree and act like himself, an infinitely wise Being. Infinite wisdom is able or sufficient to form the wisest and best plan of creation and providence, of a world or system, be it ever so large and complicated, and however many creatures, things and events, it may comprehend; and though it include innumerable existencies and events without any end. Such a plan is therefore formed and fixed upon by the divine decrees, which is of all other possible plans the wisest and the best: For if it were otherwise it would be so far disagreeable, defective, unwise, and wrong. The scripture therefore ascribes wisdom to God in all his works, by which his wise purpose and decrees are brought into effect. "O Lord, how manifold are thy works! In wisdom hast thou made them all." [52] "O the depth of the riches both of the wisdom and knowledge of God! How unsearchable are his judgments, and his ways past finding out!" [53]

The decrees of God are unchangeable; they are fixed from eternity, and cannot be altered, in any degree, or with respect to any thing, event, or circumstance. "The counsel of the Lord standeth forever, the thoughts of his heart to all generations." [54] "He is in one mind, and who can turn him?" [55] That the divine purpose is unalterable, is as evident and certain as that God is unchangeable; for alteration of God's design or decree is a change in God: And this necessarily supposes imperfection. And it is unspeakably undesirable and dreadful to suppose, that the infinitely wise and good purpose and decree of God, as all his decrees are, should be capable of any possible change or alteration; so as to fail of the most exact and perfect execution. And the more stable and fixed the infinitely wise decrees of God are, and the farther from all possible change, the more agreeable, and the greater ground of joy, are they to every one who is a friend of wisdom.

It may be farther observed, concerning the decrees of God, that they extend to every thing, and every event, though ever so small, compared with others, and every the most minute circumstance that takes place, or will exist to eternity. For every one of these are necessary parts of the most wise and perfect plan; otherwise they could have no existence in it. And if one of these had been left out of the divine plan, it would have been so far less perfect, and really defective. It is not to be supposed that of any two possible existences, events, or circumstances of existence, there should be no difference in any respect; so that one could not be preferred to the other, by infinite wisdom, as better and more suited to answer the end proposed, than the other; though we, or finite discerning, may not be able to perceive any difference: Therefore infinite wisdom discerns and fixes upon that which is preferable and best, in every instance. No two proposed or possible objects, events or circumstances, being perfectly alike or equal in the view of omniscience, there is ground of choice and preference; so that the divine determination respecting the actual existence of all these, and their taking place in all respects exactly as they do, or will, is, in every instance, most wise: and no thing, event, or circumstance, would be in any other respect otherwise consistent with infinite wisdom.

Jesus Christ teaches us that God's providence and care extend to the smallest things, and most minute circumstances, when he says to his disciples, "Are not five sparrows sold for two farthings? and not one of them is forgotten before God, or shall fall on the ground, without your heavenly Father: But the very hairs of your head are all numbered."

It may be of some importance to observe here, that there is a distinction and difference between the decrees of God, and his foreknowledge, as the words are commonly used. Divine foreknowledge is God's foreseeing future existence and events, and knowing from eternity what would take place in all futurity, to eternity, or without end. This foreknowledge is not only to be distinguished from the decree; but must be considered as, in order of nature, consequent upon the determination and purpose of God, and dependent upon it. For the futurition or futurity of all things depends upon the decrees of God; by these every created existence, and every event, with all their circumstances, are fixed and made certain; and in consequence of their being thus: decreed, they are the objects of foreknowledge; for they could not be known to be future, unless they were so; and they were made so by the divine decree, and nothing else. If we may so speak, God foreknew all things, that were to come to pass, by knowing his own purpose and decrees, by which their existence was made certain. Had God decreed nothing respecting future existences, by creation and providence, there could have been no foreknowledge of any thing whatsoever. Hence the decrees of God may be certainly inferred from his foreknowledge; for the former must be as extensive as the latter; and nothing can be foreknown or seen to have a future existence, the future existence of which has not been made certain by a divine decree.

All future existences, events and actions, must have a cause of their futurition, or there must be a reason why they are future, or certainly to take place, rather than not. This cause must be the divine decree determining their future existence, or it must be in the future existences themselves; for there is no other possible supposition. But the future existences could not be the cause of their own futurition; for this supposes them to exist as a cause, and to have influence, before they have any existence, even from eternity. And if they may be the cause of their own futurition, or become future of themselves, then they might actually exist of themselves; for by becoming future, their existence is made certain and necessary; therefore that which makes them certainly future, is really the cause of their existence. This therefore can be nothing but the divine decree, determining their future existence, without which nothing could be future, consequently nothing could be known to be future. They therefore who deny the doctrine of God's decrees, and yet acknowledge the omniscience of God, and that all future events were known to him from eternity, are really inconsistent: for if the world, or any creature, or any event, could be certainly future, without being made so by God, it can actually exist without him: for the existence of it is certain and necessary, and it cannot but exist, when once it becomes certainly future.

Therefore, because the foreknowledge of God does necessarily imply and involve his decrees, the former is sometimes put for the latter, in the inspired writings. The following are instances of it. "Him, being delivered by the determinate counsel and foreknowledge of God, ye have taken, and by wicked hands have crucified and slain." [56] "For whom he did foreknow, he also did predestinate to be conformed to the image of his Son." [57] "God hath not cast away his people whom he foreknew." [58] "Elect according to the foreknowledge of God the Father." [59]

As the decrees of God are most wise, this necessarily supposes some end in view, and that which is best, the most excellent, important, and desirable that can be; for wisdom consists in proposing and pursuing such an end, in ways and by means in the best manner adapted to accomplish that end. When no end is in view to be accomplished by any purpose or work, if this can be, there is no wisdom; and if there be an end proposed and pursued, if this be not the best that can be proposed and effected, the purpose and pursuit is not wisdom but folly. And if the end

The System of Doctrines, contained in Divine Relation, Explained and Defended Volume I
proposed be the highest and best that can be; yet if the means fixed upon to accomplish that end, be not in all respects the best suited to accomplish the end proposed, this must be a defect of wisdom. Therefore infinite wisdom discerns without a possibility of mistake, what is the best end, most worthy to be set up and pursued, and fixes on this end; and discerns and determines the best means by which this end shall in the best manner be answered. And this determination is the same with the decrees of God, and involves or comprehends every thing that comes to pass, every event, great and small, with every circumstance, be it ever so minute; and fixes them all; unerring wisdom being exercised with respect to them all; so that to make the least alteration in any thing, event, or circumstance, would render the whole plan less perfect and wise. "The work of God is perfect. Whatsoever God doth, it shall be forever: Nothing can be put to it, nor any thing taken from it." That which is perfect is not capable of the least alteration, without being rendered imperfect and defective. This is true of the infinitely wise plan of the divine operations, and all future events, which was formed by the eternal purpose and decrees of God.

If it be inquired, What that best, most important and desirable end can be, which must be proposed by infinite wisdom? The answer must be, that God himself, or that which respects him, is the end of his decrees and works. When the divine plan of operations was laid, there was nothing but God existing, or to be set up, or regarded as an end; and how could future existence be made an ultimate end with him, in proposing and causing it to exist? And when it does exist, it is infinitely less considerable and respectable than God; and as the dust in the balance; yea, as nothing, in comparison with Him. It would therefore be contrary to reason, and therefore contrary to infinite wisdom, to make creatures or the creation, considered as something distinct from God, the object of supreme respect in God's designs and works, and not God himself, whose existence is infinitely greater, more important and excellent, and who is the sum of all being. Wisdom must have supreme respect to him in every design, and in every operation, as the first and the last, and all in all. Which is the same as to say, God makes himself his end in all his purposes and operations.

Divine revelation confirms this, in which God speaks of himself as the first and the last, the beginning and the ending, by which he represents himself as the first cause and supreme or last end of all things. And this is confirmed by the following passages, "For of him, and through him, and to him, are all things. [60] For by him were all things created, that are in heaven, and that are in earth, visible and invisible, whether they be thrones, or dominions, or principalities, or powers: All things were created by him, and for him." [61] Agreeable to this it is said, "The Lord hath made all things for himself." [62]

God makes himself his end in his decrees and works, in being pleased with the exercise and expression, exhibition and display of his own infinite perfection and excellence: And determining to do this in the best manner, and to the highest possible degree, in his works of creation and providence. This exhibition, display or manifestation, is in divine revelation called the glory of God; and is there abundantly represented as the supreme end of all God's designs and works, which any one properly attentive to the Bible must have observed: It is therefore thought needless to illustrate this by a particular attention to those passages of scripture by which it is evident. This exhibition and display of the divine perfections, necessarily implies and involves, as essential to it, the communication of his own holiness and happiness to the greatest possible degree, which consists in effecting or producing the greatest possible moral excellence and felicity in his creation, or by his works. This consists hi the highest, the greatest possible good or happiness of creatures, whose capacities, circumstances, and their number, and all other things, circumstances and events, are contrived and adapted in the best manner to answer this end.

The moral excellence and perfection of God consists in love, or goodness, which has been proved in a former chapter. This infinite love of an infinite Being, is infinite felicity. This consists in his infinite regard to himself as the fountain and sum of all being; and ills pleasure and delight in himself, in his own infinite excellence and perfection; and in the highest possible exercise, exhibition and display of his infinite fulness, perfection and glory. And his pleasure in the latter, so as to make it the supreme and ultimate end of all his works, necessarily involves and supposes his pleasure and delight in the happiness of his creatures. If he be pleased with the greatest possible exercise, communication, and exhibition of his goodness, he must be pleased with the happiness of creatures, and the greatest possible happiness of the creation, because the former so involves the latter that they cannot be separated; and may be considered as one and the same thing; and doubtless are but one in the view of the all comprehending mind; though we, whose conceptions are so imperfect and partial, are apt to conceive of the glory of God, and the good of the creature, as two distinct things, and different ends to be answered, in God's designs and works. [63]

Thus whatsoever comes to pass from the beginning of time to eternity is foreordained, and fixed from eternity by the infinitely wise counsel and unchangeable purpose of God. He being infinite in understanding, power, wisdom and goodness, must perfectly know, what was the wisest and best plan of creation and providence, of operations and events, which includes everything desirable and good, and excludes whatever is not so; and he must fix upon this plan, without any possible error, and determine to prosecute it; for if any thing be left undetermined and uncertain, even the most minute existence, event, or circumstance and appendage of any existence or event, it must be owing to a defect in wisdom and goodness, or in power to execute. No truth ever was, or can be more demonstrably certain than this; and none can be more agreeable to wisdom and goodness, or more important. If a man be to contrive and make any machine or building, the end which it is to answer must be in view, and fixed; and the plan of his operation must be laid, including every thing that is to come into the composition, so as in the best manner to answer the end designed. And the more skill and wisdom the workman has, the more clear and perfect will be his idea and view of the whole plan, and of every part, even the most minute, which is included in it; and the more fixed and determined he will be to prosecute this plan, without the least variation from it. And if he have skill and wisdom sufficient to lay a perfect plan of operation, without the least mistake or error, he will be esteemed and prized above all others of less skill; and the more certain and fixed his plan of operation is, and the farther he is from a disposition to make any alteration, or a possibility of being impeded in his work or unable to execute his design, according to his present purpose, the more agreeable it will be to all who are interested in his work which he is to execute; and to all who have the least spark of wisdom and goodness; and that in proportion to the excellence and importance of the design.

What a source of unspeakable satisfaction and joy must it then be to all the children of wisdom, that the most High, omnipotent, infinitely wise, just and good, has laid a plan to express and exhibit his own character; which therefore must be wise and good, like himself; and which comprehends and fixes every thing, and all events, from the greatest to the least, from the first to the last; and which is absolutely perfect, infinitely wise, and comprehends all possible good; so that not the least thing, event, or the smallest appendage and circumstance, can be altered, left out, or added, without rendering it less desirable, excellent and perfect! And is it possible that any one who is not unfriendly to infinite wisdom and goodness, and to the most absolute perfection and excellence, should have the least objection to this? Yea, will he not highly approve of it, and make it the ground of his chief comfort and joy? And is not this infinitely preferable to a world and series of events, if this were possible, fixed by blind fate, or existing and taking place by mere, undesigning chance? Most certainly this demonstrable truth, that God has, by the infinitely wise counsel of his own will, from eternity foreordained whatsoever comes to pass, is infinitely more desirable than any other supposition whatever, were it possible; and is a foundation on which a pious mind, a true friend to God, may rest with the greatest security and satisfaction. And if he should give this up, what support and comfort could he have? Where could he fly for refuge from evil? He must fall into the most awful darkness, and horror.

Objection, It is granted that this doctrine of the divine decrees, as it has now been stated, might readily be admitted as certain and desirable, were it possible, and was it consistent with known fact, which it most certainly is not: Therefore, however great and clear the evidence of this doctrine may seem to be; and though it appear most desirable that all events should be determined by infinite wisdom and goodness; yet it cannot be true, because it is impossible and inconsistent with what has actually taken place. It is impossible, because inconsistent with moral government, and with the freedom and moral agency of creatures; and so excludes all possibility of virtue or vice, praise or blame, reward or punishment. And if this doctrine were consistent with all this; yet it is inconsistent with the evil which has taken place, both moral and natural evil, which could have no place in a plan formed and fixed by infinite wisdom and goodness, and comprehending the greatest possible good. Besides, to suppose all this evil was foreordained by God, and takes place in consequence of his purpose and decree, represents the Most High as the origin, cause or author of it all, even all the moral evil in the universe: And what can be more shocking and horrible than this!

In this objection are three distinct things, which re« quire a separate and particular consideration.

First. It is to be inquired. Whether the doctrine of God's decrees, whereby he hath foreordained whatsoever comes to pass, is inconsistent with the liberty and moral agency of creatures, by fixing all events and all actions, so as to render them infallibly certain. And here it may be proper to observe several things, in order to prepare the way to a more clear determination of this question.

1. If the doctrine of God's decrees be inconsistent with the freedom and moral agency of man; then the foreknowledge of God is equally so: Therefore the objection under consideration is as much against the latter, as it is against the former. For if it be foreknown what events and what actions will take place, then they must be fixed and certain; since it is a contradiction to say, an event is certainly foreknown, and yet it is uncertain whether it will come to pass; just as great and palpable a contradiction as to say, an event is certain and fixed, and yet precarious and uncertain whether it will take place or not. Nothing can be the object of the divine foreknowledge, which is

The System of Doctrines, contained in Divine Relation, Explained and Defended Volume I

not fixed as certainly future. If it be not fixed by the decree of God, it must be fixed by blind fate, or by something else, if this were possible; and this surely is as inconsistent with the freedom of man, as if fixed by the counsel and decree of God: Yea, infinitely more so. This is observed, to show that he who makes the objection under consideration, and yet believes the foreknowledge of God, is inconsistent with himself; and must, would he be consistent, withdraw his objection, or give up the doctrine of God's foreknowledge.

II. It being confessedly so very important and desirable that whatsoever comes to pass should be determined and fixed by infinite wisdom and goodness, if this can be done consistent with moral government; and since God is infinitely great, powerful and wise, there is reason to conclude this is not impossible; but that both are perfectly consistent: Is it not presumption and arrogance for fallen man, ignorant and deceived in a thousand things, peremptorily, and with assurance to determine that it is impossible with God to make creatures, who shall be absolutely dependent upon him, in all respects, and so as to act perfectly conformable to his most wise plan, and fulfil his counsel, and yet exercise all the freedom necessary to moral agency? If this were certainly known to imply a contradiction, it might safely be pronounced impossible: But since many things have appeared to short sighted, partial man, inconsistent and impossible, and have been confidently pronounced to be such, which afterwards have been found to be otherwise, it may be so in this case. And if both these be really and perfectly consistent, how happy! Let this point then be examined without prejudice, and with the utmost care and attention, reviewing it again and again. And if the consistence may be discovered, what matter of consolation and joy will it afford!

III. It does not appear from our feelings and experience, that a previous certainty respecting our actions in the least takes away or diminishes our freedom and moral agency. We feel ourselves free and accountable in our voluntary actions; and the supposition of a previous certainty that we should act just as we do, does not alter our feeling ourselves free, and knowing we act so, so far as our experience is to be regarded. Is not this a just ground of suspicion at least, that all objections and reasonings against this, by which it is concluded to be impossible, are fallacious and without foundation: Especially when it is considered, that a mistake respecting the divine decrees and superintendency, determining and fixing all events, which are so infinitely high, and above our reach; or about the nature of human liberty, &c. will lead to groundless and very erroneous conclusions on this point?

IV. Since it is so consonant to reason, and even demonstrably certain, that a Being of infinite understanding, power and wisdom, who is absolutely independent, and on whom all creatures and events wholly depend, must determine and foreordain whatsoever comes to pass; and at the same time it is equally certain that men are free and moral agents: And since Divine Revelation most expressly and abundantly asserts both these; he who admits and believes them both to be true, however unable he may be to reconcile them, and show or conceive how they are consistent, acts a more reasonable and wise part, than those who reject one as not true, and impossible, merely because they cannot see their consistence.

There are innumerable instances in the scriptures of God's determining and foretelling the voluntary actions of men, and the events dependent on them: And yet, in those actions, they are represented as free and accountable, as sinful or virtuous, and blameable or commendable; as much so, as if their actions had not been thus fixed and foreknown. There is not perhaps a prediction in the Bible, which is not an instance of this; and most of those predictions do fix and declare to be certain, innumerable voluntary actions of men, which are either expressly foretold, or necessarily implied in the prophecy. Only a few instances, out of the many, will here be mentioned, as sufficient to illustrate this observation. The conduct of Pharaoh and the Egyptians, towards the children of Israel, was determined and foretold long before it took place, to Abraham and to Moses: And yet they were considered and treated as moral agents, and culpable, and were punished for those very actions which were foreordained and foretold. God said to Abraham, "Know of a surety, that thy seed shall be a stranger in a land that is not theirs, and shall serve them, and they shall afflict them four hundred years. And also, that nation, whom they shall serve, will I judge." And God told Abraham that he would bring his seed from Egypt into the land of Canaan, after four hundred years, which event depended on millions of millions of voluntary free actions of that people, and of others. And he promised the same thing to Moses, and that they should hearken to him, when he seat him into Egypt to deliver them; and that they should worship God in Mount Sinai; and he said to Moses, "I am sure that the king of Egypt will not let you go. And I will stretch out my hand, and smite Egypt, and after that, he will let you go."

God told Moses that the people of Israel would apostatize after his death, and practise idolatry, &c. and that he would punish them for it. Upon which Moses said to them, "I know that after my death ye will utterly corrupt yourselves, and turn aside from the way which I have commanded you: And evil will befal you in the latter days, because ye will do evil in the sight of the Lord, to provoke him to anger, through the work of your hands."

The rise, grandeur and ruin of particular kingdoms and empires are foretold as fixed and certain, which depended on innumerable voluntary actions of innumerable men, and could not be accomplished without them; which therefore must be fixed and certain. The Persian, Grecian and Roman empires, are instances of this, as well as many other kingdoms.

The evil that Hazael did to the children of Israel was foretold, and therefore determined and fixed, long before he did it. And the particular actions of Cyrus, and of Josiah, were determined and foretold long before they were born: Yet this did not render them the less free and accountable as moral agents, in what they did.

But one instance more, among the many thousands that might be produced from the Bible, will now be mentioned. It is that of the Jews crucifying our Lord. It was before fixed and written that thus it must be; and by their voluntary conduct in this affair, God fulfilled those things which he before had shewed by the mouth of all his prophets: And, in putting Christ to death, they did the very things which his hand and counsel determined before to be done. Surely he who will well attend to this must be sensible that to say, that God's foreordaining whatsoever comes to pass, is inconsistent with the liberty and moral agency of man, does at the same time affirm, at least implicitly, that it is impossible the Bible should be from God.

Therefore, seeing the previous infallible certainty of all things which come to pass is necessarily implied in the foreknowledge of God, and the former cannot be rejected, without denying the latter: And since reason teaches that a Being of infinite power, wisdom and goodness, on whom all things absolutely depend for their existence, and every mode and circumstance of it, must determine by the counsel of his own will, and foreordain whatsoever comes to pass; and that it is infinitely important and desirable that he should do it, and that all events should be determined by infinite wisdom, rather than by any thing else: And since, according to our own feeling and experience, this is consistent with our freedom and moral agency: And since Divine Revelation abundantly asserts both these; and declares men to be moral agents, and accountable in those actions which have been foreordained and fixed by divine counsel and decrees; and therefore to deny these to be consistent, is really to renounce the Bible: When all these things are well considered, will it not appear to be amazing boldness, and the height of stupidity and arrogance, in a fallen, short sighted, ignorant man, liable to a thousand prejudices and mistakes, confidently, and without hesitation to pronounce these two doctrines absolutely inconsistent with each other? How much more modest, reasonable, and becoming us, is it to believe them both to be true and perfectly consistent? And if any have not yet been able to see how they may be reconciled; let them not rashly conclude that no man ever did, or ever will see their consistence with each other, and reduce it to a plain demonstration: Nor ought they themselves so to despair of receiving light and full satisfaction on this point, as to neglect all means and attempts to obtain it; but aught rather, with a proper sense of the importance of the matter, and their accountableness to God, for their belief and feelings respecting it; and with humble, fervent, constant application to the Father of Lights, for a wise and understanding heart; carefully to attend to the subject, and diligently improve every opportunity and advantage they may have to obtain that understanding which is pleasant to the soul, and more precious than the finest gold.

Attention to the foregoing preliminaries, it is hoped, has, in some measure, prepared the mind to a careful and candid examination of this point, about which there has been so much dispute in our world. Therefore the question will now be resumed, which is, How the divine decrees, foreordaining whatsoever comes to pass, can be consistent with the freedom and moral agency of man?

There can be no light respecting this question; nor can it be determined, without proper, precise and consistent ideas of both these subjects, about which the inquiry is made, the divine decrees, and the freedom essential to moral agency. Without this, it will be impossible to determine whether they be consistent with each other, or not; and if we affirm, or deny, we shall talk in the dark, "not knowing what we say, or whereof we affirm." My neighbour now comes into my study, and asks, whether a table he has made for me, can be introduced and have room here? I ask him, what is the length and breadth of it? He answers, it is three yards square. I tell him, it can then be of no use to me, nor can it be introduced. He is confident I am mistaken. And after some dispute, we at length conclude to take a common measure and apply it to the table, and to my door and study. Upon this the matter is soon decided, and it is found that the former agrees exactly with the latter; for his yard-stick was found to be but twelve inches long.

To prevent, as far as possible, all mistakes concerning the doctrine of God's decrees, it must be observed, that it may be justly considered as a medium between the two extremes, viz. of a supposed fatality in all things; every thing, and all events, being unalterably fixed by blind and undesigning fate on the one hand, and on the other, of a perfect contingence and uncertainty respecting all future events, there being no cause or reason of their taking place; but all things come to pass by mere chance. It would be infinitely undesirable, and dreadful, if either of these opposite extremes were true, or possible, as they certainly are not, each of them implying such absurdity, contradiction and impossibility, that it may be presumed no one ever yet had a real idea or conception of either.

All things, and every event, are indeed fixed by the decree of God; but they are wisely, and therefore most happily contrived and adjusted, as has been before observed, so as to make one most wise, consistent, and absolutely perfect plan: And in which the freedom and moral agency of rational creatures are effectually secured (if this can be done by infinite wisdom, clothed with omnipotence; and whether this be possible is now to be considered) and made a necessary and essential part of the divine plan.

This leads more particularly to observe, that this doctrine does not imply, but totally excludes a notion, which many have had of the divine decrees, which supposes that certain events, especially those which are the greatest and most important to man, are fixed and made certain, independent of the agency of man, and of any means whatsoever; and wholly unconnected with any thing of this kind; so that they will come to pass just as they are decreed, let man's conduct be what it may. For instance, they suppose that if the time of a man's death be appointed; he will live to that time, whatever means necessary to preserve his life shall be neglected, as eating and drinking, &c. and whatever may be done to take away his life. And if it be decreed that a particular person shall be saved, or he be elected to life, he shall certainly be saved, let him conduct as he will; and though he live and die in impenitence and unbelief: And if he be not elected, he must perish, let him do what he can, and though he sincerely seek salvation, and however humble, penitent and obedient he may be.--The scripture doctrine of God's decrees does not imply, but absolutely excludes, such an absurd notion and fatality as this; and makes the use of means, and agency of man, as important and necessary, in order to accomplish any proposed end, as if there were no decree respecting it: And, indeed, much more so: For if there were no appointed connection between means, and the attempts and exertions of men, and the end, then they would be of no importance, and have no tendency to the end; and there would not be the least reason or encouragement to do or attempt any thing, or use any means to accomplish any end whatsoever.

It cannot with truth be said, that according to the doctrine of God's decrees, he who is elected to salvation, shall be saved, let him do what he will, and live and die in impenitence and unbelief; for there is no election or decree inconsistent with the declaration of Christ, "He that believeth not shall be damned." They who are appointed to salvation by the decree of God are "elected according to the foreknowledge of God the Father, through sanctification of the Spirit unto obedience." And none are appointed to destruction, whether they believe or not; for "he that believeth shall be saved." This is particularly observed here, because the true scripture doctrine is so generally misunderstood in this point, and consequently misrepresented; especially by those who do not believe this doctrine, but oppose it.

The doctrine of God's decrees, including the means as well as the end, and connecting one with the other, so as to render the former important and necessary as the latter, as has been now stated and explained, in opposition to the absurd notion of fatality just mentioned, may be illustrated by a piece of history which we have in the Acts of the Apostles. [64] The apostle Paul being in a terrible storm at sea, and "all hope that they should be saved was taken away," had a revelation from heaven, that not one of them in the ship should lose his life; but they should all get safe to land. Upon which he stood forth, and declared it unto them, and his assurance that this revealed decree would come to pass. Thus Paul and his company were elected to be saved from the danger of the sea; the preservation of their lives was unalterably fixed, and certain. Yet, soon after this, while they were yet in danger, and the seamen, who only could manage the ship, were about to quit it, to provide for their own safety, "Paul said to the centurion, and to the soldiers, except these abide in the ship, ye cannot be saved." Here the doctrine of the fatalist above mentioned is contradicted, and declared not to be true; and that the decree, making their salvation absolutely certain, did not exclude the necessity of the use of means, in order to its taking place; but included this, and made their agency in the use of means important and necessary, there being a connection between these, and the end. It appears that in this instance, the means, and the exertions and agency of those who were to be saved, were as much appointed and fixed, as their salvation: and the latter could not come to pass without the former. And this is equally true of all other instances of the purposes and decrees of God; so that this instance is an illustration of all others that can be mentioned, or that do exist. And they who separate the means from the end, and say, or expect, that what God has appointed will come to pass, whether any means are used to bring it to pass or not, do separate what God has joined together by infallible connection. And they assert what is not true, and believe and trust in a falsehood.

And, by the way, if Paul and his companions were free moral agents in all they did in this affair, and which was necessary in order to their getting safe to land; and the declared decree respecting it, which fixed the whole train of actions and events that took place, was not in the least inconsistent with their acting freely, but implied it; and they felt, and really were, as perfectly free as if there had been no decree in the case: Then the divine decrees, by which all events are made certain, cannot, in any instance, be inconsistent with the free moral agency of men. But no one, it is presumed, who reads this story, or ever has read it, thought or can think, that their freedom was taken from them by this decree, so as to render them no longer moral agents; or that it could have the least influence in rendering them in any degree, less free and accountable in their exercises and conduct on this occasion: And it would not alter the case a whit with respect to their freedom and moral agency, had there been no decree determining what should take place; and had there been no previous certainty whether they should be saved or perish, or how they would conduct in those circumstances, and at that time. Does not every one who attends to this story, and consults his own sense and feeling, consider them as exercising all desirable or possible liberty of action, and blame or approve of their conduct, as much as if there had been no decree respecting it, and the event? If so, then we have the verdict of the common sense and feelings of mankind in favour of the consistence of the doctrine of the divine decrees, with human liberty and moral agency. What need is there then of proceeding any farther on this subject?

However, as more light may perhaps be thrown upon it by considering what is free moral agency, and wherein it consists; it may be of advantage to attend to this matter more particularly; by which it is hoped it may be more clearly seen, whether this moral freedom be consistent with the certainty of all events, which is implied in the doctrine of the divine decrees; and if consistent, how they are so, and may be perfectly reconciled.

It has been before observed, that nothing can be determined on this point, without forming an idea of the liberty essential to moral agency, and determining what it is, and wherein it consists: For he who knows not what liberty is, is not in a capacity to determine what is consistent with it, or what is inconsistent. Men will differ on the question before us, as they have different notions respecting human liberty; and if they be agreed in this, they will agree in the decision of it. The question then is, What is liberty? What is that freedom which is essential to moral agency?

The only way, perhaps, for any one to obtain the most satisfactory answer to this question, is to consult his own feelings, and inquire what that is: what are the exercises and exertions in which he supposes, yea, is certain, he acts freely, and is a moral agent. He will doubtless find that the internal freedom of which he is conscious, consisteth in his voluntary exercises, or in choosing and willing; that he is conscious that in all his voluntary exertions he is perfectly free, and must be accountable; and has no consciousness or idea of any other kind of moral liberty; or that the liberty he exerciseth hath any thing more or less belonging to it; or that it could be increased, or made more perfect freedom, by the addition of any thing that is not implied in willing and choosing. [65] He may indeed not be able to accomplish the thing or event which is the object of his choice; and, in this respect, be under restraint; but this is not inconsistent with his exercising perfect freedom in his choice, and in all his voluntary exertions, or in all he does with respect to such object or event. And in these exercises of will and choice his moral character does wholly consist; and therefore here he looks, even to his inclination and choice to determine what is his moral character, whether he be sinful or virtuous, and approves or condemns, according as he judges of the nature and quality of his inclination and choice; and they appear to him to be right or wrong, according as they are conformable or not to the rule or law, under which he considers himself placed.

And where can freedom, moral agency, virtue and vice be found, if they consist not in voluntary exercises? Shall we look to something which takes place in our minds antecedent to choice and voluntary action, by which acts of choice are determined, and out of which they spring, and place liberty and virtue and sin in that? This will be to place these wholly in that, in which we have no concern as agents, as we are no more active in that which precedes our exercise of will and choice, than a rock or tree; or than we were in those events which took place ages before we were born.

Shall liberty and moral agency be considered as consisting in what follows the exercise of will, or voluntary exertions, and takes place after the will ceases to act? There is indeed as much propriety and reason in placing them here, as in any thing that is antecedent to the exercise of will: But surely no man in his senses can imagine, that there is the exercise of liberty and moral action, where there is no liberty, choice or action, whether it be antecedent to these, or consequent upon them, and after they cease. When our will and choice are over, or we cease to will, our agency is at an end; and most certainly there can be no liberty exercised, when there is no exercise of any kind, no action.

If voluntary action, or the exercise of will and choice, be not freedom and moral agency: and if all virtue and sin do not consist in this, and are not to be found here, even in the will and choice itself; it will be impossible to find them any where, or that there should be any such thing: And they are therefore but empty names. Every exercise of the will in choosing or refusing is the exercise of freedom: And it is impossible for man to will and choose without exercising moral liberty; and as

The System of Doctrines, contained in Divine Relation, Explained and Defended Volume I
impossible to exercise liberty without voluntary action, or exercising choice. Therefore, to say a man is not free in exercising will and choice, is to say he is not free in that, in which freedom wholly consists, and is the only possible exercise of liberty; or that he is not voluntary or does not choose in willing and choosing: And, it is no more improper and absurd to ask, whether a man is rational in reasoning, or to say he is not, than it is to ask, whether he is free in willing and choosing; or to affirm that he is not. And that because the exercise of freedom and the exercise of will, are convertible terms, and are indeed one and the same thing; as really as reasoning is the exercise of reason; or existence is existing. And if there be any such thing as moral agency, it consists in the exercise of will and choice, and in nothing else: and virtue and vice, praise and blame, are predicable of this only, and belong wholly to the exercises of will or voluntary action, and are as the inclination, will or choice is. [66]

It may therefore be safely presumed, that no man, by consulting his own exercise and feelings, or in reasoning properly about them, ever had any other idea or conception of liberty, and that moral agency by which he is accountable for his exercises and conduct, but that which consists in voluntary action, or in will and choice; though many have confused and bewildered themselves on this point, by using words without any real meaning, and with mere chimeras and imaginations, which are perfectly inconsistent, and have no real existence.

For instance; it has been often said, that there can be no liberty in man without a self determining power; and that freedom consists in this, even in determining his own volitions, what they shall be, Sec.

Upon this it may be observed, that if it be meant, that man himself exerts his own volitions, and they are his own actions, and that he determines his own choice in actively willing and choosing; so that there can be no choice without his exertion and activity, and where he is wholly passive; and that, in this sense, he is the cause and author of his own volitions; then nothing is meant more than will be granted, and has been asserted above, viz. that he does act in willing and choosing, and is really the author, or actor of his own acts. But if by self determining power be meant, a power or capacity to determine, previous to any act of choice, what he will choose, (which must be their meaning, if they are not satisfied with that now expressed; and if that which is self contradictory can be said to have any real meaning) then what they mean to assert is, that in order to a man's being free in his choice, he must, by a foregoing act of power, exerted before he begins to will and choose, determine what his choice shall be. That is, he must act and determine, before he begins to act by choice; or he must make a choice before he begins to choose, and in order to it; which cannot be exceeded in self contradiction and absurdity: It being as absurd as to say, that a man can have no motion unless he do, previous to all his motion, move himself; that is, move himself before he begins to move. Or that his existence was produced by an exertion of his own, before he existed, putting himself into existence.

Agreeable to this notion of a self determining power, and in support of it, it is said, that a man cannot be free in his voluntary actions, unless he has a freedom to either side; that is, has a freedom to choose or refuse, to prefer one thing, or the contrary; or has power and freedom to choose that, which is directly contrary to that which is actually the object of his choice. If by this be meant that whenever any one freely chooses any particular object or act, or is inclined any particular way, he is at liberty to prefer a contrary object or act, and to incline the contrary way, if he please, or wills and chooses so to do; this is no more than to say, that in the exercise of liberty, a man must choose agreeable to his choice; or has his choice; that is, must be voluntary: And therefore is not a contradiction to that which has been above asserted, viz. that liberty consists in the exercises of will and choice, or voluntary action.

But if by a freedom to choose either side, be meant, that in order to the exercise of a free act of choice, he must, at the same time, be as much disposed or inclined to choose the contrary, or be no more inclined one way than the other; there is no need of saying any thing to expose the absurdity and inconsistence of this, to those who allow themselves to think: For it is the same as to say, that in order to a moral agent's choosing freely, he must really have no choice; or when he inclines one way, in order to be free, he must be equally inclined the contrary way, so as to make no preference of the one to the other. This assertion, thus understood, (if such an inconsistence, which destroys itself, can be properly said to be understood) is inconsistent with any possible liberty, and with all preference and choice, moral agency, virtue and vice, and utterly excludes all these out of the universe.

They who have contended for a self-determining power, as essential to the freedom of moral agents; and a freedom to either side, as now mentioned, do hold to what they call a liberty of indifference. That in order to the exercise of free choice, in the time of choosing or making a preference, or immediately antecedent to it, there must be no inclination of the mind to one thing more than to another; and that every act of choice must arise out of a perfect indifference to either side, by a sovereign determining act, turning the will one certain way, and causing or producing an inclination, where there was none before.

It is not needful to point out all the absurdities of such a notion; as supposing an exertion or act of the mind, previous to an act of will or choice (by which alone the mind can act) determining what the choice shall be; and that while the mind is perfectly indifferent, as to any preference or choice; and so inclination and choice must originate from, and rise out of that which is no inclination or choice; as its true cause, in order to be a free choice! And yet liberty does not consist in this free choice; for there is no indifference in choice; but it lies in that indifference to all choice or inclination, which is as far from choice as nonentity is from existence; and which by some inconceivable, impossible exertion of its own, produces inclination or volition, as contradictory to itself, as nothing is to something!

These things have been observed, to confirm the truth under consideration, viz. that liberty, moral agency, virtue and vice, blame and praise worthiness, consist wholly in the exercise of will and choice, made in the view of motives; and in nothing else beside, or which is antecedent to, or consequent upon voluntary action. That this is the highest and most perfect liberty in nature; and no other freedom of moral agents can be conceived of, or is possible. That this is the freedom which we feel and experience, when we consider and pronounce ourselves free; and that of which we have an idea in others, when we view them as accountable for their conduct, as virtuous or vicious, and worthy of praise or blame, reward or punishment. [67]

And now, from the view we have had of the doctrine of God's decrees, and of the nature of human liberty and moral agency, and in what they consist, it may be easily determined whether they are consistent with each other; and that their perfect consistence is demonstrably clear and certain. For if liberty and moral agency consist in the exercise of will and choice, or voluntary exertions; which is all the liberty of which we are, or can be conscious, can have any conception, or is possible, as has been shewn; then the absolute fixedness and certainty of all events is perfectly consistent with liberty: For though all events be decreed, and every motion and exercise of the will, and all moral actions, be determined from eternity, this is so far from destroying the liberty of man, that it establishes it, and makes it certain, viz. that he shall thus will and choose. The exercise of this liberty and agency is as important and necessary, as if there were no fixed certainty of events; and more, much more so. This liberty is consistent with the moral agent's absolute and universal dependence on God, while he acts freely and is under moral government and is accountable to the supreme Being, in all those exercises by which the events comprehended and fixed in the divine infinitely wise plan, do come to pass: This therefore is the only desirable as well as the only possible liberty. If there were, or could be any other liberty of moral agents, it would be infinitely dreadful! As it would be inconsistent with the real, absolute supremacy of the Deity, and with his perfect universal providence, and infinitely wise, uncontrolled government.

Secondly, It is to be considered whether the evil, both moral and natural, which has taken place, and may continue without end, be really inconsistent with the decrees of God, foreordaining whatsoever comes to pass.

It is probable that the existence of evil in God's world, and before our eyes, has been with many the chief, if not the only ground of dissatisfaction with this doctrine, and the opposition made to it. If no action or event had taken place, but such as appeared to men perfectly right, wise and good; and therefore most agreeable and desirable, none surely would object against God's ordaining every thing that was to take place, in the best manner possible. But since evil has actually taken place, both sin and suffering; and is like to continue forever, to a dreadful and amazing degree; men have been ready to think and say, "Surely this world had been infinitely better, more desirable and happy, if all evil had been effectually and forever excluded, both moral and natural; and nothing but perfect, eternal holiness and happiness had taken place. This is certainly an imperfect, disorderly, confused system, undesirably marred, and in a great measure ruined, by the rebellion of creatures against their Maker, and their consequent sufferings. How then is it possible that an infinitely wise, powerful and good God, should decree and foreordain all this? To say he has done it, is rather to represent him as unwise and evil, than wise and good; though this might be done, consistent with the freedom and moral agency of man."

It is of great importance that this difficulty and objection should be removed, if possible; for it is not only an objection against God, foreordaining whatsoever comes to pass; but is equally irreconcileable with his supreme, uncontrolled, wise and good government of the world. This leads to observe,

I. This objection does not really lie against those who hold that God has foreordained whatsoever comes to pass, more than against those who do not admit this doctrine. And therefore it is far from being just, or agreeable to truth, to consider and represent it, as militating only, or in a peculiar manner, against such a doctrine. For, if the matter be well considered, it will appear, that the objection may be with equal reason and force urged against the objector himself, or those doctrines which he professes to believe. This difficulty, if it be one, is not peculiar to

The System of Doctrines, contained in Divine Relation, Explained and Defended Volume I
predestinarians, but is common to all, who believe in one supreme, infinitely powerful, wise and good Creator and Governor of the world. It has therefore been represented as the Gordian knot in philosophy and theology, and a question above all others unanswerable, Whence cometh evil? God is infinitely good; and therefore could not be willing or consent it should take place: But it could not take place, contrary to his will; for he is infinitely wise; and therefore must know how it might be prevented; and he is almighty, and nothing is impossible with him; therefore he was able to prevent it, if he had pleased to do it. How then is it possible that evil should take place, under the government of this God; while he sits at the head of the universe; has all things in his hand, absolutely dependent upon him, and rules infinitely above all control?

This question cannot be answered, on any plan, to the satisfaction of a rational, inquisitive mind, or the difficulty in any measure solved, unless it be supposed and granted, That all the evil which does take place, is necessary for the greatest possible general good; and therefore on the whole, all things considered, wisest and best that it should exist just as it does.

All who believe the divine foreknowledge, or admit that an infinitely perfect Being made and governs the world, must adopt this solution, and grant that, on the whole, it is best that evil, moral and natural, should take place; or be left wholly without any satisfactory solution at all: And indeed, they do either expressly or implicitly grant it, however they may differ as to the mode of explaining the matter, and the reasons why it is better that evil should exist, than otherwise. They who oppose the doctrine of the divine decrees, and yet allow that God could have prevented evil taking place, had he pleased to do it, cannot account for his not preventing it, unless they allow that he saw it was on the whole best, that it should not be prevented; and therefore it was, on the whole, best it should exist.

And they who suppose that sin could not be prevented, if God made free moral agents, and continued them in the exercise of their freedom; and account for the introduction of evil in this way; yet must grant that, all things considered, it was better that there should be sin, rather than that there should be no moral agents; and that the system or plan which includes evil, is the best that was possible. For if God foresaw, that if he made moral agents, vast numbers of them would, in the exercise of their freedom, fall into sin and ruin, he would not have made them, and continued them in the exercise of their liberty, if it were not best, on the whole, that evil should take place; and if this was not preferable to any other possible plan; and he did not, all things considered, choose that evil should exist, just as it does. For to say that God made free moral agents, when he knew that they would sin, if he made them; and yet knew that it was not best, all things considered, that moral evil should exist; is to say, that he is neither wise nor good, as well as not omnipotent. This is so plain that it is needless to say any more to make it intelligible and evident to the lowest capacity.

And the same thing, in effect, must be granted even by them who deny the divine foreknowledge of the actions of creatures made free. For if God knew that sin might possibly take place, if he made moral agents; and at the same time knew that it was not, all things considered, best that it should take place; but infinitely to the contrary, it could not be best to make any such creatures, and run this dreadful venture; and open a door for the possible introduction of this infinite evil, which never could be remedied: and therefore it was not consistent with wisdom and goodness to make them free, and continue them so, on this supposition. They must therefore grant that it was, in God's view, on the whole, better that evil should take place, and to have the world fall into sin and ruin, than not to create moral agents, and have no moral kingdom; and that he preferred such a world, and to have sinful miserable creatures, rather than not to create; or they must allow that their God was deceived, and is dreadfully disappointed, and now heartily wishes he had not created; or is neither wise nor good: Which is to have no God, or something infinitely worse! It must therefore be observed,

II. It is abundantly evident and demonstrably certain from reason, assisted by divine revelation, that all the sin and sufferings which have taken place, or ever will, are necessary for the greatest good of the universe, and to answer the wisest and best ends; and therefore must be included in the best, most wise and perfect plan.

1. This appears evident and certain from the being and perfections of God. God is omnipotent; his understanding is infinite, and he is equally wise and good. He is infinitely above all dependence and control; and hath done, and can and will do whatsoever pleaseth him. It hence is certain that he will do no thing, nor suffer any thing to be done or take place, which is not, on the whole, good, wisest and best, that it should take place, and is not most agreeable to infinite wisdom and goodness. It is impossible it should be otherwise. Therefore, when we find that sin and misery have taken place in God's world, and under his government, we may be as certain that it is, on the whole, best it should be so; and that all this evil is necessary in order to answer the best ends, the greatest good of the universe, as we can be, that there is a God, omnipotent, and possessed of infinite wisdom, rectitude and goodness; and he who denies or doubts of the former, equally questions and opposes the latter. If it be once admitted that any evil, or the least event may, or can take place,

which is not, on the whole, best, and therefore not desirable that it should be, it must with equal reason be granted, that nothing but evil, and what is, on the whole, undesirable, may take place; and that the universe may become wholly evil, or infinitely worse than nothing: And all would be left without any ground or reason to trust in God, or any thing else, for the least good for himself, or any other being. The divine perfections and character are the only security against this, and are the ground of an equal certainty that nothing has taken place, or ever will, which is not on the whole best, or necessary for the greatest good of the whole. And this is a sure and ample foundation for the trusty confidence, comfort and joy of him who is a true friend to God, and desires the greatest good of the whole; and consequently is irreconcileably opposed to every event which is not, on the whole, wisest and best. If this foundation were taken away and destroyed, what could the righteous, the truly pious and benevolent do? They must be left without any possible support, and sink into darkness and wo!

There can nothing take place under the care and government of an infinitely powerful, wise and good Being, that is not on the whole wisest and best; that is, for the general good; therefore, though there be things which are in themselves evil, even in their own nature and tendency, such as sin and misery; yet considered in their connection with the whole, and as they are necessary in the best system, to accomplish the greatest good, the most important and best ends, they are in this view, desirable, good, and not evil. And in this view, "There is no absolute evil in the universe." There are evils, in themselves considered; but considered as connected with the whole, they are not evil, but good. As shades are necessary in a picture, to render it most complete and beautiful, they are, in this view and connection, desirable; and the picture would be imperfect and marred, were they not included in it; yet considered separately, and unconnected with the whole, they have no beauty, but deformity, and are very disagreeable: So moral evil is, in itself considered, in its own nature and tendency, most odious, hurtful and undesirable; but in the hands of omnipotence, infinite wisdom and goodness, it may be introduced into the most perfect plan and system, and so disposed, and counteracted in its nature and tendency, as to be a necessary part of it, in order to render it most complete and desirable, [68]

It has been said by some, that it is not becoming us, but presumption and arrogance, to say, that the system in which moral evil takes place is, on the whole, preferable to one in which it is wholly excluded; and is, all things considered, the best system, containing the greatest good. It is said, we are infinitely unable to determine this, unless we could comprehend the whole of each opposite system, and compare them together, and without error, determine the advantage of either, and see the good of each in their final issue, and exactly balance the account.

The weakness, error, and impiety of such an objection, will be sufficiently discovered and exposed, by observing, that though man is infinitely unequal to this, to take a comprehensive view of all possible systems, and determine which would be the best, and comprehend the greatest possible good; and is far from seeing all the ends that moral evil will answer; and though he could not see how it could be the occasion of any good, and why a plan, in which all evil is forever excluded, is not infinitely preferable to that in which evil exists and continues forever: Yet we know that One, infinitely able to judge and determine in this matter, has actually chosen and fixed upon a system in which moral evil takes place, and preferred it to all other possible systems; from which known fact, we may be as certain, that it is, on the whole, the best possible system, containing the most real good, as we are, that he is omnipotent, infinitely wise and good; and to question the former, is equally to deny, or doubt of the latter. If God be infinitely perfect, wise and good, his plan of operation, and all his works, must be so too; and we cannot entertain the least doubt whether it be not, on the whole, best, and for the greatest general good, that evil should take place, without impeaching the divine character and perfections. And to say that it would have been better, on the whole, if sin and all the consequences of it had never taken place, is the same as to say, that God is neither wise nor good, or had not power to execute what he saw was best, and desired to do, had he been able. It is not necessary that it should be determined and known what is the greatest good; or what is the best plan to effect this, were it known in what it consists, in order to decide this matter. It is enough, that God knows and has certainly fixed upon the wisest and best method to accomplish it; and therefore it is certain, that in order to this, it is necessary that moral evil, in all its eternal consequences, should take place. But if the greatest possible manifestation and display of the divine perfections, and the highest possible degree of moral good and happiness in the creation, be the greatest good, which it certainly is, according to reason and divine revelation: yet a great degree of moral evil and of misery may be necessary, in order to produce the highest possible degree of this good; and therefore that system which includes this evil may contain the greatest good, and be infinitely preferable to any other possible one, in which there would be no evil. And that this is really so, we may be absolutely certain, since we have the infallible evidence before our eyes in the fact which has taken place, under the direction of infinite wisdom.

It has been suggested by some, that this argument may not be conclusive: For though it be

The System of Doctrines, contained in Divine Relation, Explained and Defended Volume I
granted that infinite wisdom and goodness could not fix on a worse plan, when there was a better possible; yet there may be two or more possible systems equally good; and if one of these be fixed upon, rather than the other, we cannot hence infer that this is the wisest and best. Therefore, though the system in which evil takes place has been actually fixed upon, we do not know that a system might not be equally good, in which there is no evil. And then it will not follow that it is wisest and best, on the whole, that evil should exist. Upon this the following things may be observed.

1. If two or more possible systems be supposed to be exactly alike, in all respects, the supposition is inconsistent, and destroys itself: For if there be no kind or degree of difference , there are not two or more, but only one. There cannot be two, where there is not, in any respect, the least diversity.

2. But if there be any considerable diversity in any two or more possible systems, it is not to be supposed that they are, or can be, equally good and eligible, in the sight of infinite, unerring wisdom. The least difference must render one more eligible than the other. But if not, if two different proposed systems be equally good, and eligible in the view of infinite wisdom, and this were possible; then, by the supposition, one could not be chosen and preferred to the other; for, in such a case, it is supposed there is no ground of choice or preference: therefore no choice can be made. And if it were possible to choose the one and reject the other, there would be no wisdom in such a choice, it not being made from any reason or motive, or with any design. Indeed, such a supposed choice and preference is impossible, and therefore never did take place. It therefore could not be from choice, that one of two systems equally wise and good, exists, rather than the other, but must be from mere chance or accident, which is also impossible.

3. If two or more possible systems, though different in some respects, might be equally good and eligible, and it were possible that one of these should be preferred and chosen before the other; yet it is not to be supposed, and it is really impossible, that two systems, so infinitely diverse and opposite as those must be, in one of which is infinite evil, and from the other all evil is excluded, should be equally good and eligible. The evil which has taken place in this world will continue forever, and in this respect is infinite; and all moral evil is infinite in its nature and criminality; aid the effects of this extend to all the views, feelings and exercises of moral agents; of all the subjects of God's moral government and kingdom, without end, and render them, in many respects, vastly different from what they would have been, or could be, had there been no evil. And the divine perfections and conduct appear in a very different light to all intelligences from what they would have done; and circumstances and events in God's eternal kingdom are, and will forever be, infinitely different from what would have been, if no evil had ever taken place. If this then be a good system, and worthy of the preference and choice of an infinitely wise Being, is it supposable, is it possible, that a system infinitely different from this, and diametrically opposite to it; in the great events of it; in the divine conduct; in the displays of the perfections of God; and in the views and exercises of all his subjects to all eternity, should be equally good; as well suited to display the divine character, and promote the holiness and happiness of the kingdom of God; and answer all the infinitely important and glorious ends, which are accomplished by the divine plan, which has actually taken place?

Surely, as there is an infinite difference in two such opposite systems, that which has been actually chosen by infinite wisdom and goodness is infinitely the best; and all the evil that takes place is the occasion of infinitely overbalancing good, so that the former is wholly swallowed up by the latter; and, in this view and connection, is not evil, but good, being the occasion of infinitely more beauty, holiness, happiness and glory, in God's moral, eternal kingdom, than could have been in any possible system, in which evil has no place. The evil involves so much good, and is so absorbed in it, that, all taken together, and in the view of infinite wisdom, there appears the greatest possible beauty, perfection and glory. As shades, which appear deformed and disagreeable, when they stand alone, being introduced into a picture, by the art of a limner, add to the beauty of it, and are absorbed in the beauty and perfection of the whole, of which they are the occasion. [69]

2, That all moral evil is designed by God to answer a good end, and is overruled for die greatest good, is evident from divine revelation. This is certain, if we can find one instance of this recorded in the Bible. For, if sin may be overruled for good, so that, on the whole, there is much more good, than could have been, had not that instance of sin taken place; then an infinitely wise and omnipotent Being can do it in every instance, and an infinitely good Being certainly will do it. Therefore though numberless instances of this might be produced from scripture history, but two or three will be mentioned, as sufficient to support the argument.

The sin of Joseph's brethren, in hating him and selling him, was overruled by God for great good, and appears to be an important and necessary part of his benevolent plan to bring about the good he designed for Joseph himself, and the people of Israel: Therefore it is said God sent Joseph into Egypt, and meant to accomplish good by it. The sin of Pharaoh, king of Egypt, in refusing to hearken to Jehovah, and hardening his heart, and obstinately opposing the God of Israel, was designed by God for great good, and overruled to answer this end. The happy consequences of this instance of rebellion are too many to be mentioned here; and they will abide, and have influence, and a good effect to the end of the world; yea, to all eternity.

It is sufficient for the present purpose to recollect what God himself says of this instance. "And in very deed even for this purpose have I raised thee up, that I might shew my power in thee, and that my name might be declared throughout all the earth: And I will get me honour upon Pharaoh and upon all his host." He who is sensible of the desirableness, worth and importance of the display of the name and character of Jehovah, surely will not say that the sin and ruin of Pharaoh was not the occasion of good, which infinitely overbalances the evil. And who can say that God hath not more glorified himself by the sin and ruin of Pharaoh, and that he is not the occasion of immensely more good to the church and people of God, than if he had been perfectly obedient? Who can say, or has any reason to believe that the sin and destruction of Pharaoh has not been, or will not be the occasion of so much good, of so great a manifestation of the divine character and glory, and of so much holy exercise and happiness of the friends of God, as his obedience, holiness and happiness would have been? Is it not rather certain that the contrary is true, and that to a degree beyond all conception? And therefore he was raised up, that by his sin and ruin he might, by the all directing hand of God, answer this infinitely important end. Had not Pharaoh existed just such an one as he was, and such as he is, and will be forever, the great and good end of which he is made the occasion, could not have been answered; and had not infinite wisdom seen that such a character as that of Pharaoh was necessary in order to the greatest good of the whole, it would not have had an existence.

We have another instance of this kind in the condemnation, sufferings, and death of the Lord of glory. This is an instance of sin, the most aggravated and criminal, doubtless, of any other that has ever taken place. And yet all this sin and suffering was foreordained, and actually took place, by the wise counsel and decree of God, because it was absolutely necessary in order to accomplish the most benevolent purposes of Heaven, and produce the highest good of the universe. In order to this, it was necessary that Christ should die on the cross; but this could not be, unless he died by the hands of sinful men. Had he not been thus put to death, there would have been no redemption of man, nor any of that remarkable, glorious display of the divine character, which is exhibited in this work. It was most certainly desirable, and of infinite importance, that all the sin should take place which was necessary in order to bring to pass this event, the suffering and death of Christ, which though infinitely evil, in itself considered, is of most happy and glorious consequence. All this sin and evil sinks into nothing, when compared with the good, the glory that follows; and the whole appears to be an infinite good; the evil being covered, and vanishing, in the splendour and glory occasioned by it, and with which it is connected. Better, infinitely better is it, that the Jews should commit that sin, and that Christ should thus suffer, than that the infinitely good and glorious consequences should not take place. And may it not with safety and the greatest assurance be added, it is better that all the sin and misery that ever has been, or will be, should take place, than that there should not be such a character as that of the Mediator; such works as he has done and will do; such manifestation s of the divine character, as he has made and will make; such happiness and glory; which will be the eternal consequence of redemption? But to return.

If the sin of putting the Son of God to death was the occasion of the greatest good, which could not otherwise have taken place; and therefore God ordained that this should come to pass, for the sake of the infinitely overbalancing good J and brought it about, consistent with the freedom of man, and his own hatred of that sin, in itself considered, and the total inexcusableness and infinite ill desert of those sinners; then here is an instance of the most horrid wickedness, which is necessary to promote and bring about the greatest good; and, in this view, very desirable, and of infinite importance that it should take place. And it may be hence safely concluded, that every instance of evil that ever has been, or will be, is as really necessary to promote the greatest possible good; and, in this view, a desirable event; and therefore determined by the infinitely wise counsel and decree of Heaven, however undesirable, odious or detestable it may be, in itself considered.

But that all the sins of men are overruled by God for good, and are appointed to take place for this end, may not only be inferred from the instances mentioned, and from many others; but it is expressly asserted in the following words of Sacred Writ, "Surely the wrath of man shall praise thee: The remainder of wrath shalt thou restrain." If by the wrath of man, here be meant the furious exertions of sinners in their opposition to God and their neighbour, this comprehends all the sins of men, as they are all of the same nature. It is here declared as a most certain truth, that these sins of men, however numerous, and though they rise ever so high, shall turn to the praise of God, and promote his declarative glory. God will so overrule the sin of man, that he will get honour thereby: And that sin which would not answer this good and infinitely important end, he will not suffer to take place; but will effectually prevent it.--The following things are clearly contained in this passage,

The System of Doctrines, contained in Divine Relation, Explained and Defended Volume I

1. That God does superintend and direct with regard to every instance of sin: He orders how much sin there shall be, and effectually restrains and prevents all that which he would not have take place. Men are, with respect to this, absolutely under his direction and control.

2. That all the sin which does take place shall answer the best and most important end; even that for which all things were made, the glory of God. "Surely the wrath of man shall praise thee."

3. That therefore God wills and orders it to take place, that he may answer this end by it. If he effectually restrains and prevents that which will not praise him; it is certain that he could prevent all sin, if he pleased, and that he would do it, were it not necessary to answer this end; and that he wills the existence of it. not for its own sake, but for the sake of the end to be answered by it; or the good of which it is to be the occasion.

4. From this it follows, that the sin of man is the means of a good which so far overbalances the evil of sin, and all the evil consequences of it, that it is desirable, on this account, that it should take place: Therefore there is more good in the universe, and this is a better world, than could possibly have existed, had no evil come into it; and every instance of sin and evil is conducive, and necessary to the greatest possible good of the whole.

5. All this is here asserted in the strongest terms as a most certain and important, pleasing truth. The evidence and certainty of it are as clear and great, as of the existence of an almighty, wise and good Creator and Governor of the world. And it is a truth of the highest importance to be known, and believed with the greatest assurance, as it is implied in the exercises of true piety, especially in a joyful acquiescence in the divine government; joy in the supremacy and infinite felicity of God, and implicit cheerful trust in him: And as it is necessary to the support and comfort of the friends of God, in all the darkness and evil in this world; and the only proper ground of their rejoicing that the Lord God omnipotent reigneth; and that their God is in the heavens, and hath done whatsoever he pleased.

Thus it appears demonstrably certain, both from the being and perfections of God, and from divine revelation, that all the evil which takes place in God's world, and under the influence of his government, is necessary in order to the greatest possible good; and is made the means of this; so that in this view, it is desirable, and perfectly agreeable to infinite wisdom and goodness, that it should take place just as it does. Therefore God, infinitely wise and good, has determined and decreed that evil should exist, as necessary to the highest perfection, beauty, happiness and glory of the system which was to be formed by his hand. Consequently, the evil which does actually take place, does not afford the least ground of objection against the doctrine of God's decrees, by which he has foreordained whatsoever comes to pass; but is perfectly reconcileable to this doctrine: And this truth is the great support and ground of comfort to the truly pious mind, in the view of the abounding evil with which this world has been so long filled. God has foreordained all this, and all that ever will take place, for his own glory, and the greatest good of the universe: He superintends the whole, and brings good out of all this evil, infinitely greater good than could have been, without the evil. Therefore all is perfectly agreeable to the dictates of infinite wisdom and goodness.

It is certain that evil, both moral and natural, is in itself undesirable, and must be considered as infinitely contrary to divine holiness and goodness, viewed in this light only; and could not possibly have place in a system formed by God, and absolutely under his direction and government, were it not necessary in order to the greatest good of the whole, to make the system in the highest degree perfect, happy and glorious: And, in this view and connection, the existence of evil is desirable, and must be introduced, if infinite wisdom and goodness dictate and govern. And all the children of wisdom will approve and rejoice. And very unhappy are they who are dissatisfied with die works and ways of God in the moral or natural world; and think they have wisdom enough to see many things defective and wrong; and to have ordered matters better, had they been to contrive and direct them. This seems to be the situation of those who make the objection under consideration; which, it is presumed, will appear to all who well consider what has now been said in answer to it, to be altogether groundless and unreasonable. [70]

Thirdly, It is now to be considered, whether God's foreordaining whatsoever comes to pass, does imply that he is the origin, cause and author of sin, in a sense which is contrary to infinite holiness, and therefore very dishonourable to him. This is confidently asserted by many; and they have on this ground exclaimed against this doctrine, and all that is implied in it; and represented it in a most shocking and horrible light. Therefore, though what has been said of the nature of sin, as consisting wholly in the disposition and will of the sinner, and of the good of which it is the occasion, which renders it desirable that it should take place, may serve to throw some light on this point, and show that God's choosing and determining that sin should take place, as necessary to accomplish the greatest good, is a wise and holy choice: Yet it may be proper and important more particularly to consider this subject, and attend to it in the light in which it is set by the objection which has been introduced, and is now under consideration.

We ought to attend to this point, and think and speak of it with care and caution, and in the exercise of fear and reverence of the infinitely great and holy God, lest, under the notion of thinking and speaking for him, and to his honour, our thoughts and words should be really against him, and tend to his reproach. And this caution and reverential fear ought to possess the minds of those who make the objection under consideration, as well as of those who believe and assert the doctrine against which the objection is made. For if indeed God has foreordained whatsoever comes to pass; then all objections against it, however plausible they may appear, are really replying against God, and very dishonourable and displeasing to him. But if, on the other hand, the objection be reasonable and well founded, they who believe the doctrine of God's decrees, do really dishonour and displease him. We are happy that we have a revelation from God, in which this point, as well as every important one, is set in a clear and easy light; so that no man can, with this in his hand, run into an error concerning it, and be blameless. In the light of reason, and this revelation, let the following things be well considered.

I. It is of importance to observe here, and fix it as certain, that when the origin or cause of evil is inquired after, or is ascribed to God, or any other being; the moral evil itself is not meant by the origin or cause of it. The origin or cause of any thing is necessarily before the thing which is the effect, and must exist and take place antecedent to the evil, and before the evil can exist. It is therefore certain that there can be no moral evil in the origin or cause of this evil, in whatever and wherever it may be found: For to suppose the contrary, is a direct and plain contradiction. Moral evil cannot be the origin or cause of moral evil, any more than any effect can be the cause of itself, or a child be the cause of his father. We, in considering what is the origin of moral evil, are going back to something which is antecedent to the evil, and where, or in which, no such evil does, or can be supposed to exist, to find the cause of moral evil, or a reason why it does take place, rather than not. We must go back, therefore, till we get to that in which there is no moral evil, before we arrive to, or can find that which is the origin or cause of it. If we find an existence, object or exertion, in which there is moral evil, we may be sure, we have not yet found, or arrived to the origin and cause of it; and must yet go a step farther back, even to that in which there is no moral evil, in order to find the origin of this evil.

It hence follows that if man, or any creature is, in any instance, the origin or cause of sin, (meaning by cause, that which is antecedent to the existence of sin, and of which sin is properly the effect) that man or creature cannot be the sinful cause of that sin: And there is no moral evil in any conceptions, thoughts or exertions of such a creature, which are necessary to take place, antecedent to the existence of sin, and in order to it, whatever they may be, or if any be necessary.

It is also certain that if God, the first cause of all things, be the origin or cause of moral evil; (and this can be proved, and may be asserted, as a most evident truth,) this is so far from imputing moral evil to him, or supposing that there is any thing of that nature in him, that it necessarily supposes the contrary; and that in being the first cause of moral evil, there is no sin; and therefore that he may be the origin or cause of it, consistently with infinite holiness, and exercise it in whatever exertions or influence may be necessary or implied in being thus the cause of sin.

If any should say or imagine, that the thought, exertion, or influence, which tends to produce sin, and is in fact the cause or origin of it, must be itself sinful or wrong; this is only to contradict himself, and say that such exercise or exertion is not the origin of sin, but sin itself; consequently, as has been observed, we must go farther back to find the origin of this sin, till we find something in which there is no sin. And, according to this notion, we must go back without end, and never find the origin of sin, unless sin itself be the origin and cause of all sin; which is a contradiction. It therefore still appears demonstrably certain, that if there be any origin or cause of moral evil, which is supposed by all those who inquire after it, there is no moral evil, nothing morally wrong in this cause, wherever it may be found, and whatever it may be. Therefore God, in foreordaining whatsoever comes to pass, may be, in this sense, the origin and cause of sin, consistent with infinite holiness; and the contrary cannot be supposed without a contradiction.

If it should be said, "There is no origin or cause of moral evil except what is in the evil itself: It is the cause of itself, so far as it has any cause: Therefore the question concerning the origin of sin, meaning something antecedent to it, is groundless and vain, there being no such thing in nature. Moral evil has no cause, in this sense of cause." Upon this it may be observed,

1. If this be admitted, then the objection under consideration, against the divine decrees, foreordaining all actions and events, as making God the origin, cause or author of sin, falls to the ground, and is given up: For, according to this, sin has no cause out of itself, or previous to its existence. But this cannot be admitted, for,

2. If moral evil may exist without a cause, there being no thing antecedent to its actual existence, which had any more influence or tendency to the existence of sin, than to the contrary; and there was no ground or reason of its existence, or why it should be, rather than not be, antecedent to its actually taking place; then there is an end of arguing from any effect whatever, to a cause; and we have not the least evidence that We ourselves, or any thing around us, or the world,

have any origin or cause. For if moral evil may exist without a cause, so may every thing else which comes under our notice; and we have not the least evidence that there is a God, as the cause of the things which we behold. Which is not only directly contrary to the assertion of St. Paul, but to the reason and common sense of mankind in general. And why should one choose to embrace such an absurdity, and assert that sin has no origin or cause, antecedent to its actual existence, and is the cause of itself, rather than to admit that God is the origin of it; since by admitting this, it is not supposed there is any moral evil in him; but the contrary is necessarily implied, as has been observed above?

It will, perhaps, be farther said, "It is not meant that sin has no cause whatsoever in any sense; but that it has no positive cause: It has a negative cause; and God may be the cause, in this sense, that is, he permitted moral evil to take place, by determining not to prevent the existence of it, when he had power to prevent it, had he been pleased to do it."--Upon this the following remarks may be made.

1. If God could prevent every sin that is committed, and yet has determined to permit all that takes place, which renders the event certain; then his determining to permit it, is really decreeing that it shall take place; or foreordaining that it shall come to pass: So that the objection that God's foreordaining sin, makes him the cause and author of it, is not the least obviated by this supposition or scheme. And it may be worth while to consider whether any other supposed difficulty is removed by this. This leads to observe,

2. This does not in the least obviate what has been just observed upon the assertion that sin has no cause: For a negative cause is really no cause. Therefore to say concerning any existence, It has no cause but a negative one, is really denying that it has any cause. This therefore makes sin to exist without a cause or reason of its existence, rather than of its nonexistence. If the world has only a negative cause of its existence, then there is no cause of its existence, and no reason can be given why it does exist.

Moreover, this notion of a negative cause of moral evil supposes some positive cause, by which sin would come into existence; a cause of sufficient force, and positive energy to produce this effect, unless the operation of it be counteracted by God, by preventing the existence of it, by a positive energy; and therefore it has actual existence, as an effect of this cause, by the determination of God not to hinder it. If an effect will certainly take place upon a mere permission, or not preventing it, it is necessarily supposed there is a cause sufficient to produce this effect, if not counteracted. And it must be now asked, what is this cause? Does it exist in God, or in the creature? If in the creature, from whence is the origin of this positive cause? Is its origin in itself; or in the creature? Or must we go back to the first cause? If either of the former be admitted, then we are again involved in the absurdity of sin being the cause of itself; or of a cause and effect existing independent of the first cause.

3. Even this supposition, that God is only the negative cause of moral evil, were it consistent, and did not leave sin really without any cause; yet relieves no difficulty respecting the existence of sin. It will be asked, why God suffered sin to exist, when he could have prevented it? If we could account for its existence without any reason or cause of it, if permitted or suffered to exist, that is, if not prevented; how shall we account for God's suffering it to exist? It is presumed all must agree in the following answer. Because He, on the whole, all things considered, saw it best, or chose it should exist, rather than not. And if so, he must, he certainly did, choose things should be ordered so ns to make its existence absolutely certain; and consequently did order them so, and did every thing that was necessary to be done, previous to the existence of sin, in order to render the existence of it certain. Indeed, if it be granted that God, on the whole, chose moral evil should exist (which all must grant, who allow that he has permitted sin) and that this is a wise and holy choice; such a choice implies his doing every thing that is necessary in order to render this choice effectual; and that God is wise and holy in willing or doing all this, whatever it may be. And all this is really nothing more than his choice or will that it should exist; as all that God did in creating the world, so far as we can conceive, was to will its existence, or say, Let it be; there being a certain connection between his willing the existence of any thing or event, and the actual existence of it. He is in no other sense the origin or cause of any thing. And in this sense, it is granted by all who allow he permitted it, that he is the origin of moral evil.

Some may, perhaps, think all which has been now said of the origin or cause of moral evil may be evaded, and proved to be nothing to the purpose, by observing, that sin is purely a negative thing; that it is so, at least, in its original and foundation; and therefore has no origin or cause; or, at most, can have nothing more than a negative one.

On this it may be observed, that if it be meant that sin is a nonentity, and has, properly and in truth, no existence, and therefore is really nothing; and if this can be proved, then certainly a negative cause, or, which is the same, no cause, is quite sufficient in this case, to account for that which is not an effect, and is really nothing: And the inquiry, and all assertions about origin, cause or effect, are nugatory and absurd.

But will any man say, or can he believe, that there is nothing positive in moral evil, and that it has no positive existence? If such an one can be found, he must, if he will be consistent, say and believe that it is nothing or that there is no such thing; for not positively to exist is non-existence; and what is this more than nothing? And why is not moral good or holiness a negative, or nonentity also? Reason and divine revelation join to assert both to have a real, positive existence. Is there not as real, positive existence and exertion in selfishness, or self love, as in benevolence, or love to God? Or in enmity against God, as in the highest exercise of friendship to him?

But may it not be urged, that it is indeed granted that sin has something positive in it, when it comes to actual exercise, and is exerted in opposition to God and man: But is not this consistent with its having a negative original, or arising from a privative cause?

Answer. If there could be sin where there is not, in any sense, the least exercise, which it will be difficult, if not impossible to prove; still this must be nothing, if a mere negative or privation; and can have no existence. And a privative cause is no cause. But granting that a negative or privative cause is a real cause, and that a negative effect, is a reality; yet, this does not account for this negative becoming a positive existence of its own accord, without any positive cause. If that which is merely negative, were any such existence possible, may start into positive existence, without any positive cause; then the whole world might come into existence without any positive exertion or cause. This supposition therefore does not appear to help the matter in the least, or to remove any difficulty.

But it may still be asked, is not the true and only origin of sin overlooked in all that has been yet said? Is not the sinner himself the only true and proper cause of his sin, as he produces it, and there is no other cause or author of his sinful exertions?

Answer. If in this question it be meant, that he with whom moral evil is found is the sinner, and that we must not look beyond him, or out of him, to find the sin of which he is guilty; but that he is, in this sense, the origin, cause and author of all the sin that is found with him; it being his own act, which he has exerted voluntarily, and without any compulsion; and for which he only is blameable: If this be the meaning, it is granted the sinner is, in this sense, the sole cause and author of all the sin found with him; and we are not to look any farther for it. But still there is a reason why things were so ordered and disposed, as that he should thus sin, rather than not. Something must have taken place previous to his sin, and in which the sinner had no hand, with which his sin was so connected, as to render it certain that sin would take place just as it does. This is the origin or cause of sin, which the question we are upon respects, and concerning which inquiry is made: And in which it has been observed, there can be no sin, as by the supposition it takes place and is exerted before the existence of moral evil, of which it is the origin or cause, and in order to it. Therefore, if we find that the great first cause of all things is, in this sense, the origin of moral evil, by foreordaining whatsoever comes to pass, this does not suppose any moral evil in him, but the contrary; and is perfectly consistent with his infinite holiness, as has been before observed.

Objection. But after all the above reasoning about the origin of sin, which seems to prove that the first cause of all things is in a true and important sense, the cause of this evil; he having foreordained that it should take place, and disposed and done every thing that was necessary to be done, antecedent to the existence of sin, and in order to it, by which this event was made certain; and that in all this there can be no moral evil, but the contrary: Yet it will appear to the common sense and feelings of men, that to will the existence of sin, and to make any exertion or do any thing in order to it, in consequence of which it does actually exist, is wrong and sinful; and therefore infinitely unbecoming the supreme and infinitely holy Being. And to assert any such thing, or even to suppose that God is, in any sense, the origin of sin, is shocking, and fraught with impiety!

Ans. 1. It may be that many under the gospel, by not attending candidly and without prejudice to this subject, and not thinking closely upon it, nor making proper distinctions; and by habituating themselves to a wrong association of ideas on this point; may be shocked at the above representation; and feel as if it carried in it a degree of blasphemy; and yet, this not be any evidence that it is not agreeable to the truth, and consistent with the highest degree of real piety, and veneration for the Most High; and even the proper dictate and language of it.

The Jews had, by education, and otherwise, imbibed such prejudices in favour of their temple and worship, and had habitually formed such an association of ideas, that they thought and felt that Stephen was guilty of blasphemy, when he intimated, that their place of worship should be destroyed, and the customs which Moses delivered to them be changed. And they were shocked, and stopped their ears, when he told them that he saw the heavens opened, and the Son of Man standing on the right hand of God. And when Christ said to the Jewish council, "Hereafter ye shall see the Son of Man on the right hand of power, and coming in the clouds of heaven," the high priest was so shocked, that he rent his clothes, and they all cried out, blasphemy! The present Jews, and those of many generations past, have thought it a piece of high impiety to pronounce the

The System of Doctrines, contained in Divine Relation, Explained and Defended Volume I

Tetragrammaton, as it is called; that is, the sacred name Jehovah, and shudder at the thought of doing it; and are to the last degree shocked to hear it done. This is the effect of a false association of ideas, and superstition, introduced by the force of education, by which it comes to pass, that the pronunciation of a name, which was spoken freely, and with the highest exercise of pious veneration of the Deity, by the prophets and holy men of old, is now considered by the Jews as an instance of shocking impiety.

If we look into the popish world, we shall find innumerable instances of this kind. If a protestant pay no veneration to the host, and refuse to bow, and worship the breaden god, when it is carried in public procession, the populace will be shocked with a degree of horror: and it will be no wonder if he gets a broken head for his impiety. And if he do not worship and pray to the virgin Mary, and venerate her image; but speaks against it as idolatry, their pious feelings are most sensibly excited, and they abhor the impious wretch; while he considers himself to be following the dictates of true piety in all this, and honouring the Most High.

From these and many other instances of the same kind, it appears, that what is sometimes called the common sense and feelings of men, is not to be depended upon, in determining what is true or false; especially in those things which respect the Deity: And more especially, when the dictates of this sense and feeling are contrary to the most clear dictates of sober, sound reason, and to the plain and abundant declarations of divine revelation. For as that which is often highly esteemed among men, is an abomination in the sight of God; so that which is most important truth, in his sight, and honourable to Him, is in too many instances an abomination to men. This leads to,

Ans. 2. That God did will the existence of moral evil, in determining, at least, to permit it, when he could have prevented it, had he been pleased to do it, must be granted by all who would avoid ascribing to Him that imperfection, impotence, and subjection to that power, be it what it may, which introduced sin, contrary to his will; which is indeed shockingly impious, and real blasphemy, to every considerate, and rationally pious mind. We may infer from this, with the greatest certainty, that it is, all things considered, or in the view of the omniscient God, wisest and best that moral evil should exist. For to suppose that it was his mill that it should take place, or that he has permitted it, when he could have prevented it; and yet that it was not wisest and best in his sight, that it should exist, is beyond expression impious, and at once strips the Deity of all moral good or holiness; and gives him the most odious and horrid character!

But if God did will and choose that sin should exist, this being, on the whole, most agreeable to his holiness or his infinite wisdom and goodness; this necessarily implies, as has been before observed, ail that energy, exertion and disposal of things, that is necessary, previous to the existence of sin, in order to its actually taking place; and without which it could not have existed. For there is an infallible connection between the will of God that sin shall exist, and the actual existence of it; and this will of God is the cause or reason why it has taken place, rather than not. And if it be wise and holy to will and determine the existence of moral evil, it is wise and holy to order and do every thing which must be ordered and done, antecedent to its existence, in order to its taking place, be that what it may: And not to order, dispose and do all that, would be contrary to wisdom and holiness. Therefore, to assert that God is, in this sense, and so far the origin and cause of sin, is so far from imputing any thing dishonourable to him, that it is the only way in which his infinite wisdom and holiness can be consistently asserted and maintained: and to assert the contrary is highly impious, and very opposite to the sense and feelings of the pious mind of him who is truly judicious, sensible and discerning.

The sum of what has been said on this point may be expressed in the following words. Moral evil could not exist, unless it were the will of God, and his choice, that it should exist, rather than not. And from this it is certain, that it is wisest and best, in his view, that sin should exist. And in thus willing what was wisest and best, and foreordaining that it should come to pass, God exercised his wisdom and goodness; and in this view and sense, is really the origin and cause of moral evil; as really as he is of the existence of any thing which he wills; however inconceivable the mode and manner of the origin and existence of this event may be; and however different from that of any other. [71]

II. Divine Revelation must be examined carefully to find in what light this point is there represented; whether it does warrant any to say, God has foreordained the existence of sin: Or that he is in any sense the origin and cause of it. This ought to be done with fear and reverence of these sacred oracles; with impartial, upright hearts, and a religious concern and desire to think and speak according to this word, since they who do not "have no light in them."

In order to obtain the light which is contained in the holy scriptures, respecting this subject, it may be of advantage to observe the following particulars.

1. According to divine revelation, God superintends, orders and directs in all the actions of men, and in every instance of sin; so that his hand and agency is to be seen and acknowledged in men's sinful actions, and the events depending on them, as really and as much, as in any events and

actions whatever. Of this every person must be sensible, who has read the Bible with any proper attention and true understanding; as it is held up to view throughout the whole of it, and is suited to impress this idea on the mind of every one who reads it. All the historic part of the Bible, and the predictions of events, whether great or less, to be accomplished by the wicked agency of man; and of innumerable particular sinful actions of men, are an incontestible evidence of this. So are all the acknowledgments of the divine hand and agency, in the events brought to pass by the sinful conduct of men; which are too many to be particularly mentioned here. But the truth of this observation may perhaps be more fully illustrated, and set in a stronger point of light, by attending to the following passages of scripture.

The very sinful deed of the brethren of Joseph, in selling him, which was the necessary mean of his going into Egypt, is represented as so ordered by God, as to be as really done by him, as if it had not been done by the hands and agency of these wicked men. Joseph says to his brethren, that God did it, and that he had a particular and good design in it. "God sent me before you, to preserve you a posterity in the earth, and to save your lives by a great deliverance. So now it was not you that sent me hither, but God, who meant it unto good." [72] "He sent a man before them, even Joseph, who was sold for a servant." [73]

It is said, concerning Eli's wicked sons, that "they hearkened not unto the voice of their father, because the Lord would slay them." [74] It is here asserted that by God's ordering and direction, they disregarded the admonition of their father, as necessary in order to his destroying them.

When Shimei cursed David, he acknowledges the hand of God in it, as much as if Shimei had done it in obedience to the divine command, or it had been done immediately by God himself. "So let him curse, because the Lord hath said unto him, Curse David. Let him alone, and let him curse; for the Lord hath bidden him." [75] It is impossible David should express himself thus on this occasion, unless he viewed Shimei's wicked conduct to be ordered and directed by God, so that his hand was to be seen in it, as, in this sense, the origin and cause of what took place.

"And Absalom and all the men of Israel said. The counsel of Hushai the Archite is better than the counsel of Ahithophel: For the Lord hath appointed to defeat the good counsel of Ahithophel, to the intent that the Lord might bring evil upon Absalom." [76] This good counsel of Ahithophel was defeated by the folly of Absalom and the men of Israel; yet it is said, God had appointed it, to bring about his own purpose. His hand guided the whole affair, and superintended every motion of the hearts of those wicked men.

"Wherefore the king hearkened not unto the people; for the cause was from the Lord, that he might perform his saying, which the Lord spake by Ahijah the Shilonite, unto Jeroboam the son of Nebat. Thus saith the Lord, Return every man to his house; for this thing is from me." [77] Here it is said, that God so superintended and directed in this affair, that he was the cause of that foolish and wicked conduct of Rehoboam; and that it was from him, as necessary to accomplish an important event, which he had determined and foretold. And who can say, that God is not, in the same sense, and as much, the origin and cause of every instance of sin, that he may accomplish his infinitely wise designs? Is not this passage alone a sufficient warrant for this? And if the divine character can be vindicated, in what is ascribed to him, in this instance, how can it be dishonourable to him to say, he so directs and orders with respect to every instance of sin, as that he is, in this sense, the origin and cause of it? When the enemies of Judah came to ravage and destroy that people and country, it is said, God sent them. "And the Lord sent against Jehoiakim bands of the Chaldees, and bands of the Syrians, &c. and sent them against Judah to destroy it. Surely at the commandment of the Lord came this upon Judah, to remove them out of his sight." What can be the meaning of this, unless it be that God superintended, ordered and directed all the motions and conduct of these wicked men: and so made them his instruments to destroy Judah? "Through the anger of the Lord, it came to pass in Jerusalem and Judah, until he had cast them out from his presence, that Zedekiah rebelled against the king of Babylon," [78] Is it not here declared that God ordered the sinful rebellion of Zedekiah against the king of Babylon; and that his hand or agency was to be seen, and his anger with the inhabitants of Jerusalem and Judah, was expressed in this?

"But Amaziah would not hear; for it came of God, that he might deliver them into the hand of their enemies." [79] It appears from the story that it was owing to the pride and folly of Amaziah, that he did not hearken to the admonition and advice of the king of Israel; and yet this was of the Lord. By his determination, direction and superintending influence, it came to pass, in order to answer his own wise purposes: and his hand was to be seen in the obstinacy of Amaziah, as really as in any event which takes place by the immediate exertion of divine energy. And if this instance of sin was of God, then every instance may be, and most certainly is so: And we are warranted to assert this, by the declaration before us, as well as many others of the same tenor to be found in holy writ.

In the tenth chapter of Isaiah, God, by his prophet, addresses the king of Assyria, as the rod of his anger, and the executioner of his indignation, against the hypocritical nation of Judah and Israel; and says he would send him to punish them; though he in going and doing the work, would have no design or desire to accomplish the ends God intended to answer by his pride and cruelty; And therefore after he had accomplished his ends by him, he would punish him for that wickedness of which he would be guilty, and which was necessary to fulfil the purposes of God: And while he was as really an instrument in the hand of God, and as much under his influence and direction, and as dependent on him, in all his motions, as is the ax or saw, in the hand of the workman. There is no need of any comment to show that this passage represents God as ordering, directing and bounding the sinful actions of wicked men; so that they are answering his ends in what they do, and his hand is to be seen and acknowledged in their sinful motions and actions, as really as the hand and exertions of the workman is to be seen in the motion of the axe or saw, by which he executes his designs.

In the same manner God speaks of Nebuchadnezzar, king of Babylon. He says, he would send and fecht him, and the nations under his command; and by him utterly destroy Judah, and the neighbouring nations; and speaks of him as his instrument, or weapon in his hands to lay waste and destroy. "Thou art my battleaxe and weapons of war. For with thee will I break in pieces the nations, and with thee will I destroy kingdoms, &c." [80]

To the same purpose are the following words, "Behold, I have created the smith that bloweth the coals in the fire, and that bringeth forth an instrument for his work; and I have created the waster to destroy." [81] This is said to support and comfort the people of God, in all their dangers and troubles from evil men, telling them that they had no reason to be afraid of them, since they were made by him, to answer his ends; and they were absolutely in his hands: so that they should do nothing but what he ordered; and therefore could do them no real hurt.

"And before these days, there was no hire for man, nor any hire for beast; neither was there any peace to him that went out, or came in, because of the affliction; for I set all men every one against his neighbour." [82] This warrants us to consider God's hand, and efficacious influence, in all the hatred, quarrels and wars that take place among men.

"Wherefore I gave them also statutes that were not good, and judgments whereby they should not live. And I polluted them in their own gifts, in that they caused to pass through the fire all that openeth the womb, that I might make them desolate, to the end that they might know that I am the Lord." This has reference to the statutes and judgments which they made for themselves, and practised in their abominable idolatries, &c. yet God says, He gave them these evil and destructive statutes and judgments; and He polluted them, in these abominable sacrifices, by which they polluted themselves. This strongly expresses his superintendency and agency in all this, in order to answer a wise and important end. [83]

The crucifixion of our Saviour, and all the circumstances that attended it, are expressly and repeatedly declared to have taken place, in consequence of the divine determination and decree, foreordaining them; and by his direction and superintending hand. It was so important and useful, that this whole affair should be viewed in this light, that special care was taken to keep it in view. "Thinkest thou that I cannot now pray to my father, and he shall presently give me more than twelve legions of angels? But how then shall the scriptures be fulfilled, that thus it must be?" "But all this was done, that the scriptures of the prophets might be fulfilled." [84] "But behold the hand of him that betrayeth me, is with me on the table. And truly the Son of man goeth as it was determined." [85] "Him, being delivered by the determinate counsel and foreknowledge of God, ye have taken, and by wicked hands have crucified and slain. And now, brethren, I know that through ignorance ye did it, as did also your rulers. But those things which God before had shewed by the mouth of all his prophets, that Christ should suffer, he hath so fulfilled." [86]

Peter, in these passages, is careful to observe, that the death of Christ was part of the divine plan, which he had in his wise counsel determined; and had particularly foretold by the prophets; and which he had now fulfilled by their wicked hands, as it was necessary to be viewed in this light, in order to understand it, and see the reason and importance of this memorable event; And not consider it is an argument of the weakness and disappointment of the Saviour and his followers. Accordingly the disciples kept this constantly in view, and say, in a solemn address to God, "For, of a truth, against thy holy child Jesus, whom thou hast anointed, both Herod and Pontius Pilate, with the Gentiles and the people of Israel were gathered together, to do whatsoever thy hand and thy counsel determined before to be done. [87] "

If God had before determined, or foreordained, that all this should be done, with every act of sin which was necessarily implied in its being done; and his irresistible hand and operation was to be seen and regarded in all this; and the church did see and particularly attend to this, as matter of support, thankfulness and joy; and devoutly acknowledged all this, in a solemn address to God, in order to glorify him; all which must be owned to be true, as long as this passage is allowed to stand in the Bible: Then there can be no impiety, in believing and saying, that God has foreordained whatsoever comes to pass, and with his hand is executing his own wise purposes, in his governing providence, ordering and directing all the actions of men, even the most sinful, as well as others, for his own glory and the general good; and that his hand is to be seen in every event, and in every action of man, as really as if he was the only agent in the universe; yea, to view things in this light, and to have feelings and exercises answerable, is for the glory of God, is suited to support and comfort all his friends; and is implied in true devotion.

2. The holy scriptures represent God as, in some way or other, moving, exciting and stirring men up to do that which is sinful, and which, in itself considered, and as done by them, is very displeasing to him.

"And again the anger of the Lord was kindled against Israel, and he moved David against them, to say, Go number Israel and Judah." [88] This, to which God is said to move David, was a great sin in him, and very displeasing to God. "And the Lord stirred up an adversary unto Solomon, Hadad the Edomite. And God stirred him up another adversary, Rezon, the son of Eliada." [89] "And the God of Israel stirred up the spirit of Pul, king of Assyria, and the spirit of Tilgath-pilneser, and he carried them away, even the Reubenites, and Gadites, and brought them unto Halah, &:c."[90] "Behold, I will stir up the Medes against them, which shall not regard silver, &c." [91] These passages express a divine agency, either mediate or immediate, on the minds of these persons, by which they were influenced and moved to those actions; and God is represented to be the first moving cause of what was done by them: And what he did, be it what it may, was antecedent to their volitions and actions, and the latter the effect of the former. And if their liberty and sin consisted wholly in their voluntary exercises, as has been proved; then they were as free and as blameable, as if nothing had been determined and done, antecedent to their determinations and choice, and as necessary to their taking place, whatever it was. And whatever is implied in God's moving them, and stirring up their spirits to act as they did, it was only in order to bring to pass his infinitely wise, important and good purposes, or executing his holy decrees; and therefore was infinitely wise and holy; and directly contrary to the views, inclinations and designs of these wicked men: and therefore consistent with his abhorring their doings; his displeasure with them, and punishing them for their wickedness.

3. Agreeable to the last particular, the scriptures represent God as moving the hearts of all men, just as he pleases; and even when they do that which is sinful.

"Draw me not away with the wicked and with the workers of iniquity; which speak peace to their neighbours, but mischief is in their hearts." [92]

"From the place of his habitation he looketh upon all the inhabitants of the earth, He fashioneth their hearts alike." That is, He forms the heart of every one equally, of one, as well as another. [93]

"He turned their heart to hate his people; to deal subtilly with his servants." [94] "Incline my heart unto thy testimonies, and not unto covetousness." [95] "Incline not mine heart to any evil thing, to practise wicked works with men that work iniquity." [96] "For God hath put in their hearts to fulfill his will, and to agree, and give their kingdom unto the beast, until the words of God shall be fulfilled." [97] These are the ten kings and their subjects, mentioned in the preceding context, who join to support the beast, and make war with Christ and his people. God is here said to put it in their hearts, to do this, so far, and so long, as this is necessary, in order to answer his ends, and fulfil his infinitely wise and important designs. This cannot import less than that God has the hearts of these kings, and all under them, so in his hand and under his direction, that he turns them as he pleases, to accomplish his purposes; so that he makes them answer his ends, in all their opposition to him. Agreeable to this, it is said, "The king's heart is in the hand of the Lord as the rivers of water: He turneth it whithersoever he will." [98] If God does turn the heart of the king, whithersoever he will; then his heart, his will and choice, is always and in every instance under God's direction and control; and there can be no motion, determination, or exertion of his heart, which is not as God wills it to be. Every turn of his heart then is an event which God wills should take place, and therefore foreordained that it should come to pass just as it does. And God, in thus turning the heart, is in this sense, the origin and cause of every motion, choice or volition, in which the heart turns this way, or that. And if the heart of the king is thus in the hand of the Lord, and he turneth it whithersoever he will; then the hearts of all his subjects, yea, of all men, may be, and actually are as much in the hand of God. This is implied in the assertion under consideration. The heart of the king is mentioned, as he has great power and influence over others, and is most absolute and despotic, and commonly most obstinate and inflexible. Even his heart, as well as the heart of all others, is in the hand of the Lord; wholly under his power and influence, and is turned by him just as he pleases. The same thing is asserted in many passages of scripture, some of which have been mentioned; as that of God's representing the king of Syria as sent by him to distress Israel and Judah; and as an axe or saw in his hand, directed and moved by Him to execute his will; his speaking of other kings as raised up and sent by Him, to be his servants to do his pleasure; and putting it into their hearts to fulfil his will, &c. But, in these words of Solomon this is asserted in the most express and strongest manner, of the heart of kings and of all men; so that it seems impossible not to understand, or to evade the truth here expressed: As no words, perhaps, can be devised to convey it in a more clear,

The System of Doctrines, contained in Divine Relation, Explained and Defended Volume I
unequivocal and decisive manner.

All the objections made against God's foreordaining all the moral evil that takes place, and his being, in this sense, and so far, the origin and cause of it, as has been asserted and explained above, do equally lie, and are as strong against this passage, and many others which have been mentioned, under this and former particulars.

4. In Divine Revelation an evil spirit which is in men and takes place among them, is said to be from God; and to be sent or caused by him.

"Then God sent an evil spirit, between Abimelech and the men of Shechem: And the men of Shechem dealt treacherously with Abimelech." [99] "But the Spirit of the Lord departed from Saul, and an evil spirit from the Lord troubled him. And it came to pass on the morrow that the evil spirit from God came upon Saul." [100] "Now therefore the Lord hath put a lying spirit in the mouth of all these thy prophets." [101] "The Lord hath mingled a perverse spirit in the midst thereof: And they have caused Egypt to err in every work thereof." [102] Whatever be meant by an evil, lying and perverse spirit, whether it be no more than the evil inclination and exercise of the hearts of men; or an evil agent, distinct from their spirits, exciting them to sinful exercises; God is in these scriptures represented as superintending and ordering this spirit to take place in men, as it did. And if he did this, and yet maintained his own infinitely holy character, and these men were notwithstanding, wholly free in their evil inclinations and conduct, and accountable and deserving of blame and punishment for them; which was most certainly the case: Then all the evil volitions of men may be, in the same sense, manner and degree, from God, consistent with all these. It is therefore easy to see, that all objections against the doctrine under consideration, may with equal reason be made against such declarations as these, which are found in the holy scriptures.

5. God is said, in the scriptures, to order, send and effect the sinful deceptions and delusions of men. "With him is strength and wisdom: The deceived and the deceiver are his." [103] "O Lord, why hast thou made us to err from thy ways?" [104] "And if the prophet be deceived when he hath spoken a thing, I the Lord have deceived that prophet." [105] "And for this cause God shall send them strong delusions, that they should believe a lie: That they all might be damned, who believed not the truth, but had pleasure in unrighteousness." [106] According to these passages, the divine hand and agency are concerned in all the errors and deceptions which take place among men, by which many of them run on to destruction.

6. In the scriptures, God is many times said to blind the minds, and harden the hearts of men. This is often ascribed to him, in the most express terms, without saying any thing to qualify, soften, or explain the expressions, or to intimate that they are not to be taken in their plain, natural meaning. These will be now produced, as worthy of particular attention.

"And he said, go and tell this people, hear ye indeed, but understand not; and see ye indeed, but perceive not. Make the heart of this people fat, and make their ears heavy, and shut their eyes: Lest they see with their eyes, and hear with their ears, and understand with their heart, and convert, and be healed." [107] We have this remarkable passage quoted in St. John's gospel, in the following words, and applied to the Jews in his day. "Therefore they could not believe, because that Esaias said, He hath blinded their eyes and hardened their hearts; that they should not see with their eyes, nor understand with their heart, and be converted, and I should heal them." Here those words in Isaiah, Make the heart of this people fat and shut their eyes, have the meaning of them given in the following words, He, that is God, hath blinded their eyes and hardened their hearts, God is here said to do what Isaiah was directed to do; for the prophet was infinitely unequal to produce the effect, and could be only the instrument by whom God caused it to take place. In this view, and in no other, the Evangelist appears to have given the true sense of the passage, while he uses these strong and pointed expressions.

"For the Lord hath poured out upon you the spirit of deep sleep, and hath closed your eyes. They have not known, nor understood: For he hath shut their eyes, that they cannot see; and their hearts, that they cannot understand." [108] "Israel hath not obtained that which he seeketh for: But the election hath obtained it, and the rest were blinded," (or hardened, as it is in the original,) "According as it is written, God hath given them the spirit of slumber, eyes that they should not see, and ears that they should not hear unto this day." [109]

Those passages are now to be produced, in which hardening the hearts of men is expressly ascribed to God. This is done more than ten times, in the history of Pharaoh and the Egyptians. "But I will harden his heart, that he shall not let the people go." [110] "And I will harden Pharaoh's heart, and multiply my signs and my wonders in the land of Egypt. But Pharaoh shall not hearken unto you." [111] "And he hardened Pharaoh's heart, that he hearkened not unto them, as the Lord had said." [112] "And the Lord hardened the heart of Pharaoh, and he harkened not unto them; as the Lord had spoken unto Moses." [113] "And the Lord said unto Moses, go in unto Pharaoh: For I have hardened his heart, and the heart of his servants, that I might show these my signs before him: and that thou mayest tell in the ears of thy son, and of thy son's son, what things I have wrought in Egypt, and my signs which I have done among them; that ye may know how that I am the Lord,"[114] "But the Lord hardened Pharaoh's heart, so that he would not let the children of Israel go." [115] "But the Lord hardened Pharaoh's heart, and he would not let them go." [116] "And Moses and Aaron did all these wonders before Pharaoh: And the Lord hardened Pharaoh's heart, so that he would not let the children of Israel go out of his land." [117] "And I will harden Pharaoh's heart, that he shall follow after them; and I will be honoured upon Pharaoh, and upon all his host; that the Egyptians may know that I am the Lord." [118] "And the Lord hardened the heart of Pharaoh king of Egypt, and he pursued after the children of Israel." "And I, behold, I will harden the hearts of the Egyptians, and they shall follow them: And I will get me honour upon Pharaoh, and upon all his host." [119]

There are other passages in which God is said to harden the hearts of men, which are now to be mentioned. "But Sihon, king of Heshbon, would not let us pass by him, For the Lord thy God hardened his spirit, and made his heart obstinate, that he might deliver him into thy hands as appeareth this day." [120] "For it was of the Lord to harden their hearts, that they should come against Israel in battle, that he might destroy them utterly." [121] "O Lord, why hast thou hardened our heart from thy fear?" [122] It might be safely and with good reason argued from these instances of God's hardening the hearts of men, that God hardens every heart that is hard and obstinate; as no reason can be given why he should do this, in one instance, and not in another; or there is the same reason why the hardness and obstinacy of men's hearts in general, and wherever it takes place, should be as really ascribed to God, as these instances which are mentioned; and there can be no objection against his hardening the hearts of all men, whose hearts are hard, that may not with equal reason be made against his hardening the heart of Pharaoh, and others concerning whom it is expressly asserted. But this is made certain, as the consequence is drawn to our hand, by one under divine inspiration. "Therefore hath he mercy on whom he will have mercy, and whom he will he hardeneth." [123] The apostle in these words has reference to God's hardening the heart of Pharaoh, whom he mentions in the words immediately preceding; and from this instance of God's raising him up and hardening his heart, to answer his own infinitely wise purposes, he makes this inference: "Therefore hath he mercy on whom he will have mercy, and whom he will he hardeneth." Here every one of mankind is comprehended in those on whom God has mercy, and those whom he hardeneth; and it is asserted that he hardeneth all those on whom he will not have mercy, that is, all whose hearts are hardened. It must be farther observed,

7. In the sacred scriptures, God is expressly said to form, make, or produce moral evil.

"The Lord hath made all things for himself: Yea, even the wicked for the day of evil." [124] Here God is said to make the wicked, not considered merely as men; but as wicked: for in this character, or as wicked only, are they the proper subjects of natural evil, or punishment. What less can his making the wicked mean, than his having some hand or agency, in some way or other, in forming their character as wicked? And is this any less or more, than his willing that there should be such existences as wicked men; because moral and natural evil are necessary, as necessary as any other existence, to answer the infinitely wise and important purposes of God, in the brightest display of his perfections? He has made them for himself, to put them to his own use, and by them to manifest his own character, his holiness, hatred of sin, &c.

"I am the Lord, and there is none else; there is no God besides me: I girded thee, though thou hast not known me: That they may know from the rising of the sun, and from the west, that there is none besides me. I am the Lord, and there is none else. I form light, and create darkness: I make peace, and create evil. I the Lord do all these things." [125]

These words are addressed to Cyrus, who was not then born: But was to arise in the eastern world, to conquer the Babylonians, and to release the Jews from their captivity, and order the temple and Jerusalem to be rebuilt. He was born and educated where the God of Israel was not known, and where they were taught, that the good being who was the author of all good, was not the only power that reigned; but that there was an evil being or principle, which reigned so far as to counteract the good principle or being, and introduce all the evil, both moral and natural, which takes place; and of which he is the proper cause or author. The good principle, or being, they represented by light, and worshipped him before the sun or fire, considering it the brightest emblem of him, and in a peculiar manner possessed or inhabited by him. The evil being and the evil of which they supposed him to be the cause and author, they represented by, and called, darkness. There is an evident reference to these false and hurtful notions, in which Cyrus was educated, in the address to him, part of which has now been cited; in which Jehovah declares them to be great and dangerous delusions, and repeatedly asserts, that he is the only Supreme God. "I am the Lord, and there is none else; there is no other God besides me. I am the Lord, and there is none besides me." And then he asserts that he is the cause of all that which they ascribed to the evil being, which they believed in, and feared. "I form light, and create darkness; I make peace and create evil. I the Lord do all these things." [126]

Does not God, in these words, expressly take to himself this character, and assert that he is the origin and cause of all evil? If so, then we have no reason to be afraid to think and speak of him- as such: but may consider ourselves as promoting true piety, and the honour of the only true God, while we believe and assert, that all evil is the consequence of his determination and will, that it shall exist, and is wholly dependent upon it; as without his will that it should take place, it could no more exist, than any thing else whatsoever. No one can devise stronger terms or language to express this, than that which is here used by God himself. How this appears to be consistent with the infinite wisdom and holiness of the divine character, and most honourable to God, has been repeatedly shown, in what has been already said on this subject: and therefore it need not be again repeated here.

But it has been said by many, -that moral evil is not meant by darkness and evil in this passage; but only natural evil, or calamity and pain. Of this God may be, and is, the cause, but not of sin. To this the following reply may be made.

1. The opinion to which this passage has reference had respect to moral evil as well as natural: yea, this was chiefly in view, as the former is the origin and occasion of the latter. And the evil being was considered as having the direction and disposal of moral evil; so that it originated from him as the cause. Therefore if this was designed to be excluded in the passage before us, which is spoken to Cyrus, and has reference to that notion in the east, respecting the cause of moral evil, as well as natural, it must have been done by an express exception: For without this, and as it now stands, Cyrus, and every one else, must consider it as included and intended, as well as natural evil. Nor can it be now excluded, without doing violence to the text; and at the same time really gaining nothing by it: For if it be allowed that moral evil is intended here, as well as natural, no more is really asserted than is expressed in many other passages in the Bible, as every one may be sensible, who will attend to what has been before produced from the scriptures, under this head.

2. If it be granted that natural evil only is directly intended here; yet this will necessarily involve moral evil; for a great part of the former which takes place among men, is the natural and necessary result of the latter. It is effected by the exercise of men's selfishness and lusts. "From whence come wars and fightings among you? come they not hence, even of your lusts, that war in your members?" [127] "But if ye bite and devour one another, take heed that ye be not consumed one of another." [128] If therefore the divine Being has no direction and government of the wills and evil conduct of men, he cannot be said to create or produce, or even to regulate and superintend natural evil. If God does not will, direct and order a war, which is wholly carried on by the exercise of men's lusts; how can he be said to direct, will and order the attendant or consequent natural evil? How does he cause or produce the one, more than the other? In this view, we may turn to the words of the prophet Amos. "Shall there be evil in the city, and the Lord hath not done it?" Here evil is mentioned without restriction, confining it to natural evil: But if it be supposed that natural evil is particularly meant here; yet this implies moral evil: as the natural evil, the calamity, sufferings and distresses which take place in a city, are chiefly the concomitants or fruits of vice and folly. And if the Most High has no concern or hand in directing, ordering and producing the latter; how can he be said to produce or effect the former; or how can it be said to be done by him, since it is the necessary attendant and fruit of the sin of men; and it is really done by them, and they are as really the cause of natural evil, as they are of their own sin, as the former is involved in the latter?

3. It must farther be observed, that if natural evil only, be meant by evil in the above passages in Isaiah and Amos; yet there is as great, and the same difficulty, in accounting for God's creating and doing this, as there is in accounting for his determining and willing the existence of moral evil: Or the same objections lie, and may be urged with as much reason, against God's willing, causing and producing natural evil, which are or can be made against his willing that moral evil should exist.

If this proposition can be demonstrated, and made plain to every one who will allow himself to think calmly on the subject; then all the objections which have been made against God's foreordaining whatsoever comes to pass, and all that is necessarily implied in this, will fall to the ground; and the ways and labour which have been taken to construe the scriptures mentioned above, so as not to imply that God is, in any sense, the origin and cause of moral evil, lest they should be understood in a sense dishonourable to him, will appear to be needless, and unreasonable. Let this matter, then, be carefully considered.

Natural evil is as really contrary to infinite goodness, as moral evil is; infinite goodness cannot be reconciled to it, considered in and by itself, but is infinitely opposed to it: And to suppose that God wills and causes it to take place, for its own sake, and because he delights in it, in itself considered, is as dishonourable to him, and does as much impeach and deny his goodness, as to suppose that he wills and causes moral evil, for its own sake, and because he is pleased with it, and delights in it. Yea, to say that God causes natural evil to take place, for its own sake, and because he is pleased with it, in itself considered, is to charge him with moral evil, or that which is infinitely contrary to infinite holiness or goodness, as really as to say that he causes moral evil because he is pleased with moral evil, as such.

Therefore, if when God says in the passage under consideration, "I create darkness and evil, I the Lord do all these things," this is to be understood of natural evil only; it cannot mean, that God causes this evil, for its own sake; for this necessarily supposes him to be an evil being; but he causes it to take place, he creates it, for some good end, and for the sake of the good, of which the evil is the occasion or means; and without which evil, the good could not possibly take place; so that on the whole, there is much more good or happiness, than could have been, had there been no natural evil. If natural evil could answer no good end, and were not necessary, in order to this, it could not be created or made to take place, or be permitted to take place, by an infinitely good Being who has the disposal of all things: But if it be necessary to answer the best end, and to promote and produce the greatest good of the whole; then it may be not only permitted, but created, or caused to take place, consistent with infinite goodness; yea, it is inconsistent with infinite goodness, not to do so.

And who does not now see, that God may determine, order and cause moral evil to take place, and, in this sense, create it, consistent with his infinite holiness and goodness, if this be necessary for the greatest good of the whole, both moral and natural; yea, that God could, not be infinitely wise and good, if, on this supposition, he did not order and cause it to take place? If the divine conduct can be vindicated in causing natural evil to take place; on the same ground it can be vindicated in causing moral evil to exist; and not one objection can be made against the latter, which may not equally, and with as good reason, be made against the former. For instance, if it should be objected against the latter, that to make God the origin and cause of sin, is to suppose moral evil is in him; for there can be nothing in the effect which is not in the cause: This may with equal truth and reason be said of natural evil. If God be die origin and cause of it, this supposes natural evil to be in him, and that he is infinitely unhappy and miserable; for there can be nothing in the effect which is not in the cause. Again, if it be objected, that if it be agreeable to the will of God that sin should exist, and he chose it should take place, and is therefore the origin and cause of its existence; then sin is agreeable to his will, and he is pleased with it: It may with as much propriety, and as good reason, be said, if God wills the existence of natural evil, and causes it to take place; then he is pleased with it, and delights in the misery of his creatures; consequently he cannot be a good, but a morally evil being. If the objector, to remove the difficulty that is urged upon him, should say, that God does not cause natural evil, for the sake of the evil, but for the sake of the good end to be answered by it; he may be asked, Why this, which is as true of moral evil, does not equally remove the difficulty respecting God's being the cause and origin of that? If it solves the difficulty in one case, it must do so in the other. If God may order and cause natural evil, which, in itself, is infinitely contrary to his goodness, to exist, consistently with his goodness; then he may will and cause moral evil to exist, though it be, in itself considered, infinitely contrary to his holiness, and most odious to him: And no one can account for the former, without giving as good a reason for the latter. Is it not very unreasonable and most absurdly inconsistent, for men perpetually, and with great assurance to object and urge that against the supposition that God wills and chooses the existence of moral evil, which may be with as much reason urged against his willing the existence of natural evil; while they allow he does will and cause the latter: And at the same time cannot tell how this is consistent with the divine perfections, without offering a reason, which equally proves the other to be as consistent?

It has been said, that if it be best, on the whole, that sin should take place, as it is necessary to promote the general good, then sin is a good thing; and the more sin the better. Now, this may be with as much reason said of natural evil. If God order that, to answer a good end, then it is a good thing, and the more of it the better. The inference from the latter, is as well grounded, as from the former. In truth, it is in both instances utterly unreasonable. That which is in itself, in its own nature, evil, may by God be made the occasion of the greatest good; and this is so far from altering the nature of the evil, or making it less an evil, in itself considered, that if this should be the case, and it were possible, the end to be answered by it would be defeated, and there would be no evil, to be the occasion of good. It is indeed a good thing, that evil, both moral and natural, should take place; and the good of which this is the occasion swallows up the evil, and the whole taken together is the most complete, perfectly beautiful, and good system: But this alters not the nature of the evil, and it is still as evil, as contrary to all good, and as disagreeable and hateful, considered in itself, and as unconnected with the whole, as if it were not made the occasion of good; but of evil. But this has been often brought into view before. It is again introduced, to show the unreasonableness of the objection, and that it is as much against the existence of natural evil, in order to answer a good end, as it is against the existence of moral evil, for the same end. The infinitely wise Being most perfectly knows how much evil, both natural and moral, and what particular instances of it, are necessary, in order to accomplish the greatest possible good; and all this takes place by his decree and will, and no more. The existence of just so much, and no more, is desirable, as it is necessary to accomplish the best end: But God will not suffer any more to exist; the remainder he will effectually restrain. If he did not, and more than is necessary to answer the best ends should take place, it would be infinitely undesirable and evil, and inconsistent with the divine perfections. How unreasonable then is it to say, "If evil be necessary for the good of the whole, and thus answers a good end, then the more evil the better!"

It has been farther objected, that if God wills the existence of sin, and it is therefore agreeable to his will that it should take place in every instance, when and wherever it does; then the sinner does not resist his will in sinning, nor can be blameable for it; but rather ought to sin, that good may come. Let it now be carefully and with impartiality considered, whether this objection may not with just as good reason be urged against God's willing and causing all the natural evil which takes place. If any one, by his sin, cause natural evil to take place, by oppressing and afflicting the widow and fatherless, or by murdering his neighbour; or in any other instance; he voluntarily does that which is agreeable to the will of God, that it should take place. He has not resisted the will of God; but has complied with his will and designs: Therefore he cannot be blamed for it; but rather ought to do all this, since without his agency this natural evil would not take place, which God has determined should be done, because necessary to effect the greatest good, and accomplish his own wise design. In short, if God be pleased with the existence of that natural evil which is effected by the oppressor, murderer, &c. then he cannot blame or be displeased with the oppressor or murderer, for being also pleased with the existence of this evil, and exerting themselves to produce it. Is there any way to answer this objection, and remove the difficulty, unless it be in the words of Joseph to his brethren? "As for you, ye thought evil against me; but God meant it unto good:" [129] There was a direct and total opposition and contrariety between the will of God that this evil should take place, and the will and design of Joseph's brethren, in desiring and effecting this natural evil, consisting in his being made a slave in Egypt. God ordered it, and took measures effectually to produce the evil, not from any pleasure in the evil itself; but in the exercise of his infinite goodness, because it was necessary to accomplish the greatest good of which this evil was the occasion. "He meant it unto good." But the brethren of Joseph, thought and designed evil against him: They did it in the exercise of malevolence, or ill will towards him; which was most unreasonable, and was in the nature of it, enmity against that good, for the sake of which God ordered this evil to take place; and therefore was directly opposed to that benevolent will of God, which determined and ordered this evil. Their disposition and will in this affair were just as opposite to the disposition and will of God in determining and willing the existence of this evil, as malevolence is to benevolence and goodness, or as evil is to good; and therefore must be displeasing and hateful to God; and they as blameable in his sight, as if he had brought no good out of it, and nothing but evil had taken place. As this is the only solution of the difficulty, and fully removes the objection respecting God's willing and causing natural evil; it is easy for every one who attends, to see that it equally answers the objection against his willing and causing moral evil: And shews how the existence of both may be chosen and caused by God, not for their own sake, but for the sake of the good end answered by them; and consistent with his hating them both, in themselves considered; so that in him it is an exercise of infinite benevolence; and therefore directly contrary to the disposition and will of the sinner in sinning, and in willing and producing natural evil. And consequently shews how justly God is displeased with the sinner, and blames him for willing and choosing, both moral and natural evil.

These things have been observed to show that when God says "I create evil," in the passage above cited, moral evil as well as natural may be intended; as there can be no difficulty or objection thought of, if the former be included, which is not equally against the latter; and if the former must be excluded, as inconsistent with the divine perfections, in any sense and view, to form and create it; for the same reason must the latter be excluded: And that moral evil must be intended, as well as natural, not only because nothing is said to exclude it; but because the occasion and design of the words do necessarily include both.

The words of St. Paul seem to claim a place under this head. "Thou wilt say then unto me, Why doth he yet find fault? For who hath resisted his will? Nay, but, O man, who art thou that repliest against God! Shall the thing formed say to him that formed it. Why hast thou made me thus? Hath not the potter power over the clay, of the same lump to make one vessel unto honour, and another unto dishonour?" [130] Upon these words the following observations may be made.

1. The objection here introduced by the Apostle has reference to his assertion in the preceding verse, and is grounded upon it, "And whom he will he hardeneth." And this same objection is made now, and always has been made by men, against the truth here asserted; which is, that it is the will of God, that all the hardness and obstinacy of heart which is found amongst men, should exist just as it does; and therefore he has foreordained, according to the counsel of his own will, that it shall take place. So much, at least, is expressed in these words of the Apostle; and indeed no more than what is implied in this: For whatever God wills to take place, has a cause of its certain existence;

and this can be found no where but in the divine will. The objection is, "If all the sins of men take place by the will of God, and according to his will; then there can be no crime in sin; and men cannot be justly blamed for that, the existence of which is agreeable to his will.

2. It is observable, that the Apostle in his answer to this objection, does not say that the objector had mistaken his meaning; and that he had not said that it was agreeable to the will of God that the hardness of men's hearts, and every instance of obstinacy and sin, should take place just as it does; and therefore the divine purpose and agency was concerned in all this; but implicitly grants that this is a truth, and that he had asserted it; by not only not denying it; but proceeding to vindicate it in his answer; by which the meaning of his words is fixed beyond a doubt.

3. In his answer he is so far from palliating what he had said, or softening down his expression, to which the objection is made, that he rather heightens it, and expresses himself in a stronger manner, if possible. "Shall the thing formed say to him that formed it, Why hast thou made me thus? Hath not the potter power over the clay, of the same lump to make one vessel unto honour, and another unto dishonour?" The potter makes one vessel as really and as much as another; that which is made to dishonour, and that which is made unto honour. Therefore, if the similitude is any thing to the purpose, and does not give a very wrong idea of the matter, which it is designed to illustrate, all sinners whose hearts are hardened, who are represented by the vessels made unto dishonour, are as really formed and made such as they are, hardened sinners, as the vessel unto dishonour is made a dishonourable vessel, by the potter: And God's sovereign right to do this is here asserted; and he who objects to this, the Apostle says, speaks against God. Besides, the Apostle expressly asserts that the hardened sinner is formed and made so by God. "Shall the thing formed say to him that formed it, Why hast thou made me thus?" Thus the Apostle speaks this out, and repeats it in the most express and pointed language, without fear of hurting any one by it; and with assurance that he is espousing the cause of God, and vindicating his rights and honour, in opposition to an apostate world.

The Apostle, having asserted the sovereign right of God to form his creatures as he pleases, in the next words gives the reason of this, and mentions the important end he has in view, and answers, by making the wicked for the day of evil. "What if God, willing (or determined) to show his wrath and make his power known, endured with much long suffering the vessels of wrath, fitted to destruction: And that he might make known the riches of his glory on the vessels of mercy, which he had afore prepared unto glory? "

The following things are suggested by these words.

1. That God does not harden sinners, or punish them, for the sake of hardening and making them miserable, or because he has any delight or pleasure in their sin and punishment, considered in themselves, and unconnected with the end to be answered by them: But he does this to answer a wise and important end, which could not be answered in any other way; and to produce a good, which infinitely overbalances the evil, which is necessary in order to it.

2. We are here told what this great all important end is, which God designs to effect; the good which is produced by the persevering sin, and destruction of men, who are the vessels of wrath. It is the manifestation and display of his own perfection; "To show his wrath, and make his power known: And to make known the riches of his glory." That is, he does this for himself, for his own glory. This perfectly coincides with the words of Solomon, which have been mentioned, and serves to fix the sense of them. "The Lord hath made all things for himself: Yea, even the wicked for the day of evil."

3. It is here supposed, that what God does in hardening sinners, and making them vessels unto dishonour, and enduring with much long suffering these vessels of wrath, fitted for destruction, is consistent with their being blameable for their hardness, and every thing which renders them dishonourable: and with his being highly displeased with them for it; and that he may justly destroy them forever, for their hardness and obstinacy in sin. This is supposed, and really asserted, in the words; for, in any other view, they would be inconsistent and absurd; as otherwise, sinners could not be vessels of wrath, fitted to destruction. Whatever men have thought, and may think and assert, St. Paul, and he by whom he was inspired, knew that both these are perfectly consistent. How these things are consistent, does appear, it is hoped, from what has been said above, and may be yet farther offered, on this head.

Having thus considered what is the language of scripture on this point, and made particular remarks on the passages which have been adduced; some more general observations on the whole, in one general view of them, must now be made, hoping they may serve to throw farther light on the subject, and confirm the truth exhibited respecting it in divine revelation, which has been so difficult and intricate to many.

1. It appears from these passages of scripture, that God has foreordained all the moral evil which does take place; and is, in such a sense, and so far, the origin and cause of it, that he is said to bring it to pass, by his own agency. Therefore it is not bold or dangerous to believe and assert this;

but it is for the honour of God, and tends to promote the good of men: And to believe and assert the contrary, is directly the reverse, bold, dangerous, dishonourable to God, and hurtful to man. It is safe to speak according to the scriptures; and so far as any man does not, it is because, in that instance, there is no light in him. [131]

2. If these scriptures be understood, as many have chosen to understand them, as importing only that God permits sin, and so orders every thing respecting the event, that, he permitting, it will certainly take place just as it does; this really comes to the same thing, or if not, does not obviate any difficulty, which has been thought to attend the representation which has now been made of this matter. For they who choose this way of speaking do represent God as willing that sin should take place; or on the whole, preferring and choosing that it should exist, rather than not. And this, as has been shown, implies all that is intended by his being the origin and cause of sin; and ordering and doing every thing, that was necessary to be ordered and done, previous to the existence of sin, in order to render it certain, in every instance where it does take place. His decree turns the point in favour of the existence of sin: And his agency makes it certain, without which it could have no existence.

And if God determined to permit all the sin which does take place, and by his agency orders things so, that, he permitting it, it will be done, this is liable to all the objections that have been, or can be male against the assertion, that all the sinful volitions of men are the effect of the divine agency. For the former makes sin as certain and necessary as the latter; and it is no more consistent with the holiness of God, and his hatred of sin, to will the existence of it, and lay a plan to have it take place, upon his permission, than it is, directly to cause it to exist in the creature, by any agency or exertion whatever, which is previously necessary to the existence of sinful volitions. And the former is not only liable to all the objections that can be made against the latter; but, so far as it differs from the latter, supposes an effect without any real origin or cause, and therefore involves the greatest difficulty and absurdity imaginable, as has been shown above. Why then is it not most reasonable, safe and best, to understand these scriptures in their most plain and obvious meaning, since by a strained or forced interpretation, no difficulty is removed, and nothing is obtained; and by explaining away the most easy and natural meaning, new and inextricable difficulties are incurred? [132]

In short, there appears to be no rational or consistent medium, between admitting that God, according to the scriptures, has chosen and determined that all the moral evil which does, or ever will exist, should take place, and consequently is so far the origin and cause of it: Or believing and asserting, that sin has taken place, in every view, and in all respects, contrary to his will, he having done all he could to prevent the existence of it; but was not able; and is therefore not the infinitely happy, uncontrollable, supreme Governor of the world; but is dependent, disappointed, and miserable! No one, surely, will adopt the latter: How then can he avoid admitting the former?

3. If the scriptures which have been mentioned, where hardening the hearts of men, blinding and shutting their eyes, and inclining and turning their hearts, when they practise moral evil, &c.--if these scriptures are to be understood, as meaning no more than that God orders their situation and external circumstances to be such, that, considering their disposition, and the evil bias of their minds, they will without any other influence, be blinded and hardened, &c. then all those scriptures, which speak of God's changing and softening the heart, taking away the hard heart, and giving a heart of flesh; opening the eyes of men, and turning them from darkness to light, and from sin to holiness, working in them to will and to do, and causing them to walk in his ways, &c. may and must be understood in the same way, as not intending any special divine influence on the mind, as the origin and cause of virtuous, obedient, holy volitions; but only his using means with them in an external way; putting them under advantages, and setting motives before them; so that if they be well disposed, or will dispose themselves to obedience, they may be holy, &c. To be sure, it cannot be argued from the expressions themselves, that the latter express or intend any more real influence on the minds of men, or divine agency, by which God is the origin and cause of virtuous exercises; than the former do with respect to men's sinful exercises; for the expressions are as unlimited, plain and strong, which speak of the former, as those which are used for the latter.

The Arminian, and all of his cast, understand the latter, as they do the former, as intending no internal, decisive influence on the mind, turning the heart or will one way, or the other; but ordering external circumstances, &c. And are they not herein more consistent, than the professed Calvinist, who insists that the latter cannot be understood as expressing less, than that God, by his agency and influence on the minds of men, does actually produce all virtuous volitions, as their real origin and cause; while he as confidently asserts, that the former cannot mean any such thing; but understands them as the Arminian does: Were they consistent, they would give up the cause to the Arminian, and own that the latter expressions may well be understood, as he understands them, and must mean no more, if the former do not. This is mentioned, it must be observed, as argumentum ad hominem, to convince these professed Calvinists, or whatever they choose to call themselves, that they are really inconsistent; and, in this point, are taking a measure to strengthen their opposers, rather than to convince or confute them. This leads to another observation.

4. They who object to the divine agency being the origin and cause of sinful volitions, because, in their view, this is inconsistent with freedom and moral agency, in such volitions, and with any blame or crime in that which is the effect of such a cause; must, if consistent with themselves, reject the doctrine of the divine agency, as the cause of virtuous volitions and exercises, on the same ground, and for the same reason.

If any kind or degree of supposed influence and agency, which is antecedent to a man's volition, and the cause of its taking place, renders such volition not free, and not the man's own volition and exercise, so that he is neither virtuous nor vicious in having and exerting such a choice; then there is no freedom or virtue in the exercises of those called good men, which are the effect of powerful divine influence, causing them to take place; But if such agency and influence, producing virtuous volitions in men, be consistent with the freedom of men, in such volitions; and they are as much their own exercises, and they are as virtuous, and as much their own virtue, as if they had taken place without such previous influence; or as they could be, on any possible supposition; then all this is as true of all contrary or sinful volitions of men, whatever kind or degree of influence and agency be exerted, antecedent to their existence, and as the cause of it.

This observation is made for the sake of those, who make the above objection against there being any origin or cause of sinful volitions, antecedent to their existence; supposing this is inconsistent with man's freedom and blame in such exercises: And yet they believe and assert, that all virtuous exercises of men are the fruit and effect of divine influence, as their origin, which efficaciously causes them to take place; and that these exercises are as really and as much their own, and as virtuous, and praise worthy, as if they had taken place, without any such previous influence and cause, were this possible. It is desirable that this palpable, gross inconsistency of theirs might be discerned, and attended to by them; upon which they would drop this objection, as wholly without foundation, or urge it equally against the virtuous exercises of men, being the effect of any previous, divine, efficacious influence, as their origin and cause; and renounce it as inconsistent with the liberty a: id moral agency of men; by which they will be consistent with themselves in this point, however inconsistent they may be with the Bible.

Both the one and the other is indeed equally and altogether consistent with human liberty, and with virtue and sin. No supposeable or possible influence or agency, previous to the exercises of the will, which is the origin and cause of such exercises, can render men less free in such voluntary exercises, or the less virtuous or vicious: And that because liberty consists, and is exercised in willing and choosing; and in nothing that does or can take place antecedent to the volitions of men, or as the consequence of them: And virtue and sin consist in the exercises of the will or heart, and in nothing else; and men are sinful or holy according to the nature and quality of these. These are most certain and evident truths, which has been in some measure shown above; and which ought to be always kept ill view, when attending to this subject.

5. There is a certain connection between God's hardening the hearts of men, and shutting or blinding their eyes, whatever this may be, or imply; and their voluntarily hardening their own hearts, and shutting or closing their own eyes; so that when or wherever the one takes place, the other does also.

When God is said to harden Pharaoh's heart, he is, at the same time, said to harden his own heart. God said to Moses, that he would harden the heart of Pharaoh. [133] And it is repeatedly said, that he hardened his own heart, as the Lord had said, [134] referring to his saying, that he would harden the heart of Pharaoh. So it is said, [135] Pharaoh sinned yet more, and hardened his heart; and in the first verse of the tenth chapter, the Lord said unto Moses, Go in unto Pharaoh; for I have hardened his heart; referring to the instance just before mentioned, of Pharaoh's hardening his own heart. Hence it appears, that whenever God hardened the heart of Pharaoh, he hardened his own heart; and whenever Pharaoh did harden his heart, God did also harden it: And that this is true of every instance of hardness or obstinacy of the heart, God hardens the heart, and the sinner himself hardens his own heart.

It does not follow from this, as some have thought it did, that God's hardening the heart of Pharaoh, and his hardening his own heart, are one and the same thing. This supposition is contrary to the representation, and the express words. Here are two distinct agents, who are said to be concerned, and to act, in producing one and the same event, without which it could not take place, viz. the hardness of Pharaoh's heart. As the agents are infinitely distinct and different, and their characters directly opposite to each other; so is their agency; that of God is holy, that of Pharaoh sinful. Yet the one necessarily supposes and involves the other. The agency ascribed to God, is the origin and cause of the hardness of the heart, without which it could not take place; and of which it is the certain consequence. The agency ascribed to Pharaoh, and which is to be ascribed to every sinner whose heart is hard, is the effect or consequence of divine agency, and consists wholly in

The System of Doctrines, contained in Divine Relation, Explained and Defended Volume I
this effect, that is, in hardness of heart. The heart cannot be hardened, or there cannot be a hard heart, without the agency of the sinner, hardening his own heart; for it consists in voluntary exercise; and therefore does not, and cannot take place, while men are wholly passive and do not act, or put forth those exertions in which hardness of heart doth consist.

When God made man a living soul, the effect produced consisted in man's activity, he lived; for life is not merely a passive effect, but is itself action. Man could not be made a living soul, without life, or unless he lived, and he could not live, unless he were made to live; so that the one, is necessarily implied in the other. Yet life is as really life and activity, or man as really lives, and it is as much his own life and activity, as if he had lived without being created or made to live, were this possible. Every one cannot but see how false and absurd it would be to say, that God's making man a living soul, and man's agency in living, are one and the same thing, because one necessarily implies the other; so that to assert one, is, in effect, and really to assert the other: To say, that God breathed into man the breath of life, implies that man lived, and does really assert it: and to say that man became a living soul or lived, implies the divine agency in causing him to live, and does really assert it; though there be two different agents, and two very different kinds of agency, as distinct and different from each other, as if there were no connection between them, and the one did not imply the other.

This is applicable to the instance before us. When God hardens the heart of any man, that man certainly hardens his own heart, or that hardness is his own chosen obstinacy; and were it not so, he could have no hardness of heart, or his heart could not be hardened. To suppose the contrary, is an express contradiction. Audit is as much his own chosen obstinacy, and his own crime; and he is as odious and ill deserving, as if his Maker had no hand or concern in the matter. When God hardens the heart, or exerts any supposable or possible kind or degree of influence or power, of which sin or holiness in the creature is the consequence; this is so far from being or implying any necessitating influence, impelling or forcing men to sin, or obey, that it is absolutely impossible there should be any such thing, antecedent to the actual existence of will and choice; and it is necessarily implied, that the disposition, will and choice, in which the sinner's obstinacy consists, is the exercise of freedom, and his own choice. The will or heart is not capable of any such necessitating influence, by which it is forced to act, in opposition to acting freely; because, as has been observed, exercise of choice or voluntary action and freedom, are the same thing. To talk of a necessitating influence by which the will is forced to act, which deprives a man of freedom, is just as absurd as to say, that a man is forced to live, without having any life; and so as utterly to exclude it.--But this has been considered before.

To return, The observation to which we are now attending, viz. That whenever God hardens the hearts and blinds the minds of men, they do harden their own hearts and shut their own eyes; and the latter is necessarily implied in the former, as the former is implied in the latter; may be farther illustrated and confirmed, by several other passages of scripture; which, at the same time, will serve to throw some light upon them.

The Lord says to Isaiah, "Go and tell this people, Hear ye indeed, but understand not; and see ye indeed, but perceive not. Make the heart of this people fat, and make their ears heavy, and shut their eyes: Lest they see with their eyes, and hear with their ears, and understand with their heart, and convert, and be healed." These remarkable words are quoted, or referred to, no less than six times in the New Testament; and oftener than any other text is quoted from the Old Testament. In St. John's gospel it is expressed in the following words. "Therefore they could not believe, because that Isaiah said. He hath blinded their eyes, and hardened their hearts; that they should not see with their eyes, nor understand with their heart, and be converted, and I should heal them." In this quotation the expressions are as they are in the Prophet, though stronger and more decisively plain, if possible, representing the agency of God in blinding the eyes of men, and hardening their hearts. He is said to do this, and it is ascribed to him, as the cause; and nothing is said expressly of the agency of men in die matter. St. Paul is supposed to refer to these words, together with other passages, in the following passage. "The election hath obtained it; but the rest were blinded: According as it is written, God hath given them the spirit of slumber, eyes that they should not see, and ears that they should not hear, unto this day." [136] Here he speaks, agreeable to the words in Isaiah, and as St. John quotes them, of God as the agent, and of what he does, and he is represented as blinding men, giving them the spirit of slumber, eyes that they should not see, &c. and nothing is expressly said of the agency of men. But he quotes these words on another occasion, in a different manner. "Well spake the Holy Ghost by Isaiah, the Prophet, unto our fathers, saying. Go unto this people and say. Hearing ye shall hear, and shall not understand; and seeing ye shall see, and not perceive. For the heart of this people is waxed gross, and their ears are dull of hearing; and their eyes have they closed, lest they should see with their eyes, and hear with their ears, and should be converted, and I should heal them." [137] In Matthew xiii. 15, these same words are quoted by Christ himself, just as St. Paul quotes them here. "For this people's heart is waxed gross, and their ears are dull of hearing, and their eyes have they closed." Here they are said to close or blind their own eyes, they are represented as active in the matter, and their agency only is spoken of expressly; and the divine agency is not mentioned: Whereas in the passages above produced, these same words of Isaiah are made to express, not the agency of those who are blind, in making themselves so; but the divine agency in shutting their eyes; so that their being blind and unbelieving, is ascribed to God. It is a question worthy to be considered. How these words in Isaiah can be consistently quoted so differently, and be made to speak of the agency of the sinner hardening his own heart, and closing his own eyes, when the Prophet expresses nothing but the divine agency, in hardening and blinding them, as they are quoted by St. John, and once by St. Paul?

Is not the only solution, and satisfactory answer to this question, contained in the observation made above, viz. That whenever God hardens the heart, and closes the eyes of men, they harden their own hearts, and shut their own eyes, the one being necessarily implied and involved in the other; so that when it is expressly said that God hardens the heart of any man, or hath given him eyes that he should not see, it is as really asserted, that the man himself hardens his own heart, and closes his own eyes, as the latter is necessarily implied, it being the very thing expressly said to be produced as the effect of the divine agency. Therefore when Isaiah speaks of God as hardening men's hearts, and shutting their eyes, he equally asserts that these men harden their own hearts, and close their own eyes; and may justly, and with the greatest propriety be quoted, as asserting both of them, or either the one or the other.

This is equally true of the light, wisdom and holiness; of good men, God is certainly the origin and cause of all this, according to the scripture. He circumcises the heart, to love him: He gives a new heart, and puts a new spirit in them; creates in them a clean heart, and renews in them a right spirit: He saves them by the washing of regeneration and the renewing of the Holy Ghost: He causes them to walk in his statutes, and to keep his judgments and do them. [138] Yet the scripture speaks of them to whom God gives a new heart, and whose heart he circumcises, and whom he renews by his holy Spirit, as circumcising their own hearts; making themselves a new heart; as those who have put off the old man, and put on the new man; and renewed themselves in the spirit of their minds; and have cleansed and purified their own hearts. [139]

These passages may be reconciled by observing, that the former speak expressly of the divine agency in the renovation of the hearts of sinful men, and forming them to true holiness. The latter speak of the agency and exercises of men, implied in their renovation and holiness, and in which their turning to God, and their obedience does consist: And which is necessarily connected with the former, and involved in it. Whenever and wherever God gives a new heart, the man makes himself a new heart, in that agency and those exercises, in which a new heart consists. He renews and cleanses his own heart, and circumcises it, by turning from sin to God; hating sin and loving God, and in all that agency, and those pure and holy exercises in which he conforms to the divine law, and to the gospel, and lives a holy life. All this is necessarily implied in what God does in giving a new heart, as it is the effect which he produces by his agency; and these are connected, and involved in each other, as are the cause and effect: So that to assert one, is equally to assert the existence of the other. The sinner's heart cannot be made a clean heart, by the divine agency, in any other way, but by the sinner's cleansing his own heart; because a clean heart consists in those exercises of the man, in which he does cleanse his own heart. It is a contradiction to say, that God has circumcised the heart of a man to love him; and yet the man does not love him, or, which is the same, has not circumcised his own heart to love the Lord: And so of the rest. Therefore when God says, he will give a new heart and put a new spirit within men; it is really asserted that they shall renew their own hearts, in the proper exercises and agency, in which a new heart and new spirit consists; or that they shall walk in his ways. And on the contrary, whenever a man makes him a new heart, and becomes obedient, this implies all that divine agency, by which God gives a new heart: And therefore by asserting the former to exist, the latter is really asserted. If a man purifies himself, and cleanses his own heart, in pure, holy exercises, it is certain that God has created in him a clean, a new heart; and to assert the former or the latter, is really to assert both.

Here are two distinct agents, infinitely different; God, absolutely independent, and almighty; and a creature absolutely dependent for every thought and volition, having no power and sufficiency, that is not derived immediately from his Maker: and the agency or operation is as distinct and different as the agents. The creature's agency is as much his own as in the nature of things it can be, and as it could be, if it were not the effect of the divine agency, if this were possible. And the creature acts as freely, as if there were no agent concerned but himself; and his exercises are as virtuous and holy; and it is really and as much his own virtue and holiness, and he is as excellent and praise-worthy, as if he did not depend on divine influences for these exercises; and they were not the effect of the operation of God. All this, it is presumed, is plain, and must be evident to all who have attended to what has been said above, on this subject. And there can be no difficulty respecting God's hardening the sinner's heart, and his hardening his own heart, which does not equally attend God's making a new and clean heart, and at the same time the man renewing and cleansing his own heart; and no objection can be made against the former, which is not as much against the latter: unless it be, that in the latter instance, moral good or holiness in the creature is the effect of the divine operation: but in the former, it is directly the reverse, and moral evil or sin takes place in consequence of the divine determination and agency; which has been thought by many to be inconsistent with the infinite purity and holiness of God. It is presumed that what has been said above to this point, is sufficient to obviate this objection, and show it to be wholly without foundation. But this leads to another observation.

6. Though it be as expressly asserted in the scriptures which have been cited, and particularly considered, that God has determined the existence of all the moral evil that takes place, and does by his own operation and agency cause it to take place, as it does; as it is, that true virtue and holiness which takes place in men, is the effect of divine operation: Yet it does not follow from this, that the manner and mode of divine operation, which is the cause of those different and opposite effects, is in all respects the same; and consequently no man has a right to assert this. Indeed, this, in both instances, is inscrutable by man, and cannot be particularly explained. We know that what is produced in the latter instance, is, as it consists in the exercises of the creature, conformable to the law and nature of God. In the former, what takes place in man, is directly the reverse, contrary to God's nature and law: But as to the manner of operation, as the cause of either, we are wholly in the dark; as much as we are, with respect to the manner of the divine operation in the creation of the world, and the different and various existences. All we know is, that God willed their existence, to be just as they do exist, or said, Let them be, with which fiat their existence is infallibly connected. And he as really willed the existence of moral evil as of holiness in creatures; and the existence of both is equally the infallible consequence.

And though the effects, holiness and sin, are in their nature, and considered in themselves, so infinitely different and contrary to each other, and the latter most odious and abominable; yet the existence of them both may be equally important and desirable, and necessary for the glory of God, and the greatest possible good: And in this view God willed the existence of both, in the exercise of infinite wisdom and benevolence, even the same kind of benevolence which he requires of creatures in his holy law; and which is opposed by the sinner in every act of sin. It hence appears, that God's disposition and will respecting the existence of sin, which is the origin and cause of it, and his disposition and will revealed in his law requiring benevolence, and all that is implied in it, and forbidding the contrary, are perfectly consistent, and one and the same: And were it possible for him to will and choose that sin should not exist, this would have been infinitely contrary to the divine law. Thus it appears that God is holy in all his works and ways, even while he wills the existence of moral evil: And that there neither is, nor possibly can be, any moral evil, in being thus the origin and cause of it.

The following questions and answers will conclude this subject.

Question. Does not the doctrine which has been advanced, serve to strengthen and confirm the infidel, and others, in their belief that man is not a moral agent, and is not capable of sin or blame, whatever he may do? Many who reject divine revelation profess to believe the doctrine of universal necessity; that all things and events, from the greatest to the least, are fixed, so that there can be no alteration: And hence they infer, that man has no liberty, and is not a moral agent, so as to be in any degree criminal. And many who do not professedly renounce revelation profess to believe the absolute and universal dependence of all creatures and things on God; and hence infer and say, they are what God has made them to be; therefore they are not answerable for what they are, or do; nor are they justly blameable for any thing in their character or conduct. These will think themselves supported by the doctrine of the decrees of God, as it has been stated above. Is it wise or right to advance a doctrine which tends to produce such an evil effect? Had it not better be suppressed, if it be true.

Answer 1. If the doctrine, as it has now been stated, be clearly and abundantly asserted in the scripture; and the whole be necessarily implied in the independence and supremacy of God, and the entire dependence of the creature, in all respects, which, it is presumed, has been made evident; then there can be no good reason why it should not be asserted and vindicated: And it is certain it does not tend to any evil, or to produce any bad effect. And if it be improved to any bad purpose, and any groundless inference be made from it, it must be an abuse of the truth, and perverting it to an end to which it has no tendency; but the contrary.

Ans. 2. There is no religious or moral truth revealed in the Bible, which may not be improved to some bad purpose; and has not been so improved by ignorant and wicked men. And if no truth ought to be explained and vindicated, or mentioned, which may be abused, and will be perverted by some, even to their own destruction, all religious truth must be suppressed, and the Bible must be shut up, and no more lie open to the world.

Ans. 3. At the same time that the doctrine of the divine decrees has been stated and vindicated, it has been equally proved from scripture and reason, that man is a free agent, and accountable for his moral conduct; and in all respects as much so, and is as real and as much a moral agent, as he could be on any supposition, and if this doctrine were not true; and no events or actions were fixed and certain before they actually took place: And he is as much the former and author of his own moral character, as he could be, were there no other agent concerned in them: And all his moral actions are as much his own, and his own virtue or sins, as they could be, if nothing were previously done or determined, which rendered them certain. If any will abuse their own reason and the holy scriptures, so much as to believe but one of these equally evident truths, and reject the other, he must answer for it, and take the consequence. But must one or the other of them be given up or suppressed, lest men should abuse one, or both of them? Let the scripture and reason judge.

Ans. 4. All the difficulty in this matter appears to lie in reconciling the total, universal, and constant dependence of man on God, with his freedom and moral agency, and accountableness for his moral conduct. The scripture asserts both these in the strongest manner, from the beginning to the end, in a variety of ways. The instances are too numerous to be all mentioned here. This dependence is represented by the potter and the clay; and man is asserted to be as dependant on God for the manner of his existence, and in all his moral character and actions, as the clay is on the potter, for the shape, and kind of vessel into which it is to be formed. [140] And wicked men, in all their actions, are represented to be as much in the hand of God, and moved by him, as the saw, axe, rod or staff, are in the hand or power of a man, who uses and moves them. [141] The apostle Paul says, [142] "In him we live, and move, and have our being." [143]

And reason, or true philosophy, teaches the same. A creature cannot be made independent, in any the least degree or respect whatever; because this implies a contradiction. For if a creature can be independent with respect to any thing, or in any degree, he may be so in every degree, and in all respects; which is inconsistent with his being a creature. Therefore the constant and entire dependence of man, on God, his Creator, for existence; for every perception and thought, and every motion of body or mind, and every circumstance of these, from the least that is possible, to the greatest, is absolute and perfect, in the highest degree, and in every respect. According to scripture and right reason, this is perfectly consistent with the moral freedom and agency of man; and he is as virtuous or vicious, and as worthy of praise, or deserving of blame and punishment, as if he were not thus dependent, if this were possible; which it is hoped has been made evident. But apostate, proud man feels as if he were, in a great degree at least, self dependent, and inclines and aspires to be so. This tends to lead him to wrong ideas and speculations on this point, and to prevent his reasoning properly upon it. And it is no wonder that great mistakes are made, and that many are led aside by false reasoning on the subject; and cannot be convinced of the truth: Or if they be in some measure convinced in their judgment, or at least silenced by unanswerable arguments; yet they may feel as if it were not, and could not be true; and not submit to it, but oppose it in all the exercises of their hearts.

They who are humble, and feel their dependence on God, and are pleased with it, are most likely to understand these things, and to see the consistence of such dependence, and their freedom and accountableness to God for their moral conduct; and to be satisfied with it. And if they cannot remove every difficulty in speculation, and answer all the objections which are made to it; they nevertheless do acquiesce, and are pleased with being thus dependent, and yet wholly blameable for every deviation from the law of God; and have no doubt of the consistence of these, though they may not be able to show how, or to reason the matter out with others. "The meek will he guide in judgment; and the meek will he teach his way." [144] They will approve of the sentiments and exhortation of the apostle Paul, and feel and act accordingly. They will "work out their own salvation with fear and trembling;" that is, in the exercise of true humility, and a sense and acknowledgment of their entire, constant dependence on God for every exertion and motion of their will; knowing that "He worketh in them both to will and to do."

Ques. Do not the words of the apostle James expressly deny that the divine agency is concerned in the existence of moral evil, when he says, "Let no man say, when he is tempted, I am tempted of God. For God cannot be tempted with evil, neither tempteth he any man?"

Ans. To tempt, and be tempted, are to be understood in different senses, as they are used in the scripture. God is said to be tempted, and men are often said to tempt him. And it is said that he tempted Abraham: And in this sense he does tempt others, and may tempt all men. Sometimes to tempt, is taken in a bad sense, as it is in this passage, and means a sinful act, as it always does when Satan is said to tempt any one. In this sense God does not tempt any man; for he is holy in all his works. To be tempted, sometimes means only to be tried; and is consistent with the perfect innocence and holiness of him who is said to be tempted. In this sense God is said to be tempted, and Jesus Christ was tempted. Sometimes to be tempted implies moral evil, and actually falling into sin. In this sense, the word seems to be used in the following passages, "Considering thyself, lest

The System of Doctrines, contained in Divine Relation, Explained and Defended Volume I
thou also be tempted. Lest by some means the tempter have tempted you, and our labour be in vain." [145] In this sense the word is to be understood, when James says, "God cannot be tempted," and in the same sense he uses the word, when he speaks of a man being tempted. This is evident from his own explanation of it in the following words: "But every man is tempted, when he is drawn away of his own lust, and enticed." A man cannot be tempted, in this sense, but by the exercise and gratification of his own lusts; the existence of which is therefore supposed, and necessary, in order to his being tempted; without which he could not be so tempted. Therefore a man is not, nor can be tempted, in the sense here stated, by any thing that is, or can be done, antecedent to the existence of evil, or lust, in his heart. For the temptation applies to his lust, and is suited to excite sinful exercises, or lead men into sin. It is easy to see, that God does not so tempt any man; and that his foreordaining whatsoever comes to pass, and executing his decrees in ordering and governing all the actions of men, does not imply this. All that God does is infinitely wise and holy. And he does not exhibit any thing to the view of men, or set any thing before them, in his word or works, in false colours, or that has any tendency to deceive them, or draw them into sin; but every thing which he suggests to them, in his word and providence, has a contrary tendency, and is perfect truth. And if men view objects in a wrong and false light, it is wholly owing to their lusts, by which the light and truth which God sets before them, is perverted and abused.

Ques. Have not those who have been called Calvinists, and have professed their belief of the doctrine of the decrees of God, that he hath foreordained whatsoever comes to pass, denied the divine agency in the existence of moral evil, while they hold that God decreed to permit it? And is not this way of representing the matter safest and best, to avoid the charge of making God the author of sin? And others who hold that God is the cause of every act and volition of the sinner, have distinguished, and said that he is the cause of them, as natural actions and events, or so far as they are natural; but not of the moral depravity of them: That this is wholly from the sinner, and he alone is the cause of it? Is not this distinction proper and necessary, in order to avoid the above imputation?

Ans. 1. It has been observed, that Calvin, and the assembly of divines, at Westminster, assert that the divine decree and agency, respecting the existence of sin, imply more than a bare permission, viz. something positive and efficacious. [146] They therefore who hold to only a bare permission, do depart from those who have been properly called Calvinists; and do not agree with the confession of faith composed by said Assembly of divines, or with those numerous churches and divines, who do assent, or have assented to that confession of faith, in England, Scotland, Ireland and America.

Ans. 2. If by God's permitting sin, be meant, that sin will exist, if God do not interpose and hinder the existence of it by a positive exertion; and he only forbears such exertion, and suffers it to take])lace; this involves a real absurdity and impossibility, as it supposes sin to exist, without any proper cause, and wholly independent of the first cause. And if any one thing, or event, may come into existence, independent of the first cause, every existence may do so too , and there is no need of a first cause of all, and the being of God cannot be proved, from any existence which men behold. But if it did not involve this impossibility, and any should think such an inference not just, it does really remove no supposed difficulty with respect to making God the origin of sin: for if sin could not exist with out the will and decree of God to permit it, and nothing but a bare permission were necessary in order to its existence; yet God in determining to permit it, willed the existence of it; and this necessarily implies his choice and pleasure, that sin should exist, in every instance in which it does take place; and that he orders things so that, he permitting, it will certainly exist just as it does. And this implies the whole of the doctrine which has been advanced, as has been before observed. To decree to permit sin, in the case supposed, is to will the existence of it. And this is liable to all the objections which can be made to the doctrine which has been advanced in this chapter, as making God the author of sin, &c. And nothing worse, or more, can be said against this doctrine, as it has been stated above, which has not been said against the assertion, which has been espoused by all Calvinists, viz. That God has foreordained whatsoever comes to pass. This has always been loaded, by many, with the greatest opprobrium which they could invent, asserting that it is the most blasphemous, horrid doctrine, that was ever thought of, making God the sole author of all the sin in the world; and most unreasonable and cruel, in punishing men or devils, who, according to this doctrine, are perfectly innocent and incapable of sinning, &c. &c. And nothing will satisfy such objectors, but to give up the doctrine of the divine decrees, and admit man to be and act so as to form his own moral character, independent of God, and in every sense contrary to his purpose and will, if it be sinful.

Ans. 3. The attempt to distinguish between the sinful volitions or actions of man, as natural and moral actions, and making God the origin and cause of them, considered as natural actions, and men the cause and authors of the depravity and sin which is in them, is, it is believed, unintelligible, and has no consistent or real meaning, and gives no rational satisfaction to the inquiring mind; unless by making this distinction it be meant, that in every sinful action, God is not the sinful cause of it; but all he determines and does respecting these, is the exercise of holiness: And all the moral depravity and sin consists in the volitions and actions of men, and is their sin, and cannot be ascribed to God; men being as much the cause and authors of their own sins, as they could be, if God had not done or determined any thing respecting them. And this is the doctrine which has been vindicated in this chapter. And is it not reasonable and candid to suppose that those worthy men who have made this distinction, did really mean no more nor less than this?

On the whole, it is presumed there has nothing been advanced, as included in the doctrine of the decrees of God, which is not necessarily implied in his independence and supremacy, his infinite wisdom and goodness, or holiness; and man's necessary dependence on him; or that is inconsistent with the most perfect freedom of man, and his moral agency, and accountableness for all his moral exercises, and being justly blameable for every thing in him which is contrary to the holy law of God: And that, consistent with this doctrine, as much depends on the will and conduct of men, as if they were not dependent, if this were possible, and nothing had been done or determined, respecting their volitions and conduct, previous thereto: And that their will and conduct is as much their own, and is as deserving of praise or blame; is as virtuous or vicious, as it could be, were they wholly independent: And that there is nothing contained in this doctrine that makes God the author of sin, in any bad sense, and so as to impeach the divine holiness: And that all this has been made evident, But if the contrary can be made to appear, this doctrine, with all that is implied in it, shall be given up and renounced.

IMPROVEMENT

I. From what has been said on this high and important subject, may be inferred the truth and divine original of the holy scriptures; in that the doctrine of the divine decrees is clearly revealed, and so abundantly asserted therein; and the whole Bible is evidently formed on this plan. This doctrine is so agreeable to reason, and so essential to rational and consistent conceptions of the character and perfections, the infinite felicity, and absolute independence and supremacy and dominion of the Most High: and it is so desirable and important, that infinite wisdom and goodness should dictate, and form the plan of all existences and events; making one harmonious, absolutely perfect system; of all possible ones, the wisest and the best; that it might be reasonably expected a revelation from heaven would contain this doctrine in all its length and breadth, exhibiting it in a clear and incontestible light; and expressly or implicitly asserting the perfect consistency of it, with every truth respecting the divine character and conduct; and the liberty and moral agency of man.

If this doctrine were not contained and asserted in divine revelation, it would be perfectly unaccountable: And if the holy scriptures were formed on a contrary plan, and in opposition to this doctrine, it would be an insuperable objection against them, as coming from God. But when the children of wisdom see this contained in the Bible, they approve and are satisfied, and discern the divine stamp, in this, as well as in other things; and a perfect harmony and consistence through the whole.

It is true, that many have supposed that if this doctrine were in the Bible, it would be an unanswerable objection against the authenticity and divine original of it; and have thought they have been supporting the credit of divine revelation, by attempting to explain away those passages in which it is most expressly asserted, and to put another meaning upon them. But what has been gained by these attempts? Has one professed deist been hereby brought to think more favourably of the Bible, or to believe this doctrine is not contained in it? Not one instance of this, it is presumed, can be produced. And have not impiety and infidelity prevailed most, when and where the doctrine of the divine decrees, as above asserted and explained, has been most opposed and discarded?

All professed deists see the doctrine of the divine decrees, and the fixed certainty of all events, plainly asserted in the Bible; and some of them dislike this doctrine, and make it an argument, that it is not a revelation from God. Others believe and embrace the doctrine, and hence infer, contrary to the scriptures, that there is no such thing as liberty, moral agency, virtue or vice: And therefore dislike and oppose divine revelation, as much as the other.

But in the Bible the doctrine of the divine decrees, foreordaining whatsoever comes to pass; and the consistency of this with human liberty, moral agency, praise and blame, reward and punishment, is asserted; and he who well attends to this, will not only acquiesce and approve; but in discerning the beauty and harmony of these truths, he will have evidence in his own mind, that this is a revelation from God; as the corrupt heart of man, not guided by heavenly illumination, would not have represented the matter in this light. Thus what the wisdom of man, the wisdom of this world, calls folly, and rejects as such, the children of wisdom embrace as wiser than men, even the wisdom of God; and see and adore the finger of God in forming such a revelation.

II. This view of the divine decrees and operations tends to enlarge the mind, in high and exalting thoughts of God, and leads to adore him as the first and the last, the Almighty, who worketh all things by the counsel of his own will, infinite in power and wisdom, doing what he pleases in heaven and on earth: And this view of the Deity tends to lead the mind of man to humbling views of himself, as absolutely dependent on God, in all respects, and as infinitely little and inconsiderable, in comparison with God; and to see the reasonableness and importance of being devoted to him, in seeking his glory as the supreme end. In this view, the words of St. Paul will be naturally suggested and espoused by the pious mind. "O the depth of the riches both of the wisdom and knowledge of God! How unsearchable are his ways, and his judgments past finding out! For who hath known the mind of the Lord, or who hath been his counsellor? Or who hath first given to him, and it shall be recompensed unto him again? For of him, and through him, and to him, are all things: To whom be glory forever, Amen."

III. This doctrine is the only foundation, and a sufficient and ample one, for the support, comfort and joy of the pious friends of God, in the midst of all the darkness, sin and misery that take place. "The Lord reigneth, let the people rejoice." Infinite wisdom and goodness, clothed with omnipotence, reign, and nothing takes place but what is important and necessary to accomplish the wisest and best end, the glory of God, and the greatest possible good. God will bring infinite good out of all the evil; and for this end he hath foreordained whatsoever comes to pass. Was not this a most certain truth, and to be relied upon, the pious mind must sink in darkness, in the view of the evil that takes place, and could find no relief. But here is a source of comfort and joy, since all things are ordered in the wisest and best manner, nothing could be added, or taken away, without rendering the divine plan less wise, perfect, and excellent.

It belongs to the infinitely wise, almighty maker and owner of all things, and governor of all worlds, to order every event; especially the events of the moral world, and the moral actions of creatures, which are the most important: They must be determined and fixed by something, by undesigning chance, or by ignorance or folly, or by infinite wisdom. He who is infinitely wise and almighty can do it in a way perfectly consistent with the liberty and moral agency of his creatures; and this being every way most desirable, and the contrary supposition infinitely dreadful: when the friends of God see this is done by him, and that his counsel with respect to every event, and all actions, stands forever, and the thoughts of his heart to all generations--they rest in this, and rejoice continually, and no man can take this comfort and joy from them. Though the earth be removed, or the mountains be carried into the midst of the sea, whatever events, and however evil in themselves, take place; yet they will not fear, but drink consolation at this river, the streams whereof make glad the city of God. "Let the righteous be glad; let them rejoice before God; yea, let them exceedingly rejoice." [147]

IV. This affords a solid stable foundation, for the most unreserved, implicit confidence and trust in God. He superintends in all things. He is in the heavens, and hath done whatsoever he pleased; he will accomplish his own ends, and cannot be disappointed. Therefore his friends may trust in him with the greatest assurance, that, whatever appearances there may be against it, he will accomplish his own ends, glorify himself, fulfil all his promises to his people, and make them most happy forever. "O Lord of hosts, blessed is the man that trusteth in thee." Therefore,

V. This doctrine is suited to promote true piety and holiness. For this consists in loving God, in trusting and rejoicing in him, and his government and works, acknowledging him in all our ways, in seeing his hand in all events, in submitting to him, and obeying him. This doctrine is so far from affording any just ground of encouragement to sin, that so far as it is understood and cordially embraced, it forms the heart to hate sin and love the law of God, and to the most hearty, cheerful submission to his government. Experience proves this to be true, and the reason of it is very obvious. For they who see and approve of the wisdom of God in making all things for himself, and ordering all things, even the sins of men, for his own glory; must themselves desire and seek the glory of God; and this necessarily implies an approbation of the law of God, and a cordial submission and obedience to it.

VI. Hence may be inferred the propriety and importance of preaching this doctrine, and of explaining and vindicating it, as it is revealed in the holy scriptures.

Some who believe it is revealed in the Bible, yet think it ought not to be preached, or spoken of, as it is such a mysterious doctrine, and is so difficult and puzzling to many, and a stumbling block to them, rather than to their edification; and is liable to be misimproved to bad purposes.

But such must be under a great mistake. It is dishonourable to God, and to the Bible, to suppose any truth which he has there revealed, is of a bad tendency, and therefore ought not to be published; yea, it is implicitly denying that the Bible is from God, and taking sides with the deist. Besides, there is a contradiction and absurdity in the supposition, that it is a truth, and yet has a bad tendency; for this is impossible in the nature of things. That which has a bad tendency, is error and falsehood; but truth has a direct contrary tendency and effect, wherever it is received.

It is true, this doctrine may be preached imprudently, it may be represented in a partial and improper light; and so that the hearers will not understand it. No one can be justified for preaching this, or any other truth, in such a manner. But this is rather a reason why it should, with all other important truths, be thoroughly and fully preached, so that they who are disposed to attend, and willing to understand, may have opportunity to be instructed. It is doubtless better, if there can be a better in the case, not to preach it at all, than to do it to the halves, just mentioning it sometimes; for this is not the way to have it understood, but tends to raise prejudices against it. But the best and only wise way is, to preach it, and explain it clearly and fully, and give persons opportunity, more privately, to propose any objections they may have, that they may be removed.

And parents ought to be able and willing to teach it to their children; to explain it and show them the reason of it, and the evidence there is in the scripture of the truth of it. And though they might not fully understand it in early age; yet a foundation would be hereby laid for their making improvement in understanding, as they advance in years. It is not so difficult a doctrine, as many imagine, who perhaps never understood it themselves, through strong prejudices, which they imbibed, before they were well instructed in it. A child of twelve or fourteen years old, who is carefully instructed, and will attend, is capable of understanding and seeing the evidence and reasonableness of this doctrine; which must be believed as an important article of the christian faith, where the Bible is well understood; however it be now, and has been, rejected by many, with the greatest contempt, boldness and assurance.

Footnotes:

51. Eph. iii. 11. See also Eph. i. 4. 1 Cor. ii. 7. 2 Tim. i. 9.
52. Psalm civ. 24.
53. Rom. xi. 31.
54. Psalm xxxiii. 11.
55. Job xxiii. 13.
56. Acts ii. 23.
57. Rom. viii. 29.
58. Rom. xi. 2.
59. 1 Peter i. 2.
60. Rom. xi. 36.
61. Col. i. 16.
62. Prov. xvi. 4.
63. The point has been more particularly, and with greater care and exactness, considered and examined in the light of both reason and revelation, by the late President Edwards, than by any other author, in his Dissertation concerning the End for which God created the world. The reader, who desires to see this subject more fully explained and explored, must be referred to that ingenious, elaborate performance.
64. Acts xxvii.
65. It is to be observed, and kept in mind, in attending to what is here said on human liberty, that every degree of active inclination and moral exercise of heart, is included in willing and choosing, as well as what are called the imperate and overt acts of the will: For such inclination or exercise of heart, in every degree and instance of it, is not distinguishable from exercise of will and choice; but is really the same thing.
66. It is therefore certain that man is perfectly free, or has all the freedom that in the nature of things is possible, in the exercise of will and choice, or in acting voluntarily; and God, in forming man a voluntary agent, made him a free moral agent, and he cannot be deprived of this freedom and moral agency, unless he be made to cease from acting from motive, and exercising will and choice.
67. It was thought proper and necessary briefly to consider in what liberty and moral agency consist, in order to determine, whether real liberty be consistent with the absolute previous certainty of all events and actions, implied in the doctrine of God's decrees. But the subject is by no means exhausted here; nor is there need of it, since it has been more particularly and fully considered by those able writers. President Edwards, in his careful and strict inquiry into the modern, prevailing notions of that freedom of will, which is supposed to be essential to moral agency, virtue and vice, reward and punishment, praise and blame. And Mr. West, in his Essay on moral agency. The reader who desires to see a more thorough and clear discussion of this point, is with pleasure referred to those performances, where he will, it is presumed, find abundant satisfaction.
68. "Sin, in its own nature, hath no tendency to good, it is not an apt medium, hath no proper efficacy to promote the glory of God: So far is it from a direct contributing to it, that, on the contrary, it is most real dishonour to him. But as a black ground in a picture, which in itself only defiles, when placed by art, sets off the brighter colours, and brightens their beauty; so the evil of sin, which, considered absolutely, obscures the glory of God; yet, by the overruling disposition of his Providence, it serves to illustrate his name, and make it more glorious in the esteem of creatures.

The System of Doctrines, contained in Divine Relation, Explained and Defended Volume I

Without the sin of man, there had been no place for the most perfect exercise of his goodness." Bates, on the Harmony of the Divine Attributes, Edit. iii. p. 81

69. If any one desires to see this subject more particularly and accurately considered, he must be referred to Mr. West's Essay on Moral Agency.

70. There have been many objections to what has been here asserted and proved, viz. That sin is necessary in order to the greatest good of the whole, and is the occasion of good in every instance of it. It has been said, that such a position gives the greatest encouragement to sin; for the more sin there is, the better, the more good there will be--That sin, according to this, is really no crime--That this is therefore inconsistent with its being forbidden in the law of God, and the punishment of the sinner, &c.--The distinction which has been made between sin, considered in itself, in its own nature and tendency; and as it is connected with the whole, and as overruled and used by God for the greatest good of the universe, is sufficient, it is supposed, if well considered, to show how groundless such objections are. All sin is infinitely odious, in its own nature, and has the most evil tendency, as it consists in opposition to God, and his glory, and to all good; God's law, therefore, which requires love to him, must condemn and forbid sin, as infinitely wrong, and odious to him. The sinner cannot take encouragement to sin, from the good of which God makes it the occasion; because this is no good to him, so far as he is inclined to sin; and therefore cannot be a motive to sin: Because it is directly crossing to all inclination to sin. A son who desires not his fathers honour, but is of a disposition to be gratified in his disgrace, could not be persuaded to rebel against his father, from the consideration that his father would get honour by it: But if he be a friend to his father, and to his honour, he will not, from this friendship, be induced to act like an enemy, and do that which tends to hurt and dishonour him. Therefore man never did do evil with a desire and design to promote the good of which God makes it the occasion, it being a contradiction, and therefore absolutely impossible. And as rebellion against God is as evil in its own nature and tendency, when God makes it the occasion of good, and the disposition, views and motives of the sinner are as vile and criminal, as if no good, but infinite evil were the consequence, the sinner is as blameworthy, and deserves punishment as much, as if no good, but all the evil which his sin tends to produce, took place. It is not thought necessary or proper to give a more particular answer to these objections here. This has been done in three sermons, on the subject of the good of which sin is the occasion, published in the year 1759, and reprinted in Boston, and at Edinburgh in Scotland, in 1773.

71. "If by the author of sin is meant the permitter, or a not hinderer of sin: and at the same time, a disposer of the state of events, in such a manner, for wise, holy, and most excellent ends and purposes, that sin infallibly follows; I say, if this be all that is meant, by being the author of sin, I do not deny that God is the author of sin, (tho' I dislike and reject the phrase, as that which, by use and custom, is apt to carry another sense) It is no reproach for the Most High to be thus the author of sin. This is not to be the actor of sin, but on the contrary, of holiness. What God doth herein, is holy; and the glorious exercise of the infinite excellency of his nature And I do not deny, that God's being thus the author of sin, follows from what I have laid down: And I assert that it equally follows from the doctrine which is maintained by most of the Arminian divines." Edwards, on Freedom of Will. Edit. I. Part iv. S. xi. P. 254. "If it would be a plain defect of wisdom and goodness in a being, not to choose that should be, which he certainly knows it would, all things considered, be best should be, (as has but now been observed) then it must be impossible for a Being who has no defect of wisdom and goodness, to do any otherwise than choose it should be; and that for this very reason, because he is perfectly wise and good. And if it be agreeable to perfect wisdom and goodness for him to choose that it should be, and the ordering of all things supremely and perfectly belongs to him, it must be agreeable to infinite wisdom and goodness, to order that it should be. If the choice be good, the ordering and disposing things according to that choice must also be good. It can be no harm in one to whom it belongs to do his will in the armies of heaven, and among the inhabitants of the earth, to execute a good volition If the will be good, and the object of his will be, all things considered, good and best; then the choosing or willing it, is not willing evil. And if so, then his ordering according to that will, is not doing evil?" Idem. P. 267. It may be proper to observe here, that all which has been above asserted respecting the origin and cause of moral evil, is contained and fully expressed in the following words, in the Shorter Catechism. "The decrees of God are, his eternal purpose, according to the counsel of his own will, whereby, for his own glory, he hath foreordained whatsoever comes to pass. God executeth his decrees in his works of creation and providence. God's works of providence are, his most holy, wise and powerful preserving and governing all his creatures, and all their actions." And in their confession of faith, they say, "God, the great creator of all things, doth uphold, direct, dispose and govern all creatures, actions and things, from the greatest even to the least, by his most wise and holy providence, according to his infallible foreknowledge, and the free and immutable counsel of his own will, to the praise of the glory of his wisdom, power, justice, goodness, and mercy. "The Almighty power,

unsearchable wisdom, and infinite goodness of God, so fur manifest themselves in his providence; that it extendeth itself even to the first fall, and all other sins of angels and men, and that not by a bare permission, but such as hath joined with it a most wise and powerful bounding, and otherwise ordering, and governing them, in a manifold dispensation, to his own holy ends." It is here asserted that God hath foreordained, decreed and willed the existence of moral evil; for this has come to pass. And it is said God brings this decree or will of his into effect, by creation and his governing providence, by which he, in the exercise of wisdom and holiness, does powerfully govern his creatures, and superintend and direct, dispose and order all their actions. These assertions, which have been justly considered as essential to what has been called Calvinism, and are professed and espoused by all consistent Calvinists, have been strongly objected to by many, ever since they have been made and published, as full of impiety, and involving horrible consequences, making God the author of sin, &c. It is therefore no wonder, when this same doctrine is revived, explained and vindicated, that the same objections should come into view, and be urged, as they have been heretofore. This is observed, with a view to rectify a mistake which some seem to imbibe, while they oppose the doctrine above asserted, respecting the origin and cause of moral evil: and yet do not consider or believe they are equally opposing the Assembly of Divines, and all who have espoused the confession of faith and the catechism composed by them; and not as a proof of the truth of the doctrine; for it is presumed this has been exhibited in what has been said above; and will be yet farther confirmed b/ what is to follow; and needs not the testimony of man for its support.

72. Gen. xlv. 7, 8, to 20.
73. Psalm cvii. 17.
74. 1 Sam. ii. 25.
75. 2 Sara. xvi. 10, 11.
76. 2 Sam. xvii. 14.
77. 1 Kings xii. 15, 24.
78. 2 Kings xxvi. 2, 3, 29.
79. 2 Chron. xxv. 20.
80. Jeremiah xxv. 9.--li. 20.
81. Isaiah liv 16.
82. Zech. viii. 10.
83. Ezekiel xx. 25, 26.
84. Matt. xxvi. 53, 54, 56.
85. Luke xxii. 21, 22.
86. Acts ii. 23.--iii. 17, 18.
87. Acts iv. 27, 28.
88. 2 Samuel xxiv. 1.
89. 1 Kings xi. 14, 23.
90. 1 Chron. v. 26.
91. Isaiah xiii. 17.
92. Psalm xxviii. 3.
93. Psalm xxxiii 14, 15.
94. Psalm cv. 25.
95. Psalm cxix. 36.
96. Psalm cxli. 4.
97. Rev. xvii. 17.
98. Prov. xxi. 1.
99. Judges ix. 23.
100. 1 Samuel xvi. 4. xviii. 10.
101. 1 Kings xxii. 23.
102. Isaiah xix. 14.
103. Job xii. 16.
104. Isaiah lxiii. 17.
105. Ezekiel xiv. 9.
106. 2 Thes. ii. 11, 12.
107. Isa. vi. 9, 10.
108. Isaiah xxix. 10.--xliv. 15.
109. Romans xi. 7, 8.
110. Exodus iv. 21.
111. Chap. vii. 3.
112. Ver. 13.
113. Chap ix. 12.

114. Chap. x. 1, 2.
115. Ver. 20.
116. Ver. 27.
117. Chap. xi. 10.
118. Chap. xiv. 4:
119. Exod. xiv. 8, 17.
120. Deut. ii. 30.
121. Josh. xi. 20.
122. Isaiah lxiii. 17,
123. Rom. ix. 18.
124. Prov. xvi. 4.
125. Isaiah xlv. 5, 6, 7.

126. The Magians began first in Persia, and there, and in India, were the only places where this sect was propagated, and there they remain unto this day. Their chief doctrine was, that there were two principles, one of which was the cause of all good, and the other the cause of all evil. That the former is represented by light, and the other by darkness, as their truest symbols, and that of the composition of these two, all things in the world are made. Therefore when Xerxes prayed for that evil upon his enemies, that it might be put into the minds of all of them to drive their best and bravest men from them, as the Athenians had Themistocles, he addressed his prayer to the evil god of the Persians, and not to their good god. The good god they always worshipped before the fire, as being the cause of light, and especially before the sun, as being in their opinion the perfectest fire, and causing the perfectest light Isaiah xlv. 5, 6, 7. "I am the Lord, and there is none else; there is no God besides me; I girded thee, though thou hast not known me, that they may know from the rising of the sun, and from the west, that there is none besides me. I form light and create darkness, I make peace and create evil. I the Lord do all these things." These words, being directed to Cyrus king of Persia, must be understood as spoken in reference to the Persian sect of the Magians, who then held light and darkness, or good and evil, to be the supreme beings." Dr. Prideaux Connection, 9 Edit. p. 252, 253, 304.

127. James iv. 2.
128. Gal. v. 15.
129. Gen. l. 20.
130. Rom. ix. 19, 20, 21.

131. "Beza well expresses it, Qui sequitur Deum, emendate fane loquitur. We need not fear falling into any impropriety of speech, when we use the language which God has taught." Doddridge's Note on Luke xxii. 22.

132. Calvin represents those as very unreasonable, and perverting the scriptures, who insist that no more is meant than a bare permission, when God is said to harden the hearts of men, shut their eyes, &c. He speaks of them as frigidi speculatores, diluti moderatores; to whose delicate ears such .scripture expressions seem harsh, and are offensive. They therefore, he observes, soften them down, by turning an action into a permission, as if there were no difference between acting and suffering, i.e. suffering others to act. He says, such who will admit of a permission only, suspend the counsel and determination of God, wholly on the will of man. But that he is not ashamed or afraid to speak as the Holy Spirit does: And does not hesitate to approve and embrace what the scripture so often declares, viz. That God blinds the minds of wicked men, and hardens thei4 hearts, &c. See Calvin's Commentary on Exodus iv 21. vii. 3.--Joshua ix. 20--Rom. ix. 18. See also West's Essay on Moral Agency, page 241, 246. When the apostle Paul says, "And whom he will he hardeneth," he. refers to the words of God, when he repeatedly says to Moses, that he would, and actually did harden the heart of Pharaoh: And he does not attempt to soften or alter the expression in the least, when he applies it to all who are hardened.

133. Exod. iv. 21.--vii. 3.
134. Exod. viii. 15.--ix. 34, 35.
135. Chap. ix. 34.
136. Rom. xi. 7, 8.
137. Acts xxviii. 25, 26, 27.
138. Deut. xxx. 6. Psalm li. 10. Ezek. xxxvi. 26, 27. Tit. iii. 5.
139. Deut. x. 16. Ezek. xviii. 31. Rom. xii. 2. Eph. iv. 22, 23, 24. 1 Peter i. 22. 1 John iii. 3. Jam. iv. 8. Isai. i. 61.
140. Rom. ix. 19, 20, 21.
141. Isaiah x. 15.
142. Acts xvii. 28.

143. Dr. Doddridge gives the following translation of this text. "In him we live, (Κινουμεθα) are moved, and exist." And adds the following words. "No words can better express that continual

and necessary dependence of all derived beings, in their existence, and all their operations, on their first and almighty cause; which, the truest philosophy, as well as theology teaches."

144. Psalm xxv. 9.
145. Gal. vi. 1.--1 Thess. iii. 5.
146. See page 162, Margin.
147. Psalm lxviii. 3.

CHAPTER V - CONCERNING THE CREATION OF THE WORLD, PARTICULARLY OF MAN

GOD began to execute his infinitely wise and good plan, which he had formed and fixed, by his unchangeable purpose and decree, in the work of creation. "In the beginning God created the heaven and the earth." Heaven and earth comprehend the whole creation, both that which is visible, and invisible, to man.

This is said to be in the beginning, to denote that creation, or every thing that is created, had a beginning, in opposition to being eternal, or without a beginning; and because time and succession of existence then began; there being no other beginning of existence but this, and therefore no beginning before this, there being nothing before creation, but the Creator, whose existence is without beginning.

The creation is great, extensive and manifold, and vastly exceeds our knowledge and comprehension: But God spake the whole into existence, from nothing, with infinite ease. He said, "Let it be, and it was. He spake, and it was done: He commanded, and it stood fast." The invisible heaven, which probably is intended when St. Paul speaks of the Third Heaven, and is called by Solomon, "The heaven of heavens," was in this beginning created, and formed for the peculiar residence of God, who is said to have established his throne in the heavens, to be and dwell there; and the place where angels dwell; their creation being comprehended in the creation of heaven. And this is the heaven to which the redeemed will be received after the day of judgment, which our Saviour says, was "prepared for them from the foundation of the world." This heaven and the angels were created then; but before this lower world was formed, and brought into order. Therefore it is represented by God, that when he created this earth, the angels were spectators of the work; for these are the morning stars, and the sons of God, who are said to sing together and shout for joy, when the earth was formed. [148] God was pleased to create innumerable hosts of intelligent beings, with strong powers of mind, and large capacities, to be spectators of his works, and attend to the numerous worlds and creatures, as they rose into existence and order; and behold and admire infinite power, wisdom and goodness, manifested herein, and rejoice, adore and praise the Creator.

We have no knowledge of the existence of any other rational creatures besides angels and men: and therefore we have no reason to conclude there are any other. Men may suppose there are many other ranks or kinds of rational creatures; but this, at most, is but mere conjecture. The supposition that there are no more, seems to have a more solid foundation, viz. that divine revelation makes no mention of any such; which it is reasonable to suppose it would, if there were any; since all rational creatures, under the same moral government, must have some connection and concern with each other.

The angels are often brought into view in the holy scriptures; and they are represented as having a particular concern and interest in the future general judgment: Were there any other moral agents, they would have ah equal concern in this judgment, and be members of the same society and kingdom of God, with the holy angels, and the redeemed from among men, or share in the punishment of the wicked: therefore, it is reasonable to suppose their existence, and some circumstances relating to them, would have been revealed, had there been any such creatures. The silence of the scriptures on this head is a sufficient reason to conclude, that angels and men are the only moral agents in the created universe; or, at least, not to conclude there are any such, and to be silent about them.

If it should be said, that the supposition of innumerable ranks of rational creatures, beside angels and men, represents God's moral kingdom vastly more grand and glorious, than if there were none but the latter: It may be observed, that we are not competent judges of the number which will best answer the ends of infinite wisdom. There must be some bounds set to the number of rational creatures; and how many soever are included in this number, there would be equal reason to suppose it would be better, and render the kingdom of God still more grand a: id glorious, to have innumerable myriads added to the number, as there is to suppose it would be better there should be more than angels and men. Therefore there is certainly no reason for such a supposition.

There are "an innumerable company of angels," even when numbers, beyond our reckoning or conception, are left in sin and ruin. And who can have any adequate conception of the number of the human race, including all who have existed, and all who shall yet exist, before the end of the world! No man has any reason to think or suppose, that this number of intelligent moral agents, far beyond his conception, is not exactly sufficient, in the view of him whose understanding and wisdom are infinite, to answer all the ends of his moral government, and to render his eternal kingdom most complete, happy and glorious.

The number and magnitude of the various bodies, worlds and systems in the material universe, which we behold, or can imagine, do not render it certain, or in the least degree probable, that they are all, or any of them, inhabited by rational creatures. If we were certain that the fixed stars are all like the sun in our system, which give light and heat to as many vast bodies or worlds, as our sun does, and no more: and that there are innumerable stars or suns, of this kind, invisible to us; yet all these, and as many more as the most enlarged mind can imagine, may be no more, nor greater, than is proper and necessary to answer the ends, which infinite wisdom has in view, with respect to angels and men. It is certain no man can determine they are not all necessary to answer the best ends, though there be no other ranks of rational creatures.

God was able, and could as easily create the whole world, and all creatures and things therein, and put them in the best form, and most perfect order at once, in the first moment of their existence, as to do it gradually, and by a progressive work; but the writings of Moses inform us, that he was pleased to be six days in creating the world, and finishing this stupendous work: And we are particularly told, in what manner and order this work was carried on, until the whole was finished. We may be sure there were wise and important ends to be answered, by creating in this manner, and taking up the time of six days, and no more, in this work, though we were not able to discover or imagine what they are. But we are not left wholly in the dark, with respect to this. It is evident from scripture, that the natural world is so adapted to the moral, that the former is a representation or emblem of the latter; and that there is a designed analogy of the natural to the moral. This appears in that, in innumerable instances, reference is had to things in the natural world, and use is made of them, to represent and illustrate those of a moral kind, in the holy scriptures.

The darkness and chaotic state in which the materials of which the world was to be made, lay and were found: it being tohu bohu, without form and void, or emptiness, confusion and vanity, is a striking emblem of the moral state in which man is found, as the subject of redemption, from which a most perfect, beautiful and glorious kingdom is to be formed; which is therefore called a new creation, the new heavens and the new earth. Mankind are, in consequence of the first apostasy, m a state of moral confusion, disorder and darkness; of total ruin, emptiness and vanity. Redemption or the new creation, the kingdom of Christ, is formed out of these materials; and, when brought to perfection, will be a most bright and glorious monument of infinite power, wisdom, and goodness: and will so vastly exceed the first creation in importance, duration, worth, beauty and glory, that the former work will be forgotten, and not be worthy of mention, in comparison with the latter. This is the representation given of ii in the scriptures, particularly by the prophet Isaiah. [149] "Behold, I create new heavens, and a new earth: And the former shall not be remembered, nor come into the mind. But be you glad, and rejoice forever in that which I create; for behold, I create Jerusalem a rejoicing, and her people a joy." This is farther explained by the apostles, Peter and John. [150] Peter, speaking of the dissolution of the old or first heavens and earth, says, "Nevertheless we, according to his promise, look for new heavens and a new earth, wherein dwelleth righteousness." By the last words he fixes his meaning of new heavens and a new earth. It is that society or moral kingdom, wherein dwelleth righteousness: That is, the holy church and kingdom of Christ, consisting in moral excellency, righteousness, or holiness. John says, "I saw a new heaven, and a new earth: For the first heaven, and the first earth were passed away." He then proceeds to describe the new heaven, and the new earth: "And I, John, saw the holy city, new Jerusalem, coming down from God out of heaven, prepared as a bride adorned for her husband." This is the new heaven and the new earth, even the new Jerusalem, the holy city, wherein dwelleth righteousness, that is, the church and kingdom of Christ, formed out of the moral chaos of disorder, confusion and darkness, in which he found mankind; and adorned with righteousness or true holiness. None who attend can be insensible, that this passage is parallel with that in Isaiah, quoted above; and explains the meaning of the new heavens, and new earth, and of Jerusalem, mentioned there. In both places, Jerusalem and the new heavens and new earth are evidently put for the same thing; and the new Jerusalem is certainly the church of Christ, or the work of redemption, with all the appendages of it.

The gradual increase and advance of light and order, in creating and forming the natural material world, is analogous to the increase of light and order in the moral world, particularly in the work of redemption, and an emblem of it. This light began to dawn directly after the fall of man, and has been increasing ever since; and will continue to increase, till the Sun of righteousness, (the sun of the moral world, the Lord and Saviour, who is the light of the world, and of whom the natural sun is an emblem) shall arise, upon all nations, with healing in his beams; and the earth shall be full of the knowledge of the Lord, as the waters cover the sea; when the church shall arise, and put on her morally beautiful garments, and shine in the beauty of holiness. And the darkness in the natural world, preceding light, and night preceding day, is a representation of what takes place in the church, and will in some degree continue, till the consummation of all things. Darkness, affliction and trouble, the fruit of the original universal moral disorder, do take place in a sort of periodical succession, which is followed with a greater or less degree of light, peace and comfort; until all evil shall be banished from the church forever, and there shall be no more night there.

As God was six days in forming the natural world, in bringing it into the order which he designed, and furnishing it with the various sorts of inhabitants; and then rested on the seventh day: this was a designed emblem of the moral world, or of redemption, pointing out the length of time that it would take to bring that to such a state of order and beauty as was intended, a day being put for the period of a thousand years. During the space of six thousand years Christ is carrying on the work of redemption, and forming his church and kingdom, out of the chaotic mass of mankind, to a state of order and beauty, through various revolutions and conflicts; when it shall be brought to a state of rest and peace; and the seventh thousand years of the world shall be a day of rest, when "the kingdom and dominion, and the greatness of the kingdom under the whole heaven shall be given to the people of the saints of the Most High;" and the church shall put on her beautiful garments, prepared as a bride is adorned for her husband: And the Lord her God will rejoice over her with joy: He will rest in his love, and will joy over her with singing.

Moreover, by working six days, and resting from his work on the seventh, and consequently sanctifying that, and setting it apart as a day of rest for man, he set an example, and made an institution for man, which was useful, important and necessary, for the best good of man, and the promotion of his designs respecting his moral kingdom. [151]

According to the scriptures, there have not yet been six thousand years since the creation. And there are a variety of facts and arguments which prove the world cannot be much older than it is represented to be in sacred history: which have been mentioned by many writers: And there are no appearances or facts, which give the least evidence of the contrary.

It has been asked, Why the world was not created sooner? Why it would not have been wiser an d better, to have had it created so much sooner, or be fore it was created, as to have every thing ready for the day of judgment by this time; yea, so as to have had all the blessed in the enjoyment of complete happiness for millions of ages already? For this would have been so much clear gain of happiness, which is really lost, and never can be enjoyed, because the world was created so late.

It may be observed upon this, in the first place, that this question can never be satisfied, so that it might not still be asked with as much reason and propriety, as it is now asked; and therefore it must be an improper and unreasonable question. If the world had now existed ten thousand ages instead of six thousand years; and were this possible, still the question might be asked, with as much apparent reason as now, Why it had not been created so early, as now to have existed ten millions of ages instead of ten thousand? And so on without end. That question or demand, which in the nature of things cannot be answered or satisfied, on any supposition whatsoever, is unreasonable, and ought never to be made.

In the second place, This question is inconsistent and absurd, and can really have no meaning. Antecedent to the beginning of time there could be no succession from one minute or hour to another; for minutes and hours relate only to time. There was no before or after, sooner or later. Antecedent to the creation of the world, there was no existence but the Creator, who only exists without beginning to exist, and therefore without succession. There is no such thing, or idea, to answer the words, before or after, sooner or later, with respect to him and his existence. These are relative terms, and denote ideas that relate to time; and therefore cannot be used with propriety, to denote any thing antecedent to creation; because no such thing can be predicated of absolute eternity, which has no relation to time, and succession. Therefore it may be with truth asserted, that the world could not be created sooner than it was, or before it was actually created. Because there was no succession, and therefore nothing sooner or later, before or after, antecedent to creation.

And when it is asked. Why the world was not created so early, that from the creation to the present time, as many millions of years should have passed, as there have thousands? There is an impropriety in the question, in the use of the word early, because there was no such thing as early or late, antecedent to the creation, and therefore this is altogether inapplicable to eternity, and is a word, when used in this case, without any idea or meaning, or if any idea be affixed to it, or conveyed by it, it is a false and delusive one, or not agreeable to the truth, as has been just before proved. But, if the word early were allowed to be proper, it may upon this be observed, that the world could not be created so soon, or so early, but that there must be a time, when there have been just so many years from the creation, to that time, as there have actually been since the world was created, to this time. And whenever that time had come, and the world had been created but six thousand years, the question might be asked, Why the world was not created before, so that millions of years should have passed by that time, instead of six thousand? And on that supposition, this question would be as proper and reasonable, as it is now. And therefore it may be always asked, and never can be satisfied: Consequently is an unreasonable, absurd question, as has been shown.

Besides, the querist may be asked, since, though the world were created ever so early, even as soon as it was possible it could be created; yet there must be a time when it had existed just so many years, as it has now actually existed; how does he know, that he does not live in that very time, and that the world was created as early as his question demands; yea, as soon as it could be created, and have a beginning?

He who attends to this will doubtless perceive how unreasonable and absurd it is to suppose that the creation might have been sooner or later, or that there might now have been more or a less number of years since the creation, than there have been by creating the world sooner or later than it was actually created: And therefore, that there is no propriety or sense in the question, which has been considered. And perhaps it may be thought needless to introduce it here, and say so much, or even any thing by way of answer.

It has been a question, when, or at what time of the year, the world was created, and time began? The general opinion has been that the world was made and time began at or about the autumnal equinox. It is reasonable to suppose that the fruits of the earth, necessary for the support and convenience of man, were all ready for his use, when he was created, and therefore that the trees, &c. were created with their fruit in maturity, which they have since constantly produced, at that time of the year; which in the climate in which Adam was created, is in the latter end of our September, or beginning of October. And there is this greater evidence that time began at that time of the year, viz. that all nations began their years at that time: and Abraham and his descendants did so, until they left the land of Egypt; when God ordered them to begin their religious year at the vernal equinox, which takes place in our March. Yet even then, and after that, they continued to begin their civil year at the autumnal equinox, as other nations did. This is evident from the beginning of the seventh month, reckoning from the beginning of their ecclesiastical year, being said to be in the end of the year: That is, when the year past had ended, and another year was begun.[152] "Thou shalt keep the feast of ingatheung, which is in the end of the year, when thou hast gathered in thy labours out of the field."

When God had created the world, and furnished the earth in a manner suited for the habitation of man, he created Adam, and then formed Eve out of one of his ribs, last of all in the end of the sixth day. The particular manner of making Eve, expressed the near and intimate union which was to take place between the sexes, and their mutual relation and dependence, together with the superiority of the man to the woman. These two were so formed, that the whole human race was contained and formed in them, and to be propagated from them; so that in creating these two parents of mankind, and commanding them to multiply and fill the earth, all mankind were created. And as, in creating them he made the whole human race, and they comprehended the whole; so there was a propriety, in treating them as if they were the whole, in his transactions with them, and what he said to them; in this, having respect to all their posterity, and comprehending them as much as if they had then actually existed. As in forming the trees and plants, with the seeds in them, according to their kind, by which they were to propagate the same kind to the end of the world, he created and really gave existence and form to all the trees and plants that grow out of the earth; they being all comprehended in the original stock; and existing after their several kinds, by the same command which formed the first of the kind, and under the same regulations and laws of nature: So in creating the original stock, the first parents of mankind, with power, and under a command to propagate their kind, God created all their posterity; and by forming them, formed the whole, after their kind. And what he did for, and with them, he did for all, and they, with all their race, were put under the same regulations and laws; and what he said to these parents of mankind, he said to them and their posterity,

Man was made superior to all other creatures on the earth, being created with a rational soul, capable of understanding things of a moral nature, and acting voluntarily, from moral motives: by which he was placed in the moral world, being made capable of moral government; of being under a moral law, and of obedience, or disobedience to it; and of reward or punishment, according to his moral exercises and conduct. And he was made in the moral image of God, with a good discerning, taste or disposition, or rectitude of mind and will, or heart; by which he was perfectly conformed to the rule of his duty, or the moral law; which is the same with conformity to the moral character of God. This is to be made in the image of God, and after his likeness, in the highest and most proper sense, and to exist in the most excellent manner, and must be implied in the expression, "Let us make man in our image, and after our likeness." And in the assertion, "So God created man in his own image, in the image of God created he him:" Though that which is less perfect and excellent may be implied in this, viz. his natural faculties and endowments of understanding and will, and his being made lord of this earth, having dominion over all inferior creatures on earth, and in the sea.

The moral image of God must be implied and particularly intended, as it is asserted without any limitation or restriction to the natural image of God, and to be in his moral image, is unspeakably the greatest, most important and excellent: And without which, his natural abilities, and dominion over all other creatures, would be worse than nothing. But were there any doubt about the meaning, St. Paul puts it beyond dispute in giving the true and important sense of the image of God. [153] "And be renewed in the spirit of your mind; and that ye put on the new man, which after God (that is, after his image or likeness) is created in righteousness and true holiness." [154] "And have put on the new man, which is renewed in knowledge, after the image of him that created him." This is parallel with the passage cited from the epistle to the Ephesians, and therefore by knowledge here, is meant that true discerning which implies holiness, and which Christ says is eternal life, even to know the only true God, and Jesus Christ. Therefore, according to St. Paul, to be created after the image or likeness of God, is to be made truly holy, or to put on his moral image. To the same purpose he says, [155] "But we all with open face, beholding as in a glass the glory of the Lord, are changed into the same image." The glory of the Lord, is his holiness: therefore to be changed into the same image, is to be made like God in holiness.

    Man was not only put at the head of this world, this earth, in which he was made, and all creatures and things in it; which were all made for him: but the whole creation was made with reference to him, and in a sense for him; so that he is the end of all, under God, and next to him. It has been observed, that the material or natural creation, however large we may suppose it to be; and even though it may exceed our imagination, was made with reference to the moral world, and for the sake of that; and that angels and men are most probably the only moral agents which were created; and that God's moral eternal kingdom will consist of these only. For the sake of these then the worlds were made; they are the end of all God's works, next to himself, who is the ultimate end of all; for God hath made all things for himself. He made the material, natural world for angels and men, to promote his designs concerning them; and he made them, who are the end of all his other works, for himself.

    And though man in his natural powers and capacities, and in his situation and circumstances, was first made lower than the angels, and in many respects inferior to them; yet, we learn from the scriptures, that he is more an ultimate end in the creation, than the angels; or that the angels were made for man, and not man for the angels. We may know the particular end for which God makes any creature or thing by the use to which he puts it, or the end which he makes it to answer. And the scripture teaches us that the angels are improved to answer God's ends respecting man, and that he uses them all in the service of man. [156] "Are they (the angels) not all ministering spirits, sent forth to minister to them who shall be heirs of salvation?" It appears from divine revelation, that God designed to answer his ultimate end of the creation chiefly, and in the most eminent degree by man; and therefore all other creatures and things are subordinated to him, and made to answer the divine purposes with respect to him, even the angels, the highest and most noble order of beings that were created. The human race were the peculiar favourites of Heaven. The most important and glorious ends were designed to be answered by them. The redeemed from among men, the church, is the bride, the Lamb's wife, is to be raised in dignity and glory, far above the angels: to sit with Christ in heaven, and reign with him in a peculiar union to him, as the members of which he is the head: while the angels are represented as standing round about the redeemed, waiting upon them and ministering unto them. The Son of God took not on him the nature of angels, but of man, and has hereby laid a foundation to raise the redeemed, who were originally made below the angels, and by sin had sunk infinitely low in unworthiness, guilt and wretchedness, far above the angels in honour, glory and happiness: And hereby is made the brightest and most glorious eternal display of infinite power, wisdom, goodness, justice, mercy, grace, truth and faithfulness; in which God is glorified to the highest degree, that is conceivable or even possible. Into these things therefore the angels desire to look. They are all attention to man, and the wonderful glorious scene that is opened respecting him; and by the church of Christ, and the wonders of redemption, are made known unto them the manifold wisdom of God. Therefore the angels, with all other things visible and invisible, were made for Christ, considered in the capacity and character of the Redeemer and Saviour of the church. [157] "For by him were all things created that are in heaven, and that are in the earth, visible and invisible, whether they be thrones or dominions, principalities or powers: All things were created by him, and for him." Therefore when he came into the world to redeem his church by his obedience and death, all the angels of God received command to worship him; that is, to submit and devote themselves to him, to wait upon and serve him in the work and business which lie came into the world to perform, in favour of mankind. Accordingly, a multitude of those heavenly hosts attended upon him, when he first appeared in the world, and worshipped him; and were with gladness and joy his messengers to carry the good tidings of his incarnation to men. And they waited upon him, and ministered to him, while he was tempted of the devil, and laboured and suffered in this world; and when he rose from the grave, they were present to serve him, and to tell the good news to his friends. And when he ascended into heaven, all the angels accompanied him with veneration and joy; rejoicing in his exaltation and glory, when he sat down on the right hand of God; and they were all made subject unto him, voluntarily giving themselves to him, to be the willing instruments in promoting his cause and work in the salvation of sinners; rejoicing in the conversion of the elect, and cheerfully serving and ministering to the heirs of salvation. Therefore because the angels were made for man, and are the devoted servants of Christ in his work of redemption, and of the redeemed, constantly waiting upon them, and ministering to them, Christ speaking of the redeemed, calls the angels, their angels.

IMPROVEMENT

I. The view we have now taken of the creation of the world, though a very partial imperfect one, is sufficient to impress our minds with a belief and assurance of the being of God, and of his power, greatness, wisdom and goodness; the marks and evidences of which are every where to be seen, in the things which are made. The existence of the world, and of all things round us which we behold, and our own existence, and the manner of it, are a demonstration, constantly held before our eyes, of the existence of an invisible Being, who has power and wisdom enough to contrive and produce all these things in their order and harmony; and so as to supply the wants, and promote the happiness of the sensible part of the creation: And that this Being exists independent, necessarily, and therefore without beginning, absolutely and infinitely perfect, happy and glorious. And the more we attend to the creation, and examine the great works, the sun, moon and stars, or this globe on which we live, and the various ranks of creatures which come under our notice, the more clear and striking will be the evidence of design, and of the power, wisdom and goodness of the Creator. And we ought hereby to be led sensibly to say with the Psalmist, "O Lord, how manifold are thy works! in wisdom hast thou made them all; the earth is full of thy riches." And may well join with the four and twenty Elders, "saying, thou art worthy, O Lord, to receive glory, and honour, and power; for thou hast created all things, and for thy pleasure they are, and were created."

II. From what has been observed concerning the creation of man, his endowments and circumstances, we are led particularly to reflect upon the goodness of God to him, in making a world for him, every way furnished for his convenience and happiness; in forming him for the moral world, by giving him understanding and moral liberty, in acting voluntarily in the view of moral motives; thus making him a moral agent, capable of virtue or vice, of reward or punishment; and therefore immortal, giving him an existence never to end. He made him lord of the world in which he was placed, giving him dominion over all the creatures in the earth and sea. He formed him in his own image, after his likeness, a perfectly holy creature, which is the highest excellence in the universe, by which he was united to his Creator in perfect love and friendship, enjoying a sweet and happy intercourse and intimacy with him.

In this happy state all mankind were created and placed; for, as has been observed, all the posterity of Adam were included in him, and what was done for him was done for all. And we ought to consider ourselves as originally placed in the happy state in which Adam was created. And if Adam was under obligation to exercise peculiar gratitude to his Maker for his wonderful goodness to him, we are to consider ourselves under the same obligation to gratitude for creating goodness, and view all the kindness conferred on our first parents in their creation, as conferred on all their posterity. And if the apostasy of Adam, by which he fell from this happy state, and plunged into unspeakable wretchedness, did not dissolve his obligation to gratitude for the happy state in which he was at first placed, and the goodness of God to him herein, as it certainly did not; then, notwithstanding his and our sin has rendered us miserable, we are not for this reason under the less obligation to gratitude for the goodness of God to us in our creation, and the happy state in which he placed mankind, in which Adam and all his race would have continued forever, had they not fallen from it, by rebellion against their Creator.

III. We are hence led to see, and reflect upon, the magnitude and aggravation of the crime of the first rebellion of man against God. Man's obligations were every way infinitely great to love and obey his Creator. The greatness, excellence and infinite worthiness of God, brought an infinite obligation on man to love and obey him. His deriving his being wholly from God, and the consequent absolute propriety and right God had to him, increased his obligation to devote all he was and all he had to him, to his honour and service. And his particular and great goodness to man unspeakably increased his obligations to obedience, love and gratitude. And as it was his supreme happiness to love, serve and enjoy God, and in this way only he could secure to himself and his posterity perfect and eternal felicity, and by refusing to do this, must bring upon himself the infinite displeasure of his Maker, and sink into complete and eternal wo, with all his posterity; this brought an immense addition of obligation on him, to love and obedience. [158]

What finite mind can measure or comprehend die greatness, the aggravations of the crime, in man's violating all these obligations, by rising in rebellion against his Creator and owner, and

The System of Doctrines, contained in Divine Relation, Explained and Defended Volume I
ungratefully abusing his infinite goodness to him! Surely the crime of this is unmeasurable by man or angels. We must pronounce it boundless, or infinite; which can therefore be comprehended by God alone, who has proclaimed the infinitude of it, by threatening it with infinite evil, even endless misery.

Footnotes:

148. Job xxxviii. 4, 7.

149. Chap. lxv. 17, 18.

150. 2 Pet. iii. 13.--Rev. xxi. 1.

151. No evidence can be produced that this seventh day from the beginning of creation, is not that which is now the first day of the week; and the contrary perhaps may be supported by satisfactory evidence; And some astronomers assert that this can be demonstrated by astronomical calculations: But this will be more particularly considered in the sequel.

152. Exodus xxiii. 15, 16.

153. Eph. iv. 23, 24.

154. Col. iii. 10.

155. 2 Cor. iii. 18.

156. Heb. i. 14.

157. Col. i. 16.

158. It has been thought by some, that to suppose every sin which men commit against God, is an infinite evil, or a crime infinitely great, is to make every sin of equal magnitude, and that, according to this, one crime cannot be greater and more aggravated than another. And this objection may arise in the minds of some readers, when they attend to this representation of the many aggravations of sin, by which the crime of it is increased, while it is at the same time asserted, that every sin is infinitely criminal, as it is committed against God. All this may be easily obviated, only by observing, that every sin, and the deserved punishment of it, may be infinite in one respect; and yet some sins, and the just punishment of them, be unspeakably greater than others, there being in other respects a great difference. Two cords or cylinders may be considered as extended in length without end, or to be infinitely long, or of equal extension in length; and yet differ greatly in their diameters; and, in this respect, have vastly different degrees of magnitude. Two men may be in pain, and yet one of them may suffer an unspeakably greater degree of pain, than the other; and if the pain of each were continued without end, he who suffers the least would be doomed to infinite evil; yet the other must suffer evil, unspeakably greater, every minute.

CHAPTER VI - CONCERNING DIVINE PROVIDENCE IN GENERAL

DIVINE Providence consists in preserving, directing and governing all creatures and things which are made; or in taking the most wise and effectual care of them, so as to make them answer the end for which they are created.

God preserves or upholds all things by his powerful word; by the constant exertion of the same power, by which they were at first created, or caused to exist. Every created thing is constantly and entirely dependent on the Creator, for continuance in existence. Should that power which first caused it to exist be withdrawn, or cease to be exerted one moment, it would have no existence; it would cease to exist, and sink into its original nothing. It is impossible that a creature should be made, so as to exist one moment, in any respect or degree independent of the Creator; it must be as really and as much dependent on him for continuance in existence, as for its first existence. Therefore preservation is a constant exertion of the same power which first produced the existence of the creature, in causing or giving continual existence; and is really continued creation.

Every part of creation, and each creature and thing in it, from the greatest down to the least, is not only constantly upheld by the exertion of the same power which first gave existence; but is in all respects continually under the direction and governing power and care of the Creator, in every change, as to the place or manner of existence, and every motion, by which God orders, disposes and uses every thing in his creation, to accomplish his own infinitely wise and important designs. As God created all things for himself, in order to accomplish his own designs, being formed according to his pleasure; so he uses every thing, so as in the wisest and best manner to answer the end for which it was designed. If any the least thing were not so directed and used, as to answer the end designed, it would be created in vain; which is inconsistent with the wisdom and goodness of the Creator. God governs the world, and all things in it, by stated and fixed laws or rules, which are called the laws, or the course of nature, by which all motions and events take place, in a certain order, and constant series and connection of cause and effect. But this law, or course of nature, is nothing but divine power and wisdom constantly exerted, to cause things to take place in such a stated way and manner; or the divine will, establishing such an order in events; and does not suppose any power in creatures, or any created thing, to cause such motions and events, aside from the immediate exertion of divine power, which is the proper efficient cause of every event: so that all power is in God, and all creatures which act, or move, exist and move, or are moved in and by him.

This fixed law and course of nature, which, as has been observed, is nothing but the divine will, wisely determined to operate in a certain, steady, fixed manner, by way of cause and effect, the same cause generally producing the same effect, is necessary in order to man's gaining any proper knowledge of things around him, and obtaining any prudence and wisdom, with regard to the objects with which he is concerned, and by which he is to regulate his conduct, form his plans and prospects; and to excite his hopes, fears and exertions. Were there no settled order and fixed connection in things and events, there would be no foundation for all this; but man would be involved in total darkness and uncertainty, without any knowledge and wisdom to conduct any of his affairs, or any motive to action, in matters relating to his body. And in this established order and connection in the visible creation, not only the power, but the wisdom, and steady counsel, the goodness, truth and faithfulness of him who worketh all things by the counsel of his own will, a e constantly manifested to man; which is asserted in the sacred writings.

When this stated course of events, or these laws of nature, are interrupted and visibly counteracted, and events take place in a contrary manner; these events are called miracles, though there is no more power necessary, or really exerted and manifested in these, than there is in producing events according to the ordinary course of things. No more power is necessary or manifested in causing the sun to stand still, or move from West to East, than there is in causing it to keep a steady, uninterrupted course from East to West. The former would be a miracle, the latter is not. The Governor of the world may and does, for wise reasons, and to answer important ends, thus visibly counteract the general course of things and events; and that on such occasions, and in those instances and ways, as not to frustrate the general and important ends to be answered by the steady

The System of Doctrines, contained in Divine Relation, Explained and Defended Volume I
course of things, which he has established. And in how many instances among the inconceivable number and variety of events which take place, they are brought about and caused to exist just at such a time, and in such a manner, not according to any stated law, or course of things, no man can tell; as the agent, by whose constant energy all things are conducted, is invincible to us; and may act immediately, or by the instrumentality of invisible agents; and yet this may be done, so as not visibly to counteract the stated laws or course of nature, or be the least obstruction to the exercise of human wisdom and prudence, in every thing in which men are concerned. No one can doubt of this, who will carefully attend to the matter, and observe the representation of it in the holy scriptures. All such instances, be they ever so many, may be called miracles, though invisible to man, being out of the reach of our perception, as they are of the same nature and kind with those instances above mentioned, in which, what is called the course of nature, is visibly, or to our senses, counteracted, and events take place contrary to it, which we call miracles.

  This care and providence of God, in directing and governing all creatures and things, is universal, and constant, respecting all things at all times; and is extended to the least, as well as the greatest and more important existence; and is concerned in every event, however minute, and in our view inconsiderable. Not a sparrow, or the least bird or insect, falls to the ground, or dies, without the direction and agency of God. The hairs of our head are all carefully numbered; and so many and not one more are ordered to exist, and not one is removed or broken, without the order and operation of the divine hand. And this is equally true of every hair on men and beasts, and of each leaf in the forest, or spire of grass on the earth that ever have existed, or will exist, to the end of the world.

  In the exercise of this divine providence, some events take place by the more immediate energy and agency of God; and others by the instrumentality and agency of creatures, and by various mediums, and what are called second causes. But in all the events of the latter kind, the divine hand, power and energy, is as really and as much concerned and exerted, and is really as evident, and as much to be acknowledged, as if no instrument, agent, or second cause were used, or had any concern in the matter. Because the creature or the instrument has no power to act or effect any thing, independent of God, or which is not given to him by God. And is in the hand of God, as the axe or saw is in the hand of the workman. This is the light in which divine revelation every where represents the providence of God, as every one who carefully attends to it, must be sensible. And what has been observed shows that this is perfectly consonant to reason; and that a different and contrary idea of divine providence is insupportable and inconsistent. [159]

IMPROVEMENT
  I. From this scriptural view of divine providence, it appears, that they are in a great and dangerous error, who believe and assert, that the creation, and all creatures, when once made, have power to subsist of themselves, and stand alone by their own power, given to them in their creation; and to continue in motion and action, independent of any immediate exertion of divine energy, to support and direct them: that creation and creatures, once made and put in order, go on in a regular course of their own accord; and that God does never interpose, or take any farther care of the works of his hand. Every one who has attended to the Bible must be sensible that such a notion is very inconsistent with that: And it is most unreasonable, as it supposes that which is impossible, viz. That the creature may subsist of itself, when once made, in a measure independent of the Creator. This is contrary to all true philosophy: and at the same time dishonourable to God, as if he did not take a particular and wise care of the things he has made, and exercise and manifest his power, wisdom and goodness, in preserving and governing the world, and all things in it. And it tends to suppress and even eradicate all true piety, by leading to conceive of the Creator, as at a distance, and in a great measure out of sight; and as it obliterates a sense of our immediate dependence on God, and encourages self-dependence. In a word, it makes too much of creatures, and raises them infinitely too high, by which the Creator and Governor of the world is concealed and hid; whereas in a right view of divine providence, every creature and all events exhibit Deity to view, as constantly present in every thing, in the exercise of omniscience, power, wisdom, rectitude and goodness; and unite to impress that sense of the divine Being on the mind, and lead to that acknowledgment of him, in which all true piety most essentially consists.

  II. We are, therefore, in the next place, led to observe, that the true philosophical and scriptural account of divine providence, opens the most ample field for the exercise of piety and religion; as it leads us to see God in all things, and in every event; to fear him, trust in him, and acknowledge him in all our ways, feeling our immediate, constant, absolute dependence upon him. This leads us to hear him speaking important truths, in an intelligible language, by all creatures and things with which we are surrounded, and in all events; which calls for answerable exercises of prayer, acknowledgments, thanksgiving and praise, and a constant glorifying him, in whose hand is our breath and all our ways. Of such exercises and expressions of piety we have many examples in the holy scriptures; which, at the same time, appear perfectly rational.

III. Hence we learn the reasonableness and duty of a cheerful submission to God, and acquiescence in the events which take place under his direction and providence. Not to submit is to oppose God and his will, and to resist infinite wisdom and goodness. Every event that takes place is under the immediate direction of unerring wisdom and goodness, and ordered for the greatest good, to promote the most important and best ends; and is therefore so far from being the reasonable ground of any reluctance and regret in us, that we ought not only barely to submit, but to acquiesce with pleasure, and rejoice that God reigns, and hath done, and continues to do, whatsoever he pleaseth; and worketh all things, according to the counsel of his own will.

IV. How safe and happy are they who put their trust in God! He who directs and governs all things, and orders every event; who is infinitely above all control, on whom all things entirely depend; who does whatsoever he pleases in heaven and among the children of men on earth: He is engaged by repeated promises to them, that no evil shall come near them to hurt them: but that every thing shall work together for their good. If God be thus for them, who or what can be against them? The Lord reigneth, let them who trust in him always rejoice. Weil may they say, "God is our refuge and strength, a very present help in trouble. Therefore will we not fear, though the earth be removed, and though the mountains be carried into the midst of the sea» Though the waters thereof roar and be troubled, though the mountains shake with the swelling thereof." "Oh Lord of hosts, Blessed is the man that trusteth in thee!"

Footnotes:

159. That such a divine providence as is here described and asserted, which is rational, and every where supposed and held up to view in the Bible, is perfectly consistent with the moral agency and liberty of man, appears from a foregoing chapter on the decrees of God.

CHAPTER VII - ON THE PROVIDENCE OF GOD, AS IT RESPECTS MORAL AGENTS, ANGELS AND MEN

Section I - Concerning Divine Providence, as it respects the Angels.

AS moral agents are the highest and most noble and important part of the creation, they are the end of all the rest; and all the inferior creatures and things were made, and are preserved and governed, for the sake of these, who are the subjects of moral government; which is by far the most excellent and important. Of these, we know of none but angels and men: And it has been observed, that we have no evidence that there are any other creatures in the created universe, capable of moral government. We know nothing of the existence, number, capacity or employment of angels, but what we learn from divine revelation. We are there informed, that in their original formation, they were made a higher rank of beings than man, and with greater natural capacities; that their number is very great; that they were made perfectly holy, and under law to God, otherwise there would have been no foundation for the fall and ruin of any of them, by disobedience and sin, which we are told has been in fact the case. And. were they not at first holy, there could have been no apostasy by rebellion, or by leaving their first state.

But that they were under moral government, we maybe certain, from the reason and nature of the case. They being made rational creatures and moral agents, and so capable of moral government, must be under such a government, in order to be treated properly, or according to their nature and capacity. A moral law is essential to moral government; requiring of rational creatures those exercises, and that conduct, of which they are capable, and which are reasonable and proper. We are not expressly told what this law was, as it relates to angels, and what was particularly required of them. But we can be at no great loss about the general requirement of it. They must be under obligation, from the first of their existence, to love God with all their hearts, and their fellow creatures as themselves. This therefore was required of them. The law they were under must require this, as it was the rule of their duty; and therefore must require the whole of their duty. This law did not, strictly speaking, make it their duty to exercise and express this love; but required and commanded it, because it was their duty. And it could require no more, this being the whole of their duty; unless it were to point out in particular instances in what way they should exercise and express this love to God, and to other creatures, by express positive injunctions and prohibitions. How many, or whether any of these; or if there were any, in the law given to angels, we are not particularly and expressly informed.

In order to this being a complete law, or having the nature of a law, so as to exercise and maintain moral government, there must be a penalty expressed or implied, threatening evil to disobedience to the precept: For if the creature be exposed to no evil, by disregarding the command, more than by obeying, he cannot be said to be under any moral government; nor does God express or exercise any authority, as moral Governor, if he neither inflicts nor threatens evil to the transgressor. And if it be a perfect law, and a perfect government, as God's law and government certainly are, the evil or punishment threatened must be exactly proportioned to the crime, or the desert of the transgressor. And as the transgression of the law of God must be a crime proportioned in its magnitude, to the creature's obligation to obedience; and this obligation is great in proportion to the excellence, dignity and authority of God, which are all infinite, it follows, as certain and clear as any mathematical demonstration, that such a crime is infinitely great; and therefore deserves a punishment which is infinitely great and dreadful, that is, an endless punishment.

We therefore have sufficient light and evidence to determine, that the angels were under a law, requiring them to love God with all their hearts, and their fellow creatures as themselves; and to yield perfect obedience to every positive command which God had given, or should give to them; and threatening them with infinite evil, even endless destruction and misery, for the least single instance of disobedience: For no less than this was their duty, and therefore God must require it of them; and the least transgression, or neglect of coming up to their duty, could deserve no less than complete and endless evil; and therefore God must threaten it; or this must be the penalty of his perfect law.

That the angels were under such a law, with such a penalty, is yet farther evident, if possible, from known fact, which has taken place. Some of the angels have sinned by transgressing this law; and for one, the first, transgression, they have fallen into endless destruction. For, St. Peter says, "God spared not the angels that sinned; but cast them down to hell, and delivered them into chains of darkness, to be reserved unto judgment." And our Saviour tells us what will be their doom at the day of judgment; and that they will then be cast into everlasting fire, which is prepared for them. We therefore know by this, had we no light from any other quarter, that the angels were under a law, requiring perfect obedience, and threatening every act of disobedience with endless destruction. The experiment has been actually made, and every one that sinned, that was guilty of the least deviation from perfect obedience to the law (for every such deviation is sin) has perished; has fallen into a state of endless misery. Therefore every transgression of the divine law; every sin deserves endless punishment; and this is the only proper penalty of such a law.

The threatening of infinite evil to disobedience seems to imply a promise of good or happiness to obedience; or, at least, a continuance of existence in a state of happiness, so long as the creature continues obedient: For though annihilation be not a positive evil; yet it must appear to a happy creature, enjoying the pleasure of obedience, and of the favour of God, and having an ardent desire to serve and glorify him, to be an unspeakably great evil, though it be a negative one, to have his existence taken away; and be forever deprived of all his happiness, by annihilation. This would be to him a real and great punishment. And we have good reason to believe, that to annihilate such a creature, is not agreeable to infinite wisdom, rectitude and goodness; and therefore, that God never will do it; but we may be certain that every moral agent shall continue in existence and happiness, and enjoy the favour of God, so long as he continues in obedience; and that this is implied in the threatening: For a threatening to inflict evil on the disobedient, necessarily implies that he will not inflict any on the obedient, even the negative evil of ceasing to exist. And indeed the innocent and obedient must be considered as having a right to impunity. Hence, by the way, it appears, that moral agents must and will exist without end; as this is necessary, in order to the proper exercise of moral government, and their being the proper subjects of such government. For the moral law, which is essential to moral government, must threaten infinite evil to all who disobey it. Therefore the disobedient must exist forever, in order to suffer the evil threatened, and which they deserve. And those who never disobey can never cease to exist, consistent with the wisdom, rectitude and goodness of the Lawgiver and Governor.

It may be farther observed, that there is reason to conclude, that the best and most perfect moral government, is not consistent with moral agents being continued in a state of trial, without end, so as to be continually exposed to fall by sin, and always remain in a total uncertainty, whether they shall persevere in obedience, or fall into endless perdition, by transgression. That there should be a time for such trial, is certainly proper, and necessary to answer the best ends in moral government. How long this time shall be, and with what particular circumstances it is best it should be attended, the infinitely wise and sovereign Governor only, is able, and has a right to determine. It is also certain that God is not so obliged in justice to the obedient creature, to confirm him in holiness and happiness, after the longest term of obedience, that he would do any injury or wrong to him, if he should not grant this favour. For the creature can never merit or deserve such a reward by any obedience whatsoever; so that eternal life should be a debt due to him, for what he has done. The creature by giving all he has, that is, by perfect and constant obedience to the law of God, gives no more than he constantly owes to God, or only just pays a debt which is due; and therefore continually demanded of him. Therefore he can have no demand on his Maker, of any positive reward, or of any thing which is due to him.

But notwithstanding all this, considering how undesirable it must be to the obedient creature, to be always in suspense, knowing himself in danger every moment, of falling into sin, and eternal ruin; and that he depends wholly upon God for preservation from this evil; and that he is under no obligation to grant it: And, on the contrary, considering how very desirable and pleasing it must be to such a creature, to arrive to a state of certainty that he shall never fall into sin and misery; being confirmed by God, in a state of perfect holiness and happiness forever: And considering what a strong motive and great encouragement to obedience, it would afford to the creature, for God to promise him, that upon his continuance in obedience for a set time, which he will fix, he shall be confirmed in his favour, in holiness and happiness forever, without any possibility of falling into sin and ruin: And since such a promise, on such a condition, would be a striking manifestation of God's love of virtue and holiness, in that he grants so great a reward of the obedience of his creatures; and an expression of his bountiful munificence and infinite goodness: Considering all this, and more that might be mentioned, is there not reason to conclude that such a promise is essential to the best and most perfect moral government; and that this promise is always implied or expressed, in God's law, under which all moral agents are originally placed, and which threatens

The System of Doctrines, contained in Divine Relation, Explained and Defended Volume I
infinite evil to the transgressor? Such a law or constitution, with such requirements, promises and threatenings, may be called a covenant, in which what is required of the creature is stated and fixed; and the rule and manner of God's conduct towards him, and treatment of him, is also revealed and established.

That the angels were under such a constitution, law or covenant, which not only threatened endless punishment to the disobedient, but promised a confirmation in holiness and happiness upon their continuing obedient, through a certain time of trial, and that this time of trial is long since over, is evident from scripture, in that they were in the apostles' days called elect angels, which denotes their being fixed in holiness and the favour of God; or that they had a sure title to eternal life. And the endless torment of the wicked is represented as being in the presence or sight of the holy angels, which supposes, at least, that they will be holy and happy without end.

How long the time of trial was before they were confirmed, who continued obedient; and what was the special test and trial of their obedience, if there were any; and what was the particular temptation and sin of those who fell into rebellion and ruin, we are not expressly informed in divine revelation. Yet perhaps it will appear that we are not left wholly in the dark, respecting these particulars, if we attend to the following things, some of which seem to be suggested from the holy scriptures, and are here offered as being probable.

It has been observed, that it appears from scripture, that man is more an ultimate end, than the angels; that angels were made to answer ends respecting man, and in this sense were made for man; and that this appears from the use which God makes of the angels, in giving and subjecting them all to Christ, as the Redeemer of man, to be improved by him as instruments of promoting his designs in the redemption of sinners; and to minister to, and serve the redeemed from among mankind; and that they were therefore created for Christ, considered as God, Man, Mediator, and Redeemer of sinners, and are his angels, to be used by him in carrying on his great designs in the redemption of his church.

May we not infer from this, that when the angels and man were made, the angels were, in some way, made to know, that God had peculiar and grand designs to answer by man; that, though mankind were made so much inferior to them; yet they were to be the peculiar favourites of Heaven; and that one of that race in the human nature, even a Man, should be the head of a most glorious kingdom; and be the Lord of angels, to whom they must yield a most ready obedience; being employed by him in ministering to, and serving his friends and subjects of the human race: That this was one end for which they were made; and that their cheerfully complying with the revealed will of God, in this matter, and submitting to this person as their Lord, and serving him, and his friends of the human race, should be the particular test of their obedience and faithfulness; and if they did cordially acquiesce in this design, and persevere in obedience to this revelation and command, through the time of their trial, they should be confirmed in holiness and happiness forever. As this now appears to have been God's design, respecting the angels, and that he made them for this end; and as this was doubtless the greatest trial, whether they would be obedient in all things, is it not reasonable to suppose, that so much of this divine scheme was revealed to the angels, as was necessary to give them opportunity, voluntarily to consent, and acquiesce in it, and cheerfully devote themselves to this service?

This revelation and injunction of the Most High, made known in a degree and manner agreeable to infinite wisdom, was most probably the occasion of the rebellion of those angels who sinned; they disapproved, and refused to comply with it. Lucifer, who was at the head of all the angels, the highest and most noble creature that God had made, was displeased with such a plan: Pride entered his heart, and he was not willing, he refused to obey this command, and stoop so low as to become a servant to the inferior, diminutive creature man, and be subjected to serve and adore one in the human nature, as his lord and king. This immediately sunk him down from his high station; and by his example and influence, myriads of angels went off, and joined with him in rebellion. Thus they by sin left their first station, and were banished from heaven; and by the arm of the Almighty were cast down to hell.

This, perhaps, will in the most natural way account for the head of these fallen angels, immediately entering upon a plan to seduce and ruin man, by tempting him to sin, as he had done; supposing that he should hereby effectually defeat God's revealed designs, respecting him, against which he had rebelled. And this may also in the best manner account for his opposing with all his cunning and might, and by all his servants and angels, the redemption and salvation of men; and his hating and opposing the Redeemer, and attempting to defeat him in his designs, in every possible way, and to destroy every one of the human race; being a peculiar enemy to the church, and all the friends of Christ. To all this he is naturally led by his first sin, and is only persevering in opposing that, against which he rose, in his first rebellion.

This apostasy, whatever was the occasion of it, was a very important event indeed, the consequences of which will continue to eternity. It, with many of its consequences, are, in themselves considered, infinitely dreadful. But the designs of the Most High are not in the least frustrated by all this; but his council and plan are hereby established; and this was necessary to bring to effect, and complete his infinitely wise purposes.

It has been observed, that there is evidence from scripture, that the angels who have not sinned are now, and have been, long since, in a confirmed state; And from what has been now supposed, concerning the special trial of their obedience, it has been thought that they continued in a state of trial, until the ascension of our Lord Jesus Christ; and that they were then confirmed in holiness, and his favour, They were obedient to the divine orders, and all attention to man, particularly to the church and people of God, willingly ministering to them, and serving them and their Lord, from the fall of man to the incarnation of the Son of God. But their greatest trial did not take place, until he who was in the form of God, and thought it not robbery to be equal with God, took upon him the form of a servant, and was made in the likeness of men, being born of a poor virgin, and laid an infant in a manger; when he appeared as an outcast in the wilderness, assaulted and tempted by the devil; when he lived a poor despised man; and was finally apprehended, being betrayed by one of his disciples into the hands of men, and condemned as a malefactor, and crucified and buried in a tomb. In this time, while the Son of God was in this state of humiliation, the angels continued to own him as their Lord, they attended upon him constantly, and were his willing, faithful servants. They attended him when in a manger, and with pleasure carried the joyful news of his birth to the shepherds, and the whole multitude of them sang praises on the occasion. They were with him when in the wilderness, assaulted by Satan, and ministered to him. They assisted and strengthened him when he was in an agony in the garden. And when on the cross, and in the grave, they were his constant attendants; and proclaimed his resurrection from the dead, to his disciples. And when he ascended from earth to heaven, and sat down on the throne of the universe, ail these mighty angels came down and attended upon him, and ascended with him with joy, and added to the triumph and splendor of that event: And when they saw him seated in glory, all heaven was filled with a joy which never was known there before; and all these angels renewedly devoted themselves to the service of Christ and his church; and were made voluntarily subject unto him. Then, it is supposed probable, Christ their Lord said unto them, "Well done, good and faithful servants, you have been faithful to me through the time of my, and your greatest trial, and have persevered in the most willing and cheerful obedience: I therefore now put an end to your state of trial, and publicly confirm you in holiness and happiness, and confer on you the reward of eternal life." And as their election of God to eternal life was now made known, they are after this, but not before, called "elect angels."

Section II - Concerning the Providence of God, as it respects Man in a state of Innocency

Man being made upright, or perfectly holy, this necessarily supposes a rule of right, or that there was a right and wrong in moral character and conduct: and that God did, and could not but require or command that which is morally right, and forbid the contrary; or, in other words, that man was under moral government, which supposes a law requiring perfect obedience of him, or his whole duty, and forbidding all disobedience, on pain of suffering the just desert of it. What has been observed in the foregoing section of angels, respecting the nature of the moral government, and the law under which they were; [160] is equally applicable to man: and proves that he was certainly and necessarily under such a law, which required him to love God with all his heart, and his neighbour as himself, and to express this in all proper ways; and to obey every precept which God should give him; with a penalty annexed, threatening every instance of disobedience with a punishment exactly answerable to the crime, which must be endless suffering. So much is certainly essential to moral government, and necessary, in order to man's being treated as a moral agent, by his Creator.

We have indeed no particular account of this law, or history of man's being put under this moral government, in the inspired narrative which Moses has given of the primitive state of innocency. And there is this very good reason to be given for it, viz. because it was entirely needless. The most express narrative of this matter would not have made it more plain and certain than it now is: There is now as great and as clear evidence of it, as there is, that man was created with a capacity for moral agency, and is a proper subject of moral government, as has been proved. But if this were not so evident from the nature of the case, it might be demonstrated from what has been since revealed. St. Paul, speaking of the law under which all mankind are, asserts the tenor of it in these words, "Cursed is every one that continueth not in all the things which are written in the book of the law, to do them." [161] This law must have existed before man sinned, and while he had opportunity, and was in a capacity to continue to do every thing required by it; for if man, when in these circumstances, was not under this law, with this sanction, and bound by it, there could be no reason or propriety in making this requirement on such a penalty, when man had already violated it,

The System of Doctrines, contained in Divine Relation, Explained and Defended Volume I
and rendered it impossible to come up to, or do what is required: Which the Apostle says is the case with all mankind, since the original apostasy; for they are all under the curse of this law. It necessarily follows, therefore, that man was originally made under this law, when in a state of innocency, which denounced a curse upon him, if he failed of perfect obedience. This curse implies in it all the evil that man is capable of suffering, even endless destruction; and will take place in its fulness, and without any abatement on those to whom Christ, at the day of judgment, will say, "Depart from me, ye cursed, into everlasting fire." We must look forward to this time, to see it completely executed. This then, we may be sure, is the penalty of the law, under which man was placed, when he became a subject of moral government; which is also true of angels, as has been proved in the preceding section. So far therefore, we go on sure ground: No particular express revelation could make it more evident and certain: Therefore we may see good reason why we have no such revelation.

It has been observed, that the sum of duty required in the moral law, is love: To love God with all the heart, and our neighbour as ourselves. This we are sure of from the express declaration of Christ. [162] He has reduced the whole moral law to this, and said that, "On these two commandments, hang all the law and the prophets." This includes and enjoins obedience to all special or positive directions and commands, which God may be pleased to give at any time; for love to God implies obedience to all his particular commands, as disregard to any of his injunctions, is contrary to love to him. How many, and what particular and positive commands God gave to man, when he was at first created, and in a state of innocency, we are not told: But some of them are expressed, or may be collected from what is related. A Sabbath was instituted, God blessed and sanctified the seventh day from the beginning of the creation, which Christ says, "was made for man;" and therefore he must have been commanded to keep it holy, or dedicate it to sacred uses in the worship of God, &c. laying aside the business and employment which might be attended on other days. God instituted marriage, and consequently all the duties peculiar to such a relation; and commanded man to multiply, and fill the earth, and subdue and cultivate it. He gave him authority and dominion over all inferior creatures; which is a command to exercise government and dominion over them, and use them for his convenience and profit: But it appears from another direction, that he was forbid to kill and eat them for sustenance; and probably was not allowed to put an end to the life of any animal, on any occasion. The direction or command mentioned, is in the following words, "And God said, behold, I have given you every herb bearing seed, which is upon the face of all the earth, and every tree, in the which is the fruit of a tree yielding seed: To you it shall be for meat." Thus they were commanded to live on vegetables, and had no license to eat animal food; but a prohibition of this is implied. He was ordered into the garden of Eden, and commanded to dress, and to keep it. He was allowed to eat of every tree of the garden except one; and he was commanded not to eat of that, upon the severest penalty. "And the Lord God commanded the man, saying. Of every tree of the garden thou mayest freely eat: But of the tree of knowledge of good and evil, thou shalt not eat of it; for in the day that thou eatest thereof, thou shalt surely die."

We cannot justly infer, from this prohibition or command only being mentioned, that man was not prohibited the violation of the moral law, in every instance, upon the same penalty; or that there were no other positive commands given to him, guarded with an equally severe threatening, in case of disobedience; or that this prohibition was the only test of his obedience; or that if he had violated any other command, it would not have been attended with equally fatal consequences. The contrary has been proved above; by which it is very evident, it is presumed, to all who will properly consider the matter, that they who have supposed any of those things, have no reasonable foundation for what they have believed and asserted. This positive prohibition, with the threatened penalty, is thus particularly mentioned, for two very good reasons: First, because it was a positive prohibition or command, and therefore it could not have been known that man was forbidden to eat of that particular tree, unless it had been thus particularly narrated. Secondly, because man actually fell from his innocence and happiness, and incurred the threatened penalty, by disregarding this prohibition, and eating of the fruit of this forbidden tree. Had he sinned by transgressing any other positive command, which we know nothing of now; that, in this case, would have been as particularly mentioned, with the same penalty, as this now is, and we should have heard nothing of this, in a history so concise, as that which Moses was inspired to give, in which not a word is mentioned, which was not necessary, in order to understand the important story; leaving many things implied in the history, to be investigated or inferred from what is written, or to be farther opened and explained in some future revelation.

It has been a great question, What this threatening imports? What is meant by the death here threatened to disobedience? Those who have attempted to answer it, have done it very differently. Some have been confident, that it intends only the death of the body, or the separation of soul and body; to which all men are now condemned; to which Adam, and in him all his posterity, was sentenced, after man had transgressed, "Dust thou art, and unto dust shalt thou return." Others suppose that a total annihilation of soul and body is intended; so that if the threatening had been executed without any mitigation or remedy, Adam and Eve would have been annihilated, and none of their posterity would have had actual existence. Others have thought, that by dying is meant their becoming totally corrupt or sinful, "dead in trespasses and sins," which is denominated spiritual death. The most general and common opinion has been, that it includes the death of the body, which is called temporal death, and spiritual death, and also eternal death, or endless misery; or as it is commonly expressed, "Death, temporal, spiritual, and eternal."

Instead of attempting directly to confute all or any of these different opinions, or to vindicate any one of them, it is thought the most likely and easy way to get satisfactory evidence of the real and true meaning of this threatening, denounced against man, if he transgressed the divine prohibition, is to endeavour to find some clue which will lead us into it, so as to give all desirable evidence and satisfaction, that we have fixed on the truth. Perhaps such an one may be investigated. In this view, the following things must be observed, and carefully examined, and put together.

First, Every transgression of God's law or command, is a crime of such magnitude, that no punishment is adequate and answerable to it, so as to express the turpitude and ill desert of the sinner, but that which contains infinite evil. Or every violation of the law of God is infinitely criminal, is an infinite moral evil; and therefore deserves a punishment infinitely great and dreadful, and which contains infinite natural evil. This has been brought into view above, and the evidence of it exhibited, so that it is needless to say much upon it here. That all sin against God is infinitely criminal, every one must grant, or be inconsistent with himself, who will allow that it is a greater crime for a child to abuse his kind, excellent father, than to injure the meanest servant in the family; and that the former deserves a much greater punishment than the latter. For by allowing this, he grants that the crime of abusing another, is greater or less, according to the degree of worth and excellency of him who is injured, and to the relation in which he stands to him. And this is granting that to injure and abuse a Being of infinite greatness, authority, dignity, worth and excellence, who, in the highest sense, is our father, friend and benefactor, must be infinitely criminal. But this is true of every sin against God. Therefore every sin against God, which is an injury and abuse offered to him, is a crime of infinite magnitude; consequently the sinner must be punished with infinite evil, if he has his desert.

Again, if it be evident and certain that every criminal deserves all that punishment or natural evil, which his criminal deed tends to produce, or would certainly follow, were it not prevented by some other person or counteracting power, which, it is presumed, all will allow; then every transgression of the divine law, deserves infinite evil. Upon this ground a number of the laws given by Moses are founded, and cannot be proved to be just, if this be not admitted as a truth. It was commanded that if a man injured his neighbour, and brought any evil upon him, by depriving him of his life, limbs or senses, he should be punished, by suffering the same, or as great evil. "Thine eye shall have no pity; but life shall go for life, eye for eye, tooth for tooth, hand for hand, foot for foot." [163] And it is to be observed, that not only he who actually did evil to another, and took away his life or any of his limbs, but he who attempted or aimed to do this, and did that which tended to effect it, though it did not actually take place, but was prevented, was himself to be punished with the evil, which he willed and designed to bring on his neighbour. [164] By the same rule, if a man should murder a thousand men, or will and design to do it, he would deserve to die a thousand deaths, or lose a thousand lives, and this punishment might justly be inflicted, were he capable of suffering it, or had so many lives to lose.

Now, according to this, as has just been asserted, every transgression of the divine law deserves infinite evil. For every instance of opposition to God, which every sin is, is an attempt to destroy his being, or to take away his happiness, and make him infinitely miserable; to put an end to his government, and introduce universal confusion and misery, through the whole creation; and the rebel would be glad to effect all this, and would do it, were it in his power. Therefore he deserves to suffer infinite evil; even all the evil which he is capable of suffering.

If any proposition relating to things of a moral nature be capable of the clearest demonstration, this is such an one. And this is a chief corner stone in the science of theology. Whatever is properly built upon it must stand, and every proposition naturally and necessarily following from it, or that can evidently be deduced, must be a truth.

Secondly, It is essential to a perfect moral government, that there be a law pointing out and requiring what is right, and the duty of the subject, and threatening all transgression of it with a punishment exactly answerable to the crime.

This has been considered before, and it is hoped, has been made so evident and certain, that every one who examines it with care and impartiality, will be satisfied, that it is an important truth. However, in addition to what has been said in support of this proposition, the following things may have weight.

1. If there could be a law, and any proper moral government without a penalty threatening punishment to the transgressor, (which, as it has been observed, is impossible) yet it could not be so good and perfect a law and government, as that which threatens punishment to the disobedient, and by which the transgressor is exposed to suffer some evil, at least. This appears so evident, in itself, at first view, and is so demonstrably certain, from the many threatenings of punishment to transgressors in divine revelation, that there is no need of attempting to adduce farther evidence. If threatenings of evil to transgressors were not necessary in the most perfect government, they could not be found in the divine laws and government: Nor could that threatening which we are now considering have been made to man.

2. It is necessary in order to the most perfect government, not only that there should be a penalty, or a law threatening evil to the transgressor: but that the threatened evil should be neither more nor less than the crime deserves.

If the evil threatened be greater than the crime deserves, the law would be unjust. If it be less than the demerit of the transgressor, the ends of a threatened penalty will be wholly, or in a measure defeated; and therefore the law and government will be proportionably imperfect and defective. This will appear by considering what are the principal ends to be answered by threatening punishment.

One end is, to deter the subject from transgressing the law, and prevent rebellion. Now, it is easy to see, that a greater and more dreadful punishment is better suited to answer this end, than a less, if it be not greater than the crime deserves. Therefore so far as this end is regarded in threatening a penalty, it will require it to be as great as the sin deserves; and if a law threatens a less punishment, it is so far defective, and not suited in the best manner to answer this end of a threatened penalty: Which cannot be supposed of the divine law and government; because that is in all respects absolutely perfect.

Another end of the threatening is to state and express the evil nature of sin, and show how great the crime is, in the estimation of the legislator. The preceptive part of the law does not determine the ill desert of the transgressor. This is to be seen only in the penalty threatened. This determines how criminal sin is, in the sight of God; and what evil it deserves as a punishment. In this view, it is necessary that the punishment threatened should be as great, and contain as much evil, as sin deserves, and be exactly proportioned to it. By this, the law becomes the standard of truth, while it declares not only what is sin, but how sinful or criminal it is. It is with reference to this, that St. Paul says, "That sin, by the commandment, might become exceeding sinful." In these words he has particular respect to the penalty of the law or punishment threatened, by which he was slain, and death was wrought in him, even the death threatened to every transgressor; of which he speaks in the words immediately preceding. Sin becomes exceeding sinful, that is, appears to be criminal, beyond expression, by the infinite evil which the law threatens, as the proper desert of it. In this view, to threaten a less punishment would be deviating from the truth, and tend to deceive; or, at least, one important end of the divine law and government could not be answered.

We therefore have the greatest assurance that the law of God threatens a punishment, exactly proportioned to the desert of sin.

Another end to be answered in the divine government, by the penalty of the law, is to express the sacred authority and worthiness of the Most High, and the desert of sin and rebellion against him. The binding authority of a law, and of the lawgiver, is expressed in the threatening only; and in order to there being an expression of infinite authority, the evil threatened must be infinite; for where there is less authority and right to govern, a less evil may be threatened to disobedience, and executed; and this will be no expression of infinite authority. And the dignity, worthiness and importance of the legislator, and the greatness and ill desert of the crime, of transgressing the law, and despising him and his government, appear and are expressed in the punishment threatened to the transgressor. If treason against the king be threatened with no greater punishment, than is an attempt upon the life of a common subject, this represents the former to be no greater a crime than the latter; and instead of properly expressing the importance and dignity of the king, and the worth of his life, it degrades him, and sets him upon a level with all his subjects. The greater the evil is, which the threatening denounces against him who slights and opposes the Supreme Legislator, and his law and government, the more is his worth and excellence expressed; and the more fully is discovered and asserted the sacred importance and perfection of his law. Therefore if the law do not threaten as great a punishment as the crime deserves, it will not assert the greatness of the crime, nor the real worthiness and importance of God, and his law and government, but the contrary; and therefore must be a very imperfect, deficient law. From this, it appears most certain, that the infinitely distinguished and sacred authority, dignity and worthiness of God, and importance and excellence of his government, and infinite greatness of the crime and ill desert of rebellion, cannot be properly, and in the most clear and striking manner expressed and asserted, unless an infinitely great and distinguished evil be threatened to every transgression of the law; an evil which no other legislator ought to threaten, or is able to inflict: And therefore not to threaten such evil, or to threaten one infinitely less, is undesirable and wrong, and cannot be supposed of an infinitely wise and perfect government. If God threatens and punishes, he must threaten and punish like himself; and nothing short of infinite evil must be the threatened punishment.

Another end to be answered by the penalty of the divine law, is to manliest and express the Legislator's infinite hatred and abhorrence of ail moral evil, and how much he is displeased with the sinner. God is certainly infinitely displeased with sin, as it opposes his being and infinite felicity, and all the good of the universe, and tends to produce infinite mischief, to involve the universe in total and eternal confusion and misery. His displeasure with sin and hatred of it, must be as great as his love of holiness, and the infinite good of the universe. This is therefore essential to the divine character and perfection, in which his glory consists; and consequently it is desirable, and of infinite importance that it should be manifested and expressed in the most clear and strongest manner, in his moral government, and in his law, which is the foundation and rule of it. But this cannot be done, by merely requiring obedience, and forbidding sin. In order to the expression being as clear and strong as possible, God must threaten sin with a punishment equal to the greatness of the crime, and manifest a disposition to execute the threatening, and inflict the punishment. To threaten sin with a less punishment than it deserves, is so far from expressing a proper hatred of it, that it is, in a degree, favouring sin and the sinner. And not to threaten any punishment, or to threaten only that which is infinitely less than the crime deserves, is to manifest infinitely less displeasure with the sinner, than God has, and which it becomes him to express; and it would be favouring the sinner infinitely too much, and discouraging, and tending to prevent sin, unspeakably less than is proper and necessary in a good and perfect government; therefore would be infinitely dishonourable to God, and his government: And one great and important end of threatening and punishing the transgressor would not be answered.

And now, it must be left to the impartial, who will attentively consider what has been offered under this head, whether the evidence does not amount to a certainty, even to a clear demonstration, that in the most perfect moral government of God, his law must threaten evil to the transgressor, which is answerable to his crime, or as great as he deserves.

Thirdly, The threatening under consideration, "For in the day thou eatest thereof, thou shalt surely die," is the threatening of the divine law, and must be considered as annexed or belonging to every divine command, and expresses the punishment which every transgression deserves: And therefore is a threatening of infinite evil.

This appears from what has been observed, that there was nothing so special in this prohibition, that could be a reason why it should be attended with a peculiar and distinguished threatening. This same death was the threatened evil, as the punishment of the transgression of any command or prohibition, which was given to man; and it is mentioned with regard to this prohibition or command, because the penalty was incurred by transgressing this; and not because this was a penalty peculiar to this prohibition, which was not threatened for any other transgression, and would not have taken place on rebellion against any other command, whether moral or positive.

We have an absolute certainty of this, two ways.

1. From what has been observed under the observation preceding that, now under consideration, viz. That in the best and most perfect government, which the moral government of God certainly is, the penalty threatened in the law to the transgressor of it, must be as great an evil as the crime deserves. This prohibition, or command, was contained in the law given to man; it was the law of God, and therefore disobedience to it, deserved as great a punishment, as disobedience to other commands; and indeed, offending in this one point, was sinning against the whole law, and every command in it: But every sin, every act of disobedience, deserves infinite evil; hence it follows, with the greatest certainty, that this is a threatening of a punishment, which involves infinite evil, the just desert of every sin.

2. That the death here threatened implies and intends endless misery, we may be very certain, in that such an evil is intended by death and dying, in other parts of divine revelation. This is always meant by death, or dying, when these words are used to denote the penalty of the divine law, or the punishment which impenitent sinners will suffer, on whom the threatened penalty will fall, without mitigation. Any one may know this, who attends well to the Bible. How often are these words used in this sense by the prophet Ezekiel, in the 3d, 18th, and 33d chapters of his prophecy? It is there repeatedly said, that the impenitent, wicked man shall die, and surely die, the very words of the threatening under consideration: which death the penitent shall escape. It must therefore mean the sufferings for his sins in a future state. Christ saith, he that eateth his flesh, shall not die. Verily, verily, I say unto you. If a man keep my saying, he shall never see death. Whosoever believeth in me, shall never die. [165] Here, not to die, does not mean there shall not be a separation between soul and body: for none escape this; but, dying is put in opposition to eternal life, and therefore must mean eternal death, or endless punishment. St. Paul says, "the wages of sin is death."

The System of Doctrines, contained in Divine Relation, Explained and Defended Volume I

The wages of sin is the proper punishment of sin, or that which sin deserves. By this he fixes the meaning of the original threatening, and shews what is intended by death or dying, when threatened as the penalty of a divine law. And that by death here is meant eternal death, or endless punishment is certain, because he puts it in opposition to eternal life. "The wages of sin is death: But the gift of God is eternal life, through Jesus Christ our Lord." [166] He speaks of death in the preceding verses, as the end and consequence of sin, and puts it in opposition to life. He says, "If ye live after the flesh, ye shall die: But if ye, through the spirit, do mortify the deeds of the body, ye shall live." [167] Here he means by dying, perishing forever, in opposition to living forever; or endless misery, opposed to endless happiness. This fixes the meaning of dying, as the fruit, consequence and wages of sin; and is the same threatening with that under consideration, in the same words, ye shall die. If there be need of any farther confirmation of this point, it may be observed, that endless misery or infinite evil, the punishment which sin deserves, is expressly called death, or dying. [168] "But the fearful and unbelieving, &:c. shall have their part in the lake which burneth with fire and brimstone, Which is the second death." What can be more certain, than that the first threatening to man, if he sinned, "Thou shalt surely die," did express the proper penalty or wages due to sin, even endless misery, or infinite evil, since this is expressed often in other parts of scripture in the same language, and more than once in the same words? If the Bible may be allowed to explain itself, the matter is clearly decided.

Must not every one who will attend to what has now been brought into view on this point, be left without a doubt about the meaning of the original threatening, "Thou shalt surely die?" Is it not as demonstrably certain that it is a threatening of all the evil that sin deserves, even endless punishment, which is the second death, as any proposition in theology is, or can be?

This point being established beyond all controversy, that the threatening made to man, if he eat of the fruit of the forbidden tree, denounced the evil which sin deserves; and which was equally applicable to the transgression of any other precept; and therefore was a threatening of infinite evil, or complete and endless destruction; the following inferences necessarily follow; viz.

I. That temporal death, or separation between soul and body, is not the whole or the chief of die evil contained in the threatening. This is not an infinite evil; but a very inconsiderable one, compared with what sin deserves: Therefore something infinitely more dreadful must be implied in the threatening; even that which in scripture is called the second death, which is endless misery.

2. It farther follows, that separation of soul and body is no part of the punishment threatened. The death threatened was quite of a different kind, and not only does not include, but necessarily excludes, separation of soul and body. Had the punishments taken place and been executed without any mitigation; or had there been no reprieve and redemption for man, this separation of soul and body could not have taken place: Because the punishment deserved, and therefore the punishment threatened was, evil to the whole man, or to the man made up of soul and body. This creature, consisting of body and soul, which were essential constituent parts of the man, was threatened, and if he sinned, was to be punished; and not one part only, while the other is taken down and annihilated. Therefore, this could not take place, consistent with the full execution of the threatening. It is not so great an evil for the mind only to suffer, as it is to be miserable, or to suffer evil, in body and soul: The man is capable of suffering unspeakable evil or pain in his body; therefore, this suffering must be included in the threatening. And this proves, that separation of soul and body, could not be the subject of a threatening, that is, could not be threatened: For this would not have been an evil, in that case, but a negative good, which cannot be the subject of a threatening, but rather of a promise; for evil only can be threatened, and not good, negative, or positive. Separation of body and soul would have been a mitigation of punishment, and would have rendered man, not capable of suffering so much, as in body and soul united; therefore could not be threatened as a punishment, it being no part or kind of punishment, but the contrary. And under that constitution, under which the threatening w as made, there was no provision for a reunion if a separation once took place; nor was it indeed possible there should be a reunion, if a separation was threatened as a punishment, and had the threatening been executed. Is it not hence evident to a certainty, that separation of soul and body could not have taken place, had man been punished for disobedience, according to the threatening; and therefore this was not included in the threatening, but on the contrary, was necessarily excluded?

If any should say, as some indeed have said, that we learn what was intended by the threatening, by the sentence that was pronounced on man, after he had transgressed; which was nothing worse than temporal death: The reply will be. That it is a great mistake to suppose that the body of man, being doomed to return to the dust, and the appointment of a separation between soul and body, is pronouncing a sentence upon him, answerable to the threatening; as there is not the least evidence or appearance of this, but the contrary, in the account which is given of it, all taken together. When man had sinned, God appeared, and called him before him, and brought him to a confession of his sin. And then, instead of inflicting the threatened penalty upon him, he declared his design to reprieve him from the punishment threatened, and to exercise pardoning mercy; and promised a redemption, by which Satan should be defeated in his design, in tempting man to rebel, in the following words, to the serpent, "I will put enmity between thee and the woman, and between thy seed and her seed: It shall bruise thy head, and thou shalt bruise his heel." God having thus promised relief and redemption by the seed of the woman, proceeds to declare what shall take place in consequence of man's apostasy; and the introduction of a Saviour, viz. That the ground should be cursed for his sake, and bring forth thorns and thistles; so that in the sweat of his face, and in sorrow, he should obtain and eat his bread, till his body should return to the ground from whence it was taken. That is, this should be an evil, sorrowful world to him, and he should leave this state, and pass into the invisible world by a separation of soul and body, by the latter returning to its original dust.

This new constitution and appointment is introduced in consequence of the apostasy of man, and the promised redemption by Christ, wisely ordered to answer important ends in the new state of probation, into which man was now brought; and at the game time, to be a constant admonition to man, that he was a sinner, and had hereby incurred the displeasure of his Maker; and of his desert of endless destruction, and the certainty of its coming upon him, unless he be interested in the benefits of redemption. And it was necessary it should take place, as the best way in which man should pass out of this state of probation into the invisible state, so as to continue that state invisible, where both the redeemed, and those who die in their sins, are lodged and remain, until the general resurrection; when the body and soul shall be reunited, not to be separated again. And as this separation of soul and body, in which the latter becomes a ghastly, loathsome spectacle, and returns to corruption, and is a certain introduction to endless misery, the second death, to all who have no interest in the Redeemer, it is a striking visible emblem of endless destruction, and is connected with it to all who die ungodly; it has therefore obtained the name of death, though it be not death in the original sense of the word; eternal destruction being the only proper and real death of a moral agent, sinning against God: Therefore this is called the second death, after separation of soul and body had obtained the name of death, and with reference to that.

And as the body's returning to dust, is no part of the death threatened, and is not the real and true death of a rational creature, it is frequently represented in scripture, not to be real death; but persons are represented as escaping death and not dying, who are the subjects of this separation of soul and body, and do die in this sense. Thus in the forementioned chapters of the prophecy of Ezekiel, it is repeatedly said, that the penitent obedient sinner, shall not die. His body must return to dust, as do the bodies of the wicked, yet he should not die. Therefore this is not death. It is not the death threatened to the wicked, nor the death which the righteous escape: Therefore not death in the original and most proper sense of the word.

Solomon says, "Righteousness delivereth from death. In the way of righteousness is life, and in the pathway thereof there is no death." But the bodies of the righteous return to dust. Therefore this is not death. Our Saviour speaks the same language, and says, "Whosoever believeth in me, shall never die: shall not die, but live forever." Believing in him does not prevent their bodies returning to dust: Therefore this is not death; it is not the death threatened for sin, and is not the proper wages of it; and is not the death from which Christ came to deliver men; for there would have been no separation of soul and body, had he not undertaken to redeem man. He delivers from the second death, the only real death of a rational creature: which was therefore threatened to disobedience, and will take place in its full meaning after the day of judgment; of which the death of the body is but a shadow.

This leads to observe, as a farther evidence that the separation of soul and body is no part of the curse threatened in the divine law, that when this curse or threatened punishment shall be executed on those who die in their sins, and are not redeemed, soul and body shall be united, and they shall be miserable forever, both in soul and body, in union. The proper and full execution of the threatening does not take place, but is suspended by reason of the redemption, which brings man into a state of probation, until that is finished. During this time the wicked, who by the death of the body go out of this world into the invisible state, are represented in scripture, to be in prison, as criminals, waiting for the pronouncing and execution of the sentence against them, at the day of judgment: and then the threatening will be executed. We must therefore look there, to see what the curse of the law is, and what is meant by death when threatened as the proper punishment of sin; and this will assure us it is the second death, even that infinite evil included in the last sentence, "Depart, ye cursed, into everlasting fire."

Thus evident and certain it appears to be, that the law and constitution under which man was made, knew not of separation of soul and body, nor did admit of it; and that the death with which he was threatened, if he failed of perfect obedience to every divine command, was endless punishment, in his whole person, soul and body: And that this separation of soul and body was introduced and took place, under a new dispensation of grace by a Redeemer, as peculiar to that, and to answer important ends respecting it; and when that is over and completed, this separation shall cease, and all mankind will be united to their bodies again, in which the redeemed shall be happy forever; and the wicked suffer the penalty of the law, in everlasting misery, in soul and body united. In short, the dissolution of the body could not take place, unless man had sinned; nor then, if the threatening had been executed without remedy; and unless a new dispensation of grace had been introduced, and man had been reprieved, and put into a new state of probation, under a Redeemer. Both these must take place, the sin and rebellion of man, and redemption by a Mediator, in order to separation of soul and body being proper, necessary, or possible, consistent with the divine law. They therefore must have been greatly mistaken, who have thought and asserted that this was all that was threatened in the divine law, or as the penalty of eating of the forbidden fruit. And they have made as real a mistake who have supposed that turning the body to dust is included in the threatening, or any part of it, since the contrary is evidently true, viz. that the threatening necessarily excludes it.

3. From what has been said on this subject, it may be inferred with the greatest certainty, that death in the original threatening, does not mean annihilation, or an end to existence, as some have supposed: For this would be an infinitely less evil than sin deserves; which has been proved cannot be the penalty threatened in the divine law, because a good and perfect law must threaten a punishment equal to the crime in transgressing it. Besides, it has been shown that death and dying is never used in this sense, when it denotes the punishment or proper wages of sin. And the second death, which evidently means the death threatened to Adam, is expressly said to consist in positive, sensible punishment or pain, which is perpetual and endless, where they rest not day or night, and the smoke of their torment ascendeth up forever and ever.

4. It appears from what has been said, as well as from other considerations, that what is called spiritual death, a going into a course of total sinfulness and rebellion, is not the death threatened, when God said to man, "Thou shall surely die."

This is evident, in that it cannot be the evil which sin deserves, or the proper punishment of it. A man may be wholly a rebel and totally sinful, or contrary to the law of God, in all his exercises and conduct: and yet not be totally miserable. Of this we have evidence enough before our eyes. But rebellion deserves complete and endless misery, and must be therefore threatened, as has been proved. Besides, if going into a course of total rebellion were necessarily attended with complete and endless pain and misery; the punishment or the evil threatened, is the attendant, natural evil, pain and misery, and not the sin and rebellion itself.

This leads to observe, that sin and rebellion, or transgression of the divine law, cannot be the proper matter of a threatening, as a punishment of transgression, and the evil to be inflicted for it. For this is the evil or crime, for which punishment is threatened, and not the punishment itself. This is the crime threatened with a punishment, and not the punishment threatened. Moral evil, or sin and rebellion, is always criminal, in every instance and degree of it; and this deserves punishment, and this only can be punished. The punishment therefore cannot be sin itself, or moral evil; for to suppose this is to confound the crime and punishment, as one and the same thing, and to threaten a crime with the commission of a crime. The proper and only punishment of sin or moral evil, is natural evil, or pain and suffering; and this alone can be the proper matter of a threatening.

If sinning and rebellion be a punishment, then the first act of sin of which the man was guilty was a punishment, as really as any after acts; but this could not be a punishment, unless man was punished for his antecedent innocence: And therefore could not be threatened as a punishment. Besides, to threaten any one, that if he transgressed once, he should be left to his pleasure to go on in sin, and do nothing but sin, would be really no threatening, or a very improper one, and no more than to say, if he did sin, he should sin, and go on to do that which should be most agreeable to him, and so long as he should choose to do so, and no longer. Punishment is suffering some evil; and which is an evil in his sight on whom it is inflicted, and in which he is passive: Therefore man cannot be properly punished, by that in which he is not a patient, and really suffers nothing: but is altogether active in it, and chooses it as a good, in itself considered; which is true of every degree of sin. Therefore, in this view of it, it cannot be threatened as a punishment; for it really is none, as it has not the nature of a punishment.

God is said in scripture, in several instances, to give men up to gratify their lusts and to strong delusion, and to walk in their own ways,[169] in consequence of their having chosen to rebel against him. But this is not threatened as a punishment, nor said to be such; and for reasons just mentioned, we may be sure they are not to be considered as such, but only as instances of God's just and wise conduct, to answer important ends in his moral government. By the sins they commit who are thus abandoned to sin, they are prepared for punishment, and go on to it; but they are not the punishment itself; this consists in the destruction, the natural evil which they suffer for the sins which they are suffered, and given up to commit. It is thus expressed by St. Paul; "For this cause God shall send them strong delusion, that they should believe a lie: That they ail might be damned, who believed not the truth; but had pleasure in unrighteousness." And when he speaks of the heathen being given up by God to vile affections, and says that in this way, "They received in themselves that recompense of their error which was meet," he is not be understood to mean, that the exercise of these lusts, or their sinning as they did, was the recompense or punishment for their former sins; but this recompense consisted in the shame and disgrace, pain and misery, which were the proper, meet and constituted attendants and consequence of their vile practices. Nor does he say that this natural evil or unhappiness, which in this life attended, or followed their ways of sin, was the proper and adequate punishment of their crimes. For he goes on to observe, that they knew, or were under advantages to know, that the sins of which they were guilty deserved death; by which is meant neither temporal nor spiritual death; but eternal destruction, the second death, the death threatened, as the proper and full punishment of sin, when moral government was first instituted, and man was put under law. His words are, "Who knowing the judgment of God, that they which commit such things are worthy of death, not only do the same, but have pleasure in them that do them." [170] He proceeds in the next chapter to speak of that punishment of the sinner, which he here says is death, according to the revealed, known judgment of God. We are sure that the judgment of God is according to truth, against them which commit such things. "And thinkest thou, O man, who doest these things, that thou shalt escape the judgment of God? But after thy hardness and impenitent heart, treasurest up wrath, against the day of wrath, and the revelation of the righteous judgment of God; who will render to every man according to his deeds. To them who by patient continuance in well doing, seek for glory, honour and immortality: Eternal life: But unto them that are contentious, and do not obey the truth, but obey unrighteousness, indignation and wrath, tribulation and anguish, upon every soul of man, that doth evil." In these words he clearly, and in the most decisive manner, declares what that death is of which sinners are worthy, according to the judgment of God, and which will be inflicted on the finally impenitent. It consists in suffering the wrath of God, which shall be poured on the heads of the wicked after the day of judgment: And this indignation and wrath, tribulation and anguish, is set in opposition to eternal life, which the redeemed shall enjoy: therefore must be without end. This death therefore is not temporal, nor spiritual death, nor annihilation; but endless existence in misery, suffering that evil which is the wages of sin, and is infinitely worse than non-existence.

If all natural evil, that is, unhappiness, pain and suffering, could be separated from sin, and the sinner could have all the enjoyment and happiness he desires and seeks in the way of sin, it would be no sensible punishment, and really no punishment at all to him; but in his view, it would be a real good, perfectly agreeable to his desire and choice, to be allowed to go on in sin; and the contrary would be the object of his greatest aversion, and the greatest evil to him. Therefore there can be no propriety or reason in threatening him, to give him up to walk in his own ways, and do nothing but sin. This indeed could not be a threatening to him, but would be considered by him as a precious promise of good.

It will perhaps be said, that though living in sin be not an evil in the view of the sinner, but a desirable good; yet to innocent man, and in the perfect exercise of holiness, to whom this threatening was pronounced if he transgressed, sin appeared to be the greatest evil; and therefore nothing worse to him could be threatened, than spiritual death, which consists wholly in sin.

Upon this it may be observed, that we cannot reasonably infer from this, that spiritual death or sinning was threatened as the punishment of sin; because, for the reasons that have been given, there is an impropriety in such a threatening, as it is only threatening that if he did sin, he should continue to sin if he chose it, and be left wholly at liberty to do as he pleased. And this is really no threatening, for it is no punishment to do and to have what we choose. But this is all that would be threatened in this case, that if he once chose to sin, he should be suffered to sin hereafter, without being counteracted or interrupted. Besides, the first sin was as great an evil to innocent, holy man, as any after sin, and the most dreadful, as it was connected with all after sin, and introduced it. There is the same reason, therefore, why the first transgression should be considered, and threatened as a punishment, which is given, that any after sin should be so considered, and threatened. It will be said, this could not be, as it was improper and impossible. But it may be said with as much reason, that it was improper and really impossible to threaten any after sin, or any degree of it, as a punishment of the first sin, which appears from what has been said.

When the apostle Paul says, "sin revived, and I died," he does not mean what is called a spiritual death, for this consists in sin, or is sin itself: But Paul distinguishes the death he died from sin, and speaks of it as the effect of sin. Sin by the law slew him; and sin wrought and produced death, i.e. brought him under the curse of the law. He died, that is, found himself dead, being under the threatening and curse of that law which was given to Adam, and denounced death upon the transgressor, even eternal destruction. Is not the death originally threatened, clearly stated by this apostle?

It is granted that in a few passages of scripture, those who are wholly inclined to sin, and so

The System of Doctrines, contained in Divine Relation, Explained and Defended Volume I
under the dominion of sin, are said to be dead; and the word death is perhaps sometimes used to denote such a state. But when these words are used in this sense, they are evidently used not to express the punishment of sin; and have no reference to the original threatening, or any thing of that kind. To be dead, in this sense, is always mentioned as a crime, and not as a punishment of any crime.

5. On the whole, it appears from what has been said on this question, respecting the death threatened to the disobedience of man, that it means a being separated from all natural good and happiness, unto all natural evil or misery; continuing in endless, miserable existence, suffering the just punishment of sin against God. This is to die in the highest and most proper sense; and is the only death with which a rational moral agent can be threatened or punished, so as fully and properly to express the true desert of sin, and answer the ends of moral government.

This is the original and proper meaning of the word death, and of dying, and no other idea was affixed to it, when the threatening was denounced to man; and he was doubtless made to understand it, when the law was made known to him, if he needed any particular instruction, in order to know the meaning of the threatening. And when the separation of soul and body, which took place after man had sinned, and was restored to a new state of probation, was called death, to distinguish the death here threatened from that, it is called the second death, which is suspended, and will not take place till redemption is finished, and soul and body are restored to their original union, by the general resurrection.

Having inquired and found what was the penalty threatened to the transgressor of the law, under which man was made; it is now to be considered, whether any promise of reward was given to him, if he continued perfectly obedient.

What has been said to prove that the angels had a time of trial of their obedience, and a promise of eternal life, if they continued obedient through the time of trial, [171] is equally applicable to man, and as full a proof that the latter was not only secure in happiness and the favour of God, so long as he continued obedient; but had a time of trial appointed him, with a promise that upon his persevering in obedience to the end of that time, he should be confirmed in holiness and the favour of God. But there is a particular and decisive evidence of this, with respect to man, which we have not in the instance of the angels. This is, the tree of life, which was planted in the midst of the garden, and what is said of it. The name of this tree is significant, and points out the design and use of it. It was called the tree of life, because by partaking of the fruit of it, man was to have eternal life confirmed to him, of which this was the appointed pledge or seal. This is made certain by what is said respecting it, after man had transgressed, viz. that man was not suffered to continue in the garden, but was driven out of it, "lest he should put forth his hand, and take also of the tree of life, and eat, and live forever." This cannot be understood, without supposing that the fruit of this tree, and man's partaking of it, was the appointed sign and pledge of eternal life, or the seal of a promise that he should live forever. Man having sinned, and forfeited the promise, it was not proper that he should partake of this constituted pledge of eternal life, or continue in a situation, in which there was a possibility of his eating of this fruit. Agreeable to this, and with allusion to it, Christ says, "To him that overcometh will I give to eat of the tree of life which is in the midst of the paradise of God," which is a promise of eternal life. [172] This is still farther confirmed by what St. Paul says of the law given to man, in his primitive state, viz. that it was ordained unto life. [173] And that he that doeth the things required in it, shall live by them. [174] This must refer to the original law given to man when innocent, or before he sinned; for no such law could be ordained to life, or propose and promise life on this condition, since sin took place, it being impossible that man, since the first apostasy, should obtain life in this way. This the apostle observes in the passages just quoted. "The commandment, which was ordained unto life, I found to be unto death. For as many as are of the works of the law, are under the curse: For it is written, cursed is every one that continueth not in all the things written in the book of the law to do them." Therefore the law given to man in his primitive state, which threatened death to the transgressor, and cursed him, promised eternal life to him upon perfect obedience. And as he sinned, and so failed of obtaining this life by obedience, the death and curse threatened to disobedience is come upon him.

We are not expressly told how long man was to continue in obedience, before he might eat of the tree of life, and have eternal life made sure to him: Nor why he might not, and did not, eat of the fruit of the tree directly, and put an end to his probation state, and have eternal life sealed to him. But we may be certain there was some wise appointment and regulation concerning this. And perhaps we are not left to mere conjecture about it. Is it not very probable, if not beyond a doubt, that this tree of life had no fruit on it, when this transaction took place, and the promise was made; or the fruit had not come to maturity, so as to be eaten: And that man was told, that if he continued obedient till ripe fruit was on that tree he should then eat of it, as a token and pledge of eternal life, being made sure to him? This fixed the time of his probation, in the wisest and best manner. Man could not tell the hour nor day in which he might eat of this tree, and be confirmed; but he might see the fruit growing, and ripening every day, which would be a constant and growing motive and encouragement to perseverance. Man sinned before the fruit of this tree was produced and ripe; and therefore was not allowed to live where it might be possible for him to take and eat of it, when there should be ripe fruit on this tree.

Thus it appears that the law, or moral constitution under which man was placed, was of the nature of a cove7iant between his Creator and him; man's duty, or what God required of him, was stated, and the penalty of failing of his duty was fixed by the law with a promise of eternal life, on condition of his obedience through the time of trial, which was appointed. And man consented to this law and constitution, as good and excellent, and stood engaged to perform the condition, on which he should obtain the promised reward. This he must be supposed to do: for not to do it, when it was revealed to him by God, would be rebellion against his sovereign.

It has been observed, that the moral law, which is essential to moral government, and by which man was bound as soon as he existed a moral agent, is epitomised by Christ, who says it requires nothing but love, to love God with all our heart, and our neighbour as ourselves. It hence appears, as well as from the reason of the case, that this law respects the heart, or wall and affections. It is with the heart, in the exercise of perfect love, that this law is obeyed; and the smallest contrariety to this love, in the exercises of the heart, or the least defect in the degree and strength of it, is a violation of this law, and must bring the curse or penalty on the transgressor. If there be no degree of exercise of love in the heart, there is no obedience to this law: and where this love is exercised constantly in a perfect manner and degree, or without any defect, there is perfect obedience. This docs indeed necessarily imply, that this love is expressed in all proper ways, in external conduct, so far as it is in the power, and under the government of the will; but the obedience consists wholly in the exercises of the heart or will, producing what is external, in proper expressions of love. And where there is no love exercised in the heart, there is no real obedience or holiness, whatever be the external appearance, in words or conduct. The resolving the whole law into love by Christ, and St. Paul's saying that love is the fulfilling of the law, and that without love he was nothing, whatever were his external conduct, sufficiently establish this point, if it were not capable of demonstration from the reason and nature of things.

This law being founded in reason, and as perfect and excellent as is the moral government of an infinitely wise and good Being, must be, in its own nature, unchangeable; so that it cannot be abrogated or set aside, or abated; nor can any moral agent be released from obligation to obey it constantly and perfectly. There may be particular positive precepts given on special occasions, and with reference to particular circumstances; which may not be always binding, but may be temporary, and cease to be in force, when the end of them is answered, and the reason of their being given ceases. The law requiring love to God and to our neighbour will oblige man to obey all such positive temporary commands, while the reason of these injunctions continues; but when the reason of them ceases, they become obsolete, and the obligation to obey them is at an end. Many of the laws given to Israel by Moses are instances and an illustration of this. But the law requiring love is reasonable and binding on all, at all times, and cannot cease or be made void in any degree. The least disregard paid to it, even in thought or heart by a moral agent, for one moment, in any circumstances, must be wrong and criminal. And it would be infinitely wrong, were it possible, as it is not, for the Legislator and Governor of the world, to express or show any disregard to this law, and not to support and maintain it at all times, and in every respect, by all his authority.

Therefore the penalty of it must always be regarded as reasonable, important and sacred, it being an essential part of the law, and necessary in order to guard, support and enforce it, and clothe it with the authority of the supreme Legislator. A disposition not to execute the threatening, or to mitigate the punishment; and consequently the manifestation of such a disposition would be infinitely unreasonable and wrong, as it would be dishonourable to a most reasonable and righteous law, worthy to be maintained and honoured; and which must be regarded and supported, in order to exercise moral government in the best manner. In the most perfect and excellent government, the penalty of the law must be as much regarded and supported as the precept; because to disregard, abate, or set aside the former, is equally shewing disrespect to the latter, and really repealing it. A proper regard cannot be shewn to the penalty, without manifesting a disposition and determination to punish agreeable to the threatening, by inflicting infinite evil for transgression, and actually punishing so as to answer all the ends of the penalty, and fully support the threatening.

Jn what particular way and manner this law was communicated to man, with all the positive precepts which were given to him, we are not informed. It appears that God conversed familiarly with him; but whether he put on a bodily shape, and appeared like a man, or what was the appearance, or the way in which he communicated to Adam the commands and instructions which he revealed, cannot be certainly determined. However, we are certain this was done in the most wise and proper way; and so as that man had clear and decisive evidence that his Maker did converse with him, and understood all that was said or revealed to him, respecting the moral

The System of Doctrines, contained in Divine Relation, Explained and Defended Volume I
government under which he was placed, the covenant made with him, and the state of probation, into which he was put, and when it should be ended, &c.

Adam, when he first came into existence, though in a state of manhood and maturity, as to his faculties of body and mind, stood in need of instruction, and doubtless had the knowledge of many things communicated to him by immediate inspiration, or otherways from his Maker, as he could have no other instructor. Among these the knowledge of language was one; and how to communicate ideas by words. He was not left to learn this art, and form a language without help, but had the immediate assistance of God.

In this transaction between God the Creator and Governor, and man the creature, in which the law, with the promises and threatenings of it, was declared and established in the form of a covenant between God and man, Adam was considered and treated as comprehending all mankind. He being, by divine constitution, the natural head and father of the whole race, they were all included and created in him, as one whole, which could not be separated: And therefore he is treated as the whole in this transaction. The covenant made with him was made with all mankind, and he was constituted the public and confederating head of the whole race of men, and acted in this capacity, as being the whole; and his obedience was considered as the obedience of mankind; and as by this, Adam was to obtain eternal life, had he performed it, this comprehended and insured the eternal life of all his posterity. And, on the contrary, his disobedience was the disobedience of the whole of all mankind; and the threatened penalty did not respect Adam personally, or as a single individual; but his whole posterity, included in him, and represented by him. Therefore the transgression, being the transgression of the whole, brought the threatened punishment on all mankind.

This point will be more particularly considered, explained and proved in a following chapter; but it seems proper to bring it into view in this place, in order to give a clear and full representation of the law and moral government, under which man was originally placed. That Adam was considered and treated in this respect, as being, or comprehending all mankind, is evident, in that almost every thing which is said to him, in the three first chapters of Genesis, has respect to the whole race of mankind, and not to Adam personally; and is spoken to them, or of them. The first time man is mentioned, it evidently means mankind, and not any particular man. [175] "And God said, Let us make man, and let them have dominion over the fish of the sea, and over the fowl of the air, and over the cattle, and over all the earth, and over every creeping thing that creepeth upon the earth." By man here must be meant mankind, which is denoted by the following words, "And let them have dominion over the whole earth," that is, mankind; the whole human race. All mankind were created, in creating the first man; for they were all included in him, and to be propagated from him, and arise and grow out of him, as the branches of a tree are included in the original stock, root or seed. God in creating the first herbs and trees, with the seed in themselves to propagate their kind, really created all the herbs and trees which shall exist to the end of the world. So he created all mankind, in creating the first man; and in giving dominion to him, he gave dominion to all. They were all made like him, in kind, and their state, condition and circumstances were fixed, as much as that of the race of plants and trees. All mankind were created in the image of God, and to them was given dominion over all the earth. "And God blessed them, and God said unto them, Be fruitful, and multiply, and fill the earth, and subdue it." This blessing and this command respected mankind, and not the first man personally, in distinction from the rest; for he alone was not to fill the earth, and subdue it, but the human race. God is therefore represented as blessing them all, and speaking to them all, and not to a single person. It hence appears, that the posterity of Adam were so connected with him, and included in him, that they might properly be considered as one; and that he was so far the head, and representing father of the whole, that in creating him all mankind were created, and in blessing him, all were blessed; and what was said to him, and done for him, was said to, and done for the human race; that the law given, and covenant made with him, with the blessing and the curse, the promise and the threatening, was given to all, and made with all, having respect to all mankind, included in their father and head: And what he did as a moral agent, was done for them, as much as himself; so that they, even the whole human race, must share equally with him an his obedience, and the promised, consequent blessing, or in his disobedience, and the curse. But the evidence and certainty of this, is more fully established, by what took place, and has been revealed since the apostasy of man. What God said to Adam after he had sinned, was said to, and of all mankind; and the calamity or evil to which he was doomed in this world, as the consequence of his transgression, equally falls upon his posterity. "And unto Adam he said, Because thou hast eaten, &c. Cursed is the ground for thy sake; in sorrow shalt thou eat of it all the days of thy life. In the sweat of thy face shalt thou eat bread, till thou return unto the ground: For out of it was thou taken: for dust thou art, and unto dust shalt thou return." As this sentence, "Unto dust shalt thou return," did not respect Adam only, but all his posterity, we are naturally, if not necessarily led to understand the same language in the threatening, as having respect to all mankind, "In the day thou eatest thereof thou shalt surely die." But this is reduced to a certainty by St. Paul. [176] "Wherefore, as by one man sin entered into the world, and death by sin; and so death passed upon all men, for that all have sinned. Through the offence of one, many are dead. By the offence of one, judgment came upon all men to condemnation. By one man's disobedience many were made sinners." Here Adam is asserted, in the most plain and strongest terms, to be constituted the public covenanting head of mankind, so that sin, condemnation and death, came upon all his posterity, by his disobedience. The threatening, therefore, respected all mankind, and consequently the promises did also. And all depended on Adam's conduct, to determine whether his posterity should be holy and happy forever, or sinners and miserable.--But this subject will be more particularly considered in the next chapter.

This covenant or constitution, in which Adam was considered and treated, as the father and public head of his future posterity, was more than mere law: and in this respect different from the covenant made with the angels. It is supposed they acted every one for himself, and that they all existed at once, and there was no such peculiar union between them, like that between the first man and his posterity, which rendered such a constitution with respect to the latter, proper and wise; yea, necessary, in order to the exercise of the most perfect and excellent moral government.

Should any object to this, and say, that as the posterity of Adam had no opportunity to consent to this constitution, it was not consistent with wisdom or righteousness to include them in it, and fix it for them. And as it was not the best and most likely way for them to obtain eternal happiness, by making it depend on the conduct of the first man, it was not consistent with goodness, and really unjust, and injurious to mankind. In answer to this, it must be observed,

1. The creature has no right to object to any law or constitution which God sees fit to make respecting him; but is obliged to acquiesce in what he orders. God has a right to prescribe the particular method in which he will govern his creatures, and this belongs to him; and for a creature not to approve and consent to what God prescribes, is rebellion against his Maker. Therefore there was no need to wait, to see if Adam's posterity would approve of such a constitution, before it could be with justice and propriety fixed for them. This therefore cannot be the ground of a reasonable objection. Indeed, if it can be proved to be an unjust, or unwise constitution, we may be sure no such constitution was ever made by the Governor of man. This brings to observe,

2. Such a constitution does not appear, and cannot be proved not to be just and good. There was as great a prospect and probability, that the first man would not sin, but persevere in obedience, as that any one of his posterity would; yea, much greater, seeing he was created an adult, in the full exercise of all his rational faculties: whereas they must come into existence infants, and gradually rise to manhood, through the weak state of childhood and youth, in which they would be more exposed to fall by temptation. And the father of mankind had a strong motive to obedience, which none can have who only act for themselves, as the interest of all his posterity was put into his hands, and he acted for them all. Before the consequence was known, had any one, capable of viewing all circumstances, been to judge, he would doubtless have concluded that such a constitution was the most eligible, and the best that could be formed for mankind, and most likely to secure their holiness and happiness. Now the event has proved to be evil, and by this constitution, Adam and his posterity are fallen into a state of ruin, we may view it as bad, and injurious to us; especially since we are become prejudiced against the dictates of wisdom, and enemies to the wise and good government of Jehovah. But this is not the least evidence that it is not wise and good. Mankind, while in a state of rebellion, are disposed to think and say, "The ways of the Lord are not equal." And they will find fault with any constitution, which infinite wisdom and goodness can form. Witness their disapprobation of the gospel, and opposition to it. It ill becomes those who choose to live in sin, and when they have the offer of pardon, and deliverance from sin, and of eternal life, will not accept of it, but spurn it from them, to find fault and complain that they were originally placed under a constitution, by which they are fallen into that sin and ruin, from which they cannot be persuaded to accept deliverance, but choose to live in sin, as a privilege, and constantly approve of the original transgression, by obstinately persisting in that rebellion, which their first father began, when he sinned.

3. It must be observed, that if it could be proved, as it cannot, that such a constitution was not the most favourable to every individual, it will not follow that it is not, on the whole, the wisest and best constitution that could be formed. If no injustice be done to any one by it, and it be best suited to answer the most wise and important ends, it is certainly the best possible constitution. If it were evident that mankind did not enjoy so great advantages to be holy and happy forever, under such a constitution as they would have under some other, it does not follow that any injustice is done to them; for they had no right to these advantages; and God was not obliged to grant them: If he were, there could be no state of trial, and eternal life must be made sure to them all, which God was able to do. But this would not be wise, it would not have been suited to answer the most important ends, and for the greatest general good. Therefore if this constitution is suited to answer these ends, and is the best that could be for the general good, then it is the wisest and best that could be devised.

The System of Doctrines, contained in Divine Relation, Explained and Defended Volume I
There is certainly no evidence that it is not so: But abundant evidence of the contrary, which may more fully appear by what is farther to be said on the subject, in attending to the consequences of this constitution, or the ends actually answered by it.

IMPROVEMENT

I. From what has been brought into view in this chapter, we are led farther to reflect on the goodness of God, and our obligation to gratitude. The goodness of God appears in his forming angels with such high and noble capacities, and under advantages to be proportionably happy, in the exercise of their powers, under the good and excellent moral government, under which they were placed. God's goodness appears in the moral constitution formed for angels, which was, as has been observed, more favourable than mere law, as they had the promise of a reward of eternal life, inconsequence of their obedience during a temporary trial. The infinite goodness and munificence of God is expressed in this, and will be forever celebrated by them, who are confirmed in holiness, and have actually received this reward. And herein is to be seen the goodness of God towards them who fell into sin and endless ruin. Their rebellion, and their being treated according to their desert, and falling under the threatened punishment, did not render the goodness of God to them in their original formation, and in placing them under so good a constitution, in any respect or degree the less; but was and continues to be as great and perspicuous, as it would be if they had continued in this goodness, and had obtained eternal life. And were their hearts right, as they ought to be, they would never cease to exercise gratitude, and be thankful for the goodness of God to them, and to acknowledge that the infinite evil which is come upon them, is the just consequence of their abuse of God's goodness to them.

And the goodness of God to man was great and wonderful, in forming him with a capacity to be a moral agent, and under moral government, and to enjoy endless life in the favour of God. And the constitution and form of moral government, which has been considered, was an expression of infinite goodness; and could not have been formed by any being, but one infinitely good. The law requires nothing but what is necessary for the good of man: The highest happiness consisted in obedience to this law. The time of trial was to be short; and man was under every desirable advantage, and had every conceivable motive to persevere in obedience. The reward promised was infinitely great, infinitely more than the longest obedience could merit or deserve. And the sanction or penalty threatened was necessary in order to its being a good law, and was an instance of goodness, as it was a guard to the law, and tended to secure obedience, as it rendered disobedience infinitely dreadful, in the consequence of it; and so was an unspeakably powerful motive to obedience.

The appointment of a public head, and Adam, to act for the whole, as he was, in a sense the whole of mankind, they being all included in him, was a wise and good constitution; even the best, and the most in favour of mankind of any that can be conceived: Unspeakably more favourable to man, than if every one of the human race were to act for himself, and be in a state of trial, as they should successively rise into existence. There was a possibility that Adam would transgress; it was highly probable he would not. And, as has been observed, he had every desirable and possible motive to obedience, and a very powerful one which could not have existed, had he not acted as a public head, for all his posterity.

All this, as has been observed, was in our favour, and goodness to us. This is the happy state in which mankind were placed under moral government; the best, the happiest situation which could be devised by infinite wisdom and goodness. And it may be demanded, What could have been done, that was not done for mankind, in placing them in such circumstances, and under such a good law and constitution, consistent with being placed in a state of probation?

The goodness of God ought to be celebrated by us, and to excite our constant, fervent gratitude and praise. For, as has been before observed, this goodness is not the less, nor are our obligations to gratitude and praise in the least diminished by the abuse of it; by which we have lost all the benefit of it, and are become most miserable.

II. The sin and eternal ruin of the angels who fell, is suited to give conviction to all, of the vanity, weakness and insufficiency of the highest and most excellent creatures; and of their absolute and constant dependance on God: And consequently, that there is no creature, in whom we may safely put any trust, however great and dignified.

This event taught the angels who did not sin this lesson more fully, than otherwise they could have learned it. In this they saw their own insufficiency for themselves; that they were liable to ruin themselves every moment, and depended on God entirely for preservation from infinite evil; and that they were wholly indebted to him for this favour, which must be sovereign goodness, to which they had no claim, and which God was under no obligation to grant. This they will see more clearly, and acknowledge with greater sensibility forever, than they could have done, if none of them had sinned, and fallen into endless ruin: And by it God will be more loved, praised and glorified, and they will be unspeakably more holy and happy, throughout their endless existence.

God, in his wisdom, ordered it so, that the highest, and most excellent part of the creation, should become morally corrupt, and infinitely worse than nothing, by sinking into irrecoverable and endless ruin and misery, to shew, that the creature, in its best state, is nothing but vanity, considered in itself, independent of the power, goodness and all-sufficiency of God; which could not be discovered to creatures, to the best advantage, in any other way. Which discovery is of the utmost importance, and absolutely necessary to the highest good of the universe. This will remain an everlasting lesson, by which all holy creatures will be taught humility and gratitude; and God will receive a revenue of praise and glory forever, which could not have existed, had not this event taken place.

III. By the view we have had of the divine law and moral government, we may learn, what is the rule of our duty now, and consequently, what is sin in us, viz. every deviation of heart from the rule of duty, by omission of what it requires, or doing what it forbids.

The particular covenant made with man in his original state; by which the head and father of the human race was considered as including all mankind, and was constituted to act for the whole, being violated, ceased to exist any longer, except in the consequences of the violation of it. But the law pointing out and requiring duty, and threatening the transgressor, is still the rule of our duty, and binding on us; and in the threatening we are told what every transgression of ours deserves; and learn what is the curse under which we are, as sinners. For this law, as has been shown, is unchangeable in its nature, and must be binding on every moral agent. Transgressing it, though ever so often repeated, does not in the least absolve us from obligation to obey it; and however great is our aversion from what it requires, and however strong and fixed it be, this does not in the least excuse us in our disobedience, and remove or abate our obligation to obedience; bat the stronger and more fixed our hearts are in opposition to what is required, and the more and longer such opposition is indulged, the more criminal we are. There is no other law given to us, which requires less than this original law, or that is not virtually contained in it or enforced by it. To love God with all our heart, soul, strength and mind, and our neighbour as ourselves, is always our duty; and all opposition to it, and every omission of this duty, in the least degree, is sin. We must therefore look into this perfect law and rule of duty, and no where else, in order to know what is our duty, and what is sin; and by this alone can we obtain the knowledge of, and ascertain our own moral character.

Footnotes:

160. Page 208, 209, 210.
161. Gal. iii. 10.
162. Matt. xxii. 37, 40.
163. Deut. xix. 21.
164. Deut. xix. 16-21.
165. John vi. 50.--viii. 51.--xi. 26.
166. Rom. vi. 23.
167. Rom. viii. 8.
168. Rev. xxi. 8.
169. Psalm lxxxi. 12.--Rom. i. 26.--2 Thess. ii. 11.
170. Romans i. 32.
171. Page 211, 212, 213.
172. Rev. ii. 7.
173. Rom. vii. 10.
174. Chap. x. 5.--Gal. iii. 12.
175. Gen. i. 26.
176. Rom. v. 12.

CHAPTER VIII - ON THE APOSTASY OF MAN, AND THE EVIL CONSEQUENCE TO HIM

MAN, who was placed in a happy and honourable situation, did not continue in it; but by transgressing the divine command, and violating the holy covenant, plunged into a state of infinite guilt and wretchedness, under the curse and threatened penalty of the law of God.

Moses gives a particular history of this first apostasy of man, in the third chapter of the book of Genesis. He does not tell us how long man continued innocent and obedient, after he was created; or give us a history of what passed, and of all the particular events and transactions which took place in a state of innocency; such a history being of no use and importance to us, while we continue in the present state. The whole will doubtless be revealed to all mankind at the day of judgment.

The Serpent is said to be the tempter, by whom Eve was deceived, and led to eat of the fruit of the forbidden tree; and then gave it to Adam, and he eat of it also. It is said, "The serpent was more subtle than any beast of the field which the Lord God had made." He appeared to have more sagacity than any other of the brute creation. Probably he had an erect and very beautiful form, and had nothing of the appearance and form of serpents since the fall of man. He appeared near the forbidden tree, or on it; perhaps eating of the fruit of it. It seems probable that Eve, seeing him there, and eating of the fruit of the tree, was surprised; upon which the serpent spoke, "Hath God said, ye shall not eat of every tree of the garden?" Eve replied, that God had given them full liberty to eat of every tree in the garden, except that one; but had forbidden them to touch that, upon the severest penalty. The serpent said, "Ye shall not surely die. For God doth know, that in the day ye eat thereof, then your eyes shall be opened; and ye shall be as gods, knowing good and evil." It is most probable that the serpent told the woman that by eating of the fruit of that tree, he had obtained the use of reason, and the faculty of speech, which she saw him now to exercise; and therefore said, that from his own experience, he could assure her, that if she would eat of this fruit, she should be so far from dying, that she should arrive to a much higher degree of perfection and knowledge. The first motion in her mind disposing her to regard and believe the serpent, rather than God, who had said, she should surely die, if she eat of that tree, was wrong and sinful: so that she really fell from her innocence, before she actually took of the fruit, and ate. Her doing the latter was completing her apostasy, by a full exertion of her will in open rebellion. And the first motion of Adam's heart, which implied the least degree of inclination to hearken to the woman, and eat of the forbidden fruit, was a sinful one; and he was a rebel in heart, before he actually ate.

Nothing is spoken of as the tempter but the serpent; because nothing else was visible but the serpent speaking and reasoning; or rather deceiving and lying. But the story itself, when properly considered, will necessarily lead us to conceive of some superior, invisible agent, speaking and acting in and by the serpent, making him the instrument, by which he effected his design. And as it could not be a good spirit, which by the serpent acted this part, it must be an evil one; which is confirmed by what God said to the serpent, after the apostasy of man, which will be considered more particularly in its place. But this is reduced to a certainty in succeeding divine revelation, where the devil and his angels are brought into view: And Christ evidently alludes to this instance of ruining mankind by deceit and lying when he says, "The devil was a murderer from the beginning; and he is a liar, and the father of it." And the devil is repeatedly called the dragon, and the serpent, "That old serpent called the devil, and satan which deceiveth the whole world," plainly alluding to the serpent which in the beginning deceived and seduced our first parents. [177] The devil, in order to carry on his design, made use of the serpent as his instrument, he being a creature best suited to answer his purpose. And God saw fit to suffer him to do it.

By this act of disobedience, our first parents violated the covenant which God had made with them, and forfeited all the good promised to obedience, and brought upon themselves the penalty threatened. It was not, indeed, completely executed upon them immediately. They fell under the divine displeasure and wrath, which was sufficiently great to destroy them forever; and which, if fully executed on them, must make them miserable, without end. They were condemned, and fell into a state of complete eternal ruin, being totally and forever undone and lost, without any help or hope. Thus they died immediately on sinning: Though the full execution of the punishment did not take place immediately; yet as they were condemned and cursed, and utterly undone, and had nothing in their reach or view to prevent infinite evil coming upon them, the evil threatened in a true sense fell upon them, and they died in the day on which they transgressed. The sentence of death, and the penalty threatened in the law under which the angels were, fell upon those who sinned immediately; but it will not be completely executed till the day of judgment; nor will it ever be, because it is endless punishment, to which they are condemned. It will be in execution without end, and so, strictly speaking, will never be fully executed: And yet the execution is according to the threatening. So it is in the case of man; he fell under the threatening immediately on his sinning, though the full and complete execution of it, do not take place for many ages.

St. Paul says, "When the commandment or law came, sin revived, and I died:" That is, he found himself dead. He found himself under the curse of the law, which was contained in the original threatening, "In the day thou eatest thereof, thou shalt surely die." If Paul found himself dead, agreeable to the threatening of the law, then Adam did really die in the same sense, or the same death: and sin, even the first act of disobedience, wrought this death in him. The evil which the law threatened, "Thou shalt surely die," in this sense, came upon him. He fell under the curse. This sentence fell upon him, and he was a dead man. Paul calls this death, or dying; and by this tells us what dying means in the threatening; and that Adam did die on that day in which he ate the forbidden fruit.

Bat if this were not so, and Adam did not die the death threatened on the day he sinned, this may be consistent with the execution of the threatening, according to the true intent of it. The threatening, "In the day thou eatest thereof, thou shalt surely die," expresses two things, viz. The certainty of the punishment, as infallibly connected with transgression; and that the threatened penalty should follow on one or the first act of rebellion. We find much the same language used, to express one or both these; and not that the threatening should be immediately executed, or on the day in which the crime was committed. "The righteousness of the righteous shall not deliver him in the day of his transgression. As for the wicked less of the wicked, he shall not fall thereby in the day that he turneth from his wickedness: Neither shall the righteous be able to live in the day that he sinneth; but for his iniquity that he hath committed, he shall die or it." [178] This does not express the time when death should be executed or take place; but the certainty of the punishment. "For it shall be that on the day that thou goest out, and passest over the brook Kidron, thou shall know for certain, that thou shalt surely die." [179] This does not mean, that he should die on the same day in which he should pass over Kidron; but that he should certainly be put to death for this offence, without any farther trial.

This apostasy of our first parents, was a total apostasy: That is, by giving themselves up to this sin, an inclination to sin took the dominion in their hearts, and they wholly lost all their moral rectitude and holiness, or the moral image of God, in which they were created. This is not expressly asserted in the history of their sin; but it may be inferred from the nature of the case. By this transgression they forfeited all favour from their Maker, and fell under his displeasure, and were cursed, according to the law and constitution, under which they were when they sinned; and it was inconsistent therefore to shew them any favour; especially such a favour, as preserving them from total apostasy, or their being continued in the exercise of love to God, while they were under that constitution, and antecedent to the revelation of the dispensation of grace. Moreover, the first act of sin carried in it an inclination to universal sinfulness, and opposition to holiness in general, or to all and every degree of holiness; and according to the natural course of things, would issue in total depravity, in the exclusion of all moral good, and the complete possession and reign of moral evil in their hearts. This consisted in their ceasing to love God, and loving themselves only; which self love, or selfishness, was in every degree of it opposed to the law under which they were, and the fruitful source of all sin; which will more fully appear, when this subject will come more particularly into view, in its proper place. There was nothing therefore that could prevent their total apostasy, or becoming wholly sinful, and opposed to the law of God, and all holiness, unless God had miraculously interposed, contrary to the law and constitution under which they sinned, to prevent it, and exercised mere sovereign favour, which, as has been observed, would be inconsistent with the constitution under which they sinned.

The above reasoning, to prove that the apostasy of man was total, appears to be confirmed by the apostasy of the angels who sinned. It is presumed all will grant that their first apostasy was not partial, but total. If the angels fell totally in their first rebellion, why not man also? It is true that under another and a new dispensation of grace through a Mediator, holiness is introduced and maintained in the heart of the believer, in a small and low degree, while there is also a degree of sinful exercise; and both these, sin and holiness, continue through life; and particular acts of sin of which believers are guilty, do not bring on total depravity, and wholly extinguish every degree of divine love: But this may with propriety be called a miracle, being contrary to the course of nature, and the constitution of things, which originally took place, and is the effect of the new constitution,

The System of Doctrines, contained in Divine Relation, Explained and Defended Volume I
by which the original order or course of nature is counteracted by the introduction of a gracious dispensation; and the nature and natural course of sin is interrupted and opposed, by special divine interposition: But this is so far from an evidence that our first parents could go into an overt act of rebellion, consistent with retaining any degree of love to God, that it is a proof of the contrary, and that man, by the first apostasy, sunk into total depravity, and became wholly a rebel, and altogether opposed to the divine law.

It has been observed, and it is thought proved in the foregoing chapter, that all mankind were created and comprehended in the first man; as much as were all the trees and plants, in the first trees and plants which were made, with the seed in themselves, to produce a succession of trees and plants after their kind, to the end of the world. Therefore in what God said to Adam, and his transactions with him in giving him law, and forming a covenant with him, he was considered and treated as comprehending all mankind; and he was the real and constituted head of the whole race, so that his obedience or transgression should affect all mankind, as it affected him, and was to be considered as the obedience or disobedience of all. It is proposed now, to attempt to explain this point more fully, and show how far, and in what respects, all Adam's posterity are comprehended in the first transgression, and affected by it.

I. By the constitution and covenant with Adam, his first disobedience was the disobedience of all mankind. That is, the sin, and consequent ruin of all the human race, was by this constitution infallibly connected with the first sin of the head and father of the race. By the divine constitution, the appointment of God, if the head and father of mankind sinned, the whole race of men, all his posterity, should sin; and in this sense it should be the sin of the whole. Accordingly, when the head became a sinner, and moral corruption took possession of the heart, a sure foundation was laid, by the constitution under which man was, for the same sin and moral corruption to take place and spread through all the human race: Just as by a divine appointment, or a law of nature, the $ap of the root or original stock of a tree passes into the numerous limbs, twigs and the fruit of the tree, as they successively grow out of it. If the sap or nature of the root or stock be bad, sour or poisonous, the same is communicated to the whole, and every branch, and all the fruit and seed of the whole tree, is corrupt, sour, or poisonous, and of all the trees which spring from that, or are produced by the seed of it. Thus, if any tree was, when first created, of a poisonous nature, and produced such fruit, all that race of trees, or all that should spring from it, would of course be of the same nature. And if a tree or plant, which was created al first good and wholesome, did degenerate, and become corrupt and poisonous, all that should proceed from that, would, of course, be equally corrupt.

The disobedience of Adam decided the character of all his natural posterity; and rendered it certain, according to a divine, revealed constitution, that they should be born, and rise into existence as moral agents, in disobedience and rebellion: And that the same moral corruption which then took place in his heart, should spread through the whole race of mankind. In this sense, the first sin carried in it the sin of all mankind, and contained the seed, and was the foundation of all the moral corruption of the human race; as by this they were all constituted sinners,

II. As the first sin was, in the sense just explained, the common sin of all mankind, as the disobedience of them all was infallibly connected with it, and by it all the human race were constituted or made sinners; so as this first sin brought condemnation, or the penalty of the law on Adam, it fell equally on all mankind. For as the sin of Adam inferred and implied the disobedience of all, the consequent condemnation of all was equally implied and involved in the condemnation of Adam. Or the condemnation and penalty which fell on Adam, the father and head of mankind, really came upon all his posterity. As the sin was common to all, so was the curse. And it is here particularly to be observed, that as Adam first disobeyed, and condemnation and the curse came upon him, for his disobedience and in consequence of it; so these take place just in the same order in his posterity, their sin, or the moral corruption, which is common to all mankind, first takes place, as the ground and reason of their condemnation, and liableness to the threatened penalty.

The evidence that this was the original constitution under which mankind were placed has been in some measure given in the foregoing chapter. But there is more clear and certain evidence, that things have actually taken place in this manner and according to such a constitution; and that the sin of all the posterity of Adam, and the consequent condemnation and curse, were thus connected with the first sin of their common father and head, and come upon all mankind as the certain and appointed consequence of the original apostasy of man; the former being implied, and involved in the latter. This is now to be brought into view, and carefully considered.

1. The pain, sorrow, and train of evils in this world, which issue in the death of the body, to which all mankind are sentenced, and which actually came upon them all, in consequence of the original transgression, are a standing evidence, and full demonstration, that the sin and condemnation of all the posterity of Adam were infallibly connected with that first sin, and involved in it.

Though these evils were denounced to the first parents of mankind on their disobedience, and they only are addressed in the sentence; yet it is evident from fact, that all their posterity were included in them, and fell under the same sentence, and were doomed to the same evils. This is not only an evidence that Adam was considered, as including his posterity as their common head, so that what was said to him and of him, was said to, and of all mankind; but also renders it certain, that all his children were considered as sinners, in consequence of the apostasy of their first father; and that there was a certain connection between the first sin, and the sin and guilt of all mankind. For surely it would not be proper or just to sentence all mankind to these evils, when considered as perfectly innocent. There is therefore no possible way to account for this, consistent with the righteousness and equity of the divine government, but by supposing and granting that all the posterity of Adam were constituted, and considered to be sinners, in consequence of his sinning, or by his first offence, there being a certain constituted connection between his first transgression, and the sinning of all the human race.

Separation of soul and body, and the numerous particular natural evils which now take place among mankind in this life, could have had no existence, if the original threatening had been executed without mitigation; or had not the redemption taken place, by which mankind are put into a new state of probation, as has been before observed. Nevertheless, had not man sinned, these evils which issue in the death of the body could not have taken place, as redemption also could not. Therefore these evils are introduced, and afflicted on man, in consequence of sin, and as a standing testimony of God's displeasure with him, and consequently cannot be inflicted on any but sinners. We are therefore sure that as the death of the body, with other attendant evils, are inflicted on all mankind, they are all considered and treated as sinners; and consequently, that they are really sinners; and that their being such had a certain connection with the first sin, upon which they were condemned to these evils.

Adam is sentenced to the death of the body, and all the train of preceding evils, because he had sinned, and offended his Maker; and this is expressly declared to be the ground of the sentence. And as this sentence was extended to all his posterity, and they were included in it, as much as Adam himself, they were considered and treated by this as being sinners, whenever they should exist; which could not be, unless there were a certain established connection between the sin of the first man, and the sinfulness of all mankind. If it were possible that any of Adam's natural posterity should be innocent, this sentence could not be extended to them; but they must have been excepted. Therefore as all are included in the sentence, not one of mankind can possibly be innocent; but the sinfulness and guilt of all are infallibly connected with the sin of Adam, and included in it, by an established constitution.

Many particular instances of the death of men, who have been cut off in divine providence, are represented to be expressions of God's displeasure with them for their sins, such as the drowning of the old world; the destruction of the inhabitants of Sodom, &:c. and innumerable other instances. How much more must the sentence of death upon all mankind, be an expression of God's displeasure with them, for their sinfulness and guilt!

2. That the sin, and the consequent guilt and condemnation of all the human race, were by divine constitution connected with Adam's sinning, is very particularly and expressly asserted by St. Paul.

"Wherefore, as by one man sin entered into the world, and death by sin; and so death passed upon all men, for that all have sinned. Through the offence of one, many died. For the judgment was by one, to condemnation. By one man's offence, death reigned by one. By the offence of one, judgment came upon all men to condemnation. By one man's disobedience, many were made sinners." [180]

Here sin, condemnation and death, are expressly said to be introduced into the world, upon all mankind, by one offence, one act of disobedience of one man, that is, Adam. When it is said that sin entered into the world by one, the meaning cannot be merely that one man sinned first, or that Adam committed the first sin, sinned before any of his posterity did sin; for this would be to assert nothing to the purpose. But by sin entering into the world, is meant its taking place among mankind, and spreading or extending to ail the posterity of Adam. Death entered into the world as sin did, as the consequence of it, by one man; and this passed or came upon all men, just as sin did. This is expressly asserted in the words immediately following, "For that all have sinned." By one man sin entered into the world of mankind, as the common sin of all, and extended to every one of his posterity, and by this sin, death entered also, and came upon all mankind, in that by this one offence all became sinners; there being an established connection between the sin of this one man, and the sinning of all. That this is the truth, and what is asserted in those words, is made certain beyond dispute, by the repetition of the same assertion, in other and more express words, in the 19th verse. "By one man's disobedience, many were made sinners." Here the disobedience of Adam is said, in this sense, to be the disobedience of all his posterity, that their sinning was connected with his disobedience, or implied and involved in it; so that by his sinning, they were all made sinners, or constituted sinners, as the Greek word properly signifies. That is, by a fixed, divine constitution, if Adam sinned, all his posterity were to become sinners; so that by his disobedience, he fixed this character upon all mankind.

Condemnation and death, or judgment to condemnation, came upon all men, considered as sinners, or as a consequence of sin, as it came upon Adam. It is represented in this light in this passage. Death entered into the world by sin, and came upon all men, because, or inasmuch as all men were sinners, being made sinners, by the disobedience of Adam their head, by virtue of the divine constitution and covenant made with him, they all fell under condemnation to death, considered in this character, or as sinners. "By one man's offence death reigned." All mankind being constituted offenders, or sinners by one offence of Adam, death took place, and held dominion and reigned over all. Again he says, verse 21, "As sin hath reigned unto death." Death is asserted to be the consequence of the reign of sin in the world, or among mankind.

It has been observed, that by death, which is mentioned six times in this passage, is evidently meant eternal destruction, or the second death, as it is put in opposition to eternal life, and is the wages of sin; unless death mentioned in the 14th verse, be an exception. But if it be, and it were granted that the death of the body is intended whenever death is mentioned in this paragraph; yet this would not evade or weaken the evidence and proof it contains, that the posterity of Adam are constituted sinners by his first sin, so as by it to fall under condemnation, and become justly exposed to the second death. For if a moral agent be in such a sense a sinner, as to deserve any evil, he must deserve infinite evil, that is, endless punishment; for this, as has been proved, is the just wages of sin, and what every sin deserves. Therefore if any evil, even that of the death of the body, be inflicted on mankind, in consequence of Adam's first act of disobedience, it carries in it a certain evidence, that they become sinners by that sin of his, there being an established connection between his sin and their being sinners, and that they deserve all the evil which the first sin deserved, and was threatened to the first act of disobedience, which was endless misery, the just wages of sin. In this view, the death of the body, to which all mankind are subjected, is a standing evidence that they are sinners, and consequently that they deserve endless punishment: For if they were not sinners, they could not be sentenced to this evil; and if they are sinners, and deserve this evil, they deserve infinite evil, which is the just desert of every sin. And as this death comes on all mankind in consequence of one act of disobedience of the first man, the head and father of all, it is a certain evidence that by his sin, all his posterity are constituted and become sinners, and were considered as such, as soon as Adam sinned; otherwise his sin could not have brought this death upon all mankind, or upon any but the first sinner. And their being condemned to this death, necessarily implied their personal sin in consequence of Adam's sinning, and just desert of the second death, as has been shown.

Hence it appears, that as long as this passage of scripture is to be found in the Bible, we have good evidence that the sin and ruin of all mankind was implied, and certainly involved in the first act of disobedience of Adam.

3. This is also demonstrably certain, in that the posterity of Adam are all considered and treated as sinners, and deserving and exposed to endless ruin, in the method which has been opened and prosecuted for the recovery and salvation of man, by Jesus Christ. In the revelation of this salvation, and all that has been done to effect it, it is supposed that all mankind are lost in sin; that every one of the natural posterity of Adam who has been born, has been a sinner; and that every one that shall be born and exist to the end of the world, will exist a sinner, and in a state of condemnation and ruin. The gospel is represented as providing relief for all who believe, and the only way in which mankind can be saved, all being condemned and infallibly lost forever, who are not saved by Christ. There could be no reason for this, unless it were certain that all mankind would rise into existence sinners, and so be involved in condemnation and ruin, and stand in absolute need of the revealed Saviour. But this could not be, unless this was implied in the apostasy of the father of mankind, and upon this was fixed and made certain. [181] How could a Saviour from sin and destruction be provided and revealed for mankind, immediately upon the sin of Adam, if this sin did not involve the sin and ruin of all? for the innocent could have no need of such a Saviour. And with what propriety could the gospel be ordered to be preached to all nations, and to every one of the human race to the end of the world, if it were not certain that every one was in a state of sin and ruin? This can be well accounted for, if the sin and ruin of Adam's posterity were connected with his first sin, and involved in it, by virtue of the covenant and constitution made with the father of mankind; and the whole is consistent and easy to be understood: But no consistent, rational, satisfactory account can be given of this, on any other supposition.

4. Agreeable to this, mankind are represented in the scripture, to be universally depraved and morally corrupt; and this appears to be true from fact and experience. It is needless to adduce all the passages of scripture in which this is asserted. St. Paul asserts this in such express and strong terms, when he is attending particularly to this point, that it will be established sufficiently for the present

purpose, by appealing to his words.[182] "We have before proved both Jews and Gentiles, that they are all under sin: As it is written, There is none righteous, no, not one. They are all gone out of the way, they are together become unprofitable, there is none that doeth good, no, not one,--That every mouth may be stopped, and all the world may become guilty before God." This witness is supported, and appears to be true from the character mankind have given of themselves, by their general conduct in all ages, as there never has appeared to be one perfectly upright, sinless person; and in general all nations and generations, of every age, have been exceeding corrupt and sinful; and that while many of them have had great light and advantage to be wise and virtuous, and when great and special means have been used with them in the best manner suited to make them so. By a great variety of experiments which have been made, it appears that mankind are so sunk into sin, and strongly inclined to evil, that no external applications, means, motives, and advantages are sufficient to reclaim them. And children, as soon as they are capable of manifesting any moral disposition or inclination, universally discover that which is contrary to the law of God.

If what the scripture asserts on this head, wanted any support from fact, this character which mankind have themselves drawn by their practice would be a sufficient one.

When St. Paul had asserted and proved in the words just quoted, that all mankind are become wholly corrupt and sinful, that "all have sinned, and come short of the glory of God," he proceeds to account for this, and show the ground and origin of the universal sinfulness of the posterity of Adam, in the paragraph which has been considered. "By one man sin entered into the world, and death by sin: and so death passed upon all men, for that all have sinned. By one man's disobedience, many were made sinners."[183] And there is the greatest reason to believe, and rest satisfied in this account, not only as it is given by divine inspiration, but as it is the only rational, consistent and satisfactory account of this interesting affair, that can be given.

That such a constitution is just and wise, and that mankind have no reason to object to it as injurious to them, is evident from what has been observed upon it in the foregoing chapter.[184] But that this may appear yet more evident, and all objections be obviated, a particular explanation of this matter, and vindication of the divine conduct herein, will be now attempted.

It is carefully to be observed, that sin does not take place in the posterity of Adam, in consequence of his sin, or that they are not constituted sinners by his disobedience, as a punishment, of the penalty of the law coming upon them for his sin: It is not to be supposed that the offence of Adam is imputed to them to their condemnation, while they are considered as in themselves, in their own persons innocent: Or that they are guilty of the sin of their first father, antecedent to their own sinfulness. But all that is asserted, as what the scripture teaches on this head is, that by a divine constitution, there is a certain connection between the first sin of Adam, and the sinfulness of his posterity; so that as he sinned and fell under condemnation, they in consequence of this became sinful and condemned. Therefore when Adam had sinned, by this the character and state of all his posterity were fixed, and they were by virtue of the covenant made with Adam, constituted or made sinners like him; and therefore were considered as such, before they had actual existence. It was made certain, and known and declared to be so, that all mankind should sin as Adam had done, and fully consent to his transgression, and join in the rebellion which he began; and, by this, bring upon themselves the guilt of their father's sin, by consenting to it, joining with him in it, and making it their own sin.

This cannot be objected to as an unjust appointment, or a constitution injurious to mankind, without equally objecting to God's willing and ordering things so as to make it certain that any of his creatures should sin. If it was his will that Adam should sin, and he constituted and ordered things so that it was certain that he would sin, and he had a right to do this; then it was right and just to will and determine that all the posterity of Adam should sin, and to form a constitution, which established a certain connection of the latter with the former. The disobedience of Adam was connected with something which preceded it, and of which it was the consequence; and it was determined and fixed by God, as has been proved, and which all must grant who hold that God did permit Adam to sin: But none will say or think that this was a punishment inflicted on Adam, thus to determine, and form and fix a constitution which made his sinning certain; or that this was injurious to Adam, or in the least degree improper or unwise. And if this was just and wise and good, then it was equally so, to form a constitution which connected the sin of all mankind with the first sin of the father of the human race. Or, if he might and did permit Adam to sin, consistent with justice, wisdom and goodness, he might, consistent with all these, permit everyone of his posterity to sin, and therefore determine to do it. And if God had a right to order things so that all mankind should sin, independent of their connection with Adam and his sin, and this be no more unjust or injurious to them, than to order things so that Adam and myriads of angels should sin; then certainly no wrong is done to them, by ordering that this should depend upon, and take place in consequence of this sin of Adam. No objection can be made to this, which ib not equally an objection to God's ordering things so that sin should take place, and has taken place in any instance,

The System of Doctrines, contained in Divine Relation, Explained and Defended Volume I
among angels or men.

The following propositions must be granted, as axioms of indubitable truth, and may serve to give light to the point under consideration.

1. Every creature capable of moral agency and holiness is entirely dependent on God, not only for his continuance in existence, but for all his moral exercises; and especially for his moral excellence or holiness. This is a greater and higher gift than mere existence, and when it is given, the continuance of it is entirely dependent on the will of God. The most excellent creature in the exercise of perfect holiness, is, in his own nature changeable, and may become sinful; and nothing can secure him from this but the will and agency of the infinite, unchangeable Being.

2. God is under no obligation to preserve the moral agents which he creates, from sinning. If this proposition were not self-evident, the actual existence of sin is a demonstration of the truth of it.

3. God may, therefore, for wise reasons, will and determine not to prevent the sin and consequent ruin of his creatures; which is really willing that sin should take place. The truth of this proposition is also demonstrated by the sin which has actually taken place; for this could not have been, unless God, all things considered, willed it should be, otherwise it must have taken place contrary to his will, or while he was not willing it should exist, which is infinitely impossible.

4. If God may, and has actually exercised his will and choice about the existence of sin, and determined in favour of its actually taking place, and this be consistent with his wisdom, holiness and goodness, as it certainly is; then it is consistent with his glorious moral character, to dispose, order and do every thing which is necessary to be, ordered and done independent of the creature, and previous to their actually sinning, in order to the certain existence of this event. This has been observed in a former chapter; where it has been also shown that the former, viz. that God's willing the existence of sin, does necessarily imply the latter: and that these are not really two distinct things; but one and the same. [185]

From all this, it appears, that God, being under no obligation to preserve any of his rational creatures from sinning, may, consistent with his righteousness, wisdom and holiness, order things so that any number of them shall become sinful, when this is most for his glory and the general good. Accordingly, it was agreeable to his will and purpose that vast numbers of the angels should fall into sin: And had this will and purpose reached all of them, they would have had no reason to complain of any injustice or wrong done to them. And therefore those who have not sinned, must ascribe it to the sovereign, distinguishing, undeserved favour of God, that they have been preserved innocent and holy, when so great a number of them went off into a state of rebellion. And he had a right to order it so that any number, or all of mankind, should become sinners, as they rose into existence, had there been no constitution connecting their sinning with the sin of Adam; and no injustice or injury would have been done to any. And since God has seen fit to order and constitute things so that the universal sinfulness of man should take place, in connection with the sin of Adam, and as the unfailing consequence of it, which he might have ordered without doing them any wrong, had not Adam first sinned, or without any consideration of his sin, or connection with it, surely there is no ground or colour of an objection to it, as being injurious to them. If mankind had no claim to be exempted from sin, had there been no connection between them and Adam, or had they no common head or father; then surely they have no reason to complain, that they are become sinners by a constitution, appointing Adam to be their public head, and connecting their becoming sinners with his sinning.

It is a notorious and acknowledged fact, that all mankind are sinners; sinning is infallibly connected with their existence. There is certainly some unfailing constitution or law, which constantly and effectually operates to produce this effect in all Adam's posterity. We are sure this is just, and no wrong is done to man, that sin does thus infallibly take place in all, by some steady, efficacious cause, though we were not able to tell by what means, or in what way this universal corruption of man has been introduced, and taken place. And shall we complain as being injured by this, because God has seen fit to favour us with a revelation, informing us how, and in what way this universal sinfulness of the human race has been introduced and taken place; "That by one man sin entered into the world: And by one man's disobedience, many (even all his posterity) are made sinners?"

And to complain of this, is not only to find fault with that which is just, by which no wrong is done to us; but to object to a most wise and good constitution. This constitution is perfectly agreeable to the natural relation in which Adam's posterity stood to their common head and parent; and all mankind were so comprehended and included in the first man, that it was natural, proper and wise to deal with him as including all his posterity, and to constitute him to act for them all, as being in him. And there farther appears a natural propriety and fitness in such a constitution, if we consider the nature and tendency of sin, and the inclination, wish and attempt of the sinner who rebels against God. Adam's first rebellion contained in it a desire and wish that all his posterity might sin as he did. This became agreeable to his heart as soon as sin entered into it; and so far as he had power and influence, it would certainly take place. To suppose the contrary, is inconsistent and absurd. The corruption and rebellion of all Adam's children therefore must be the consequence of his sinning, unless his inclination, desire and attempt were crossed and counteracted. And his sin had a mighty and almost irresistible tendency to lead all his posterity into the same rebellion; and who can say this would not be the consequence, without one exception, had things taken their natural course, without being opposed and prevented by divine interposition? Adam's sin had a natural tendency to corrupt the world of mankind, and according to the natural course of things would spread to every individual of his posterity. And this was agreeable to the inclination and choice of the father of mankind. The language of his transgression was, "Let all my posterity sin as I do, and be as I am; let them rise into existence in my own image and likeness: So far as I have power to beget and produce them, they shall be rebels like myself."--Therefore, according to the natural course of things, and the nature and tendency of sin, and agreeable to the inclination and choice of Adam, the first act of sin by the common father and head of mankind, contained in it the infection and sin of all the human race; and must corrupt the whole, and issue in the rebellion and ruin of every one, unless counteracted and prevented by divine interposition. Hence it appears that the divine constitution connecting the sin and ruin of all mankind with the first sin of their common father, is so far from being arbitrary and unnatural, that it is an establishment, agreeable to the natural course, tendency and connection of things, and perfectly consonant to the nature of sin, and serves to make a display of this. And that a contrary constitution, which should prevent the spreading of the sin of Adam to his posterity, or corrupting any one of them, would be unnatural and improper, as it would counteract and prevent the natural tendency, and the nature, course and connection of things; and therefore would not have been wise and good--while the constitution which has taken place is agreeable to the nature of things, and both wise and good. It appears most wise and best that if any of mankind sinned, all should be sinners, and constituted so by the first sin, as this has laid a proper and ample foundation for the glorious work of redemption, for the character and works of the Redeemer, of whom Adam in this way was made a type,--the Redeemer and his works, and the consequent glory, being the grand design and end of all. But this will rise more clearly into view as we proceed.

It must be farther observed, that there is no reasonable objection to this constitution, in that it not only establishes a connection between the sin of Adam and the sinning of his posterity; but that the latter should be born in sin, so as to begin to sin, as soon as they begin to act as moral agents. For if a moral agent may begin to sin at any time, he may begin to sin as soon as he begins to exist with a capacity of sinning. And if God is not obliged to prevent his sinning at any time of his existence, he is under no obligation to prevent it the first moment of his existence. Therefore he had a right to determine the sinfulness of all Adam's posterity as soon as they should exist, as a certain consequence of his disobedience: And there is no more ground of objection to this, than there is to Adam's posterity sinning at any time of their existence, in consequence of his sinning.

If a person can have no reason to complain of any one but himself, if he be inclined to sin, and actually disobeys the divine command, at any time, at whatever distance from his beginning to exist, he will be equally without reason to complain that he is injured by any one, but by himself, if he be inclined to sin as soon as he begins to exist, and though he never were otherwise inclined. If any one should say, if he had not sinned early, even from his beginning to act, he should not have sinned now; or if he had not been always inclined to sin from his first existence, he should not have been inclined to sin since, with a view to exculpate himself, would this be any excuse? Was not his first inclination to sin, his own inclination, and as really blameable as if it had not been the first, or so soon? And because he began to sin so soon, does this excuse his sinning afterwards, and continuing to sin?--

It seems proper, if not necessary, that if moral corruption be derived from Adam to his children, by a fixed law or constitution, it should take place from the beginning of their existence. If by their being his children, they become corrupt, they must of consequence be corrupt as soon as they exist, or become his children. If it were not so, it would not appear from fact, that they became sinful by being the posterity of Adam, or that their moral corruption was, by divine constitution, connected with his sin, by their being his children.

Agreeable to this, the scripture represents all mankind as sinful from the beginning of their existence. "The imagination of man's heart is evil from his youth." [186] That is, his infancy, from the beginning of his existence. "David says of himself, "Behold, I was shapen in iniquity; and in sin did my mother conceive me." [187] This must be as true of all mankind, as of David. "The wicked are estranged from the womb, they go astray as soon as they be born, speaking lies." [188] Here it is asserted at least, that as soon as they begin to act, they sin. And though it cannot be precisely determined how soon this is; yet it hence appears that they are by nature corrupt, and they begin to exist with that moral corruption, which is the same thing that appears as soon as there is

The System of Doctrines, contained in Divine Relation, Explained and Defended Volume I
opportunity, in visible action, in opposition to the rule of truth and duty, the divine law. The words immediately following these are "Their poison is like the poison of a serpent." The serpent is generated a poisonous creature. Poison is in his nature from the beginning of his existence, and when he begins to bite that is acted out, with which he was born. There appears to be evident reference to this, in these words. The wicked are said to be estranged from the womb; to go astray, speaking lies, as soon as they be born: And in this respect their poison, their wickedness, is like the poison of a serpent. Solomon says, "Foolishness is bound up in the heart of a child." By folly and foolishness in his writings, he generally means sin, or moral corruption: And certainly this is meant here, because he says, "The rod of correction will drive it far from him." The rod of correction can drive no other foolishness away, but that which is of a moral kind. The expression is very strong and emphatical, and asserts that sin has gotten fast hold, and is firmly fixed in the heart of a young child, and that this is true of every child which is born. How could the early, native corruption of children be more fully expressed?--The same is asserted by Christ, when he says to Nicodemus, "That which is born of the flesh, is flesh." [189] It is abundantly evident from the whole passage in which these words are found, that by flesh here is meant moral corruption, or sin, in which sense this word is frequently used in the scriptures, especially in the writings of St. Paul. According to this, man is born in a state of moral corruption.

A child, an infant, as soon as he exists, may have moral corruption or sin. As soon as he has any mental motion, which is of the nature of inclination, this motion, disposition or inclination, may be wrong, and have in it the foundation and seeds of every sin, being of the same nature with the sinful motions and inclinations of the hearts of adult persons. These motions, though invisible and unperceived by us, do really, and in the sight of the Omniscient Being, fix the actual moral character of the child, which discovers itself to men, as it has opportunity, and there is capacity to express it in actions and words. This is confirmed by observation and experience. Children commonly, before they can speak, discover that selfishness, that wilfulness and obstinacy, which is the root and source of all the sin which takes place among mankind. This, therefore, is of the same nature with moral evil in general, and was in the heart or mind when it first existed; and has grown up to a greater degree of strength, as the mind has been enlarged, and appears and is acted out, as the capacity increases, and opportunity and occasion are offered.

This sin, which takes place in the posterity of Adam, is not properly distinguished into original and actual sin, because it is all really actual, and there is, strictly speaking, no other sin but actual sin. [190] As soon as sin exists in a child of Adam, though an infant, it consists in motion, or inclination, of the same nature and kind with sin in adult persons; all the difference is, the former is not so strong, and has not opportunity to be acted out, as the latter is. Sin, or an evil inclination, took place and existed in the heart of Adam, before he determined to eat, and did eat of the fruit which was forbidden. The very first motion in his heart, tending that way, was a sinful motion, though it was not perfected or completed till it produced the overt act. Who can say that this motion or inclination, which may be called lust, was stronger or had more activity in it, than the evil motion which may exist in the heart of an infant; which may be sufficient to produce the most horrid mental and external acts of sin, when capacity and opportunity are given? St. James says, "Every man is tempted, when he is drawn away of his own lust, and enticed. Then when lust hath conceived, it bringeth forth sin." He does not mean that lust is not sin; for this is contrary to all reason, and cannot be true. And if we should suppose this to be asserted or implied, we should make this apostle contradict St. Paul, who says, "I had not known sin but by the law: For I had not known lust, except the law had said. Thou shalt not covet." Here he speaks of lust and sin, as synonymous, by which he means one and the same thing. St. James, when he distinguishes lust from sin, intends by the latter, what is called, an overt act of sin, or sin when it is finished or completed in overt acts, agreeable to the following expression. "Sin, when it is finished." It is begun in the first and least motion of lust, or evil inclination and motion in the heart, and finished by being acted out in an overt act of the will. Both are actual sin, yet there is a distinction which maybe made.

The existence of sin in the heart of a child, as soon as it is capable of any thing of a moral nature, can be as well accounted for, and as easily, as the sin of an adult person, or as the first existence of sin in the heart of Adam. The former being as consistent with the divine perfections, and the nature of man, as the latter. What has been said in the fourth chapter on the origin and cause of moral evil, may serve to illustrate this. And it takes place in the hearts of all the posterity of Adam, by virtue of the divine constitution, which has been considered and explained above.

On the whole, it is presumed that none but those who assert that the sin of man does take place, contrary to the will and purpose of God, and that it is not, all things considered, agreeable to his will that it should exist, can have any objection to the doctrine of original sin, as it has been stated above, which asserts the universal sinfulness of Adam's posterity, to be connected with his first sin by a just, wise and good constitution, made by God, when he created man. And of these, it is hoped, there are but few, since they must, by such assertion, contradict the truth plainly delivered in the holy scriptures, and deny the supremacy and absolute independence and infinite felicity of the Most High God; as has been observed in the forementioned chapter.

In order to set this important scripture doctrine in a yet more full and clear light, the following things must be observed.

I. Mankind are born totally corrupt or sinful, in consequence of the apostasy of Adam. That is, they have naturally, as the children of Adam, no degree or kind of moral rectitude, and their hearts are full of moral evil. That the first apostasy was total, and that man became immediately wholly sinful, having no degree of moral rectitude, has been shewn to be, at least, probable, if not certain; and therefore when he begat a son in his own likeness, he must come into existence wholly sinful. But that this is in fact true of all mankind, is expressly and repeatedly asserted in divine revelation. It was early declared that "God saw that the wickedness of man was great in the earth, and that every imagination of the thoughts of his heart was only evil continually." [191] The total corruption and depravity of mankind cannot be asserted in stronger and more decisive language than this. With reference to this assertion, it is said, "The imagination of man's heart is evil from his youth." [192] Agreeable to this, Solomon says, "The heart of the sons of men (that is, of all mankind) is full of evil. [193] If it be full of evil, there can be no good in it. Again, it is said, "The heart is deceitful above all things, and desperately wicked." [194] St. Paul asserts the total depravity of man, and that there is nothing in him naturally which is morally good and right, in very express and strong terms, repeated over and over again. He quotes the following words from the Old Testament, and expressly applies them to all mankind, both Jews and Gentiles. "There is none righteous, no, not one. There is none that understandeth, there is none that seeketh after God. They are all gone out of the way, they are together become unprofitable, there is none that doeth good, no, not one. There is no fear of God before their eyes." [195] This truth is implicitly asserted in many passages of scripture. Only a few will be mentioned, since it is so clearly asserted in what has been quoted. When Christ says, "That which is born of the flesh, is flesh," that is, nothing but flesh, he really asserts that man, as he is born, in his natural state, is destitute of all moral goodness: For by flesh is meant that which is opposed to the holy Spirit, or holiness; and is put for moral corruption; which is abundantly evident by the writings of St. Paul. Christ says, "Him that cometh unto me, I will in no wise cast out." All under the gospel are invited to come. "Whosoever will, let him come." Yet Christ says, "No man can come unto me, except the Father, which sent me, draw him." All this put together proves that all mankind are wholly opposed to the character of Christ, which they could not be, if they had the least degree of moral rectitude, or inclination to that which is right. Oar Lord further says, "Whosoever shall give you a cup of water to drink, in my name, because you belong to Christ, verily I say unto you, he shall not lose his reward." [196] If he who exercises so much regard to Christ, as to give a cup of water for his sake, to one of his disciples, shall be saved; then men have not by nature the least inclination to embrace him, but must be his enemies, which indeed is abundantly declared, both by Christ and his apostles. "He that is not with me, is against me. Ye shall be hated of all men, for my name's sake. If the world hate you, ye know that it hated me before it hated you." By the world, is meant mankind in general. To hate Christ implies a mind not only destitute of all right disposition; but under the dominion of a strong evil propensity. St. Paul says, "The carnal mind is enmity against God. In me, that is, in my flesh, dwelleth no good thing." The carnal mind and the flesh are the same, and stand opposed to the mind renewed by the Spirit of God in regeneration. It is said, "the natural man receiveth not the things of the Spirit of God: For they are foolishness unto him; neither can he know them, because they are spiritually discerned. But he that is spiritual, judgeth all things." As the natural man is opposed to the spiritual man, that is, a true christian, it must mean man in his natural state in which he is born, or the world of mankind; which is confirmed by our Saviour's saying the same which is here said of the natural man of mankind, as distinguished from his disciples. "I will pray the Father, and he shall give you another comforter, that he may abide with you forever; even the spirit of truth, whom the world cannot receive, because it seeth him not, neither knoweth him; but ye know him, for he dwelleth with you." [197] This represents man as not having the least degree of true taste and discerning of mind with respect to things of a moral, spiritual nature, which is the same with being destitute of all moral rectitude, or holiness. Nothing but total depravity .can render men wholly blind to spiritual things, and so as to be opposed to them, and refuse to receive them. This is confirmed by what Christ says, "Except a man be born again, he cannot see the kingdom of God." [198] He has no true discerning and understanding respecting it; but is wholly in the dark. Nothing but viciousness or depravity of mind can thus blind them; and a being destitute of every degree of conformity to the law of God, This is asserted by St. John, "Every one that loveth, is born of God, and knoweth God. He that loveth not, knoweth not God." [199] "Love is the fulfilling of the law," which requires nothing but love. It is necessary to have this love, in order to see and know God. And consequently this is necessary in order to see the Spirit of God; for he is God; and in order to know the things of the Spirit of God, and see the kingdom of God. And he who has this love does know God, and receives the things of the Spirit. But all who are not born of God and saved by the washing of regeneration, and renewing of the Holy Ghost, are wholly without every degree of this kind of love; for every one that loveth, is born of God. Therefore all who are not born of God are wholly without every degree of conformity to the law of God, or of real holiness; consequently, are wholly depraved or sinful.

This fact, the total depravity of mankind, is confirmed by experience and observation. Mankind have given this character of themselves, in all ages of the world, not only that they are sinners; but that there is none that doeth good, no, not one, unless he be renewed by divine grace, and is made a new creature, by being created in Christ Jesus, unto good works. [200]

II. It is of importance to observe, That the total moral depravity and sinfulness of mankind, which by divine constitution takes place in consequence of the sin of their common father, is as much their own sin, and they are consequently as answerable and blameable for it, as if this their sinfulness had taken place in any other or different way that is conceivable or possible.

Indeed, it is a plain contradiction to say, or suppose, that any person's moral depravity or sin is not his own sill, and that all the blame and ill desert of it does not lie upon him; for if it be not his sin, and he is not answerable for it, it is not sin or moral depravity, but must be of a different and contrary nature, and consistent with innocence and moral perfection; and consequently cannot subject the person to any blame or desert of evil.

Therefore to talk, or think, of the total or partial moral depravity of mankind, as not being wholly their own depravity or sin, and they not wholly accountable for it, and as if they are not odious and ill deserving in proportion to the degree of their moral corruption or sinfulness, is most absurd, and tends only to blind and delude.

If the natural capacity and powers of mankind were debased and sunk, and become much less, and more feeble, independent of any moral depravity or sinfulness of theirs, this would not be their sin; nor could they be answerable or blamed for it. And if, in consequence of their being the children of Adam, and of his sin, they had lost their rational powers, and all natural capacity, necessary to constitute them moral agents; this could not render them sinful or blameable in the least degree; and, by the supposition, they would be utterly incapable of either. The constituted consequence and effect of the sin of Adam, as it respects his posterity, is their total moral depravity or sinfulness; and not the removal or debasing their natural powers of mind in the least degree, any farther than the corruption and sinfulness of their hearts has influence to prevent the proper use of their understanding, and natural powers of mind with which they are endowed; and they are by this moral depravity, perverted and improved to the purpose of sin and rebellion against God. Therefore nothing is necessary in order to restore man to the perfect possession of his natural powers, and the proper exercise and use of them, but the removal of the moral corruption of his heart, and restoration to the perfect exercise of holiness: Which moral corruption is in every instance and degree of it, wholly his own corruption and sin, in whose heart it takes place, and he is blameable and answerable for it all, be it more or less; and it is impossible it should be otherwise, as has been observed and proved. But as this matter is liable to be misunderstood, and many difficulties respecting it have much embarrassed the minds of not a few, it is proper to give it a more particular attention.

1. The sinfulness of mankind being connected with the sin of Adam, as the constituted consequence of it, does not in any respect, or in the least degree, make it less their own sin, or render them the less answerable and blameworthy for it.

The previous certainty that they will all sin, however, and in whatever way this becomes certain, whether by the divine decree, or constitution, or whatever, cannot render it less their own sin, or them less guilty, than if there were no certainty that they would sin antecedent to their actually sinning. This has been considered and proved in a former chapter, and cannot be consistently denied by any who admit the foreknowledge of God, and believe in divine revelation. If the previous certainty that men will act wrong, and sin, renders their conduct not wrong and sinful, which is indeed a contradiction; then, according to the Bible, neither Pharaoh, nor the Israelites, nor Judas, nor the Jews in crucifying Christ, were guilty of any sin; and others innumerable, whose actions were predicted in holy writ. Yea, according to this, there is, there can be, no sin in the universe, since all the actions of creatures were foreknown and therefore certain from eternity. It was certain that Adam would sin before he was a sinner. This did not render his transgression, no sin, or not his own sin, or in the least exculpate him for what he did: So far from this, that it necessarily implied, that he would be a sinner, and that he should be wholly answerable for that which was his own sin. And if the sinfulness of all the posterity of Adam was certainly connected with his sinning, this does not make them sinners, before they actually are sinners; and when they actually become sinners, they themselves are the sinners, it is their own sin, and they are as blameable and guilty as if Adam had never sinned, and each one were the first sinner that ever existed. The children of Adam are not answerable for his sin, and it is not their sin any farther than they approve of it, by sinning as he did: In this way only they become guilty of his sin, viz. by approving of what he did, and joining with him in rebellion. And it being previously certain by divine constitution, that all mankind would thus sin, and join with their common head in rebellion, renders it no less their own sin and crime, than if this certainty had taken place on any other ground, or in any other way; or than if there had been no certainty that they would thus all sin, were this possible.

2. The moral corruption or sin of mankind, is not the less their own sin and crime, because they begin to sin so early, and are morally depraved as soon as they exist, capable of any thing of a moral nature. It is evident from scripture and from fact, as has been shown, that this is true of all the children of Adam. They are sinful as soon as they are capable subjects of any thing of a moral kind, and their first moral exercises are wrong and sinful: But nevertheless, it is their own depravity, and all their moral exercises are as much their own, and this corruption and these exercises are as really criminal, as they could be, did they not take place so soon; but in any supposeable aftertime. The time in which a person begins to have moral exercises, right or wrong, whether earlier or later, does not alter the nature of those exercises. If his exercises be wrong and selfish, from the beginning of his existence, they are in their own nature as really wrong and sinful, as if he had been holy a thousand years, and after that had fallen into a course of the same wrong and sinful exercises and conduct. It is not necessary, in order to a creature's being sinful, that he should first be virtuous, or free from moral corruption. The first sin of Adam would have been as really his own sin, and his own crime, had he sinned sooner than he did; yea, if that had been the first act of his, and he had never had one virtuous exercise: His previous holy exercises might be the means of rendering his sin which he afterwards committed, more criminal than otherwise it would have been; but had there been no such holy exercises previous to his sin, and his first exercises had been contrary to holiness, they would have been as much his own exercises, and as really criminal, as was his first sin, which he committed after he had been holy for a time. The plain, incontestible reason has been given for this, viz. That all sin consists in the nature and quality of the exercises which take place in a moral agent, and not in any thing which goes before, or follows after them, and which is not of the same kind.

If a person finds himself now a sinner, and that from the heart he approves of, and chooses rebellion against God and his laws, he is not the less a sinner, because he has been of the same disposition many years, and has always sinned, since he has been conscious of any of his own exercises; yea, has in fact had the same disposition, from the beginning of his existence. His having sinned before, and done nothing else but sin, since he began to act, is no excuse for his sinning now, and going on to sin, nor does it make his present sinful exercises less his own sin, nor any of the precedent ones, than if he never had such exercises more than at one time of his life. Yea, according to the common sense of mankind, he is the more criminal, and his character is the worse and more odious, for his being always given to wickedness, and to do evil, from a child; so that it is natural, or in his very nature, to do evil. It has been often said of persons, in order to represent them very criminal, and set their character in a bad and odious light, "Their conduct has been always bad and mischievous, their character has been bad from children, they sprang from very wicked families; they are vicious by nature; and mischievousness runs in their very blood, &c."

King David represents himself in this light, and speaks of his native corruption as his own, and as an aggravation of all his sins, and the odiousness of his own character, in that remarkable penitential psalm of his, [201] "Behold I was shapen in iniquity, and in sin did my mother conceive me."

It is not necessary to determine when or how soon the children of Adam became moral agents, or what is necessary to constitute them such, in order to decide the point now under consideration; since it is only asserted that the moral corruption of mankind, is not the less their own sin and fault, because it takes place as soon as they are capable of moral exercise, be that when it may. Many have supposed that none of mankind are capable of sin or moral agency, before they can distinguish between right and wrong, and know what the law of God requires, and what it forbids: But this wants proof, which never has been yet produced. And it appears to be contrary to Divine Revelation: For that speaks of sins committed ignorantly, and supposes a person may sin and be guilty in those exercises, and that conduct, in which he has no knowledge or consciousness that he is doing wrong. Hence it appears, that persons may be moral agents, and sin without knowing what the law of God is, or of what nature their exercises are; and while they have no consciousness that they are wrong. And if so, then as soon as children are capable of the least motion and exercise of the heart, which is contrary to the law of God, such motions and exercises are sin in them, and their sin, though they are ignorant of it: And of such sinful inclinations and exercises, they may be capable as soon as they exist the children of Adam. It is certain no one can know it not to be so: And this is agreeable to the representation the scripture gives of the matter, which puts it beyond all doubt. This has been particularly considered, page 273, &c.

3. The corruption of mankind is not the less their own moral depravity and sin, and they are not the less culpable and guilty, because it is so deeply fixed in their hearts, and they are totally corrupt and sinful.--This observation might be thought quite needless, and as only saying, that a greater degree of sinfulness is not less than a small degree; or that ten or a thousand degrees of moral corruption are not less than one degree; or that sin is not the less sinful, because it is so great. I say, this observation would be needless and but trifling, were it not too common to believe and assert the contrary, though not in plain and express terms; however unreasonable and absurd.

If one degree of sinfulness, or opposition of heart to the law of God in any person, be wholly his own sin, and he is justly accountable for it, and the blame and guilt of it lies upon him; then, if he has ten, or a thousand degrees of evil inclination and opposition to the law of God; this must be all still his own sin, and he proportionably more criminal and blameworthy. If inclination to oppose the law of God be wrong and criminal; then it must be criminal in proportion to the strength of such inclination. And if this be the constant reigning inclination and choice of his heart, so as wholly to exclude every degree of opposite inclination and choice, he is wholly sinful, and criminal in proportion to the strength and constancy of his evil disposition, by which his heart is obstinately fixed and bent to do evil. This is the clear dictate of reason, and the contrary is most absurd, and supposes that the more strongly the heart is inclined to oppose God and his law, the less criminal the man is; and that when the heart is wholly and constantly fixed in opposition to the law of God, this opposition of heart to God becomes wholly innocent, so that a man cannot be justly condemned for it; whereas if he had less opposition to God, and a very small degree of it, it would be very odious and sinful! That the greatest possible degree of moral corruption does not excuse, but increase the odiousness and guilt of the man so depraved, is not only demonstrable by reason, but is the dictate of common sense, and feelings of mankind. If a person appears wholly and constantly inclined to falsehood, and to injure his neighbours; and if no means and arguments used with him, or motives set before him to desist from his evil conduct, have the least impression or effect upon him, to reclaim him; but he obstinately persists in his evil practices, we consider him not as innocent and blameless, because his moral depravity is so deeply fixed that he is incurable by any possible means; but as more odious and criminal in proportion to the degree and obstinacy of his incurable and unalterable inclination to do evil.

It has been thought and urged by many, that fallen man cannot be wholly blameable for his moral depravity, because he has lost his power to do that which is good, and is wholly unable to change and renew his depraved heart. But what has been before observed, must be here kept in mind, that man has not lost any of his natural powers of understanding and will, &:c. by becoming sinful. He has lost his inclination, or is wholly without any inclination to serve and obey his Maker, and entirely opposed to it. In this his sinfulness consists; and in this lies his blame and guilt, and in nothing else; and the stronger and more fixed the opposition to the law of God is, and the farther he is from any inclination to obey, the more blameable and inexcusable he is, as has been observed and proved. So that when it is considered what must be meant by man's losing his power, and having no ability to do right, if there be any real meaning, and any thing be meant that is agreeable to the truth, the objection and difficulty vanishes entirely; and it appears that man is under no inability to obey the law of God, but what consists in his inclination to disobey. And it is easy to see that if inclination to disobey God, be it ever so strong, will excuse disobedience, and render it blameless; then there cannot possibly be any such thing as sin and blame in the universe; unless creatures may commit sin contrary to all their inclination and choice.

It is certain that every degree of inclination contrary to duty, which is and must be sinful, necessarily implies and involves an equal degree of difficulty, and inability to obey. For indeed, such inclination of the heart to disobey, and the difficulty or inability to obey, are precisely one and the same. This kind of difficulty or inability, therefore, always is great according to the strength and fixedness of the inclination to disobey; and it becomes total and absolute when the heart is totally corrupt, and wholly opposed to obedience. But this inability to obey, being, the same in kind and degree with opposition of heart to obedience, does not excuse disobedience, or in the least remove the blame of it, unless opposition of heart to obedience renders disobedience no crime: Which none, it is presumed, will assert or believe.

This leads to observe, that the holy scriptures speak frequently of this kind of inability, or want of power to do good; and always represent it as inexcusable and blameable. Our Saviour said. "No man can come to me, except the Father, which hath sent me, draw him." And yet apparently blamed the Jews for rejecting, and not coming to him, and said to them, "Ye will not come to me, that you might have life." From whence it appears that the cannot, the inability mankind are under to come to him, is precisely the same thing with their unwillingness, or opposition of heart to come to him, as the matter has been stated above. Nothing but the opposition of the heart, or will of man, to coming to Christ, is, or can be in the way of his coming. So long as this continues, and his heart is wholly opposed to Christ, he cannot come to him, it is impossible, and will continue so, until his unwillingness, his opposition to coming to Christ, be removed by a change and renovation of his heart by divine grace, and he made willing in the day of God's power. And yet this inability, and impossibility to come to Christ, consisting wholly in the opposition of his will or heart to Christ, is the man's own sin, and he is criminal in proportion to the degree of his inability, or the strength and fixedness of the opposition of his heart to Christ.

This kind of inability, therefore, is so far from being an excuse for not coming to Christ, that it is in its own nature criminal, being nothing but sin, a strong fixed opposition of heart to that which is most reasonable and right. No man can act contrary to his present inclination and choice. But whoever imagined that this rendered his inclination and choice innocent and blameless, however wrong and unreasonable it might be?

St. Paul says, "the carnal mind is enmity against God, for it is not subject to the law of God, neither indeed can be." None can think the Apostle means to excuse man's enmity against God, because it renders him unable to obey the law of God, and cannot be subject to it. The contrary is strongly expressed, viz. that this enmity against God is exceeding criminal, in that it is directly opposed to God and his law, and involves in its nature an utter inability to obey the law of God; yea, an absolute impossibility.

On the whole, it is hoped that by what has been said above on the apostasy of man, it will appear that the doctrine of original sin has been stated and explained agreeable to the holy scripture; and that it does not imply any thing unreasonable and absurd, or injurious to mankind; but is the result of a constitution which is perfectly agreeable to the nature of things, reasonable, wise and good; that the children of Adam are not guilty of his sin, are not punished, and do not suffer for that, any farther than they implicitly or expressly approve of his transgression, by sinning as he did: And that their total moral corruption and sinfulness is as much their own sin, and as criminal in them, as it could be if it were not in consequence of the sin of the first father of the human race, or if Adam had not first sinned: And that they are under no inability to obey the law of God, which does not consist in their sinfulness and opposition of heart to the will of God: Therefore are wholly inexcusable, and may justly suffer the wages of sin, which is the second death,

III. This subject of the introduction of sin into the world, and the total moral corruption of all the natural posterity of Adam, cannot be properly finished without observing, and more particularly considering, what is the nature of sin, and wherein it consists.

The most express and concise definition of sin, which, perhaps, we have in the Bible, is in the following words, "Sin is the transgression of the law." Or, as it might perhaps more properly be rendered. Sin is a violation of the law; or a deviation from law. Sin supposes a law; "For where no law is, there is no transgression." And every motion or exercise of the heart of a moral agent, which is not perfectly conformed to the law of God, which requires all love to God with all their heart, soul, mind, and strength, and to love their neighbour as themselves, is sin, as it is a deviation from this law. As the law requires love, and nothing but love, it may be determined with great certainty that sin consists in that which is contrary to that love which the law requires, be it what it may. There can be no neutral moral exercises, which are neither conformable to the law of God, nor contrary to it; therefore every exercise of the heart of a moral agent, which is not agreeable to the law of God, is contrary and opposed to it. It must be also observed, and kept in mind, that sin. as does holiness, consists in the motions or exercises of the heart or will, and in nothing else. Where there is no exercises of heart, nothing of the nature of moral inclination, will or choice, there can be neither sin nor holiness. Nothing external or out of the heart, or will, and which has no connection with that, can be of the nature of morality, either virtue or sin: External motions or exertions, in words and actions, are virtuous or sinful, only as they are connected with the heart, and are the expressions, fruits or effects of inclination, design and choice; and all the virtue or sin consists wholly in the latter. This observation, the truth of which none can dispute, is made in order to direct us where to look for sin, even into the heart, and no where else; when we are inquiring after the nature of it, and wherein it consists.

Therefore if we would find what sin is, and what is that in which it consists, we must look for these exercises of heart, that disposition, inclination or choice, in which there is no love to God and our neighbour; and which are contrary to loving God with all the heart, and our neighbour as ourselves. And if we can find, and on sure ground determine, what these are, we shall know what is the nature of sin, and wherein it essentially consists.

Love to God, and love to our fellow creatures, is of the same nature and kind, and differs only as it is exercised towards different objects. It consists most essentially in benevolence or good will to being in general: In this is necessarily included all virtuous love, or all the love which the law of God requires, such as love of complacency in moral beauty and excellence, and love of gratitude to benevolent beings, &c. Love to God, who is infinitely the greatest, and the sum of all being, consists primarily and essentially in good will or friendship of heart towards him, in acquiescing and rejoicing in his existence, glory, and infinite felicity, and in seeking the promotion of his

The System of Doctrines, contained in Divine Relation, Explained and Defended Volume I
interest and honour, &c. And this implies all the virtuous love required in the divine law: And where there is no degree of this kind, disinterested affection, there is no virtuous love to God or man. If this were not so evident from the nature of things, it is capable of being proved from scripture many ways. The apostle John says, "God is love." And then proceeds immediately to say, "In this was manifested the love of God towards us, because that God sent his only begotten Son into the world, that we might live through him." This is love of pure, disinterested benevolence, to creatures infinitely odious and guilty. This is the love meant when he said, "God is love;" for this is introduced to illustrate that assertion. Hence it follows with certainty, that disinterested benevolence is primary and essential in the divine moral character. Consequently, this is the love which is required of creatures in the divine law: For the law of God is a transcript of his own moral perfection; and so far as creatures are conformed to this, they are like God in his moral character, and partakers of the divine nature; and exercise the same kind of love and holiness which forms the moral character of God. St. Paul gives a particular description of the love in which holiness consists; [202] and he says, "It is kind," that is, it is benevolent, and good will to others, consequently to being in general, and to God, the first and sum of all being. He also says, "It seeketh not her own," by which assertion he sets it in direct opposition to self love, for in the exercise of this a man seeketh his own, and nothing else; and he makes it wholly a disinterested affection; for if holy love seeketh not her own, it seeketh the good of being in general, as her only object, and cannot have the least degree of selfishness in its nature; but is directly opposed to it.

That the love to our fellow creatures required in the law of God, is love of benevolence, which is disinterested, is certain, as it is a love which will extend to those who have no moral excellence, even those of the worst moral character, and to our greatest enemies, towards whom a virtuous love either of complacence or gratitude cannot be exercised. And it follows from this also, that the love to God which is required, is love of disinterested benevolence: for, as has been observed, the love to God, and to our neighbour, which the law of God requires, is of the same nature and kind, and the one implies and involves the other. And this is the farther evident and certain, from the apostle's considering the love of christians, as of the same nature and kind with this disinterested love of God, in this passage; and from his exhorting them to imitate God in this his disinterested benevolence, by loving as he does. "Beloved, if God so loved us, we ought also to love one another. If we love one another, God dwelleth in us, and his love is perfected in us."

It being thus evident that the love required in the divine law, in which holiness consists, is disinterested benevolence, which is primary and most essential in all virtuous love; and in which all is included; it appears from what has been observed, that sin consists in that affection and those exercises, which are directly opposed to disinterested benevolence to being in general, and all those affections and exercises which are implied in true benevolence or good will to others. And this must be self love, or selfish affection and exercises; for this, and this only is, or can be opposed to disinterested regard and good will to other beings; and to all those exercises which are implied in true benevolence. If a person has no other exercises but self love, or the love of his own self, and those moral inclinations and affections which are implied in this, he does by the supposition regard himself only, and has respect to nothing but his own supposed good or interest; and cannot exercise the least degree of disinterested affection to any other being. And as that heart whose exercises may be all resolved into self love, being implied in it, and flowing from it, does not, and cannot exercise any true benevolence to other beings, but is wholly opposed to it; so every degree of self love, be there more or less, is in its own nature opposed to the love required in the divine law: And therefore is in its nature, and in every degree of it, sin, being contrary to true holiness. And if a person be not wholly selfish, but exercises some degree of disinterested regard and good will to other beings; yet every degree of self love which he exercises is as opposite to disinterested affection, as if he had no benevolence; and therefore as sinful. The nature of self love is not changed from sin to holiness, nor does it become an innocent affection, by the exercise of a degree of opposite disinterested affection, or by being diminished, as to the degree of it, so as to be exerted with less strength and vigour, and in a measure counteracted by opposite affection. Still every exertion of self love is as really sin, as if it were exercised in a higher degree, and were not restrained and counteracted by opposite, disinterested love. No one does or can suppose that benevolent affection changes its nature, and becomes wrong and sinful, by being exercised in a low degree, and counteracted, and kept very much under by selfishness: But this might be as reasonably supposed, as that selfishness does become innocent and virtuous, when exercised in a small degree, and under the restraints of benevolence to being in general. Yea, if the latter be true or possible, the former must be so too.

Hence it is evident, that sin consists in sell love, and those affections and exercises which are implied in this, and naturally flow from it as their root. This is in its own nature opposite to all virtuous, holy affection, to all truth and reason; and is of a criminal nature, in every degree of it, wherever it is found; and where there is nothing of this, there is nothing criminal or wrong. Self love pays a supreme and sole regard to an infinitely small and inconsiderable part of existence, and the feeling and language of all the exercises of it is, "I am, and there is none else! There is no other being worthy of any regard, but myself." "Self love regards nothing but self, as such, and subordinates every being and every thing to this; and opposes every thing which, in the view of the selfish person, opposes him, and his selfish interest. He who is under the government of this affection, takes all to himself, and gives nothing to any other being, as if he was the greatest, the best, and only worthy and important being in the universe.

Self love is the root of all pride; or rather is pride itself, as there is no distinction to be made of which there can be any conception. Pride is self love exercised in self esteem, and desire to exalt self, &:c. Self love is blindness and delusion itself, as it is a contradiction to all truth; and is the source of all the blindness and delusions with respect to things temporal and spiritual, which have or can ever take place. This sets man against God, and his fellow creatures, and against himself, that is, against his true interest, and renders him really miserable; and prepares him to be completely miserable forever, unless it be removed. In short, there can be no kind or degree of moral depravity which has appeared among men, or of which there can be any conception, which does not consist in self love, in the various exercises and fruits of it: And where there is no selfishness, there is no sin, there can be no deviation from the law of God.

Therefore when the apostle Paul speaks of the nature of sin, and that in which he found it to consist when he came to the knowledge of it, he comprehends it all in selfishness, or coveting, which is the same. He says, "I had not known sin, but by the law: For I had not known lust, except the law had said, Thou shalt not covet." He refers to the tenth command in the decalogue, "Thou shalt not covet thy neighbour's house, &c. nor any thing that is thy neighbour's." Coveting that to ourselves, which belongs to others, is an exercise of self love. In this the apostle represents sin to consist; even in the inmost latent exercises of this selfishness in the heart, being the root and fountain of all sin. Agreeable to this, the same apostle, when he describes the great degree of vice and wickedness which shall take place in the last days, sets self love at the head, as the source and root of the whole. "This know also, that in the last days perilous times shall come. For men shall be lovers of their own selves; covetous, boasters, proud, &:c." [203] Any one who will attentively read over this catalogue of iniquity, will see, that every vice here mentioned, is implied in the self love which is first introduced, and is only a different modification of that which men will practise because they are lovers of their own selves: and consequently act out this self love in a variety of forms, which therefore are called by these different names.

It therefore appears, that as holiness is, in the holy scripture, reduced to one simple principle, love, and made to consist wholly in this, by which is evidently meant disinterested good will to being in general, capable of happiness, with all that affection necessarily included in this; so sin is there represented as consisting in the simple principle or exercise of self love, which, in its own nature, comprehends all sin, every exercise and affection which is a deviation from the divine law; and is directly and wholly opposed to that love which this law requires. [204]

It has been said, that every degree of self love cannot be sin, but must be lawful and right, since it is reasonable that we should have some regard, at least, for ourselves, and desire and seek our own interest and happiness, not inconsistent with that of others; and were there no self love, men could not be influenced by promises and threatening; and there would be no propriety in these, of which the Bible is full. Besides, the command to love our neighbour supposes and enjoins self love. "Thou shalt love thy neighbour as thyself." Here the love of our own selves is mentioned as the stated measure, by which our love to others is to be regulated. If we are forbid to exercise any degree of self love, the command is inconsistent, and comes to nothing.

Upon this it may be observed, that a person may have and exercise a proper regard for himself, and desire and seek his own interest and happiness, without the least degree of the self love which is opposed to disinterested benevolence, or which is not implied in it. The person who exercises disinterested good will to being in general must have a proper and proportionable regard to himself; as he belongs to being in general, and is included in it, as a necessary part of it. It is impossible he should love being in general, or universal being, and not love himself; because he is included in universal being. And the more he has of a disinterested, universal benevolence, and the stronger his exercises of it are, the more regard will he have to his own being, and the more fervently will he desire and seek his own interest and happiness. But here it must be observed, that he will not desire and seek it as his own, or because it is his own interest, considered as distinct and detached from the interest of the whole, or of being in general; but as included in it. Thus disinterested benevolence to being in general loves our neighbour as ourselves; in which there is nothing selfish, but ourselves are loved as included in the general object of disinterested love. The least degree of selfish love necessarily destroys all due proportion, and sets up a selfish interest detached from that of others, and injurious to the whole. It is in the very nature of it an enemy to the harmony and happiness of the whole, and breaks in upon it, and tends to spread confusion and evil through the whole, in opposition to universal benevolence; and is inconsistent with our loving our neighbour as ourselves; but, by the supposition, loves self and nothing else. Hence it appears that the command, "Thou shalt love thy neighbour as thyself," excludes and forbids all self love, or selfishness, and enjoins that disinterested love to the whole, which necessarily includes a proper and proportionable love and regard to our own existence and interest, as implied in that of the whole. And in this view of the matter, it appears that he who has disinterested benevolence to the whole may be influenced by promises and threatenings, and is as proper a subject of them, and more so, than the most selfish person in the world. [205]

Thus it appears from scripture, and the reason and nature of things, that the sin which entered into the world by one man, the father of the human race, and has spread to all his children, by which they are totally corrupted, and involved in guilt and ruin, consists wholly in self love. Nothing but that which has the nature of selfishness is sin; and this is in its own nature, and in every degree, a transgression of the law of God, and contrary to true holiness. It is useful and important that we should have this scriptural idea of holiness and sin, as it will put us under advantage to know how far we ourselves are sinful, or what is sin in us, as well as to judge of the moral corruption of mankind.

IMPROVEMENT

I. IN the part the devil acted in seducing man, and leading him off into rebellion against God, may be seen the nature and tendency of sin, and what is the disposition or inclination of the sinner. When Satan became a rebel against his Maker, his inclination and desire was to disappoint and dethrone him, if possible, and to spread rebellion through the universe; and he wished to have every creature that existed, or ever should exist, to join with him, and do as he had done: And his sinning had a mighty tendency to this, and did accomplish it, so far as his influence reached, and had its natural effect. He actually drew off into rebellion with him myriads of angels. And had it been in his power, and had not God prevented it, he would have drawn them all off from obedience to God. He wished to extinguish all holiness from the universe. He acted out this disposition, this enmity against God and man, and all holiness, in seducing man, and spreading sin and ruin through this world.

Sin in man is of the same nature and kind with the sin of the devil, by which man is inclined to do as he does, and in which man has joined with him, to desire and pursue the same thing which he seeks; and it tends to produce the same effects, the sin and ruin of the whole universe. Therefore our Saviour says to the Jews, "Ye are of your father, the devil, and the lusts of your father ye will do." [206] That is, ye are of the same disposition with the devil, and desire and pursue the same things. "He that committeth sin is of the devil." [207] Here we are to look to see the nature and tendency of sin, when acted out, and the inclination and choice of the sinner; and to learn our own character as sinners, in which we imitate the devil, and exercise the same desires and lusts of self-love and pride, in which his first rebellion consisted; and in which consists his obstinate perseverance in disobedience, and all his attempts against God and man. This, if properly considered, will lead us to view ourselves, and the character of mankind, in a much worse light than that in which men generally view themselves; and will serve to discover the infinite evil of all sin, as tending, and desiring and attempting, to spread unbounded mischief, and infinite natural evil through the universe. The consequence is, that the sinner deserves to be punished with infinite evil, or everlasting destruction.

Doubtless one reason why it was so ordered that one, the first act of sin, should spread total corruption and ruin over all the countless myriads of the human race, was to discover to all intelligent creatures the evil nature and tendency of sin. This constitution, as has been observed, was only ordaining that sin should, in this respect, have its natural course, and spread, agreeable to the inclination and desire of the first transgressor, through all his posterity; And hereby the evil there is in every act of sin, is held up to the view of men and angels, discovering to all that it deserves the endless punishment threatened in the divine law.

Let no one then condemn Satan for his rebellion and persisting in sinning, while he justifies himself, or even thinks better of himself, who is doing the same thing, and rendering himself like the devil, and joining with him, and justifying him, by every act of sin of which he is guilty. Nor let any of the children of Adam object to the constitution which connects their sin with his; nor complain of the sin of their common father, while they are disposed to excuse and justify themselves in that conduct by which they consent to his sinning as he did, and imitate him, and desire to spread sin and ruin as far as he has done, and would do it, were it in their power; and which they are attempting to do, even in making the objection. Rather let all condemn, and humble themselves in the sight of the Lord, for their joining with Satan in rebellion, and imitating and justifying Adam in his transgression, and doing what they could to spread and perpetuate disobedience. And let all adore and give glory to almighty power, infinite wisdom and goodness to that glorious Being, who does in any degree counteract sin and the sinner; and in any instance prevent the just and natural consequences of it; and turn all to his own glory, and the greatest good of his kingdom.

II. From the history of the apostasy of man, and the way in which sin entered into the world, we are warned of the folly and danger of disregarding divine revelation, and giving the least heed to any assertions or suggestions which are contrary to the revealed will of God, or which are not warranted by that.

The first suggestion which Satan made was contrary to that which God had declared; and by giving heed to that, sin was introduced, and has brought sin and ruin on all mankind. And this same deceiver and father of lies has at all times since, and does now, in various ways, attempt to lead men to disregard what God has said in his word, and believe those things which are not warranted by it, but are really contrary to those divine oracles. And so far as he succeeds, he gets the advantage of men; and in this way they fall into his snare, and are led captive by him. This is the continued source of all the sinful practices in the world, and of all the delusions and false religions which take place among mankind.

With what care and circumspection does it become us to examine every doctrine and practice which is proposed or suggested to us as right and true; and to reject with resolution and abhorrence every thing of this kind, which is not agreeable to the oracles of God! Upon this law and testimony we ought to keep our eye, with constant, painful care and study, to understand it, and a readiness immediately to reject every thing which is not warranted by that, as dangerous delusion, from whatever quarter, or by whomsoever it may be proposed, and however plausible and tempting it may be.

III. The particular suggestion of Satan, contrary to revealed truth, by which he tempted our mother Eve to transgress, is worthy to be considered as a warning to us. "The serpent said unto the woman, Ye shall not surely die." By hearkening to this lie of Satan she fell into sin and ruin. We may be sure the devil has been ever since urging this same lie upon men, as the great and principal delusion by which he holds them secure in his snare, and tempts them to go on boldly in rebellion. Those who are persuaded to believe this lie, which Satan tries by all means and ways in his power to propagate, are fallen into his snare; and in their attempts to promote it, they are his instruments and servants; and he influences them to the utmost of his power to make their bands strong, and to heighten their confidence, that they shall have peace, and no evil shall come upon them, though they walk after the imagination of their own hearts: And they have his assistance in searching and studying the scriptures to find passages, and to pervert them, so as to strengthen themselves and others in this dangerous delusion, by which their hearts are steeled against any impression by the many awful threatenings in the word of God.

And where he cannot persuade men to believe there is no future punishment for impenitent sinners, he does all he can to keep them stupid and thoughtless, with respect to it, and make them feel and act as if they were exposed to no such punishment; and to flatter themselves with peace and safety, until sudden destruction cometh upon them. This is one special mean of holding men in security and ease in sin, in the christian world. And Satan has great advantage against mankind, in promoting this delusion, because it is agreeable to their hearts, and it is the nature of sin to be pleased with it, and to make men stupid and unbelieving with respect to the reality and dreadfulness of future punishment, and the danger in which they are of falling into it.

Let all beware of this delusion, by which sin first entered into the world, and which has been the mean of thousands and millions falling into that endless punishment, which they have not believed, or not realized, that it would ever come. "Though hand join in hand, the wicked shall not be unpunished." "Wo unto the wicked, it shall be ill with him; for the reward of his hands shall be given him: Who shall be punished with everlasting destruction from the presence of the Lord, and the glory of his power."

Let the ministers of the gospel, the watchmen on the walls of Jerusalem, not be silent, but cry aloud, and warn the wicked, to whom God has said, Ye shall surely die; and sound an alarm to all the secure in their sins, if by any means, they may be awakened from their deadly sleep, and delivered from their delusions, and fly from the wrath to come, before it shall be too late.

IV. This subject leads us to see and reflect upon the infinitely guilty, miserable and lost state into which mankind are fallen by sin. They begin to sui, as soon as they are capable of moral exercise; and by one sinful exercise, were they guilty of no more, they undo themselves forever, if not delivered by mere sovereign grace. All their exercises are wrong and sinful, by which they are growing more and more guilty and ill deserving; and all the light they have, and the favours they enjoy, being abused, render them unspeakably criminal. They are so wholly inclined to sin, and with such strength and obstinacy of heart, fixed in enmity against God and his law, that they stand ready to oppose all means and every method that can be taken and used to recover them from sin and reclaim them; and if left to themselves, will only wax worse and worse, until they plunge into endless ruin, and intolerable misery. They are continually provoking God to cast them into

The System of Doctrines, contained in Divine Relation, Explained and Defended Volume I
everlasting destruction, on whose sovereign mercy they depend every moment, to save them from dropping into hell; and by whose forfeited grace, and almighty power alone, they can be recovered to repentance, and from sin and infinite evil. And at the same time they are flattering themselves in their evil ways, involved in the darkness and delusion of sin; loving darkness, and hating the light, and cannot be told in what an infinitely evil and dangerous case they are; that is, cannot be made to believe it, though they be told, and are ready to hate their best and only friends, and look upon them as their enemies; while they love their enemies, who are doing all they can to destroy them forever. But who can describe, or fully conceive the sinful, miserable, ruined condition into which mankind are fallen; and in which we all naturally are, and shall be forever, unless delivered by infinite, sovereign grace!

Footnotes:

177. Rev. xii. 9, 14, 15.--xx. 2.
178. Ezekiel xxxiii. 12, 13.
179. 1 Kings ii. 37.
180. Romans v. 12, &c.
181. It is granted that all mankind might have been in a state of apostasy, had not this been the consequence of the sin of Adam, and connected with this, and made certain by it; but that they should be considered and treated as in such a state, and a Saviour be provided for them, and ordered to be preached and offered to them, when nothing had taken place with which this was connected, and by which it was rendered certain, appears to be highly improper and inconsistent.
182. Romans iii. 9, &c.
183. Romans v. 12, &c.
184. Page 247, &c.
185. See chap. iv. p. 129, 130, &c.
186. Gen. viii. 21.
187. Psalm li. 5.
188. Psalm lviii. 3.
189. John iii. 6.
190. What has been meant by this distinction may be agreeable to the truth, if by actual sin be meant the expression and acting out of the depravity or sinful disposition of the heart, in distinction from the sin of the heart, while not thus expressed. But the latter is as really actual sin, as the former. Therefore there is no ground for calling one actual sin, and the other not. Original sin is that total moral depravity, which takes place in the hearts of all the children of Adam, in consequence of his apostasy, which consists in exercise or act, as really as any sin can do, and therefore cannot be distinguished from actual sin.
191. Gen. vi. 5.
192. Chap. viii. 21.
193. Eccl. ix. 3.
194. Jer. xvii. 9.
195. Romans iii. 10, &c.
196. Mark ix. 41.
197. John xiv. 16, 17.
198. John iii. 3.
199. 1 John iv. 7, 8.
200. That those appearances and things which are found in mankind in general, which have been by some considered as true virtue and real goodness, and produced as an argument that mankind are not wholly depraved, are not true virtue, is proved in President Edwards's Dissertation on the nature of true virtue.
201. Psalm li.
202. 1 Cor. xiii.
203. 2 Timothy iii. 1-5.
204. Our Lord says, all which the law requires is love, therefore holiness consisted wholly in this (Matt. xxii. 37-40) And St. Paul says, "He that loveth another hath fulfilled the law; therefore love is the fulfilling of the law." (Rom. 13) And, as has been observed, he represents sin as consisting in the coveting what belongs to others, which is forbidden in the tenth command; which is self love. The love required, gives all to being in general, and reserves and desires nothing to self, as self, or as an object distinct from universal being. The self love forbidden, covets and seeks all to self, as such, as distinguished from being in general, and opposite to it. It gives nothing to any other being, but, so far as its grasp can reach, takes and holds all good to self, as such, and as opposed to every other being; and seeks to subordinate every other being and thing to his own self, will and interest. The former is required as that in which all holiness consists. The latter is forbidden, as the

root and essence of all sin.

205. This subject is more particularly considered in "An Inquiry into the Nature of True Holiness," published in the year 1773, and reprinted at New-York, in the year 1791 To which the reader is referred, who shall desire to see it more fully discussed.

206. John viii. 41.

207. 1 John iii. 8.

PART II

CHAPTER I - CONCERNING THE REDEMPTION OF FALLEN, LOST MAN, BY JESUS CHRIST

Some general Observations on the Redemption of Man.

1. WE depend wholly on divine revelation for all we know concerning the redemption of man. By this only we learn, that it is possible that man may be recovered from a state of sin and ruin; and that God has determined to redeem man, and is prosecuting this design. And by this only we can know what is implied in this, and what is the way and manner in which it is effected.

Man might justly be left to endless destruction, without any remedy, having fallen under the curse of the divine law, which is righteous and good. And that he could be saved consistent with this law, and the maintenance and honour of divine government, could not be known by any creature. And if it were known that it was possible for man to be delivered and saved, consistent with the honour of the divine law and government, it could not be known that God would see fit to do it, until he revealed his will and design in this matter. God was infinitely far from being under any obligations to show favour to man; it depended upon his sovereign will to determine whether man should be redeemed, or not: and if he were redeemed, it must be by the most free, undeserved sovereign mercy. Therefore that God Would show any mercy to sinners, could not be known by men or angels; or that this was possible, consistent with the holy law of God, and with wisdom and righteousness. This was hid in God from all creatures, until he was pleased to reveal his design. This indeed was done immediately upon the apostasy of man; and this important and glorious purpose of God has been opening more and more from that time to this: Which has been suited to excite and increase the attention and wonder of men and angels, through all ages.

In this revelation is comprehended what God has made known by declarations, promises and predictions in the holy scriptures, and by his providence, in ordering the events recorded in the historical part of scripture, and accomplishing many things which he has promised or predicted; by which the declarations, promises and prophecies are opened and explained, and light is thrown upon this grand design; while the word of God, and his providence in governing the world, and ordering all events, do most exactly agree and illustrate each other.

And the providence of God, as it respects the natural world, considered by itself, unconnected with his word in the holy scriptures, in preserving mankind, and giving them ease and health, and so many comforts and good things in this life, carries a language in it, and is a kind and degree of revelation of the disposition and will of God, declaring not only the being of God, and his universal and particular providence, and care of all his creatures; but also that he is good and kind to man in a sense and degree which is inconsistent with his being cast off without hope; and is a standing evidence to all who have proper discerning, that God is propitious to the human race; and that there is some way in which he may be reconciled, and show mercy to sinners. This seems to be the sentiment expressed by St. Paul in the following words. "Who in times past suffered all nations to walk in their own ways. Nevertheless he left not himself without witness, in that he did good, and gave us rain from heaven, and fruitful seasons, filling our hearts with food and gladness." [208]

The witness or testimony of which the apostle here speaks, which was given to mankind in general by God, in his doing them good, and which was constantly held up in divine providence, was not merely of his existence, but of his kind care of man, and his readiness to be reconciled to him, without particularly pointing out the way and method in which this could be effected. This was a sufficient ground to excite their hope, and induce them to seek after him, and make all possible inquiries and search after the way in which they might obtain mercy; and to find what was necessary in order to their being saved. And God has so ordered the situation and bounds of mankind, both under the Mosaic and christian dispensation, that all who would take proper notice of this witness in divine providence, and improve it as they ought, and might do, might come to the knowledge of the truth They who lived before the incarnation of Christ could not fail of coming to the knowledge of the revelation given to the Israelites. And all mankind who have lived since might have come to the knowledge of the truth revealed by Christ and his apostles. This is asserted by St. Paul. "And hath made of one blood all nations of men, to dwell in all the face of the earth; and hath determined the times before appointed, and the bounds of their habitation; that they should seek the Lord, if haply they might feel after him, and find him." [209]

Many who pay no regard to a written revelation have supposed that the dictates of reason, without any particular revelation from God, did assure them that he must pardon and receive to favour every penitent sinner, as it would be inconsistent with his goodness not to do it; therefore mankind want no other revelation from God to give them a certainty of this. But they have never been able to give any satisfactory evidence of this to those who properly attend to the matter; and what they call reason, appears to be presumption, when examined by impartial enlightened reason. There is nothing within the reach of the reason and knowledge of creatures that can afford the least evidence that God will pardon the penitent sinner, merely because he repents; or that this could be done consistent with the most perfect moral government; but the contrary appears most reasonable, viz. that the repentance of the criminal is not sufficient to give him any claim to forgiveness. And it is very evident and certain that such an opinion is inconsistent with real repentance; and that while a sinner thinks that his repentance will give a claim to forgiveness and favour, he is a stranger to true repentance, and never will repent, until he gives it up. Nor can he have the least evidence that any of mankind will ever repent, if left to themselves, and are not the subjects of those divine influences to which they have no claim, and which they have no reason to conclude God will grant. But this matter will be made more evident as we proceed on the subject of redemption.

II. Redemption does not extend to all sinful, fallen creatures, but many are left to suffer the just consequence of their rebellion, in everlasting punishment. No mercy has been extended to the fallen angels, of whom there are vast numbers. "For God spared not the angels that sinned, but cast them down to hell, and hath reserved them in everlasting chains of darkness, unto the judgment of the great day," [210] when they are to receive their final sentence to eternal punishment. [211] And it is expressly and repeatedly declared in divine revelation that a part of mankind shall also be punished forever. To which they shall be sentenced, together with the fallen angels, at the judgment of the great day. [212]

This distinction, made between the fallen angels and mankind, and in favour of the latter, is not because man might not have been justly left to eternal ruin, or because he was less unworthy of mercy, and not so ill deserving, as the apostate angels; but for reasons in the view of infinite wisdom, which may, at least the most of them, be wholly out of our sight at present. As light and knowledge shall increase in the churchy the wisdom of God in this dispensation of sovereign grace will be more and more seen; and there will be an increasing discovery of this to angels and the redeemed in the eternal kingdom of God.

We are also certain that infinite wisdom saw it best that redemption should not extend to all mankind, so that every one of the human race should be actually saved, though we were not able to see the reason of this, and the contrary should appear to us to be most wise and best; for we are infinitely far from being competent judges in this case; and there is the highest reason that we should acquiesce, and be satisfied with the declaration and conduct of the infinitely wise and benevolent Being, who is able, and to whom it belonged to determine whether all the human race should be saved or not. For we are sure that it is determined perfectly right, and that all mankind could not be actually redeemed, consistent with the good of the whole, or consistent with wisdom and goodness.

It also belongs to the supreme, infinitely wise and benevolent Being to determine what number and proportion of mankind shall be saved, and fix upon every individual person, since all this depends upon him, and he has a right to do as he pleases, and he only knows what is most wise and best. "Hath not the potter power over the clay, of the same lump to make one vessel unto honour, and another unto dishonour?"

We are not in express words of revelation informed what proportion of mankind shall be saved, whether the greater or less part of them, on the whole. But perhaps more is revealed with respect to this than has been supposed, and which is contrary to what has been generally thought to be asserted in the scriptures. It has been thought by many, that when Christ says, "Strait is the gate, and narrow is the way which leadeth unto life, and few there be that find it. Many are called, but few chosen. Fear not little flock," he declares that but few, a very small part of mankind, shall be saved. But when we attend to these words of Christ, we shall find that they are spoken of the then present time; and nothing is asserted concerning that which shall take place in future ages; and therefore have no relation to the point before us, and determine nothing about it. When this question was put to him, "Lord, are there few that shall be saved?" He did not think proper to answer it then, by expressly affirming or denying; but only said, that many should not be saved; and improved this truth to excite all to secure their own salvation, without delay: Which is consistent with there being many more saved than lost.

The System of Doctrines, contained in Divine Relation, Explained and Defended Volume I

When we attend to the many predictions of the flourishing, greatness and extent of the church and kingdom of Christ in the last days, so as to fill the whole world, when "the kingdom and dominion, and the greatness of the kingdom under the whole heaven, shall be given to the people of the saints of the Most High;" and are assured that this state of prosperity shall continue, at least a thousand years, we shall find no reason to conclude that but few of mankind will be saved, in comparison with those who shall perish; but see ground to believe that the number of the former will far exceed that of the latter. [213] But were there nothing revealed by which we could determine any thing with respect to this, we might well rest satisfied that God, who is infinitely wise and good, has fixed the number of those who shall be saved, and of those who shall not be saved, so as exactly to answer the best end, and promote the greatest general good; and may be as certain that many of mankind will perish forever, as we can be that the Bible is a revelation from God, since this is there so expressly, abundantly, and in such a variety of ways declared and established.

III. The Redemption of man is the greatest instance of the exercise and manifestation of the benevolence, or the love and goodness of God, that ever took place, or that ever will. It is the greatest possible exercise and display of divine benevolence; in which there is the best and most ample ground and scope for the highest increasing and endless discovery of the love and goodness of the infinitely benevolent Being.

The benevolence of the Deity is exercised, and appears in all his works; but in the work of redemption is the fullest, most perfect and bright display of the divine love, as all the works of God have reference to this as their result and end, in which his design in all is manifested. This is every where set in this light in the Holy Scripture. "God so loved the world, that he gave his only begotten Son, that whosoever believeth in him should not perish, but have everlasting life." [214] God is love. In this was manifested the love of God towards us, that God sent his only begotten Son into the world, that we might live through him. Herein is love, not that we have loved God, but that he loved us, and sent his Son to be the propitiation for our sins. Behold! What manner of love the Father hath bestowed upon us, that we should be called the sons of God." [215]

Thus the sacred oracles celebrate the work of redemption as the highest and most remarkable instance of divine love, and direct us there, to behold it acted out in the highest degree, and to the greatest advantage, to be seen and admired by creatures; as an inexhaustible and endless object of gratitude and praise.

The reason and propriety of this representation in divine revelation, and that the work of redemption is infinitely the greatest instance and display of divine benevolence, will in some measure appear, if the following things be well considered.

1. Benevolence exercised in the bestowment of favour, is greater or less, according to the greater or less unworthiness and ill desert of those who are the objects of the benevolence. If those on whom good is bestowed, be worthy or deserving, the granting that good or benefit, is really paying a debt, and is an act of justice. And though benevolence may be exercised in doing this, as it is contrary to benevolence not to give what is deserved; yet the goodness exercised in this case is not so apparently disinterested; nor does it require so great a degree of goodness, as it does to bestow favours on the unworthy and ill deserving. The latter is free grace, sovereign, disinterested goodness: the former may not be so. And the more unworthy and ill deserving they are to whom favour is shown, the greater is the degree of benevolence exercised in granting the favour: For it requires a greater degree of benevolence to shew kindness to those who deserve no good, but evil, than to be kind to those who have no ill desert; and the degree of benevolence exercised in granting favour, is in proportion to the degree of ill desert of those who are the subjects of it.

In this respect the divine benevolence appears to be unbounded and wonderful in the redemption of man. Man, by rebellion against his Maker, is become infinitely unworthy and ill deserving, as he is infinitely criminal. And he does not only sin in one, or a few instances, but is wholly a rebel, and become a total enemy to God. Mankind have taken up arms against Heaven, and they are universally and constantly acting out their opposition and enmity against God, with great strength, obstinacy and violence. "Every imagination of the thoughts of man's heart is only evil continually. The heart of the sons of men is full of evil, and madness is in their heart, while they live. There is none that doeth good, no, not one. They are all gone out of the way. Their throat is an open sepulchre. The poison of asps is under their lips. Their mouth is full of cursing and bitterness. Their feet are swift to shed blood. There is no fear of God before their eyes." They will not be reclaimed from their rebellion and enmity against God by any methods that can betaken to bring them to submit and return to obedience, short of taking away their rebellious heart by almighty power immediately exerted, and creating them anew. But the more favour is shown to them, and the greater the kindness is which they receive, the more will they rebel and act against their greatest benefactor, abusing, despising, and trampling upon all his goodness to them; they being "desperately wicked," and wholly irreclaimable by any means, provoking their Maker to destroy them, to the utmost of their power. This was all seen by the omniscient Jehovah. And no benevolence short of infinite could be disposed to spare, and show favour to such infinitely criminal, ill deserving, odious, and God provoking, obstinate enemies as men were. Therefore the redemption of such creatures calls for the strongest exercise, and gives the brightest display of divine, infinite benevolence or goodness. St. Paul sets it in this light in the following words. "Scarcely for a righteous man will one die; yet, peradventure, for a good man some would even dare to die. But God commendeth his love towards us, in that while we were yet sinners, and when we were enemies, Christ died for us." [216]

2. The greater the evil is from which any one is delivered by undeserved goodness, the greater and the more perspicuous is the benevolence which is exercised in such deliverance; and the more gratitude to the benefactor is due from him who is delivered. In the case before us there is the most ample room for the exercise and display of benevolence, in this respect. Man was fallen into a state of infinite misery and wretchedness, under the curse of the divine law, which implies separation from all good and happiness, and the suffering all the evil of which he is capable, without end. This man must have suffered forever without the least mitigation or relief, had not redemption taken place. By his apostasy man was become a vassal to Satan, and his heart was wholly under the power of moral depravity, from which nothing could deliver him but the mighty arm of Omnipotence. From this complicated, infinitely evil state, every one is completely delivered, who shares in redemption by Christ. Nothing short of the exertion of infinite, omnipotent, all sufficient benevolence, is sufficient to rescue man from this infinitely guilty, miserable state.

3. The exercise and expression of benevolence is strong and great in proportion to the degree of positive good and happiness which is bestowed.

Deliverance from evil is a benefit, and may be called a negative good; and this benefit is great in proportion to the degree of evil from which deliverance is granted. And the degree of benevolence expressed in such deliverance is great, in proportion to the greatness of the evil from which the miserable subject is delivered. This has been considered under the foregoing particular. What is now brought into view is the degree of positive good which is bestowed by benevolence. A less degree of benevolence may procure and give a small benefit, which is insufficient to prompt to bestow a much greater benefit. Therefore the greater the benefit is, which is given, the greater is the exercise and manifestation of that goodness which wills and procures it. In the redemption of man, the positive good procured and bestowed is infinitely great, being great and increasing in degree, and in duration endless. It is everlasting life, in the most happy and honourable circumstances possible. Nothing short of the infinite love of the omnipotent, all sufficient jehovah, can give such infinite good to infinitely ill deserving rebels. In this view, infinite benevolence is exercised and most conspicuously displayed in the redemption of man. Inspired with the view and sense of this, St. John exclaims, "Behold, what manner of love the Father hath bestowed upon us, that we should be called the sons of God! Beloved, now are we the sons of God, and it doth not yet appear what we shall be: But we know that, when he shall appear, we shall be like him." In the redemption of man an unbounded field is opened in which divine benevolence is displayed to the best advantage, and God "fulfils all the good pleasure of his goodness," in bestowing infinite happiness and glory on the redeemed; unspeakably greater than man could have enjoyed, had he not sinned, and rendered himself infinitely unworthy of the least favour; and infinitely more "to the praise of his rich and glorious grace."

4. The greater the difficulties and obstacles are, which must be removed or surmounted, in order to bestow a favour, and the greater the expense, cost and trouble, which are necessary, in order to procure it, the greater and more strong is the exercise of goodness in procuring: and bestowing the benefit. This is so evident that no proof or illustration is necessary.

There were difficulties and impediments which must be removed, and such infinite expense and sufferings were necessary, in order to redeem man, which could not be effected by any thing short of infinite power, wisdom and goodness. Man had fallen under the curse of the righteous and perfect law of God. It was inconsistent with rectoral righteousness, and infinite goodness; to set aside, or disregard this law, in favour of rebellious man, so as to pardon and receive him to favour, without paying any regard to the execution of the curse threatened, in any sense or degree. It was of infinite importance that the law and moral government should be maintained, and the curse threatened, properly and fully executed. This put man out of the reach of divine infinite goodness, Unless some expedient could be found, some way be devised, in which the law of God might be regarded and maintained, and the penalty of it executed, consistent with pardoning and shewing favour to man. This rendered it necessary that God himself, in the second person of the adorable Trinity, should assume human nature into a personal union, so as to form one person, who is both God and man; and that this person should, in the human nature, be made under the law, and support and honour it by obeying the precepts, and suffering the curse of it, in the room and stead of man. In this way only could man be delivered from the curse of the law, and obtain complete redemption, consistent with divine truth, rectoral righteousness, wisdom and goodness. Had not all this been necessary in order to redeem man, and might he be saved consistent with the divine law, without such a Mediator, doing and suffering all this, the love and grace exercised in redeeming and saving him would have been infinitely less, and as nothing compared with that benevolence which is expressed in the incarnation, humiliation, death and sufferings of the Son of God, which are necessarily implied in this redemption. God the Father giving his Son, and the Son of God giving himself, to suffer an ignominious, cruel death, and be made a curse, that sinners, his enemies, might be redeemed from the curse, and have eternal life, is an infinitely greater gift, and higher exercise and expression of disinterested love or benevolence, than merely to save man from eternal destruction, and give him endless life, could the latter be done without the former.

This is the light in which the holy scripture sets this matter. There this is represented as the greatest, most remarkable and glorious instance and display of divine benevolence, that God has given his Son to die, and Christ has given himself unto death as a ransom, to deliver sinners from hell, and procure eternal life for them. "God so loved the world, that he gave his only begotten Son, that whosoever believeth in him should not perish, but have everlasting life." [217] "God commendeth (displays in the most amiable, and brightest light) his love towards us, in that while we were yet sinners, Christ died for us." [218] "Hereby perceive we the love of God, because he laid down his life for us. In this was manifested the love of God towards us, because that God sent his only begotten Son into the world, that we might live through him. Herein is love! Not that we loved God, but that he loved us, and sent his Son to be a propitiation for our sins." [219]

5. There is something yet farther necessary in order to the salvation of men. Though by the atonement which Christ has made by his death, a way is open for the pardon and salvation of sinners, consistent with rectoral righteousness, and the honour of the divine law; yet man is so obstinate in his rebellion, and such an enemy to God, that he cannot be persuaded to embrace the gospel; but will dislike and oppose Christ and the way of salvation by him, unless his heart be renewed by the omnipotent influences of the holy Spirit. Christ has therefore obtained by his obedience and sufferings, the holy Spirit to be given unto men to recover them from their total depravity, and form their hearts to true holiness. This is an infinite gift. It is no less than God giving himself to men, in the third person of the adorable Trinity; uniting himself to them, and dwelling in them, as the principle and author of all their holiness and happiness forever. Did man need no such gift and grace, the divine goodness and beneficence in his redemption would be unspeakably less, and would not be so gloriously displayed, as now they are. In order to redeem man, God not only delivers him from infinite wo, and gives him infinite happiness and glory, when man in himself is infinitely odious, guilty and ill deserving; but, in order to this, gives himself repeatedly, and in different ways. He gave himself to die on the cross, a ransom for man, to be a propitiation for their sins. The Father gave the Son, and the Son gave himself. He gives himself also in the third person of the Trinity, the Holy Ghost, in renewing and sanctifying the redeemed, and dwelling in them forever. The Mediator said, "I will pray the Father, and he shall give you another Comforter, that he may abide with you forever; even the Spirit of truth." [220] And God, in a Trinity of Persons, gives himself to the redeemed as their infinite, everlasting portion and happiness. Thus divine benevolence is exhausted, and gives all away: Infinite goodness can give no more. God gives himself, and all he has for the redemption of man! This is, in the highest degree, an "unspeakable gift."

6. This benevolence and goodness appears greater, and is more illustrious in the salvation of man, in that all is given freely, without money and without price, as man is infinitely unworthy of it; and, as such, receives this redemption as a free gift, the whole being offered and given to every one who is willing to receive it. Men obtain an interest in this salvation, not by works of righteousness which they do; not by any worthiness in them, or by any thing they offer, as the price of the divine favour; but by believing in the Mediator, receiving the record which God has given concerning his Son, and accepting salvation, as it is freely offered and given, trusting wholly in Christ, and receiving all from him, as a free gift, to such who are not only wholly without any desert of the least favour; but are infinitely odious and ill deserving. This is to be saved by faith, by which the free grace of God in the salvation of sinners is exercised and displayed to the highest degree, as is abundantly represented in divine revelation. St. Paul insists much upon this. He having proved from scripture that all men are sinners, consequently infinitely ill deserving, says, "Therefore by the deeds of the law there shall no flesh be justified in his sight; for by the law is the knowledge of sin. But now the righteousness of God, without the law, is manifested, even the righteousness of God, which is by faith of Jesus Christ unto all, and upon all them that believe. Being justified freely by his grace, through the redemption that is in Jesus Christ: Whom God hath set forth a propitiation, through faith in his blood. Now to him that worketh, (that is, in order to offer his works as the price of God's favour,) is the reward not reckoned of grace, but of debt. But to him that worketh not, (that is, has nothing to recommend him, and acknowledges he has done nothing by which he deserves the divine favour, more than any other man,) but believeth on him

that justifieth the ungodly, his faith is counted for righteousness. Therefore it is of faith, that it might be by grace." [221] "By grace are ye saved, through faith, and that not of yourselves, it is the gift of God." [222]

The above particulars, put together, and taken into one view, serve to illustrate the observation, that the redemption of man is the highest instance of the exercise of the love of God, in which divine, infinite benevolence has an object equal to itself, and is acted out and displayed to the highest degree, and best advantage to be seen and celebrated by the redeemed and all holy creatures, with increasing views and happiness forever and ever. In the redemption of man, the infinitely benevolent Jehovah, "fulfils all the good pleasure of his goodness, [223] and mercy is built up forever." [224] In this work God shows his glory by causing all his goodness to be displayed before the redeemed; while his name is proclaimed and celebrated. "The Lord, the Lord God, merciful and gracious, long suffering, and abundant in goodness, keeping mercy for thousands, forgiving iniquity and transgression and sin." [225] This goodness, this love of God, is in scripture celebrated as great love. "But God, who is rich in mercy, for the great love, wherewith he loved us, &c. Love which passeth knowledge." [226] It is called the riches, the exceeding riches of his grace. "In whom we have redemption through his blood, the forgiveness of sins, according to the riches of his grace. And hath raised us up together, and made us sit together in heavenly places, in Christ Jesus. That in the ages to come, he might show the exceeding riches of his grace, in his kindness towards us through Jesus Christ." [227]

The love of God is exercised in the redemption of man in its infinite strength, in overcoming difficulties and obstacles infinitely great, which were in the way of the exercise of it towards man, and opposed it; in delivering from infinite evil, and giving him infinite good. This benevolence is infinite mercy and compassion to the infinitely miserable. It is exceeding rich, free and sovereign grace, which gives such deliverance, such salvation, not only to the undeserving, but infinitely guilty, vile and ill deserving.

IV. This design and work, the redemption of man, has been gradually introduced and opened from the first apostasy to the coming of Christ, and from that time down to this day; and will be carried on until it shall be completed, at the end of the world, and the day of judgment.

Every thing, and all events which took place in the world, from the beginning of it, during four thousand years, were preparatory to the coming and incarnation of the Redeemer; while other ends, respecting redemption, were in view, and answered. And since that event, and the resurrection and exaltation of Christ to the throne of his kingdom, what has taken place is to be considered as the first fruits of redemption, and preparatory to much greater things, which are yet to take place in the accomplishment of this great work, which will not be completed till the day of judgment. This has been represented by our Saviour in a number of similitudes, such as the following. "The kingdom of heaven is like to a grain of mustard seed, which a man took and sowed in his field; which indeed is the least of all seeds; but when it is grown, it is the greatest among herbs, and becometh a tree: So that the birds of the air come and lodge in the branches thereof. He spoke another parable. The kingdom of heaven is like unto leaven, which a woman took and hid in three measures of meal, till the whole was leavened." [228] "And he said. So is the kingdom of God, as if a man should cast seed into the ground, and should sleep, and rise night and day, and the seed should spring and grow up, he knoweth not how. For the earth bringeth forth fruit of herself, first the blade, then the ear, after that the full corn in the ear: But when the fruit is brought forth, immediately he putteth in the sickle, because the harvest is come." [229]

V. The work of redemption is the greatest and most glorious work of God, and, indeed, the sum and end of all his works.

This is abundantly evident from divine revelation; which revelation itself originated from this design, and has been formed and given to man, in order to promote and accomplish it. It is of no importance or worth, any farther than it answers ends which respect the redemption of man. This asserts that the new creation, by which is meant the work of redemption, or the church of the redeemed, which is the New Jerusalem with the inhabitants, is so superior to the old creation, or the natural world, and so much the end of it, that the first creation shall be swallowed up and forgotten, in the existence and glory of the latter. "Behold, I create new heavens, and a new earth: And the former shall not be remembered, nor come into mind. But be you glad and rejoice forever, in that which I create: For behold, I create Jerusalem a rejoicing, and her people a joy." [230] This is most expressly asserted in the following words. "For by Him were all things created that are in heaven, and that are in earth, visible and invisible, whether they be thrones, or dominions, or principalities, or powers: All things were created by Him, and for Him."

All the created universe, containing every creature and thing, visible and invisible, greater and less, are here said to be created for Christ, considered as God, Man, and Mediator, the Redeemer of man; for in that character and capacity he is considered, described and spoken of in these words, and the context, as being "the head of the body, the church, who have redemption through his

The System of Doctrines, contained in Divine Relation, Explained and Defended Volume I
blood." For Him, as the Redeemer of the church, and for the sake of the work of redemption; for Christ, the Son of God, and his redeemed church, were all things made, and to this end they are all subordinated, in the works of creation and providence. He is therefore "appointed the heir of all things," [231] and made head over all things to the church; all things being put under his feet. [232]

It is hence most certain, that all the works of God have reference to the work of redemption, as their end, being all subordinated to this, in order to promote and perfect it, and really belong to it, as parts and appendages of it. All things are created for the sake of Christ and his church, and therefore they are all used and improved for this end in the course of divine providence; which consists in ordering and disposing all events, and using all things so as completely to answer the end for which they were made.

And that the work of Redemption is the greatest and most glorious of all the works of God, and the end of all, will be evident, if we consider what it is, and the things which it comprises. To this belong the character and works of the Mediator. There could have been no such character as this, and no such works as he has done, had there been no redemption of man. And his character, and his works, are infinitely greater and more glorious than any could have been, had not redemption taken place. There is an unspeakably greater and more illustrious display of the divine character and perfections in "God manifest in the flesh," than could have been in any other way. And to redeem the church by giving himself a ransom for it, even his life on the accursed cross; to recover man from the power of sin and Satan; to sanctify the church and make it a perfectly holy and most beautiful society, is, beyond all comparison, a greater work of power, wisdom and goodness, than creating and upholding all worlds, or the government of all possible moral worlds, exclusive of this. Therefore in this work is the proper and full display of the divine perfections, which is the highest end of all God's works.

And by the redemption of the church and the eternal kingdom of Christ, the greatest possible happiness of the creation is effected, as an eternal monument of the infinite power, wisdom and goodness of God. All intelligent creatures who are friends to God, will be, beyond expression, more holy and happy, than they could have been, had there been no such person and character as that of the Redeemer, and no redemption. Though holy angels be not redeemed, yet they behold the works of redemption, and the Redeemer with holy love, admiration and joy; and see and enjoy unspeakably more of God, than otherwise they could have done, and are happy in their activity to promote it. "Into this the angels desire to look." [233] "To the intent that now unto principalities and powers in heavenly places, might be known by the church, the manifold wisdom of God." [234] "Are they not all ministering spirits, sent forth to minister for them who shall be heirs of salvation?"[235] By this they have a song to sing which otherwise they never could have known. "Glory to God in the highest, and on earth peace, good will to men." [236]

Thus we have abundant evidence from scripture, and from the reason and nature of it, that the work of redemption is not a secondary purpose, detached from the original plan of divine operations; but is itself the first and original design and end of all the works of God, to which all things in creation and providence, in the divine purpose, have respect, and are subordinated. "Jesus Christ, the Lamb slain from the foundation of the world, was himself foreordained before the foundation of the world." [237] And all the favour, good and happiness bestowed on the church, was, by the divine purpose and decree, "given to them, in Christ Jesus, before the world began;"[238] they being "chosen in him, before the foundation of the world, according to the eternal purpose, which he purposed in Christ Jesus our Lord." [239]

IMPROVEMENT

I. We learn, particularly from the third observation, what an ample foundation is laid in the work of redemption, for the highest and endless gratitude of the redeemed.

As in the work of redemption is the highest exercise and most perfect and glorious display of divine, infinite benevolence, in delivering from infinite, deserved evil, and bestowing infinite, undeserved good and happiness; by such infinite labour, cost and suffering's of the Son of God, the redeemed are laid under infinite and endless obligations; suited to excite the highest exercise of that gratitude which consists in a proper view, sense and admiration of this benevolence and goodness of God, and in feeling and expressing their obligations to him, in eternal thanksgiving and praise. And in this a great part of the beauty, glory and happiness of the redeemed church will consist. In order to raise creatures to the highest happiness, there must not only be objects in the best manner suited to excite the exercises of benevolent and complacential love; but they must be in circumstances suited to call forth the warmest, and most sweet exercises of grateful love to him, who by his sovereign goodness has laid them under the greatest obligations. The work of redemption is in the highest degree suited to this; and the redeemed will be forever immensely more happy in the exercise of this sweet happifying love, than any creatures could have been had not the redemption of man taken place. This will be the sweet, animating subject of the new song which none but the redeemed can learn, and which they will sing with increasing delight forever. "O give thanks unto the Lord, for he is good; for his mercy endureth forever. Let the redeemed of the Lord say so." [240] They will say so forever with unceasing, growing pleasure. In this, in a great measure, the happiness of heaven will consist.

II. We also learn from the fourth particular, and what has been said to illustrate it, that they have made a great mistake, who have thought that the divine goodness and grace do not appear so great in the pardon and salvation of sinners for Christ's sake; it being obtained and procured by his suffering in their stead, and hereby making atonement for their sins; as it would, had pardon and salvation been granted without any such consideration, as that of the atonement and merits of Christ.

It appears from what has been said above, that the salvation of sinners by the obedience and sufferings of Christ, is so far from rendering the benevolence and grace of God less in saving them, that it enhances and magnifies the divine goodness to an amazing degree. Could sinners have been saved without such a Mediator, and such atonement as he has made, consistent with the honour of divine government, and the greatest good of the universe; their pardon and salvation would have required and manifested very little benevolence, compared with that which is exercised and appears in their salvation, when it could not be effected consistent with wisdom and righteousness without the humiliation, obedience and sufferings of the Son of God; as has been observed and shown above. How contrary to all reason and truth, how very absurd is it to assert or suppose, that divine grace in the salvation of men, is greatly lessened and obscured by the Son of God suffering the curse in their stead, and making atonement for them that they might be delivered and saved, consistent with rectitude and wisdom!

A number of the subjects of a certain king rebelled against him, were apprehended, and justly condemned to die for their crime. The circumstances of the case were such that they could not be pardoned consistent with the proper support of government, and the good of the kingdom, unless the king's only son, who was the most honourable and excellent person in the kingdom, and whom he loved as himself, should willingly take their place, and die in their stead. The son consented and chose to do it, in order to obtain pardon for them. The king himself made the proposal, and was well pleased with his son's readiness to die for them; and freely gave him up to the most ignominious and painful death, that he might, consistent with propriety and wisdom, pardon those rebels, who deserved themselves to die.

An equal number of the subjects of another king were condemned to a deserved death for rebellion. But the case was such that they might be pardoned and restored to favour, consistent with the support of government, and the highest good and happiness of his kingdom, without any one dying in their stead. He therefore gave them a free and full pardon, and restored them to the enjoyment of life and liberty in his kingdom.

Shall it now be asked, Which of these kings exercised and expressed the most, the highest degree of benevolence or grace towards the rebels, in pardoning and saving them from deserved death? It is presumed no . rational creature, who will properly attend to the case, can possibly hesitate a moment; but must pronounce the former to have exerted and discovered unspeakably more benevolence and goodness, than the latter; and that die latter is inconsiderable and as nothing, compared with the former.

How then can any one, in the instance before us, which is in all respects infinitely more grand, clear and striking, say or imagine there would have been more grace manifested in the pardon and salvation of sinners, if this could have taken place, without an atonement by the Son of God dying for them, and no such sufferings had been necessary! How can any man suppose this without contradicting the reason of man, and the clearest dictates and feelings of common sense!

III. How great is their guilt who slight and oppose the great and wonderful works of God in the redemption of man; who neglect this great salvation, and abuse this highest and most astonishing instance of the goodness of God! All are under this awfully aggravated guilt, who do not thankfully embrace this salvation which is freely offered to all. And this is the great and chief aggravation of all the sins of men under the gospel, that they express or imply a rejection of Jesus Christ, who has procured, and offers salvation to them; and a refusal to believe on him. Therefore he says, when the Holy Spirit reproves mankind of sin, he discovers that it all consists in unbelief, and is an expression of that, and because they believe not on him. [241] Every sin is a sin of unbelief, as it opposes the Saviour, and is a rejection of him, and in this the great and chief criminality of it does consist. Had there been no Saviour for man, and no redemption, he would be justly punished forever for his sin against God, as his rebellion deserved this infinitely great evil. But the sins of man in this case would have been as nothing compared with what their sins now are who live under the gospel, and oppose, slight and abuse all that astonishing benevolence and grace of God and the Redeemer, which is exercised and expressed in the work of redemption. The rebellion and obstinacy of a creature is aggravated and rendered more criminal by every instance and degree of benevolence and kindness exercised towards him by his Creator, as every instance of his goodness increases the obligation of the creature to love and obey him, and that in proportion to the greatness and degree of that goodness. Hence it follows that man is laid under the greatest obligations to love and obedience by redemption, and the benevolence of God exercised therein; which is by far the greatest, and most remarkable and affecting instance of love that has been shown to creatures, or of which we can have any conception; consequently an obstinate refusal to embrace this salvation, and abuse of all this goodness, is the greatest and most aggravated crime that men can commit, and swallows up all other supposeable crimes, as nothing in comparison with this.

And this discovers the great and total depravity of man, and the exceeding wickedness of the human heart, in that it has so much enmity against God and his laws, and is so hard and obstinate, as not to be won by such love and kindness; but is disposed to slight God the more for all his love, and to abuse and trample upon Christ, and all the grace discovered in the gospel. Scripture and experience join to teach us that man can do this, and that all have done it, who have had opportunity; and that all would persevere in this most aggravated wickedness, whatever methods were taken to reclaim them, did not God by his immediate, almighty power interpose, and take away the rebellious heart, and give a new obedient heart.

IV. From this subject, and particularly from the foregoing remark, we are led to reflect upon the ignorance and insensibility of persons who live under the gospel, of their greatest crime and guilt. They in general will acknowledge that they are sinners; some are led to this acknowledgment from their living and being educated where it is granted and inculcated that all men are sinners, and this confession is constantly made in public; and where particular practices, of which they know they are guilty, are considered and condemned as wrong and sinful. Others are convinced in their consciences that they are guilty of many actions which are forbidden in the Bible, and that they live in the neglect of many duties which are there commanded; and that therefore they are criminal. But few have any conviction of the evil nature of sin in general; and especially of the greatest sin, and which is the chief aggravation of all their sins, viz. their opposition to Jesus Christ, and constant abuse of the grace revealed in the gospel. Most men who live in gospel light are so far from feeling themselves guilty of any crime by not embracing the Saviour, that they have not the least idea of this, and stand ready to oppose it, and to exculpate themselves, when they are charged with it, and the magnitude of the crime is laid before them: And they cannot be brought to a proper conviction of their crime and guilt in this, by any arguments and light which may be set before them; or by all possible means that may be used with them. This leads to another inference.

V. Hence we see the reason why our great Prophet and Teacher has represented it as the work of the Holy Spirit to convince men of this sin, and cause them to be thoroughly reproved for it. He says, "And when he (the Holy Spirit) is come, he will reprove the world of sin, because they believe not on me." [242] Nothing short of the almighty agency of the Holy Spirit, renewing the heart, and forming it to true discerning in spiritual things, can produce this conviction and efficacious reproof. The criminal darkness and delusion which is essential to the reign of sin in the heart cannot be removed by any agent but the Holy Spirit giving a new heart which admits the true light, and sees and confesses the exceeding sinfulness of the human heart, this being the fountain and seat of all sin; and especially the great sin of all sins, the chief of all crimes, the sin of unbelief, in rejecting and abusing Jesus Christ, and the love and grace exhibited in him. When men have such an heart given them, they will submit to the divine reproof: confess this sin, and feel and own that they are wholly without any excuse for not believing on Christ: That in this they have been monsters of wickedness, which has been expressed in all the sins they have committed; and thus they will humble themselves in the sight of God, and fly to the Redeemer for refuge, for pardon and redemption.

Footnotes:

208. Acts xiv. 16, 17.
209. Acts xvii. 26, 27.
210. 2 Peter ii. 4.--Jude 6.
211. Matt. xxv. 41.--Rev. xx. 10.
212. Matt. XXV. 41. 46.--Rev. xx. 10, 15.--2 Thess. i. 8, 9.
213. The reader may see this more fully considered in Dr. Bellamy's discourse on the Millennium. Some attention is also paid to this point; and the reasons are suggested, why redemption does not include the salvation of all men, in "An inquiry concerning the future state of those who die in their sins." Page 182, &c.
214. John iii. 16.
215. 1 John iii. 1, 4, 8, 9, 10.
216. Rom. v. 7, 8, 10.
217. John iii. 16.

218. Rom. v. 8.
219. 1 John iii. 16. iv. 9, 10.
220. John xiv. 16, 17.
221. Rom. iii. 20, &c. iv. 4, 5, 16.
222. Eph. ii. 8.
223. 2 Thess. i. 11.
224. Psalm lxxxix. 2.
225. Exod. xxxiii. 18, 19. xxxiv. 6, 7.
226. Eph. ii. 4. iii. 19.
227. Eph. i. 7. ii. 6, 7.
228. Matt. xiii. 31, 32, 33.
229. Mark iv. 26-39.
230. Isaiah lxv. 17, 18.
231. Heb. i. 2.
232. Eph. i. 22.
233. 1 Peter i. 12.
234. Eph. iii. 10.
235. Heb i. 14.
236. Luke ii. 14.
237. 1 Peter i. 20.
238. 2 Tim. i. 9.
239. Eph. i. 4.--iii. 11.
240. Psalm cvii. 1, 2.
241. John xvi. 8, 9.
242. John xvi. 8, 9.

CHAPTER II - CONCERNING THE PERSON AND CHARACTER OF THE REDEEMER

WELL may we, with fear and trembling, enter upon this high and important subject, the person and character of the Redeemer of men. This person is so great and wonderful, that he passes knowledge; and so does his character, consequently; which is singular, and infinitely distinguished from all others, being excellent and glorious beyond conception. And yet there is no salvation for men, without a degree of true knowledge of his person and character; and such knowledge is connected with eternal life. "This is life eternal, that they might know thee, the only true God, and Jesus Christ, whom thou hast sent." [243]

He who knows Jesus Christ, the Son of God, knows God. He therefore said to one of his disciples, "Have I been so long time with you, and yet hast thou not known me? He that hath seen me, hath seen the Father." [244] The knowledge of Jesus Christ is the sum of all christian knowledge, and includes the whole of true divinity. Hence St. Paul says to christians at Corinth, "I determined not to know any thing among you, save Jesus Christ crucified." [245] And again, "Yea, and I count all things but loss, for the excellency of the knowledge of Christ Jesus my Lord: That I may know him." [246] The apostle Peter exhorts christians to strive to make advances, and to increase in the knowledge of this person. "Grow in grace, and in the knowledge of our Lord and Saviour Jesus Christ." [247] This is an endless theme, an inexhaustible subject, which the redeemed will study and explore forever, and will grow and increase in the knowledge of this boundless, glorious, and most entertaining object, with unspeakable and ever fresh delight and joy, without any end. Happy are they who with St. Paul have the true revelation of Jesus Christ; it will lead them on, in the only path of wisdom, to endless stores of knowledge and happiness; when they shall be where he is, and behold his glory: dwelling in the New Jerusalem, whereof the Son of God, the Lamb, shall shine forever with increasing lustre, and be the light thereof. But they who have not the true knowledge of Christ are exposed to run into error and fatal delusions respecting this person, and while they profess to acknowledge and honour him, really deny and reject him. This was the case with the Jews, when the Son of God was in the flesh on earth. "For they that dwelt at Jerusalem, and their rulers, because they knew him not, nor yet the voices of the prophets, which were read every Sabbath day, they have fulfilled them in condemning him." [248] This proved fatal to them, of which our Lord warned them, when he told them, "If ye believe not that I am he, ye shall die in your sins." [249] And there soon arose in the christian church those who denied the Lord that bought them, even our Lord Jesus Christ. [250] And as ignorance of the person of Jesus Christ, and mistakes respecting his real character, were so dangerous and fatal to Jews and professing christians, in that day, they have been equally so in every age since, down to this day; and will be as mischievous to us, if we are so criminal and unhappy as to imbibe them, or any other, as contrary to the truth.

Professing christians have differed, perhaps, in nothing so much as they have about the person and character of Jesus Christ. The opinions which have been imbibed and professed are so many and various, that it would take volumes, and be an almost endless task, particularly to mention and describe them; which, therefore, will not be undertaken here. All that will be attempted, is to ascertain the truth, as revealed in the holy scriptures, concerning this high and important point, and great mystery of godliness, God manifest in the flesh.

The variety of different sentiments and gross errors into which men have run on this point, to their own destruction, have not been owing to any darkness or defect in divine revelation, respecting this. We may be certain that the person and character of the Redeemer is there so fully, and with so much perspicuity ascertained and fixed, that every honest, unprejudiced person, who is willing to know and embrace the truth, and will properly study the Bible, will come to the knowledge of the truth, and form right conceptions of Jesus Christ, in every important article respecting him. All the mistakes and errors, therefore, which have been embraced on this point, have originated from the evil biases, prejudices, and inattention of sinful man, together with the influence which Satan, "who deceives the whole world," has been suffered to exert on the minds of men. The depraved minds of men love darkness rather than the light; yea, hate the. truth; and are more ready to embrace error and delusion, than the pure truth, with relation to the Redeemer: And Satan, the great enemy of Christ, and of men, is unwearied in his attempts to blind and deceive them, especially respecting the Saviour, and lead them to embrace damnable errors concerning him, and such as are very dishonourable to him, and rob him of all his glory, as the Redeemer of sinners. This will fully account for the various and multiplied errors which have been, at one time and another, invented and propagated in the christian world, consistent with the utmost clearness and perfection of divine revelation on this head.

Ever since the gospel has been preached to the world to this day, the person and character of Christ, Christ crucified, has been to the Jews a stumbling block, and to the Gentiles foolishness: To all the unbelieving and disobedient he has been, and is now, and will continue to be, "a stone of stumbling and rock of offence." While to them who believe he is precious, the only sure foundation, and chief corner stone, on whom they build all their hopes. These true friends to Christ do know him, having some degree of true acquaintance with his person and character: But their knowledge is very imperfect, and, it is to be feared, in most, if not all of them, is attended with great darkness, and more or less mistakes and wrong conceptions of him. This, however, is no matter of discouragement to attend to this subject with great care, diligence and circumspection; but rather a weighty motive to it; and to attempt to confirm the truth, and throw all the light upon it which may have been obtained, by a long and careful study of the holy scriptures; leaving it with them who shall come after with more clear heads, better hearts, and a more unprejudiced, and engaged study of the Bible, to detect the mistakes which may now be made, and remove present darkness, by bringing forth more abundant light from the divine oracles, on this important subject.

It is not designed to attempt a particular refutation of any of the many different opinions which have been advanced concerning the person of the Redeemer, or to answer all the objections which have been made to that representation which shall now be given as warranted by the scriptures of truth; since stating the truth, and supporting it by divine revelation, is the shortest and most effectual way to discover and confute the opposite errors, and silence all the objections which have been made to it

The following things appear to be revealed in the holy scriptures, concerning this wonderful person; and therefore may be safely believed and asserted.

I. That Jesus Christ, the Redeemer of men, is truly God, or a divine person. This has been so much insisted upon, and abundantly proved from scripture, by so many writers, that it is needless to attend here to all the evidence there is of this truth in scripture. It will be sufficient briefly to note the following particulars.

1. This is expressly asserted of him, and he is often called God in the Scripture. The following passages are instances of this. "In the beginning was the Word, and the Word was with God, and the Word was God." This is the Word, which took flesh, or the human nature, into a personal union with himself. "And the Word was made flesh, and dwelt among us; and we beheld his glory, the glory of the only begotten Son of the Father." [251] The Word, which is asserted to be God, is the second person in the Trinity. "There are three that bear record in heaven, the Father, the Word, and the Holy Ghost." [252] Therefore, "his name is called the Word of God." [253] "Unto us a Child is born, unto us a Son is given, and the government shall be upon his shoulders: And his name shall be called, Wonderful, Counsellor, The mighty God." [254] "And this is the name whereby he shall be called: The Lord (Jehovah) our righteousness." [255] "Behold, a virgin shall be with child, and shall bring forth a Son, and they shall call his name Emanuel, which, being interpreted, is God with us." [256] "And Thomas answered and said unto him, My Lord, and my God." [257] "Whose are the fathers, and of whom, as concerning the flesh, Christ came, who is over all, God blessed forever." [258] "Looking for that blessed hope, and glorious appearing of the great God, and our Saviour Jesus Christ." [259] The words in the original might, with propriety, be rendered Our Great God and Saviour. Mr. Fleming, in support of this interpretation, observes, that we never read of the Father's appearance. [260] "Through the righteousness of our God, and Saviour Jesus Christ." [261] "But unto the Son, he saith. Thy throne, O God, is forever and ever." [262] "Great is the mystery of godliness; God was manifest in the flesh." [263]

2. What is in one part of the Bible said of Jehovah, and ascribed to him, as the only true God, this being the name which is appropriated to him in distinction from all other beings, is, in other passages, ascribed to the Redeemer of man, Jesus Christ, and applied to him.

"Mine eyes have seen the King, the Lord (Jehovah) of hosts." [264] This Jehovah, Lord of hosts, is said by St. John to be Jesus Christ, as he applies this passage to him--"These things, said Isaiah, when he saw his (Christ's) glory, and spake of him." [265]

"Thus saith the Lord, the King of Israel, and his Redeemer, the Lord of hosts, I am the first, and I am the last, and besides me there is no God." [266] Here Jehovah takes this character to himself, as peculiar to him. The first, and the last. But Jesus Christ, the Redeemer of the true Israel, the church; who redeems his people from the curse of the law, by his blood, takes this same character to himself, and therefore must himself be Jehovah, besides whom there is no God. "I (Jesus Christ) am Alpha and Omega, the beginning and the end, the first and the last." [267] This same person takes

The System of Doctrines, contained in Divine Relation, Explained and Defended Volume I

this to himself repeatedly in the first chapter of this book, "saying, I am Alpha and Omega, the first and last." [268] "I am the first and the last: I am he that liveth, and was dead, and, behold, I am alive forevermore." [269] "I am Alpha and Omega, the beginning and the ending, saith the Lord, which is, and which was, and which is to come, the Almighty." [270] "I, even I, am the Lord, and besides me there is no Saviour." [271] This title and character, which Jehovah takes to himself, exclusive of all others, the Saviour of Israel, his church and people, is constantly given to Jesus Christ in the New Testament. He is called Jesus, which signifies a Saviour, because he saves his people from their sins. [272] "Christ is the head of the church, and he is the Saviour of the body," that is, the church. [273] He is called, "our Lord and Saviour Jesus Christ." [274] This title is given to him in other places, too many to be particularly recited. And this is needless, since one instance of his being called, by way of eminence, the Saviour, is sufficient to prove the point now in view. It may be proper and useful, however, under this head,. to observe, that as this title. The Saviour, is claimed as peculiar to Jehovah, the only true God, in the passage just quoted from Isaiah; and since Jesus Christ is called God, and asserted to be God, in many instances, which have been mentioned above, we are hence warranted to apply the expression, God our Saviour, which is so often used, to Jesus the only Saviour and Redeemer of his church. Among other instances of this, the following may be particularly noted. "And Mary said, My soul doth magnify the Lord, and my spirit hath rejoiced in God my Saviour. For unto you is born this day, in the city of David, a Saviour, which is Christ the Lord." [275] "According to the commandment of God our Saviour, That they may adorn the doctrine of God our Saviour in all things. Our great God and Saviour Jesus Christ. But after the kindness and love of God and our Saviour appeared. [276] Through the righteousness of our God and Saviour Jesus Christ." [277] In our translation it is God and our Saviour, but this is not so agreeable to the original, as that now given. "Now unto him that is able to keep you from falling, and to present you faultless before the presence of his glory, with exceeding joy, to the only wise God our Saviour, be glory and majesty, dominion and power, both now and ever, Amen." [278]

That Jesus Christ is the person here intended by the only wise God our Saviour, is farther evident, because this same thing is expressly ascribed to him by St. Paul. "That he (Christ) might present it to himself, a glorious church, not having spot or wrinkle, or any such thing; but that it should be holy, and without blemish." [279]

Again, Jehovah, the Lord of hosts, is called the husband of the church, and claims this relation, "Thy Maker is thine husband, the Lord of hosts is his name." [280] "Thou shalt no more be termed forsaken, &c. for the Lord delighteth in thee, and thy land shall be married--And as the bridegroom rejoiceth over the bride, so shall thy God rejoice over thee." [281] This same character and relation is ascribed to Jesus Christ. He is the bridegroom, the husband of the church. John Baptist, speaking of Christ, says, "He that hath the bride is the bridegroom." [282] St. Paul says to the Corinthian church, "I have espoused you to one husband, that I may present you a chaste virgin to Christ." [283] St. John heard them rejoicing in heaven, and saying, "The marriage of the Lamb is come, and his wife (the church) hath made herself ready." [284] "And I saw the holy city, New Jerusalem, (which is the church) coming down from God out of heaven, prepared as a bride adorned for her husband. And there came unto me one of the seven angels, and talked with me, saying, come hither, I will shew thee the bride, the Lamb's wife." [285] Thus it appears that Jehovah, the only true God, is the church's husband; and so is Jesus Christ. Therefore Jesus Christ is Jehovah; or the only true God, and Jesus Christ, are the same: For the church hath not, and cannot have two husbands: Nor are there two brides or wives, who can each of them have a husband: For there is but one church; but one bride, who, as a chaste virgin, is espoused to one husband, Jesus Christ. "There is one body," that is, the church, of which Christ is the only head and husband. [286] "My dove, my undefiled, is but one." [287]

"Sanctify the Lord (Jehovah) of hosts himself, and let him be your fear, and let him be your dread: And he shall be for a sanctuary; but for a stone of stumbling, and for a rock of offence to both the houses of Israel." [288] This, which is spoken of Jehovah, is applied to Jesus Christ by St. Peter. "The stone which the builders disallowed, the same is made the head of the corner, and a stone of stumbling and rock of offence." [289] It is said, "The Lord God of the holy prophets sent his angel to shew unto his servants the things which shortly must be done." [290] And in the sixteenth verse Jesus Christ says, "I Jesus have sent mine Angel to testify unto you these things in the churches." Here the Lord God of the holy prophets, which must be Jehovah, and Jesus Christ, are said to be the same thing. Therefore Jesus Christ and the Lord God, are one and the same.

Not half the instances of this kind, which might be adduced under this head, have been mentioned; but these are enough, it is presumed, to illustrate and make evident to every attentive, impartial person, the truth of the particular observation, to prove which they have been cited.

3. That Jesus Christ is God, is evident from the divine attributes being ascribed to him, even those which are peculiar to the Deity.

Eternity, or existing without beginning, is ascribed to him. "But thou, Bethlehem--out of thee shall he come forth unto me, that is to be ruler of Israel, whose goings forth have been from old, from everlasting." [291] This is expressly applied to Christ. [292] He is represented in that remarkable type of him, Melchisedec, to be without beginning of days, or end of time. [293] He is "the beginning and the ending, the first and the last, which is, and which was, and which is to come." [294] Which words strongly express eternal existence, without beginning or end.

Immutability is ascribed to him, which is an attribute peculiar to God. Speaking to the Son of God, it is said, "Thou art the same," as opposed to all changeable existence. [295] This is expressed more strongly in the following words, "Jesus Christ, the same yesterday, to day, and forever." [296] Here both his eternity, his existence from everlasting to everlasting, and his immutability are expressed.

He is omnipotent. "And Jesus came and spake unto them, saying, All power is given unto me, in heaven and in earth:" [297] He is "head over all things to the church. " [298] He is "able to subdue all things unto himself." [299] He is "the first and the last, which is, and which was, and which is to come, the Almighty." [300] "He upholds all things, by the word of his power." [301] His creating and upholding all things, and other works which are ascribed to him, are, without controversy, the work of Omnipotence. But these will be more particularly considered under another head.

That he is Omnipresent, he himself declared, "Where two or three are gathered together in my name, there am I in the midst of them." "And lo, I am with you alway, even unto the end of the world." [302] "And no man hath ascended up to heaven, but he that came down from heaven, even the Son of man which is in heaven." [303] Surely these things cannot be said with truth of any one but Him, whose presence fills heaven and earth. Omniscience is also one of his attributes. This Peter ascribes to him, without reserve, and with the greatest confidence. "And Peter said unto him, Lord, thou knowest all things." [304] It is asserted, agreeable to this, that "He knew all men, and knew what was in man." [305] And it is often said that he knew the secret thoughts of men. And he says, "And all the churches shall know that I am he which searcheth the reins and hearts, and will give unto every one of you according to his works." [306] This is elsewhere spoken of as the attribute and prerogative of the omniscient God alone. Solomon, speaking to Jehovah, says, "Thou only knowest the hearts of the children of men." [307] "The righteous God trieth the hearts and reins." [308] "I, the Lord, search the heart, I try the reins, even to give every man according to his ways." [309] If Jesus Christ were not the only true God, it is impossible he should take to himself this attribute, prerogative and work, which Jehovah, the God of Israel, claims to himself exclusively; and which is infinitely too much to be ascribed to any mere creature. Jesus Christ is declared to be incomprehensible, which is an attribute peculiar to Deity. He says of himself, "All things are delivered unto me of my Father; and no man (no one, it is in the original) knoweth the Son but the Father." [310] And it is said of him, "He had a name written that no man (no one) knew but he himself." [311] Equality with God is ascribed unto him. St. Paul, speaking of his person, says, "Who being in the form of God, thought it not robbery to be equal with God." [312] Jesus said to the Jews, "I and my Father are one." [313] The Jews understood him as hereby claiming to be God, and charged him with making himself God. [314] Nor does Christ, in his answer to them, renounce this claim. Jesus said, "My Father worketh hitherto, and I work." [315] Upon this the Jews charged him with making himself equal with God. Nor does he deny this charge, or say that it is unjust: but goes on to say, in a yet stronger manner, "What things soever the Father doeth, those also doth the Son likewise. For as the Father raiseth up the death, and quickeneth them; even so the Son quickeneth whom he will. For the Father hath committed all judgment unto the Son; that all men should honour the Son, even as they honour the Father." Surely this is making himself equal with God. He moreover says, "All things that the Father hath, are mine." [316] Thus he claims to be equal with the Father, the owner and possessor of all things. This is consistent with his saying, "The Father is greater than I," as he was man as well as God, and agreeable to the economy of redemption, in the human nature, was become a servant, to obey and suffer, in order to effect the redemption of man. In this capacity and work he was sent, and to be justified and exalted by the Father. In this view his words have a plain meaning, consistent with his claim of equality with the Father, as God. "If ye had loved me, ye would rejoice, because I said, I go unto the Father; for my Father is greater than I." [317]

4. The divinity of Jesus Christ is asserted by ascribing to him those divine works which God alone can do.

He puts himself upon an equality with the Father in this respect, and says, that he does whatsoever the Father doth. "My Father worketh hitherto, and I work. What things soever he doth, those also doth the Son likewise." [318] The works of creation and providence are ascribed to him. "All things were made by him, and without him was not any thing made that was made." [319] "For by him were all things created that are in heaven, and that are in earth, visible and invisible, whether they be thrones, or dominions, or principalities, or powers; all things were created by him, and for him." [320] God hath made all things for himself: All things were made by Jesus Christ, and for him;

Therefore he is God. "And he is before all things, and by him all things consist." [321] "Who being the brightness of his glory, and the express image of his person, and upholding all things by the word of his power, when he had by himself purged our sins, sat down on the right hand of the Majesty on high." [322] And he is addressed in the following words, "Thou, Lord, in the beginning, hast laid the foundation of the earth; and the heavens are the works of thine hands."[323] Bat these are the works of God, of Jehovah, and peculiar to him. "In the beginning God created the heaven and the earth. By the word of the Lord were the heavens made; and all the host of them by the breath of his mouth." [324]

Jesus Christ raiseth men from the dead, which is a work of omnipotence as great as that of creation. When he was on earth he raised man from the dead, by his own powerful word. And he claims power and authority to raise all the dead of mankind, at the last day. He hath said, "The hour is coming, in the which all that are in the graves shall hear the voice of the Son of God, and shall come forth, they that have done good, unto the resurrection of life; and they that have done evil, unto the resurrection of damnation. And this is the will of him that sent me, that every one which seeth the Son, and believeth on him, may have everlasting life: and I will raise him up at the last day. I am the resurrection and the life." [325]

Jesus Christ will judge the world, angels, devils, and all mankind. This is often asserted in the scripture. All judgment is committed unto him. A work infinitely too great for a mere creature to perform; and therefore infinitely too great for him, and too high and honourable, were he not the most high God, possessed of infinite power, knowledge, wisdom and rectitude.

But one thing more will be added under this head. Jesus Christ is Governor of the world. He has all things in his hand; upholds all things by the word of his power; is head over all things to the church, having all power in heaven and on earth. He executeth a particular providence; his care and power orders and effects every event, and extends to every creature and thing in the created universe, whether great or small. He alone, therefore, is able to take the book of the divine decrees, and open the seals thereof, by governing the world, and bringing to pass all things agreeable to the eternal purpose. None can do this but he who has omnipotence, infinite knowledge, wisdom and goodness.

5. It is certain that Jesus Christ is the supreme God, in that he is the object of the divine worship, which would be idolatry, if offered to any being but the only true God.

Nothing can be more evident and certain than that God is the only proper object of religious worship. Jesus Christ is, in the holy scriptures, asserted to be the object of such worship; therefore he is God.

All the angels of heaven are commanded to worship him. "When he bringeth the first begotten into the world, he saith. And let all the angels of God worship him." [326] John saw and heard him worshipped in heaven, and represented as the object of prayer and praise. "And when he had taken the book, the four beasts, and the four and twenty elders, fell down before the Lamb, having every one of them harps, and golden vials full of odours, which are the prayers of saints. And they sung a new song, saying, Thou art worthy to take the book, and open the seals thereof; for thou wast slain, and hast redeemed us to God, by thy blood. And I beheld, and I heard the voice of many angels round about the throne, and the beasts and the elders; and the number of them was ten thousand times ten thousand, and thousands of thousands: saying, with a loud voice, Worthy is the Lamb that was slain, to receive power, and riches, and wisdom, and strength, and honour, and glory, and blessing. And every creature heard I saying, Blessing, and honour, and glory, and power, be unto him that sitteth upon the throne, and unto the Lamb, forever and ever. And the Tour beasts said» Amen. And the four and twenty elders fell down and worshipped him that liveth forever and ever;" even Jesus Christ, who was dead, and is alive, and behold, he liveth forever and ever. [327] Thus all in heaven and on earth "honour the Lamb, the Son, even as they honour the Father." [328]

Agreeable to this, St. Paul says of Jesus Christ, "God hath highly exalted him, and given him a name which is above every name; that at the name of Jesus, every knee should bow, of things in heaven and things in earth, and under the earth; (or angels, and men, both the living and the dead) and that every tongue should confess that Jesus Christ is Lord, to the glory of God the Father."[329]

These words express the involuntary subjection of his enemies, and the voluntary submission, adoration, and worship of his friends, which is given only to God. And that such subjection, submission and worship, is here intended, which is due to God alone; and that Jesus Christ is this God, is evident both from this same apostle's quotation of these words in another place, and from the passage in the prophet Isaiah, from, whence they are taken. "For we shall all stand before the judgment seat of Christ. For it is written, As I live, saith the Lord, every knee shall bow to me, and every tongue shall confess to God." [330] This homage is here said to be paid to Jesus Christ, as Judge of the world, and as God. And this bowing the knee and confession, is claimed by Jehovah, the God of Israel, and he says it shall be given to him, as the only true God, in the passage quoted from Isaiah, "I am God, and there is none else. I have sworn by myself, the word is gone out of my mouth in righteousness, and shall not return, that unto me every knee shall bow, and every tongue shall swear." [331]

Stephen, the first martyr, prayed to Jesus Christ, and committed his spirit, himself, to him, when he was expiring under the hand of his persecutors. And they stoned Stephen, calling upon God, and saying. Lord Jesus, receive my spirit. [332] The word God is not in the original, and the words might be with propriety rendered, calling upon Jesus Christ, saying, Lord Jesus, &c. Such a solemn prayer to Jesus Christ, putting his whole trust in him, and committing his soul to him, with his last breath, is an act of worship, which would be gross idolatry, if offered to any but God.

And as Stephen worshipped Jesus Christ, and called upon his name, making his last prayer to him when he was leaving the world, he was not singular and alone in this; but thus calling on the name of Christ was practised by all christians, and therefore mentioned as expressive of their character, and an essential branch of it, and by which they are denominated, and distinguished from others. St. Paul thus addresses them: "Unto the church of God, which is at Corinth, to them that are sanctified in Christ Jesus, called to be saints, with all that in every place call upon the name of Jesus Christ, our Lord, both theirs and ours." [333] Ananias, speaking to the Lord Jesus Christ, says, "And here he (Saul) hath authority from the chief priests to bind all that call on thy name." [334] That is, all christians. And of Saul it is further said, "And straightway he preached Christ in the synagogues, that he is the Son of God. But all that heard him were amazed, and said, Is not this he that destroyed them which called on this name in Jerusalem, and came hither for that intent, that he might bring them bound unto the chief priests." [335]

And when he was on earth he was worshipped--By the wise men from the east--By a ruler of the synagogue--By a woman of Canaan--By a leper--By a man born blind, whom he had restored to sight--By all who were in the ship with him--By the women, when they saw him, after his resurrection--By the multitude of his disciples, when he appeared to them in Galilee; and by his disciples who saw him ascend from Mount Olivet into heaven. Yet in none of these instances did he forbid this worship to be paid to him, or shew the least disapprobation of it; but the history of it leads us to suppose that such worship was proper; and that he accepted it with approbation, and was pleased with it: Whereas, when Cornelius the centurion, offered to worship Peter, he forbid and reproved him, saying, "Stand up, I myself also am a man." [336] And when St. John offered to worship the Angel who spake to him, he received a rebuke from him. He said unto him, "See thou do it not; for I am thy fellow servant. Worship God." [337] Plainly declaring that God only is the proper object of such worship; which worship was paid to Jesus Christ, with his approbation, as has been observed; which he must have rejected, and rebuked those who offered it, as Peter and the Angel did, had he not been a divine person, that is, God. He himself rebuked the devil when he proposed to Christ to worship him; not because he was an evil being; but because he was not God, and such worship was to be given to God only. "Then saith Jesus unto him, Get thee hence, Satan; for it is written, thou shalt worship the Lord thy God, and him only shalt thou serve." [338] The word in the original translated serve, is found in above twenty places in the New Testament, and always means religious service, implying devotion and religious worship, and is in a number of places translated to worship.

The disciples of Christ and the christian church, by thus worshipping him as their Lord, and their God, obeyed the prophetic direction and command given in the 45th psalm. "So shall the king greatly desire thy beauty; for he is thy Lord, and worship thou him."

Jehovah had abundantly expressed his peculiar displeasure with idolatry, and done much to guard his people, and warn them against it, and all approaches to it: and did often strictly forbid their worshipping any creature, idols, or any god besides himself. And he had often punished them for this sin, as peculiarly provoking to him. He had said, "Thou shalt have no other gods before me: thou shalt not bow down thyself to them, nor serve them; for I the Lord thy God am a jealous God. Thou shalt worship no other god; for I the Lord, whose name is Jealous, am a jealous God. I am the Lord, that is my name, and my glory I will not give unto another, neither my praise to graven images." If Jesus Christ were not God, even this same God, who has said these things, what a contradiction to these declarations and commands, and how inconsistent is it with them to set him so high, as worthy of equal honour with the Father; to call him God, and give him all the power in heaven and earth, and make him head over all things to the church; to represent him as praised, adored, and worshipped, by all the inhabitants in heaven; and to command all the angels in heaven, and the church in earth, to worship him! Were he not the true God, this would be the greatest imaginable, and even an irresistible temptation and encouragement to the most gross idolatry; to worship and trust in him who is not God, but a mere creature. We cannot reconcile the Old Testament with the New, or the New Testament with itself, unless we believe and grant, that Jesus Christ is the true God; for in both, men are repeatedly forbidden to worship, or pay religious homage to any but the only true God: And yet in both, they are commanded to worship Jesus Christ, the Son of God, the King of Israel. And the latter teaches us that he who of old was

The System of Doctrines, contained in Divine Relation, Explained and Defended Volume I
worshipped by the Seraphim under the name and character of Jehovah, the Lord of hosts, was Jesus Christ. [339] But if Jesus Christ be the true Son of God; God with us; God manifest in the flesh, as he is expressly declared to be, all the Bible can be reconciled with itself, and appears perfectly consistent, on this head: While we there behold him who was in the form of God, and thought it not robbery to be equal with God; who appeared and acted from the beginning of the world, and under the Old Testament dispensation, in the form of God, who took to himself the name Jehovah, and the attributes and character of the most high God, and claimed the worship and honours which belong to God alone: While we behold him laying aside his former appearance and glory, and making himself of no reputation; taking upon himself the form of a servant, instead of the form of God, in which he appeared before; being made in the likeness of man: In this view, we shall see the whole scripture to harmonize on this point, and be constrained to say with Thomas, "My Lord, and my God!" and join to honour him, even as the Father is honoured; ascribing, with the heavenly hosts, praise, blessing, wisdom, power, dominion and glory, unto him that sitteth upon the throne, and unto the Lamb, forever and ever.

And, indeed, if he be not the true God, and to be worshipped as God, who has created all things that ever were created; and upholds them all continually by his powerful word; who has all the power in the universe, and sustains and governs all creatures and things, being head over all things to the church; it will be impossible to find any proper object of worship, or any God to be trusted and adored.

It may be further added, that the religious rite of baptism, instituted by Christ, is a solemn and important act of devotion and worship, in which the name of God is invoked, and the person baptized is dedicated to him with awful solemnity. This religious act of worship is commanded to be done in the name of Christ, in which he joined with the Father and the Holy Ghost. "Go teach all nations, said Christ to his disciples, baptizing them in the name of the Father, and of the Son, and of the Holy Ghost." [340] This, properly considered, will appear a demonstration of the divinity of the Son of God, and that he is equally God with the Father; and cannot be accounted for on any other supposition. If Jesus Christ were not God, what a profanation of the sacred name would this be, and what a gross act of idolatry, to join his name with that of the only true God, as equal with him in such a solemn act of covenanting, and religious worship!

The priests in Israel, Aaron and his sons, were appointed and directed to bless, in the name of the Lord, and to say, "The Lord bless thee, and keep thee: The Lord make his face to shine upon thee, and be gracious unto thee. The Lord lift up his countenance upon thee, and give thee peace." This was an act of solemn, religious worship, invoking the name of Jehovah, and calling on him.[341] St. Paul blesses christians, in the name of the same Lord, doubtless, even in the name into which they were baptized, saying, "The grace of our Lord Jesus Christ, and the love of God, and the communion of the Holy Ghost, be with you all, Amen." [342] This is an act of devotion and worship, in which God is called upon to bless; or he asks this blessing from God. If Jesus Christ were not God, thus to bless in his name, and join him with the true God in this invocation, and act of worship, would be real idolatry. And it is remarkable that as the name Jehovah, or Lord, is mentioned distinctly three times, in the blessing which Aaron and his sons were ordered to pronounce, denoting, as is reasonably supposed, the three, included in that name; so the apostle, blessing in the same name, mentions three, as included in this name, each of which is elsewhere expressly called God, and Lord. And it is worthy of observation here, that as the baptism which Christ ordered to be administered in the name of the Father, Son, and Holy Ghost, is afterwards said to be administered in the name of the Lord, and in the name of Jesus Christ because one of these supposes and comprehends all; so this apostle, who blessed in the name of these same three, does more commonly bless in the name of Jesus Christ. "The grace of our Lord Jesus Christ, be with you;" because he is God, and the whole Trinity is implied in his name: And this is to bless in the name of the adorable three, as really as when they are distinctly mentioned.

Much more may be produced from the holy scriptures to prove and confirm this truth, that Jesus Christ is God; but surely what his been now collected from the sacred oracles on this head, is sufficient to establish this important doctrine in the mind of every honest, unprejudiced person, who is willing properly to attend to it, and to know the truth.

There have been, and now are, indeed, many professing christians, who do not believe; but deny and oppose this doctrine of the divinity of Jesus Christ. These appear to be led to renounce this doctrine, principally for two reasons. First, because they are disposed to reject every doctrine in Christianity, which they cannot comprehend, and fully understand, with their boasted reason. They therefore deny the doctrine of the Trinity, as well as this of the divinity of Christ, and many other doctrines, which to them are incomprehensible, and which they therefore pronounce unreasonable. And would they be consistent, they must renounce Christianity itself, and even the belief of the being of a God, and of almost every thing else; for the existence of God is as incomprehensible as the divinity of Christ: And it is above our reason or conception, and contrary to reason as some would improve it, that any being should exist without any cause out of himself; and without beginning to exist; and unchangeable, &c. If the being of a God be admitted, which must be admitted, unless we renounce all reason, we must admit innumerable mysteries, which our minds cannot fathom and comprehend.

And what object is there in universal nature, which can be fully comprehended by us? And what truth is there which respects God or the creature, which can be perfectly understood by us, and which is not attended with seeming contradictions; at least, in the view of some?

Secondly, Another reason of their rejecting the doctrine of the divinity of Christ, is, their not seeing any need of his being God, in order to be the Saviour of men. They entertain such notions of God, the divine law and government, of the nature and demerit of sin, the state of fallen man, &c. that they cannot see any need of atonement for sin, which a creature cannot make, or of any thing to be done by the Redeemer of man, which a mere creature cannot do. Therefore they are resolved not to admit a doctrine which in their view is so incomprehensible and absurd, and at the same time so perfectly useless. They therefore think they find many things in divine revelation inconsistent with this doctrine; and have attempted to explain away those passages of scripture adduced to support it, and to put such a sense upon them as to make them assert no such thing. Their objections, and manner of explaining the scriptures, so as to make them consistent with their believing Jesus Christ to be a mere creature, will not be particularly considered here; as this has been done by many able divines. What has been now produced from the scriptures, to prove that Jesus Christ is the true God, it is presumed, is sufficient to satisfy every humble, modest inquirer after the truth, that this doctrine is clearly revealed in the Bible; and in such a manner, that the evidence of it is incontestible, and must be admitted, if we admit the scriptures to be the standard of truth. And this evidence will rise higher, if possible, as we proceed, and when we come to consider the importance and necessity of this doctrine; and that none but a divine person could be the Redeemer of man, consistent with other doctrines and truths of divine revelation; and do and suffer what was necessary to be done and suffered, in order to redeem sinners: That a person who is not God, would be infinitely unequal to this work.

But there is another truth equally important, and plainly revealed, with that which we have been considering, concerning this wonderful person.

II. The Redeemer of sinners is truly and really man. This person is both God and man. The Word, who was God, and created all things that are made, became, and was made flesh, and dwelt among men. He was made in the likeness of men, and was found in fashion as a man, that is, was really man, "the son of man." He is therefore denominated man, that man, the man Christ Jesus, &c. This necessarily implies that he had a real body and soul; for these are essential to human nature; so that none can be a real man, who has not both these. The history of his conception, birth, life, death and resurrection, states this truth in a clear and unequivocal light. Therefore there is need of nothing farther to be said, to prove that Jesus Christ is really man. But it seems needful to observe and attend to the following things concerning this wonderful, incomprehensible person, God man, and the union of these two natures, in this one person.

1. The human nature of Jesus Christ is not a distinct person, separate from the divine nature, or his Godhead. The human nature exists, and began to exist, in union with the sacred person in the Trinity, the Word; so that both natures are but one person. As the soul and body of a man, though different and distinct in their nature; or are two different natures, considered in themselves; yet in union with each other, are but one person.

2. What is true and may be affirmed of either nature, divine and human, is true, and may be affirmed of this person, Jesus Christ, the Redeemer. This same person is God, and he is man. This person was in heaven, and was visible on earth at the same time. "No man hath ascended up to heaven, but he that came down from heaven, even the Son of man which is in heaven." [343] This person who is God-man, Immanuel, God with us, God manifest in the flesh, was put to death in the flesh, that is, in the human nature. He died on the cross, and his blood was poured out there. This being the death, the blood of this person, it was the blood of God, because this person was God.[344] This person is omniscient and unchangeable in his divine nature; but the human nature of this person is not omniscient, nor unchangeable, but did increase in stature, knowledge and wisdom. [345] As God, he is omnipotent and independent; as man, he is altogether dependent. Many other instances of this kind might be mentioned; but these are sufficient to illustrate the observation which has now been mentioned concerning this wonderful, complex person, including two natures perfectly distinct, and infinitely different one from the other.

This matter may be farther explained, and rendered more intelligible, perhaps, by considering the person of a man. Every man is a complex person, consisting of body and soul, of very distinct and different natures, and yet so united, as to make one person. What is true of one of these two parts or natures of man, is not true of both. The body is mortal, the soul is not. The body has dimensions, and visible shape and countenance; the soul has nothing of these, and is not capable of them. And yet, what is true of either of these different parts or natures, is true of the person consisting of these parts. The same person is mortal, as to his body; but is immortal, as to his mind. The person dies, but it is only in one of the constituent parts of his person, his body. Therefore this same person may live, when his body is dead. This person, consisting of body and soul, is intelligent, does think and reason. This is true of the person, because his mind is intelligent, thinks and reasons; while his body is not capable of this, &c. &c.

3. These two distinct and infinitely different natures, united in the person of Jesus Christ, are not transformed into each other, so that one becomes the other by this personal union; but remain as distinct and different, in this respect, as if there were no such personal union. The human nature is not God, and has not any of the attributes peculiar to divinity, any more than if it were not united to divinity. And the divine nature of Christ is no more a creature, and has no more the peculiar properties of a man, than if no such personal union of these natures had taken place. Therefore,

4. This personal union of the divine nature, or of God in the second person of the Godhead, with the human nature, does not cause or suppose any change in the former: But as God, this person is unchangeable. The human nature is assumed, or taken into a personal union with the second person of the Trinity, without any change in the divinity or divine nature; And all the change, or that is changeable, is in the human nature.

5. The personality of Jesus Christ is in his divine nature, and not in the human. Jesus Christ existed a distinct divine person from eternity, the second person in the adorable Trinity. The human nature which this divine person, the Word, assumed into a personal union with himself, is not, and never was, a distinct person by itself; and personality cannot be ascribed to it, and does not belong to it, any otherwise than as united to the Logos, the Word of God. The Word assumed the human nature, not a human person, into a personal union with himself, by which this complex person exists, God-man. Had the second person in the Trinity taken a human person into union with himself, and were this possible, Jesus Christ, God and man, would be two persons, not one. Hence, when Jesus Christ is spoken of as being a man, "the son of man, the man Christ Jesus, &c."--these terms do not express the personality of the manhood, or of the human nature of Jesus Christ; but these personal terms are used with respect to the human nature, as united to a divine person, and not as a mere man. For the personal terms, He, I, and Thou, cannot, with propriety, or truth, be used by, or of the human nature, considered as distinct from the divine nature of Jesus Christ.

6. The mode or manner of the union of the two natures, divine and human, in one person, cannot be described nor conceived by us, it being entirely above our comprehension. This does not, however, render it in the least degree incredible. For could it be comprehended, it would not be a real union, much less a union of the divine nature with the human. For if we cannot comprehend, or have any clear conception of the personal union of our own souls with our bodies; how much more inconceivable must this high and singular union be to us, by which Deity and humanity are united, and become one person!

7. The human nature of Jesus Christ is doubtless unspeakably greater and more excellent than any other creature. This individual of the human race, being raised up to a personal union with him who is God, is the first and chief of all elect creatures, the greatest and most peculiar favourite; and is under the greatest advantages to advance in knowledge and holiness, being brought nearest to God of any creature, and receiving peculiar and more copious communications from him. It is with respect to his human nature, that John the Baptist speaks, when he says of Jesus Christ, "God giveth not the spirit by measure unto him." [346] As Jesus Christ increased in wisdom, in knowledge, and holiness, in the human nature, when in this world; so he will doubtless increase in this, and in degrees of existence without end; and make more rapid advances than any mere creature in proportion to the greater favours, and the special advantages enjoyed in the near and peculiar union to the Deity, and the high and important station and offices to which the human nature is advanced. May we not from this, and other considerations which might be mentioned, safely conclude, that the human nature of Jesus Christ, is greater in capacity, in knowledge and holiness, and has, or will have, without end, more or a greater degree of existence, worth and happiness, not only than any mere creature, but more and greater than the whole redeemed church, and even all the elect angels, were the latter summed up together? The former, when put in the balance, may exceed it, to a degree beyond all our present conceptions.

8. The human nature of Jesus Christ began to exist when it was conceived in the virgin Mary, and not before. The scripture history of his conception and birth, or the incarnation, and all that is said of it, naturally leads to this conclusion. The reader will have no other idea suggested to his mind, unless he has some particular end to answer by rejecting it; or puts a sense on some other passages of scripture, which is inconsistent with it. Such there have been in former ages, and such there are now in the christian world, who are confident that the soul, or rational creature, which was united to a body in the incarnation, did not then begin to exist, but is the first creature that was made, &c. And they have thought that this sentiment is supported by a number of passages in the

Bible. But the writers who have opposed them in this, it is thought, have made it evident that the passages which they allege assert no such thing; but are perfectly consistent with the human nature of Jesus Christ beginning to exist at his incarnation.

The doctrine of the pre-existence of the soul of Jesus Christ, or of that created nature which took a body in the womb of the virgin Mary, appears first to be invented and propagated by Arius, in the fourth century, and, since his time, by his followers. He denied the divinity of Jesus Christ, or that he is the true God equal with the Father; and asserted that he is a mere creature. And in order to support his notion of the Redeemer, and make it consistent with many passages of scripture which represent him as existing before his incarnation, and from the beginning, and speak of his creating the world, &c. which his opposers used, to prove that he is a divine person, or the true God, he invented this scheme, and applied them to this pre-existing creature.

This creature, they suppose, was the first creature that was made, and the greatest and most exalted of all creatures, and in this sense is "the first born of every creature; and the beginning of the creation of God." That he made the world, and had the government of it, at least in some degree, before his incarnation. That he is the Logos, or the Word, which became flesh, and dwelt among men, by taking a body in the womb of the virgin Mary, and being born of her. Thus this glorious creature, who was greater and more honourable than the angels, and placed far above them, in the highest and most dignified station, and made in a sense, a God, and appeared in the form of God, being nevertheless, but a mere creature, made himself of no reputation, and took upon him the form of a servant, and was made in the likeness of men, &c.

There are others, especially of late, who, though they profess to believe that Jesus Christ is God, in a sense in which the Arians deny it; and that the human nature has a personal union with Deity; yet hold with the Arians, that the created nature of the Redeemer, his body excepted, existed before his incarnation, and was the first creature that was created, &c. They think this to be asserted in several places of scripture; and that many others cannot be well explained on any other supposition. It has been observed, that the divines who have opposed this scheme, have shewn that all these passages of scripture which have been adduced in favour of it, import no such thing; but are perfectly consistent with the human nature of Christ beginning to exist at his incarnation. The labour of repeating what has been written to this purpose, will not now be undertaken, as it may be found in most commentators on the Bible, and in their writings who have opposed the Arian scheme. It may be proper, however, to take notice of two expressions in scripture, which the favourers of this notion have thought to be most express in their favour. Jesus Christ says of himself that he is, "The beginning of the creation of God." [347] That is, say they, the first creature that was created by God. But these words do not, by the most natural construction, express any such idea. If he existed before the creation of any thing, and did himself begin and finish the creation of God; and is the head and Lord of the creation, and head over all things to the church, all which we have seen the scripture affirm of him; what words could more clearly, and in the most concise manner, express all this than these, "The beginning of the creation of God?" Jesus Christ says of himself repeatedly, in this book of the revelation, "I am the beginning and the end, the first and the last." By which, is not meant that he began to exist, or was created the first of all; but directly the contrary, viz. that he existed without beginning, and without end, and is the author, the creator, or beginner of all things. [348] Jesus Christ is called, "The first born of every creature," or, as it might be more properly rendered, The first born of the whole creation. [349] This, they plead, imports that he is the first creature that was made. But the scripture no where expresses creation by being born: nor is this the natural import of the word. Therefore, these words do not appear to suggest that the Son of God, of whom the apostle is speaking, was created the first of all creatures. There is a more natural and easy sense, consistent with the human nature of Christ beginning to exist at his incarnation. The first born had the preeminence in the family, and was in a peculiar sense the heir. In ancient times, the first born was much distinguished from the rest of the family. He was of course, after his father, the ruler, the king, and priest in the family. Agreeable to this, Jacob addresses his first born son in the following words; "Reuben, thou art my first born, my might, and the beginning of my strength, the excellency of dignity, and the excellency of power." [350] The first born was, in a peculiar sense, the heir; and by his birth had a right to the blessing, and a double portion. Thus Esau, being the first born of Isaac, was heir to the blessing of his father, and to pre-eminence in all respects, as his birth right. In Israel, the first born were in a peculiar sense appropriated to God, and heirs of a double honour and portion, the peculiar favourites. These, in the family of Aaron, were heirs to the high priesthood; and the first born of the kings were heirs of the kingdom. With reference to this, the redeemed are called, "the church of the first born," [351] God says to Pharaoh, "Israel is my son, even my first born." [352] And he says, "I am a father to Israel, and Ephraim is my first born--My dear son, a pleasant child." [353] In these passages first born has no reference to priority of existence; but to pre-eminence, and their being subjects of peculiar favours, honours, and privileges. In this sense, it is predicted of Christ, "I will make him my first born, higher than the kings of the earth." [354] When all

The System of Doctrines, contained in Divine Relation, Explained and Defended Volume I

this is considered, who can be at a loss about the meaning of the expression before us? "The first born of the whole creation." He is the highest, most honourable, the peculiar favourite, the king, the head and the heir of the whole creation; in all things having the pre-eminence above every other creature; for all things were created for him. [355] The apostle fully explains himself in these and the following words, "And he is the head of the body, the church, who is the beginning, the first born from the dead; that in all things he might have the pre-eminence." In this sense, "he is the first born among many brethren." [356] But if we understand his being the first born of every creature, as expressing his priority of existence to the whole creation, it must be understood not of his human, but of his divine nature; for this person exists before all, worlds, and without beginning, as has been proved. Agreeable to this, the apostle goes on to say,[357] "And he is before all things, and by him all things consist." This is true of this person, but cannot be true of the human nature, that it exists before all things, that is, all created things.

But it may be farther observed, that it is not only consistent with the whole of divine revelation, to consider the human nature of the Redeemer, as beginning to exist at his incarnation; and not only that no important or good end is answered by the contrary supposition: But it appears to be contrary to the current of scripture, and of a dangerous and bad tendency. For,

First. This notion appears inconsistent with the true and real manhood of Jesus Christ, or with his taking upon him the human nature, and being a real man, which the scripture abundantly asserts, as we have seen» If the creature w4iich took a body by the incarnation were the first and greatest creature that was ever created, he was no more a man, no more like and akin to the human race, or the nature of man, than the angels; but was more distant from man than they, as he was much greater and higher than they. But if an angel should take upon him a real human body, this would not make him a man, or one of the human race. Gabriel, indeed, who was sent from heaven to Daniel, is called "The man Gabriel;" and the angels which appeared to Lot, and to the women who visited the sepulchre where Christ had been laid, are called men; because they appeared in the shape of men: But no one supposes they were real men; nor would they have been any more so, had they been united to real bodies. A man has not only a human body, but a human soul; both these are essential constituents of human nature, and necessary to make a man. The angelic nature, or superangelic, as such a supposed creature may be called, does not, and cannot be made human nature, or be made a real man, so as to be one of the human race, by uniting to a human body. He still will be an angel, or a creature of a higher order, and not a man. A distinction is made between angels and men, or the seed of Abraham, and it is said, that Jesus did not unite himself to the former, but to the latter. "For as much as the children are partakers of flesh and blood, he also himself likewise took part of the same. For verily he took not an him the nature of angels; but he took on him the seed of Abraham." [358] Had the Eternal Word united himself to an angel, and taken a human body, he would have been an angel, and not a man; not the seed of the woman, or of Abraham. This would not have formed the relation of brethren between him and mankind; but between him and angels.

"It behoved him to be made like unto his brethren in all things;" [359] which he could not have been, had he not taken upon him human nature, consisting in a human soul and body. Had he united himself to an angel, or any other creature of an higher order, and then that creature, united by the Word, have taken a human body, he would not have been made in all things like unto his brethren; but on the contrary, he would have taken but a very inconsiderable part of the human nature; and be far from being a man. This supposed first and greatest creature cannot, with any propriety or truth, be called a human soul, more than any other supposable, or possible creature that could be made: Nor would his union to a human body make him any more a human soul, than if he were not so united. A human soul comes into existence in union with the body, by which human nature, or the human creature, comes into existence.

If this argument has any weight in it, is it not a sufficient reason for rejecting a scheme which does not appear to have any foundation in the sacred Oracles, and will not give any better or more exalted conceptions of the Redeemer, than the common opinion, which views his human nature as beginning to exist at the incarnation? But there are other objections to this scheme: For,

Secondly, If only the body of Jesus came into existence, and was formed in the womb of the virgin Mary, he could not be really her son, or the Son of man, conceived by her, in her womb, as the scripture says he was. She who conceives and brings forth a son, is as really, and as much the mother of his soul, as of his body, and the former is conceived and formed in her womb as much as the latter; and is the greater and chief part of the child or son; yea, the most essential part, without which he would not be a son; but a monster, a body without a soul. Therefore, Mary's conception of her son did imply the conception of soul and body, otherwise she could not be said to conceive a son. The virgin Mary, and Elizabeth, are each of them said to conceive a son. [360] All must allow that the latter conceived a child, with a human soul and body; otherwise it would not have been the conception of a son. And why must not Mary's conception of a son imply the same? If not, how could he be her son, conceived by her?

It is a mistake which some have made, who have supposed that the parents of a child, are the parents or authors of the body, and are instruments of producing that only, and not the soul of the child. They are the cause of one as much as the other, and no more. They are not the efficient cause of either. God is the cause of the existence of both soul and body; of the latter just as much as the other; both come into existence according to a law of nature, by which parents are made the instrumental cause of the production of the child, consisting of both soul and body. The mother, therefore, according to a law of nature, conceives both the soul and body of her son; she does as much towards the one, as towards the other, and is equally the instrumental cause of both; and God is as much the efficient, and immediate cause of the existence of the one as of the other. The human nature of Jesus was conceived not according to a stated law of nature; but in a miraculous way: Yet Mary as really conceived him, and he was as really her son, as if he had been conceived, according to the ordinary course of nature. But he was not conceived by her, neither could he be her son, if his soul, or that creature which took a body in her womb, had existed a mighty, glorious creature, thousands of years before this, as in this case she must have conceived nothing but a body; which is no conception, according to the proper use of the word; and could not be a son.

Thirdly, We find it is the way and manner of the governor of the world, first to put his creatures, who are moral agents, upon trial, that through the appointed time of trial they may exercise and manifest submission to him, and obedience to the law and commands under which they are placed, before he admits them to glory, and publicly confirms them in happiness, that the latter may be the reward of the former, as a testimony of his approbation of their obedience; and this appears highly reasonable and proper. To make a creature and set him above every other creature, and confer upon him great and distinguishing honours, as being the greatest favourite, without putting him in a state of trial, and before he had performed any signal act of obedience, would be contrary to God's way of dealing with his creatures, so far as our acquaintance reaches, and would be very unreasonable, and altogether unbecoming the moral governor of the world, so far as we can judge. But the notion of the pre-existence of the human nature of Jesus Christ, (if on this plan it can be properly called human nature, or a human soul, which indeed it cannot) supposes that God has dealt so with this creature. He made him the first and highest of all creatures; and honoured him by making him the creator of all things, visible and invisible, angels and men; or using him as the great agent or instrument in this work; and set him over all creatures and things, as the director and governor of all worlds, in a state of high exaltation and glory; in which he continued four thousand years, before the great trial of his obedience took place. This therefore, is not to be admitted as true, or any part of the divine plan and conduct, without some cogent reasons which have not yet been produced; or unless it be plainly asserted in divine revelation, which is so far from being true, that it seems to speak a contrary language.

But if, contrary to this notion, the human nature of Jesus Christ first began to exist at the incarnation, and he increased in wisdom and stature until he arrived to manhood, in a state and circumstances of trial; and persevered in a state of temptation, trial and suffering, and in obedience, in the form of a servant, unto death, even the death of the cross; and after this, and as a reward for such obedience and sufferings, "God hath highly exalted him, and given him a name above every name;"--This is perfectly agreeable to God's conduct as moral governor of the world in other instances; and appears to be most reasonable and proper, and is suited to answer the best ends.

Fourthly, The doctrine of the pre-existence of the creature, which was united to the human body in the womb of the virgin Mary, not only has no foundation in divine revelation, and is useless and unreasonable; but appears to be of a dangerous and bad tendency.

Arius, and his followers, have espoused this notion in order to support, and render more plausible their denial of the divinity of Jesus Christ, or that he is truly God as well as man. By applying those passages of scripture to this supposed creature, which their opposers adduced to prove his divinity, and applied to Christ as God, and the second person in the Trinity; which has occasioned so much dispute in the christian world, in the fourth century, and since. It was therefore first advanced and improved to support an error, which really subverts Christianity. This gives just ground of suspicion, that it is itself an error: And it ought not to be received, until it be carefully examined and found to be well supported, and clearly asserted by divine oracles.

And though many who now embrace this notion of the pre-existence of the human nature of Jesus Christ, do not consider themselves as giving up his divinity; or that they are doing any thing in the least inconsistent with this doctrine, or that tends in any degree to weaken or injure it; but hold that this pre-existing creature was united to the Deity, so as to be a divine person, and not a mere creature; yet they, by applying all or most of those passages of scripture to this dignified creature, which they who do not admit this opinion consider as properly applicable to the second person in the Trinity, who in the fulness of time took upon him human nature, do, in a measure, at least, obscure and weaken the doctrine of the divinity of Christ; and that of the Trinity of persons in the Deity; and hereby give great advantage to those who deny and oppose these doctrines.

And this is rather confirmed, than otherwise, by fact and experience; since many, if not most of those who have embraced this sentiment of the pre-existence of the human nature of the Redeemer, give up the doctrine of the Trinity, of three distinct persons subsisting eternally in one God, independent of his works, or manner of operation, or at least doubt about the truth of it; and are rather inclined to consider this first and greatest creature, as a divine person, by a peculiar union to Deity, or to God; not considering him as subsisting in three persons, or in any sense three, considered in himself; but only in his different manner of acting, and distinct offices in his relation to his creatures, and works respecting them. And as this notion takes away and annihilates the divinity of Christ, as a distinct person in the Godhead, it tends to obscure and even remove the idea of his being really and properly God, and to consider him as a creature no otherwise united to God, than by having the divine presence and assistance in a peculiar and extraordinary manner and degree; and enjoying the peculiar favour and love of the Deity: That his divinity consists in this, and nothing more; and that his personality consists wholly in his nature, as a creature, as a distinct person from all other creatures, and vastly superior to them all; and not in his divinity, or divine nature. And as this scheme makes the Logos, or Word, to be the first and greatest of all creatures, they apply all those passages of scripture which speak of Jesus Christ before his incarnation to this creature, who, by taking the human body, became a man. Thus they are naturally, and even necessarily, led to give up the divinity of Jesus Christ, as it has been held by those who have acknowledged and adored him as the true God; and find themselves not to differ in their idea of the Redeemer, in any thing essential or important from the Arians, who have always denied the divinity of Christ, as it has been held by the greatest part of professing christians, in all ages. And this has been realized by fact in too many instances, of those who have embraced the notion of the pre-existence of the human nature of Christ. They have gone on to disbelieve and deny that he is truly God, or at least, to hesitate and doubt of it. And there is reason to fear, and even to expect, that if this notion prevails, a denial of the real divinity of the Redeemer will keep pace with it, and Jesus Christ, instead of being honoured by it, will be degraded infinitely below what he has been believed to be by the christian church in general, in all ages, and deprived of the honours which have been given to him; and which are ascribed to him in the divine oracles, as has been proved above.

When all this is well considered, viz. That the doctrine of the pre-existence of Jesus Christ, as a creature, is no where expressly, or by implication, asserted in the scripture, and is not so consistent with it, as the contrary doctrine;--:hat it is at best a useless notion, and can answer no good end;--that it is not reasonable, and is contrary to the divine conduct, as moral governor;--that it is inconsistent with his being a real man, or the son of the virgin Mary;--that it appears in theory, and from fact and experience, to be of a dangerous and bad tendency; even to the dishonour of Christ, and the denial of his divinity; and consequently to sap the very foundation of christianity;-- that it has been invented and propagated by those who have denied that the Redeemer of men is the true God, equal with the Father, in order to render their opposition to this doctrine more plausible;-- that the best and most sound part of the church, and those who have been most eminent for wisdom and grace, and a conduct most agreeable to the gospel, have not received but rejected this doctrine:- -If all this appears to be true; or if it be in part, and in some measure agreeable to the truth; may not this notion be rejected with safety and a degree of confidence? Yea, ought we not to renounce it, and embrace the contrary, which has been received by the christian church in general, from the days of the apostles, and supported by the best divines?

9. The human nature of Jesus Christ never was tainted with the least moral corruption; but is perfectly holy. This is repeatedly asserted of him in the scriptures; and was absolutely necessary in order to his being the Redeemer of man. "For such an high priest became us, who is holy, harmless, undefiled» separate from sinners, and made higher than the heavens." [361] But how he could be a man, descend from Adam, and be really one of the human race, and not partake of the common corruption of mankind, has been a question of no small importance. This inquiry is answered by observing. That though by a divine constitution, all the posterity of Adam in a constituted natural way, or according to the established course of nature, are born in a state of total moral corruption, in consequence of his apostasy; which has been proved in a former chapter; yet this did not reach or affect the human nature of Jesus Christ, as he was conceived and born in a supernatural and miraculous way, and had no human father.

When the constitution and covenant was made with Adam, and his natural posterity, it was not determined by any thing in this constitution, that there would be any such person as that of the Mediator, as it did not appear by any thing in that covenant, that there would be any need of a Redeemer; he was not, therefore, included in this constitution and covenant, as all the natural posterity of Adam were; but was introduced in consequence of the breach of that covenant; consequently, he did not partake of the moral pollution and depravity which came upon the natural posterity of Adam, who were included in that covenant. And he is not only not one included in the covenant made with Adam; as he does not descend from him in the ordinary, natural way; but he is "the Lord from heaven." The human nature of Christ began to exist in a personal union with the second person in the Triune God, and so is infinitely distinguished from the rest of the children of Adam." [362]

10. The incarnation of Jesus Christ, or his becoming man, by his taking the human nature into a personal union with the divine, is no part of his humiliation, nor is, in itself, in any respect or degree, degrading, laying aside, or hindering his glory. The manner and circumstances of his incarnation, in his being born of a poor virgin, in an infant state, and lodged in a stable, and attended with the innocent infirmities of the human nature, and in it suffering disgrace, pain and death, are all parts of the humiliation of Christ; but the incarnation itself is no part of it. If it were, he would be in a state of humiliation now, and forever hereafter; for he is a man now, and will continue to be such a person eternally.

The union of the divine nature with the human, is an instance of wonderful condescension and grace, and will be celebrated as such, by the redeemed forever. But the second person in the Trinity will not be less, but more honoured and glorious forever, than if he were not man, as well as God.

III. The Redeemer is the Son of God, in a peculiar and appropriated sense, and by which he is distinguished from every other person in the universe. He is therefore called the first begotten, or first born son of God: his only begotten son; his own son; and eminently The Son, and The Son of the Father. His dear Son; or, as it is in the original, The Son of his love; His beloved Son, in whom he is well pleased. "For he received from God the Father, honour and glory, when there came such a voice to him from the excellent glory. This is my beloved Son, in whom I am well pleased." [363] He is "The only begotten Son, which is in the bosom of the Father." [364] Who only knows the Father; and none does or can reveal and make him known but the Son. [365] He being the brightness of his glory, and the express image of his person; he that hath seen the Son, hath seen the Father. [366] Which epithets and declarations distinguish him from all other sons; as much as his Father is distinguished from all other fathers. He is mentioned as the Son of God above an hundred times in the New Testament; and fifty times by the apostle John. And the Father of Jesus Christ, the Son, is mentioned above two hundred and twenty times; and more than one hundred and thirty times in the gospel and epistles of St. John. Jesus Christ often makes use of the epithets, The Father, My Father, &c. This character is represented as essential to the Redeemer and peculiar to him, and is an essential article of the christian faith. This confession Peter made as the common faith of the disciples of Christ. "We believe, and are sure that thou art that Christ, the Son of the living God."[367] This was the Eunuch's faith, required in order to his being baptized. "I believe that Jesus Christ is the Son of God." [368] And he who believes with all his heart, that Jesus Christ is the Son of God, hath the Son, and with him eternal life. When Peter made this confession, "Thou art Christ, the Son of the living God," Christ said to him, "Blessed art thou; for flesh and blood hath not revealed it unto thee, but my Father which is in heaven." [369] "He that believeth on the Son hath everlasting life, and he that believeth not the Son, shall not see life." [370] And John says, "Whosoever shall confess that Jesus is the Son of God, God dwelleth in him, and he in God. Who is he that overcometh the world, but he that believeth that Jesus is the Son of God! He that hath the Son, hath life; and he that hath not the Son of God, hath not life. These things have I written unto you that believe on the name of the Son of God: that ye may know ye have eternal life, and that ye may believe on the name of the Son of God." [371]

It must be farther observed, that this title, the Son of God, is the highest title that is given to the Redeemer, and denotes his divinity, or that he is himself God, and therefore equal with the Father, if his divinity be any where expressed in the Bible; and that it is there abundantly declared, we have before shewed. He styles himself, and is called The Son of Man, more than eighty times in the New Testament, by which epithet his humanity is more especially denoted, but not excluding his divinity. And, on the contrary, he is called the Son of God, more particularly to express his infinitely superior character, his divinity or godhead. In this view, let the following passages be considered. When the angel who declared to the virgin Mary that she should be the mother of the Messiah, expressed to her the greatness of this her Son, he does it by saying that he should be called the Son of the Highest, the Son of God. "He shall be great, and shall be called the Son of the Highest. Therefore also that holy thing which shall be born of thee, shall be called the Son of God."[372] If this were not his greatest, his highest title and character, he most certainly would have given him a higher, and one that did fully express divinity. This, therefore, did express it in the fullest and strongest manner. And no one who believes in the divinity of Christ, can, consistently, have any doubt of it. And when the Father gives him the highest encomium, and recommends him to men, as worthy of their highest regards, implicit obedience, and unlimited trust and confidence, and commands them thus to regard, love, trust in, and obey him, this is the highest character he gives him, by which his divinity is expressed, "This is my beloved Son, in whom I am well pleased: Hear ye him." If this does not express his divinity, we may be sure divinity is no part of his

The System of Doctrines, contained in Divine Relation, Explained and Defended Volume I

character; and that he is not God. So, when Peter undertakes to express the idea he had of the high and glorious character of his Lord and Master, he does it in the following words, "Thou art the Christ, the Son of the living God." If Peter believed the divinity of Christ, he certainly expressed this in these words; for he did not conceive of any higher character, that could be given in any other words. This also appears by Nathaniel's using this epithet, when he was struck with wonder and surprise at the omniscience of Christ. "Rabbi, thou art the Son of God, thou art the King of Israel."[373] When our Lord Jesus Christ proposed himself to the man whom he had restored to sight, as the proper object of his faith and trust, he said to him, "Dost thou believe on the Son of God?" And when he told the man that he himself was the person, he said, "Lord, I believe. And he worshipped him."[374] It appears from this, that Son of God, was the highest title which Jesus assumed, and that this had special reference to, and expressed his divinity; and therefore in this character, and as the Son of God, this pious man paid him divine honour, and worshipped him. When the disciples of our Lord, and all that were in the ship with them, had seen him walking upon the sea, in the midst of a terrible storm, and reducing the boisterous winds, and raging waves, to a calm, by his word and presence, they were struck with a fresh and affecting conviction of his divinity, that he was God, and expressed it by coming to him, falling down and worshipping him, "saying, of a truth, thou art the Son of God."[375] In which words they expressed his divinity, and gave a reason for their worshipping him, as their Lord and their God, viz. that they were sure from clear and abundant evidence, that he was the Son of God. The apostle John, when he would represent Jesus Christ in his highest and most glorious character, gives him this title, and adds, "This is the true God." He says, "We know that the Son of God is come, and hath given us an understanding, that we may know him that is true: And we are in him that is true, even in his Son Jesus Christ. This is the true God, and eternal life."[376]

It is to be farther observed, that when our Lord said to the Jews. "My Father worketh hitherto, and I work," the Jews, therefore, sought the more to kill him, because he said that God was his Father, (his own proper Father, as it is in the original) making himself equal with God." This is to be understood as the sense which St. John the Evangelist puts upon the words of Christ, "My Father worketh hitherto, and I work." For this was making himself equal with God the Father, as doing the same work with him: And this is represented as implied in God's being his own Father; or in his being the Father's own Son, the Son of God. But if we understand it as the sense which the Jews put upon the words of Christ, and that they said this was making himself equal with God, it amounts to the same thing; for it appears that their inference was just; and our Saviour is so far from denying it to be true, that in his reply to them, he confirms it, and asserts that whatsoever the Father does, the Son does the same; and instances in his raising the dead, and judging the world, and having all things, and all power in his hands. "That all men should honour the Son, even as they honour the Father."[377] Thus he makes the Son equal with the Father. Hence it appears that to be the Son of God, and God's own Son, is the same with a divine person, and denotes one who is truly God; and that this title is used to express the divinity, rather than the humanity of Jesus Christ.

The same appears from what passed between our Lord and the Jews at another time. He said to them, "I and my Father are One." This, they said, was blasphemy, because being a man, he made himself God. It is plain from the answer which he makes to them that they considered him as a blasphemer, because he claimed to be the Son of God, by calling God his Father. "Say ye of him, whom the Father hath sanctified, and sent into the world, Thou blasphemest, because I said, I am the Son of God?" This was the blasphemy with which they charged him; because they considered his saying, that he was the Son of God, by calling God his Father, as an assertion that he was God.[378] And it appears, not only from this passage, but from others, that the Jews, and others, did affix the idea of divinity to the Son of God, and considered this title as expressing a character infinitely above a mere creature. When Jesus was arraigned before the Jewish council, the High Priest charged him with the solemnity of an oath, saying, "I adjure thee by the living God, that thou tell us, whether thou be the Christ, the Son of the living God." And when Jesus answered in the affirmative, he with all the members of the council, charged him with blasphemy; and pronounced him worthy of death for making this claim.[379] And they brought this accusation against him to Pilate, "We have a law, and by our law he ought to die, because he made himself the Son of God. When, therefore, Pilate heard that saying, he was the more afraid."[380] By this, it is evident that Pilate considered the Son of God, to imply divinity. When the Centurion, and the guard who were with him, saw the earthquake and the other supernatural events which attended the crucifixion of Jesus Christ, "they feared greatly, saying. Truly this was the Son of God."[381] From this, it is evident that they considered the Son of God to be more than a man, at least, if not really God.

There was some idea and belief propagated among other nations, as well as the Jews, of an extraordinary personage, a divinity, who was denominated The Son of God, and who was to make his appearance in the world. To this, Nebuchadnezzar doubtless had reference, when he said, that in a vision, he saw a fourth person, walking in the midst of the fire of the furnace into which he had cast three men; and that none of them had been hurt by the fire; and the form of the fourth was like the Son of God. [382] And who but this divine person can be meant by Agur, when he says, "Who hath ascended up into heaven, or descended? Who hath gathered the wind in his fists? Who hath bound the waters in a garment? Who hath established all the ends of the earth? What is his name, and what is his Son's name, if thou canst tell?" [383]

This epithet and character we find expressly mentioned by David, the divinely inspired king of Israel, in the second Psalm. And he is there introduced and described, as a divinity, who claims divine homage, trust, and worship, as the Omnipotent heir, possessor and ruler of the world. "I will declare the decree. The Lord hath said unto me, Thou art MY SON, this day have I begotten thee. Ask of me, and I shall give thee the heathen for thine inheritance, and the uttermost parts of the earth for thy possession. Thou shalt break them with a rod of iron; thou shalt dash them in pieces like a potter's vessel. Be wise now, therefore, O ye kings; be instructed, ye judges of the earth. Serve the Lord with fear, and rejoice with trembling. Kiss the Son, lest he be angry, and ye perish from the way, when his wrath is kindled but a little. Blessed are all they that put their trust in him."[384] From this ancient oracle in Israel, and from a revelation which was made upon the first apostasy, and handed down by tradition, not only the Jews, but also those of other nations who had any particular connexion with them, were taught to consider the expected Messiah as the Son of God in a peculiar and appropriated sense; and as implying real divinity. Therefore, it was supposed on all hands, that this person, the Son of God, the King of Israel, the King of the Jews, was to be worshipped as worthy to receive divine honours. Hence the wise men from the East, being admonished of the birth of this glorious personage, came to worship him, to pay him divine honours; for which they had a particular warrant, having had him pointed out to them by a star, which was a known symbol, or hieroglyphic of the Divinity, or a God. And Herod took it for granted, that this person was to be worshipped, and receive divine honours. For he said to the wise men, "When ye have found him, bring me word again, that I may come and worship him also."

All this will be of no weight, indeed, and as nothing with the Anti-trinitarians, the Sebellians; and with all those who deny the divinity of Jesus Christ, the Arians and Socinians. But they who believe in a Trinity of persons in the Deity, and that Jesus Christ is God, the second person of the Trinity, must be sensible that he is called the Son of God, the Son of the Father, with a special reference to his divine nature, and to denote his Godhead, as the second person in the Triune God.-- The Arians and Socinians hold that he is the Son of God, considered as a mere creature, being by this distinguished from all other creatures; and consequently that there was no Son of God before this creature did exist. The latter, or Trinitarians, believe that the Sonship of Jesus Christ, necessarily includes his divinity; but are not all agreed as to the foundation of his Sonship, and in what it consists. It has been generally believed, and the common doctrine of the church of Christ, from the beginning of the fourth century, and so far as appears from the days of the apostles to this time, that Jesus Christ is the eternal Son of God: That his Sonship is essential to him, as the second person in the Trinity, and that in this sense he is the only begotten Son of the Father, antecedent to his incarnation, and independent on it, even from eternity. But there are some who think that the Sonship of the Redeemer consists in an union of the second person of the Trinity, or the Word, with the human nature; and that he became the Son of God by becoming man; and therefore before the incarnation, there was no Son of God, though there were a Trinity of persons in the Godhead. This opinion seems to be rather gaining ground, and spreading, of late.

Those on each side of this question differ in their opinion of the importance of it, and of the bad tendency of either of these opposite sentiments. Some suppose that the difference is of little or no importance, as both believe the Redeemer to be God and man, in one person, and that he is the Son of God, and that this implies his divinity, though they differ in opinion respecting the time and manner of his filiation. Others think this is a difference so great and important, and attended with such consequences; and that those who are opposed to them on this point embrace such a great and dangerous error, that they ought to be strenuously opposed: and consequently do not desire an accommodation, or think it possible.

Though it be needless and improper here to undertake the labour of entering into all the arguments which have been produced, or may be mentioned in support of each side of this question; yet the following observations may not be altogether useless; but may be of some help to form a judgment upon this point, agreeable to the scriptures.

1. As this question respects the character of the Redeemer, it may justly be considered as an important one; as every thing relating to his character is very important and interesting. Who would be willing to be found at last taking the wrong side of this question; and always to have entertained so unbecoming ideas and conceptions of the Redeemer, which his must be, if on this point he embraces and contends for that which is directly contrary to the truth? Though such an error should not be fatal to him who embraces it, but be consistent with his being a real christian; yet it must be a very criminal mistake, and dishonourable to Jesus Christ; as every idea of him must be, which is

contrary to his true character: For that is so perfect and glorious, that nothing can be taken from it, or added to it, which will not mar and dishonour it. His character, as it respects the question before us, is without doubt properly and clearly stated in divine revelation, and if we embrace that which is contrary to the truth, it must be wholly our own fault, and a very criminal abuse of the advantages which we enjoy, to know the only true God, and Jesus Christ his Son, whom he has sent. Those considerations ought to awaken our attention to this subject, and excite a concern and earnest desire to know and embrace the truth; which will be attended with a modest, humble, diligent inquiry, sensible of the danger in which we are, through prejudice, or from other causes, of embracing error; and earnestly looking to the great Prophet to lead us into the truth.

2. What has been observed above, and, it is believed, made evident, viz. that the term, Son of God, so often given to Christ, is used to denote his divine nature, and to express his divinity, rather than his humanity, seems naturally, if not necessarily, to lead us to consider this character as belonging to him independent of his union to the human nature, and antecedent to his becoming man; and therefore, that it belongs to him as God, the second person in the Trinity. For if his Sonship consists in his union to the human nature, and he became a son, only by becoming a man; then this character depends wholly upon this union, and is derived from his being made flesh: Therefore this epithet could not be properly used to denote his divinity, independent of his humanity, or what he is as a divine person, antecedent to his incarnation; or to express his divine, rather than his human nature. And Son of God, would be no higher a character, and express no more than Son of man; which is contrary to the idea which the scripture gives us on this head, as has been shown.

This may, perhaps, be in some measure illustrated by the following instance. The son of a nobleman of the first honour and dignity, came from Europe, and married the daughter of a plebeian in America, by which he became his son: But as his honour and dignity did not consist in his marrying this woman, or in his being the son of the plebeian, by this union with his daughter, but in his original character; no man thought of expressing his highest and most dignified character by which he was worthy of the greatest respect, by using an epithet which denoted only his union to that woman, and which was not applicable to him in any other view; or by calling him son, as expressing this new relation: But the highest title which they gave him, was that which had a special respect to, and expressed his original character, which he sustained antecedent to this union; and in which his highest dignity consisted. And he being the son of a nobleman and a lord, in which all his honour and dignity did consist, they used this phrase, My noble Lord, to express their highest respect, and his most worthy character. This epithet was always used to express his original and highest character and relation, and could not, with propriety, be used to express any thing else. He was often called, indeed, the son of the plebeian, when they designed particularly to express his union to his wife, and speak of him as standing in this relation.

3. The Son of God is spoken of in many instances, if not in every one where this term is used, so as will naturally lead the reader to consider him as sustaining this character and relation antecedent to his incarnation, and independent of it. "God so loved the world that he gave his only begotten Son." [385] Do not these words seem to express this idea, viz. that there existed an only begotten son, antecedent to his being given; that God gave this his Son to the world by his becoming flesh, and being united to the human nature; and not that he became his Son by this union? "In this was manifested the love of God towards us, because that God sent his only begotten Son into the world, that we might live through him. Herein is love, not that we loved God, but that he loved us, and sent his Son to be a propitiation for our sins." [386] If God sent his only begotten Son into the world, does not this suppose he had a Son to send, antecedent to his sending him; and that he did not become his Son by his sending him into the world, or only in consequence of this? This is expressed in the same manner by St. Paul. "But when the fulness of time was come God sent forth his Son, made of a woman, made under the law." [387] The Son was sent forth. Does not this seem at least to imply that there was a Son to be sent forth antecedent to his being made of a woman, and that he was not made a Son, by being made of a woman, or becoming man? "No man hath seen God at any time: The only begotten Son, which is in the bosom of the Father, he hath declared him." [388] Do not these words naturally lead us to conceive of the only begotten Son as existing in the nearest union with the Father as his Son, independent of the human nature?

It is said, "God was manifested in the flesh." [389] It would be unnatural and absurd to suppose, from this > expression, that Jesus Christ was not God, antecedent to his being manifested in the flesh, and that by his becoming man, he became a God. Directly the contrary to this is asserted, viz. that he who is God from eternity, did in time appear in the human nature, and manifested himself to be God, independent of the flesh, in which he appeared. It is also said, "For this purpose, the Son of God was manifested, that he might destroy the works of the devil." [390] These two passages appear to be parallel. God manifested in the flesh, and the Son of God manifested, are two expressions of the same thing. From this it may be inferred, that the Son of God, and God, are synonymous here, and of the same import. This serves to confirm what has been said above of the use and meaning of the term, Son of God. And may it not with equal certainty be inferred from these two passages, compared together, that the Son of God existed in this character as the Son of God, antecedent to his manifestation in the flesh, and independent of it; and that he did not become the Son of God by being made flesh? If God be manifested in the flesh, there must be a God to be manifested antecedent to such manifestation, and independent of it. And is it not equally certain that if the Son of God be manifested, he must have existed the Son of God, antecedent to such manifestation, and independent of it? Consequently he did not become the Son of God by his being manifested in the flesh: His Sonship does not consist in the union of the divine and human natures in one person. His personality existed before this union with the human nature; and he was the Son of God before this: This same Son of God, this same person who existed without beginning, assumed the human nature, not a human person, into a union with himself, his own person, and so appeared, was manifested in the flesh. ?

When David speaks of the Son of God, and represents the Father as saying, "Thou art my Son, this day have I begotten thee," so long before his incarnation, the idea which most naturally arises in the mind from this is, that there was then such a person as the Son, who did at that time declare the decree, by the mouth of David; and not, that there should in some future time be a Son begotten, who should then declare the decree. "I will declare the decree: The Lord said unto me, thou art my son, this day have I begotten thee." It is very unnatural, and contrary to all propriety of speech to suppose, "this day have I begotten thee," means I will beget thee in some future time; and that the Son should be made to declare the decree, long before any such person existed; and when there was in fact no such Son. The decree which the Son declares is not that declaration, "Thou art my son, this day have I begotten thee;" but what follows, "ask of me, and I will give thee the heathen for thine inheritance, and the uttermost parts of the earth for thy possession. Thou shalt break them with a rod of iron, &:c." "This day," that is, now, not in time which is passed, or which is to come; for with God there is no succession, no time passed or to come; but he exists, as we may say, in one eternal, unsuccessive now. Therefore, when he speaks of an eternal, immanent act, it is most properly expressed thus, "This day, or now, have I begotten thee." This therefore is the sense in which the best divines have generally understood it.

St. Paul cites this passage as being illustrated and verified in the resurrection of Jesus Christ.[391] But he cannot mean that he by the resurrection became the Son of God, and was then begotten: for he had this title before that. His meaning is explained by himself in his epistle to the Romans. "Declared lo be the Son of God, by the resurrection from the dead." [392] That is, this was a fresh and open manifestation and declaration that he was indeed what had been often asserted of him, and what he always was: The only begotten Son of God.

What the angel said to the virgin Mary, "He shall be great, and shall be called the Son of the highest--The Holy Ghost shall come upon thee, and the power of the highest shall overshadow thee: Therefore also that holy thing which shall be born of thee, shall be called the Son of God," cannot reasonably be understood as a declaration that his sonship consisted in his miraculous conception, or in the union of the second person of the Trinity with the human nature, thus conceived: But that this child, conceived in this manner, and born of a virgin, should appear, and be known to be the Son of God, that very person who had been spoken of and known in all past ages by this title; of whom Isaiah had particularly spoken, when he said, "Behold, a virgin shall conceive, and bear a Son, and shall call his name Immanuel. Unto us a Son is given, and the government shall be upon his shoulder: And his name shall be called, Wonderful, Counsellor, the mighty God:" [393] That this Son was now to be born of the virgin Mary: The long expected Messiah, who is considered and spoken of by the people of God, by the title of the Son of God, which title he shall bear, as he is indeed the mighty God.

We are naturally lead to consider the Son of God as existing in this character before his incarnation, and the same with the Word, by what is said of him in the first chapter of John. "The Word was made flesh, and dwelt among us; and we beheld his glory as of the only begotten of the Father. No man hath seen God at any time. The only begotten Son, which is in the bosom of the Father, he hath declared him. John bare witness of him, and cried, saying, this was he of whom I spake, he that cometh after me, is preferred before me: For he was before me. And I saw, and bear record that this is the Son of God." Here John is represented as asserting that the Son of God, concerning whom he bore witness, did exist before him, which therefore must be before his incarnation; for John was conceived before the incarnation of Jesus. But how can this be true, if there were no Son of God, before John existed? But if we consider the Word and the Son of God as synonymous, who was in the beginning with God, and who was God, and created all things, this whole chapter will be plain and easy to be understood; and we shall see John bearing witness to the Son of God, who existed before him in this character, and was now come in the flesh.

We find the same representation made in the epistle to the Hebrews. "God, who spake in time past unto the fathers, by the prophets, hath in these last days spoken unto us by his Son, whom he hath appointed heir of all things; by whom also he made the worlds. Who being the brightness of his glory, and the express image of his person, and upholding all things by the word of his power," &c. How could God make the worlds by his Son, four thousand years before he had a Son; and on this supposition, where is the propriety or truth of this assertion? And how could the Son be said to uphold all things by the word of his power, thousands of years before any Son existed? "And again, when he bringeth the first begotten into the world, he saith, And let all the angels of God worship him." This expression naturally suggests the idea that God the Father had a first begotten Son to bring into the world, whom he commanded the angels to worship. How can he be said to bring his first begotten Son into the world, when he had no such Son to bring into the world; and indeed never did bring this his Son into the world, if he was begotten, and received his sonship in this world, when he took the human nature in the womb of the virgin, and was not a son before?

Again, speaking of Melchisedec, he says, he was "Without father, without mother, without descent, having neither beginning of days, nor end of life; but made like unto the Son of God."[394] If there were no Son of God till the human nature of Christ existed, then the Son of God did begin to exist; consequently there was a beginning of his days; and Melchisedec was not made like him, but unlike to him, by having no beginning of days.

Since there are so many passages of scripture, (and there are many more than have now been mentioned) which seem to represent the Redeemer as the Son of God, antecedent to his incarnation, and independent of it, which will naturally lead those who attend to them to this idea of him; and some of them cannot be easily reconciled to the contrary opinion; this will fully account for the generally received doctrine in the christian world from the earliest ages to this time, viz. That the Redeemer of man is the second person in the Trinity, the eternal Son of God, who in the fulness of time was made flesh, by a personal union with the human nature.

4. It is worthy of consideration, whether the contrary opinion, viz. That the Redeemer is the Son of God, only by the second person in the Trinity being united to human nature, and becoming man, does not naturally lead to dangerous and evil consequences; and what good end is to be answered by it? If it be not agreeable to scripture, we know it must be dangerous and hurtful in a greater or less degree, (as all errors respecting the person and character of the Redeemer are) and naturally tends to lead into other mistakes, still greater, and of worse consequence. And if it be agreeable to scripture, it certainly has no bad tendency. If, therefore, it does appear from reasoning upon it, or from fact and experience, that this opinion tends to evil consequences, and has a bad effect; we may safely conclude that it is wrong, and contrary to divine revelation.

1. Does not this sentiment tend to lower our ideas of the Redeemer, and lead into a way of thinking less honourably of him? It has been observed that it appears from scripture, that this title, Son of God, was used to express the highest and most honourable idea which his friends had of his person and character. But if we understand by it, nothing but what takes place by his union to man, by taking flesh upon him, and consider it as signifying nothing but what took place by his becoming man, nothing is expressed by it more than by Son of man: And we are left without any epithet or common scripture phrase, whereby to express the divinity, the Godhead of the Redeemer, and his equality with the Father. Thus, instead of raising our conceptions of the Redeemer, does it not tend to sink them? Does not the sonship of Christ become an infinitely less and more inconsiderable matter, upon this plan, than that which has always been esteemed the orthodox sentiment on this point, which considers his sonship, as wholly independent of the whole creation, as eternal, and altogether divine?

We live in an age when the enemies of the Redeemer lift up their heads, and are suffered to multiply and prevail. The deists attempt to cast him out as an imposter. Arians and Socinians strip him of his divinity: And the careless, ignorant, immoral and profane, treat him with contempt or neglect. This is agreeable to his great enemy, Satan; who seems now to be let loose in an unusual degree, and has uncommon power among men, to lead them into gross errors, and those especially which are dishonourable to Christ, and injurious to his character. And if this sentiment now under consideration, concerning the sonship of the Redeemer, should spread and prevail now, this would be no evidence in favour of it; but, considering what has been now observed, concerning it, would it not give reason to suspect, at least, that it is dishonourable to the Son of God, and leads to other errors yet more dishonourable to him?

This leads to observe,

2. It is worthy of consideration, whether this doctrine of the filiation of Jesus Christ, does not tend to reject the doctrine of the Trinity, as it has been held by those who have been called the orthodox in the christian church, and leads to what is called Sabellianism; which considers the Deity as but one person, and to be three only out of respect to the different manner or kind of his operations.

This notion of the sonship of Christ, leads to suppose that the Deity is the Father of the

Mediator, without distinction of persons; and that by Father so often mentioned in the New Testament, and generally in relation to the Son, is commonly, if not always, meant Deity, without distinction of persons. If this be so, it tends to exclude all distinction of persons in God, and to make the personality of the Redeemer to consist wholly in the human nature; and finally, to make his union with Deity no more, but the same which Arians and Socinians admit, viz. the same which takes place between God and good men in general; but in a higher and peculiar degree.

But if there be no tendency in this doctrine of the sonship of Christ, to the consequences which have been now mentioned; and it can be made evident that none of those supposed evils do attend it, or can follow from it; yet it remains to be considered what advantage attends it, and the good ends it will answer, if it were admitted to be true. None will say, it is presumed, that it is more agreeable to the general expressions of scripture relating to this point, than the opposite doctrine; who well considers what has been observed above. The most that any one can with justice say with respect to this is, that the scripture may be so construed and understood, as to be consistent with the sonship of Christ, commencing at the incarnation, however inconsistent with it some passages may appear at first view.

It may be thought, perhaps, that this notion of the sonship of the Redeemer is attended with two advantages, if not with more, viz. It frees the doctrine of the Trinity from that which is perfectly incomprehensible, and appears a real contradiction and absurdity; that the second person should be Son of the first, who is the Father; the Son being begotten by the Father from eternity; than which nothing can be more inconceivable, and seemingly absurd. And this appears inconsistent with the second person being equal with the first; for a son begotten of a father, implies inferiority, and that he exists after his father, and consequently begins to exist, and is dependent. Both these difficulties are wholly avoided, it is thought, by supposing that the second person in the Trinity became a son by being united to the human nature, and begotten in the womb of the virgin. And it is probable that these supposed advantages have recommended this scheme of the sonship of Christ, to those who embrace it, and led them to reject the commonly received opinion; and not a previous conviction that the former is most agreeable to the scripture. This therefore demands our serious and candid attention. And the following things may be observed upon it.

1. If we exclude every thing from our creed, concerning God, his existence, and the manner of his existence, which to us is incomprehensible and unaccountable, we must reject the doctrine of the Trinity in unity, and even of the existence of a God. The doctrine of three persons in one God is wholly inconceivable by us, and Unitarians consider it as the greatest contradiction and absurdity imaginable. And those Trinitarians, who have undertaken to explain it, and make it more intelligible, have generally failed of giving any light; but have really made it absurd and even ridiculous, by "darkening counsel by words without knowledge." If we reasoned properly on the matter, we should expect to find in a revelation which God has made of himself, his being and manner of subsistence, mysteries which we can by no means understand, which are to creatures wonderful, and wholly unaccountable. For the being of God, and the manner of his existence, and of his subsisting, must be infinitely above our comprehension: God is infinitely great, and we know him not. And if we attempt to search out these mysteries by reason, we are prone to think they are contradictions and absurdities, merely because our reason cannot fathom them; and they appear more unintelligible, the more we try to understand them. "Canst thou by searching find out God? Canst thou find out the Almighty to perfection? It is as high as heaven, what canst thou do? Deeper than hell, what canst thou know? The measure thereof is longer than the earth, and broader than the sea." [395] "Teach us what we shall say unto him, (and what we shall say concerning him;) for we cannot order our speech by reason of darkness. Shall it be told him that I speak?" and attempt to comprehend and explain the mysteries that relate to his existence? "If a man speaks surely he shall be swallowed up." [396] If a man undertake thus to speak, instead of giving any light, he will be involved and overwhelmed in impenetrable darkness.

They, therefore, who do not believe the eternal sonship of Jesus Christ, because it is mysterious and incomprehensible, and to some it appears to be full of contradiction, will, if they be consistent with themselves, for the same reason, reject the doctrine of a Trinity of persons in one God. [397]

2. If the doctrine of the eternal generation and sonship of the second person in the Trinity be soberly and modestly considered in the light of the foregoing observation, and with a proper sense of our own darkness and infinite inferiority to the divine Being, and how little we can know of him; we shall not be forward to pronounce it inconsistent with reason, and absurd; but be convinced, that to do thus, is very bold and assuming; and that it may be consistent and true, notwithstanding any thing we may know; though it be mysterious and incomprehensible. This is a divine generation, infinitely above any thing that takes place among creatures, and infinitely different. It is that of which we can have no adequate idea, and is infinitely out of our reach. What incompetent judges are we then of this matter? What right or ability have we to pronounce it absurd or inconsistent,

The System of Doctrines, contained in Divine Relation, Explained and Defended Volume I

when we have no capacity to know or determine what is true, consistent, or inconsistent in this high point, any farther than God has been pleased to reveal it to us? There may be innumerable mysteries in the existence and manner of subsistence of the infinite Being, which are, and must be, incomprehensible, by a finite understanding. God has been pleased, for wise ends, to reveal that of the Trinity, and this of the eternal generation and sonship of the second person: And he has done it in a manner, and in words best suited to convey those ideas of it to men, which it is necessary they should have: And we ought to receive it with meekness and implicit submission, using our reason in excluding every thing which is contrary to, or below infinite perfection, and absolute independence; without pretending to comprehend it, or to be able to judge of that which is infinitely high and divine, by that which takes place among creatures, with respect to generation, and father and son.

God is said in scripture, to repent and be grieved at his heart; to be angry, and to have his fury to come up in his face; and hands, feet, eyes, mouth, lips and tongue, &c. are ascribed to him. These words are designed and suited to convey useful ideas, and important instruction to men. But if we should understand these expressions as meaning the same thing in the Divine Being, that they do when applied to men; we must entertain very unworthy, and most absurd notions of God, and wholly inconsistent with other declarations in the sacred Oracles. But if we exclude every thing that is human, or that implies any change or imperfection from these expressions when applied to the Deity, they will convey nothing absurd or inconsistent, or that is unworthy of God. And it will doubtless be equally so in the case before us; if it be constantly kept in mind that the only begotten Son of God denotes nothing human, but is infinitely above any thing which relates to natural, or creature generation, and does not include any beginning, change, dependence, inferiority, or imperfection. This will effectually exclude all real absurdity and contradiction.

It will be asked, perhaps, when all this is excluded from our ideas of generation, of Father and Son, what idea will remain in our minds, which is conveyed by these words? Will they not be without any signification to us, and altogether useless? To this, the following answer may be given: From what is revealed concerning this high and incomprehensible mystery, we learn, that in the existence of the Deity, there is that which is high above our thoughts, as the heavens are above the earth, infinitely beyond our conception, and different from any thing which takes place among creatures, which is a foundation of a personal distinction, as real and great as that between father and son among men, and infinitely more perfect: Which distinction may be in the best manner conveyed to us by Father and Son, to express the most perfect union and equality; that the Son is the brightness of the Father's glory, and the express image of his person, and that there is infinite love and endearment between them; and that in the economy of the work of redemption, the Son is obedient to the Father, Sec. All this, and much more, our minds are capable of conceiving from what is revealed on this high and important subject; which is suited to impress our hearts with a sense of the incomprehensible, infinite, adorable perfection and glory of the Father and the Son; and is necessary in order to give us a right understanding of the gospel; of the true character of the Redeemer, and of the work of redemption.

What has been now said under this second particular, may serve to remove the other supposed difficulty in admitting the eternal filiation of the second person in the Trinity, viz. that it represents the Son as inferior to the Father, and as existing after him, and therefore his existence had a beginning. This is obviated by the above observations; and particularly by this, that it is a divine filiation, and therefore infinitely unlike that which is human; and above our comprehension. Besides, to suppose eternal generation admits of before or after, or of a beginning, is inconsistent. It may be further observed,

3. That the opinion that Jesus Christ is the first and only begotten Son of God, by the second person in the Trinity becoming incarnate, and united to the human nature, is, perhaps, attended with as great difficulties as the other which has been considered, if not greater. If so, the inducement to embrace it, and reject the other, which we are examining, wholly ceases.

If the Son was begotten by the miraculous formation of the human nature; then the Holy Ghost begot the Son and is the Father, as much as the first person in the Trinity. For the angel said to the virgin, "The Holy Ghost shall come upon thee, and the power of the Highest shall overshadow thee: Therefore also that holy thing which shall be born of thee, shall be called the Son of God." If we take these words as referring only to the production of the human nature, and if it be granted that by the highest, is meant the first person in the Trinity, of which there does not appear to be any evidence, yet the third person, the Holy Ghost, is represented as doing as much, and being as active in this production as the first person. But if this were no difficulty, and the first person of the Trinity be supposed to produce the human nature, and in this sense to be the Father of Jesus Christ; yet this will make him his Father in no other and higher sense than he is the Father of angels, and of Adam; and Jesus Christ will be the Son of God in no other, or higher sense than they; for they were created and formed in an extraordinary, miraculous way.

If the Son was begotten by uniting the second person of the Trinity with the human nature, and the filiation of the Son is supposed to consist wholly in being thus united to man; this is attended with the following difficulties, as great, perhaps, if not greater, than those which attend the eternal Sonship of the second person.

1. This is as different in nature and kind from natural or creature generation, as eternal divine generation; and the one bears no analogy or likeness to the other.

2. This union of God with the creature so as to become one person, is as mysterious and incomprehensible, as the eternal Sonship of the second person of the Trinity; and as inexplicable: So that nothing is gained with respect to this, by embracing this scheme.

3. It is not agreeable to scripture to suppose that the first person of the Trinity only, united the second person to the human nature, and so became a Father by thus begetting a Son. The third person, the Holy Ghost, is represented as doing this, or at least, being active in it; and there is nothing expressly said of the first person doing any thing respecting it as such. "The Holy Ghost shall come upon thee, and the power of the Highest shall overshadow thee: Therefore also, that holy thing which shall be born of thee, shall be called the Son of God." "Now the birth of Jesus Christ was on this wise. When his mother, Mary, was espoused to Joseph, before they came together, she was found with child of the Holy Ghost." And the angel of the Lord said unto Joseph, "Fear not to take unto thee Mary thy wife: For that which is conceived in her, is of the Holy Ghost." [398] And this uniting the divine nature with the human, is expressly ascribed, not to the first, but to the second person. "For as much as the children are partakers of flesh and blood, he also himself took part of the same. For verily he took not on him the nature of angels; but he took on him the seed of Abraham." [399] Do not they speak not only without scripture, but contrary to it, who say that the first person of the Trinity became a Father by uniting the second person to the human nature, in the womb of the virgin Mary; by which the latter became the only begotten Son of the Father? That the relation of Father and Son began in the incarnation of Christ, and consists wholly in this? And do they by this supposition avoid any difficulty, and render the filiation of the Redeemer more consistent, intelligible, or honourable to him? Let the thoughtful, candid, discerning reader judge.

IV. The Redeemer of man, who is God-man, the Son of God, sustains the character of Mediator between God and man. That such a person only is equal to this, to mediate between God and rebellious man, so as to effect a reconciliation, will be made evident when we proceed more particularly to consider the work of redemption, what is implied in it, and what was necessary in order to effect it. And it will also appear that he is every way qualified to sustain such an office and station, and in the best manner complete the arduous, the glorious work; and the character of this infinitely high, important, and wonderful personage will be more fully investigated and displayed in the sequel.

IMPROVEMENT

1. By attending as above, to the person and character of the Redeemer, we are in some measure prepared to see the folly of that pride which has led many to reject every thing in divine revelation which does not comport with their boasted reason, and is to them, dark and unintelligible; and to be sensible of the reasonableness and importance of modesty, humility and self diffidence; while we think and inquire concerning the being and character of God, and the Son of God, the Redeemer. Many by this pride, and trusting to what they call their own reason, have been led to renounce divine revelation, the only light and sure guide, in the high and important business of religion; and have plunged themselves into darkness and delusion. And others, though they profess to believe the Bible to be a revelation from God, reject the most essential and peculiar doctrines contained in it, on the account of which, men principally stand in need of a revelation from heaven.

When we are once convinced, by undeniable, clear and abundant evidence, that the Bible contains a revelation from God; if we make a right use of our reason, we shall expect to find in it, declarations concerning God, his character and works, which are beyond our comprehension, and in this respect perfect mysteries to us; and that we shall not, at first, understand many things; yea, they may appear inconsistent and contradictory to us, which afterwards, by farther study and increase in the knowledge of divine things, we may understand, and see them to be plain and perfectly consistent. The things of God, or heavenly things, are so infinitely high, great and wonderful, that the greatest created, finite mind, falls infinitely short of fully comprehending all or any of them. The angels do not perfectly understand them. They may make swift advances in the knowledge of them, without end, and yet will forever fall infinitely short of reaching to their infinite height, so as to comprehend all. How ignorant and short sighted, then, must man be in those things, who not only has less natural capacity, but is sunk down in that moral depravity which is blindness itself, with respect to the things of the Spirit of God, and carries in the nature of it strong prejudices against them. How unreasonable, how arrogant, is it in him to imagine, that he can, by his own scanty,

The System of Doctrines, contained in Divine Relation, Explained and Defended Volume I
corrupted discerning, at once understand, and fully comprehend, all he needs to know and believe concerning God and heavenly things! Such a conceit, such pride and arrogance, can take place no where, but among such fallen, apostate creatures as mankind are; and serves to verify the ancient declaration, "Vain man would be wise, though man be born like a wild ass's colt." [400]

If a philosopher should undertake to teach children of eight or ten years old, a system of philosophy, would he think himself well treated by them, if they were disposed to call in question the truth of every proposition of his, which they did not directly understand; and immediately conclude that every thing he delivered to them for truth, was inconsistent and absurd, which they were not able to reconcile? So long as they were of this disposition, they could receive no instruction from him. They would find many things perfectly dark and unintelligible to them, and others would appear to their narrow, childish conceptions, inconsistent and impossible. But the objects of natural philosophy are not so much above the understanding and capacity of these children, as heavenly things are above the understanding of men. There is an infinite difference; especially if we take into the account, man's moral depravity, which blinds him to the things of the Spirit of God.

There are many things in natural philosophy, which men of the greatest capacities, and who have attended most to them, and made them their chief study, cannot understand; but remain unintelligible mysteries: Yea, there are propositions which appear to be inconsistent, and yet both of them must be received as true. For instance, it can be demonstrated that matter is infinitely divisible: And that matter is finite, is equally demonstrable; which two demonstrable propositions appear to be perfectly inconsistent.

And shall we, to whom earthly things are, in so many instances, unintelligible, and appear inconsistent, imagine, that when God speaks to us of heavenly things, things infinitely great, high and wonderful, we are able to comprehend them all; and are warranted to reject every thing as not true, and not revealed to us by him, which we do not understand, or are not able to reconcile with each other!

Let us rather become fools, that we may be wise. Sensible of our ignorance, and proneness to imbibe error, to love darkness rather than light; and put light for darkness, and darkness for light, let us study the Bible with a modest diffidence in our own reason and wisdom, and implicit confidence in our divine Instructor, looking to him to open our eyes to understand the scriptures, and behold the wonderful things revealed in those sacred oracles. "The meek will he guide in judgment; the meek will he teach his way." [401]

II. This subject brings into view the infinite fulness and sufficiency of God. A fulness equal to the wants of sinners, and suited to relieve and save them. In order to this, he must be not only infinitely powerful, wise and good; but subsist in a manner, of which we could know nothing, had he not revealed it, viz. a Trinity in unity. And when revealed, it is infinitely above our comprehension. And if it were not so, we should have no reason to believe this was the true God: For the true God must be incomprehensible both in his existence and manner of subsistence. Had there not been a God subsisting in three persons, so distinct as to covenant with each other, and act a separate and distinct part in the work of redemption, man could not have been redeemed, and there could have been no Redeemer. They, therefore, who disbelieve the doctrine of the Trinity, and that the Redeemer is the second person in the Triune God, do really, though ignorantly, exclude the possibility of the redemption of man, and of a Redeemer equal to such a work; which will appear as we proceed in our inquiry into the work of redemption.

But let us believe this revealed mystery, God the Son, manifest in the flesh, and adore, and rejoice in the infinite fulness and sufficiency of God, which appears in the person and character of the Redeemer, for the redemption of sinners: which fulness and sufficiency never could have been known to men or angels, had it not been revealed, and the redemption of man had not taken place.

III. We are led by this subject, with wonder, gratitude and joy, to contemplate the ability and sufficiency of Jesus Christ to redeem sinners; and see that he is just such a Saviour as we need.

Were he not a person of infinite greatness, dignity and worthiness, were he not God, his sufferings and obedience would have been of no avail to make atonement for the sins of men; to procure pardon, and merit eternal life for us. And were he not man, he could neither suffer nor obey. But being both these, he was equal to this. "Such an High Priest became us, who is holy, harmless, undefiled, separate from sinners, and made higher than the heavens." [402] And were he not almighty, infinitely wise and good, he would not be able and willing to rescue sinners from the power of sin and satan, and completely sanctify them, and make them meet for the inheritance in heaven. But being all this, he is a complete Redeemer: "For it hath pleased the Father that in him all fulness should dwell. Who is made of God, unto his people, wisdom, and righteousness, and sanctification, and complete redemption." [403] And all the redeemed must know and say, "Surely in the Lord have I righteousness and strength: In the Lord Jesus Christ shall the seed of Israel be justified and shall glory." [404]

They who know their own state and character, as sinners, being wholly lost in sin, infinitely guilty and miserable; and believe in Christ, see all this in some degree. To such Christ is all-sufficient, most honourable and precious. But to them who are ignorant of themselves; the nature and ill desert of sin, and their own guilt and misery, who are unbelieving and disobedient, Jesus Christ, considered in his true character, is "a stone of stumbling, and rock of offence." [405]

His sufficiency also includes his inexhaustible, unbounded fulness, as the glorious object of knowledge, contemplation and love, and of enjoyment and happiness. The redeemed will attend forever to their Redeemer, who is infinite, and whose person and character are full of wonders, with ever fresh and increasing delight. They will spring forward, in the full employ and strongest exertion of all their powers, and make swift progress in the knowledge of their Saviour, and in holiness and happiness, without ever coming to an end. Whatever wonders and glories they may have seen, and however high their love and happiness may be at any supposed future period, the Redeemer may with truth say to them as he did to Nathaniel, "Ye shall see greater things than these." St. Paul entered upon this endless, progressive and happifying knowledge of Christ, when he commenced a christian, and was admitted into the school of his Lord and Master; which he expresses in the following words. "What things were gain to me, those I counted loss for Christ. Yea, doubtless, and I count all things but loss for the excellency of the knowledge of Christ Jesus, my Lord: That I may know him," &c.

IV. The view we have now had of the person and character of the Redeemer is suited to enlarge our ideas, and excite a sense of the infinite, wonderful condescension and love exercised and manifested in the work of redemption. The love of the Father is expressed in giving his only begotten, dear Son, to descend to such a low state of humiliation, of poverty, disgrace, and sufferings; even unto a most cruel death, to redeem man. And as this his own Son was equal to himself, and infinitely dear to him, the degree of love and goodness expressed in giving him up to redeem man, by suffering the curse under which he had fallen, must be infinite, and the greatest possible instance and exercise of disinterested benevolence, that can be conceived, or that ever did or can take place. And the more the greatness and dignity of the Son of God is known, and how dear he is to the Father, the greater will his sufferings appear to be, and the higher and more affecting will be the view and sense of the goodness of the Father, in giving up his Son to such sufferings. "God so loved the world that he gave his only begotten Son." Herein is love!

And the condescension and love of Christ in his humiliation and sufferings for the redemption of men, appear in the most affecting and striking light, when we take into view his greatness and dignity, and the infinite height from which he descended, to such an amazing scene of debasement, ignominy and sufferings: And the more our ideas are enlarged in the view of the former, the greater sense shall we have of the latter. Hence it follows, that as his greatness, dignity and excellence are infinite, there is a foundation for increasing, endless views and admiration of "The love of Christ, which passeth knowledge."

V. By considering the person of the Redeemer we are led to infer the height to which the redeemed are raised, the great honour which is conferred upon them, by their union to him. In the personal union of the human nature to the Son of God, the greatest honour is put upon it; and they who are united to this person as the redeemed are, rise to a degree of honour and exaltation, far above the angels, and unspeakably beyond all our present conceptions. They are the bride, the Lamb's wife, and share in all his honours and riches. They are "Raised up together with him, and made to sit together in heavenly places with Christ Jesus." [406] In his exaltation, they are exalted, as members of his body, of which he is the head; and shall sit with him, on his high throne, and reign with him forever. This honour have all the saints.

VI. We may hence see the warrant we have to worship and pray to Jesus Christ, and call upon his name. We have seen that he is worshipped by all the inhabitants of heaven; that the apostles and primitive christians prayed to him, and called on his name: And there is the same reason why his people should do so in all ages, and at all times. He is God manifest in the flesh, Immanuel, God in our nature. He has all power in heaven and on earth; and is head over all things to the church. He can do all things for us that we want; why should we not ask him for what we want, and constantly pray to him, acknowledging our absolute dependence on him, and his sufficiency and ability to do all for us? And is not a neglect to do this putting a slight upon him?

It will be asked, perhaps, whether this be not expressly forbidden by Christ, when he says, "In that day ye shall ask me nothing: Verily, verily, I say unto you, Whatsoever ye shall ask the Father in my name, he will give it you." [407]

Ans. When he says, "In that day ye shall ask me nothing," the word in the original is commonly used for asking questions. And not to make a petition. The disciples had been asking him a number of questions for their information about things which they did not understand. Christ tells them in these words, that after his ascension they should have no opportunity or occasion to ask him any questions; for they should then have sufficient knowledge by the holy Spirit teaching

The System of Doctrines, contained in Divine Relation, Explained and Defended Volume I
them all things they should have need to know. When he says, "Whatsoever ye shall ask the Father," he uses another word for asking, which always signifies to make a petition.

But from these last words there arises another question. Here Christ directs to ask the Father in his name. Is not this an implicit prohibition to ask any thing of him directly?

Ans. This cannot be understood as a prohibition to pray to Jesus Christ, and call on his name, because the apostles and primitive christians did this, as has been shown. And perhaps, if the matter be properly considered, it will appear that praying directly to Jesus Christ, and asking him, is asking in his name, and asking the Father, as really, though not expressly, as when we ask the Father directly, in the name of Christ. Jesus Christ says, "I and my Father are one. What things soever the Father doth, these also doth the Son likewise." [408] He hath, and exerciseth all the power that is in heaven and earth. It hath pleased the Father that all fulness should dwell in him. And the Father says to wretched man, "This is my beloved Son, hear ye him." Whatever you want, go to him for relief and a supply; as Pharaoh said to the starving people, "Go to Joseph." He then, who goes to Christ and asks the things which he wants of him, does really and in truth go to the Father, and asks of him, as he is the appointed governor and steward, and has all things in his hands. "The Father loveth the Son, and hath delivered all things into his hand. All things that the Father hath, are mine." [409] As the people by applying to Joseph, with whom all the authority and supplies u ere lodged, did really apply to Pharaoh; so they who apply to Christ and ask him, do really apply to the Father through him, and ask of the Father as really as if they expressly applied to him: For he and the Father are one, and what he does, the Father doth, and what the Father doth, the same doth the Son likewise. Therefore what our Saviour says in one passage the Father will do; in another he says, he himself will do the same. In the text under consideration he says, "Whatsoever ye shall ask the Father in my name, he will give it you." At another time he said, "Whatsoever ye shall ask in my name, that will I do." If ye shall ask any thing in my name, I will do it." [410] And we ask the Father in the name of Jesus Christ, when we go to Christ, and ask him; for in this way we approach to the Father, through him. We ask in the name of Christ, when we go immediately to Jesus Christ, and through him as a medium to the Father, as really and as much as if we apply expressly to the Father, and ask expressly in the name of Christ: For to ask in the name of Christ, is to rely on the atonement he has made, and on his merit and righteousness for the favour we ask. And this may be done when we apply immediately to Christ, as really and as much as if we apply expressly to the Father in his name.

VII. This subject is suited to excite in our minds a conviction, and impress a sense of the amazing, infinite crime and folly of slighting and rejecting the Redeemer of men. The crime of this is great in proportion to the greatness, worthiness and excellence of this person, and his amazing condescension and goodness exercised and manifested in what he has done and suffered for man.

And the folly of it is great, in proportion to the greatness of the evil from which he offers to deliver us; and of the good and happiness which he has obtained for man and invites him to accept, both of which are infinite. How unspeakably great then must be this wickedness and folly! They are to us as incomprehensible in their magnitude, as are the person and works of the Redeemer; they are truly boundless and infinite! They are attended with innumerable other aggravations, which far exceed our thought. How much more guilty are they who reject and cast contempt upon Christ, than they could have been, had there been no such person, no such Redeemer! And their endless punishment who persist in slighting him and neglecting this salvation, and die impenitent, will be inconceivably greater. They slight, they reject and despise God, the Father, Son, and Holy Ghost, and declare themselves to be irreconcileable enemies to him, while he is offering to be reconciled to them, to pardon their multiplied and infinitely aggravated offences, and bestow on them eternal life, in consequence of the Redeemer's undertaking in behalf of man, and obeying, and suffering unto death, for them. This serves to discover the universality, the exceeding greatness, and the malignity of the moral depravity of man. Jews and Gentiles acted this out, in the horrid action, never to be forgotten, in condemning and crucifying the Son of God, the Redeemer, when he was in their reach and power. And every man and woman who have lived since, and had opportunity to know the person and character of the Redeemer, have been guilty of the same crime, in a greater or less degree; as we have all slighted and abused him more or less; and so have, in this way, in some measure at least, joined with them who put him to death.

Footnotes:

243. John xvii. 3.
244. John xiv. 9.
245. 1 Cor. ii. 2.
246. Phil. iii. 8, 10.

247. 2 Pet. ii. 18.
248. Acts xiii. 27.
249. John viii. 24.
250. 2 Pet. ii. 1. Jude 4.
251. John i. 1, 14.
252. 1 John v. 7.
253. Rev. xix. 13.
254. Isaiah ix. 6,
255. Jer. xxiii. 6.
256. Matt. i. 23. Isaiah vii. 14.
257. John xx. 28.
258. Rom. ix. 5.
259. Tit. ii. 13.
260. Doddridge's Note on the place.
261. 2 Pet. i. 1.
262. Heb. i. 8.
263. 1 Tim. iii. 16.
264. Isaiah vi. 5.
265. John xii. 41.
266. Isaiah xliv. 6.
267. Rev. xxii. 13.
268. Verse 11.
269. Ver. 17.
270. Ver. 8.
271. Isaiah xliii. 11.
272. Matt. i. 21.
273. Eph. v. 28.
274. 2 Peter i. 11. ii. 20. iii. 2, 18.
275. Luke i. 45, 47. ii. 11.
276. Tit. i. 3. ii. 10, 13. iii. 4.
277. 2 Pet. i. 1.
278. Jude 24, 25.
279. Eph v. 27.
280. Isaiah liv. 5.
281. Isaiah lxii.4, 5.
282. John iii. 29.
283. 2 Cor. xi. 2.
284. Rev. xix. 7.
285. Rev. xxi. 2, 9.
286. Eph. iv. 4.
287. Cant. vi. 9.
288. Isaiah viii. 13, 14.
289. 1 Peter ii. 7, 8.
290. Rev. xxii. 6.
291. Micah v. 2.
292. Matt. ii. 6.
293. Heb. vii. 3.
294. Rev. i. 8, 17. xxii. 13.
295. Heb. i. 12.
296. Heb. xiii. 8.
297. Matt. xxviii. 18.
298. Eph. i. 22.
299. Phil. iii. 21.
300. Rev. i. 8.
301. Heb. i. 3.
302. Matt. xviii. 20. xxviii. 20.
303. John iii. 13.
304. John xxi. 17.
305. John ii. 24, 25.
306. Rev. ii. 23.
307. 2 Chron. ix. 30.
308. Psalm vii. 9.

309. Jer. xvii. 10.
310. Matt. xi. 27.
311. Rev. xix. 12.
312. Phil. ii. 6.
313. John x. 30.
314. John x. 33.
315. John v. 17.
316. John xvi. 15.
317. John xiv. 28.
318. John v. 17, 19.
319. John i. 3.
320. Col. i. 16.
321. Col. i. 17.
322. Heb. i. 3.
323. Psa. cii. 25. Heb. i. 10.
324. Gen. i. 1. Psa. xxxiii. 6.
325. John v. 29, 26. vi. 40. xi. 25.
326. Heb. i. 6.
327. Rev. i. 18. v. 8, 9, 11, 12, 13, 14.
328. John v. 23.
329. Phil. ii. 9, 10, 11.
330. Rom. xiv. 10, 11.
331. Isaiah xlv. 22, 23.
332. Acts vii. 59.
333. 1 Cor. i. 2.
334. Acts ix. 14.
335. Verse 20, 21.
336. Acts x. 26.
337. Rev. xix. 10. xxii. 9.
338. Matt. iv. 10.
339. Isaiah vi. 1, 2. John xii. 37-41.
340. Matt. xxviii. 19.
341. Num. vi. 23, 24, 25, 26. 1 Chron. xxiii. 13.
342. 2 Cor. xiii. 14.
343. John iii. 13.
344. Acts xx. 28.
345. Luke ii. 52.
346. John iii. 34.
347. Rev. iii. 14.
348. Rev. i. 8, xxi. 6, xxii. 15.
349. Col. i. 15.
350. Gen. xlix. 3.
351. Heb. xii. 23.
352. Exod. iv. 22.
353. Jer. xxxi. 9, 20.
354. Psalm lxxxix. 27.
355. Verse 16.
356. Rom. vii. 29.
357. Verse 17.
358. Heb. ii. 14, 16.
359. Heb. ii. 17.
360. Luke i. 31, 36.
361. Heb. vii. 26.
362. 1 Cor. xv. 47.
363. 2 Peter i. 17.
364. John i. 18.
365. Matt. xi. 27 John i. 18.
366. John xiv. 9. Heb. i. 3.
367. John vi. 69. Matt. xvi. 16.
368. Acts viii. 37.
369. Matt. xvi. 16, 17.
370. John iii. 36.

371. 1 John iv. 15. v. 5, 12, 13.
372. Luke i. 32, 35.
373. John i. 49.
374. John ix. 35, 38.
375. Matt. xiv. 33.
376. 1 John v. 20.
377. John v. 17-18.
378. John x. 30, 33, 36.
379. Matt. xxvi. 64, 65, 66.
380. John xix. 7, 8.
381. Matt. xxvii. 54.
382. Dan. iii. 25.
383. Prov. xxx. 4.

384. This is an incontestible proof that the Son is God, even Jehovah The Psalmist often says, "Blessed are they, blessed is the man who trusteth in the Lord." And here he says, Blessed are all they who trust in the Son of God. And yet forbids us to put our trust in any but God. "Put not your trust in princes, or in the son of man, in whom there is no help. Happy is he that hath the God of Jacob for his help, whose hope is in the Lord his God." [Psalm cxlvi. 3, 5.] And he says, "My soul, wait thou only upon God; for my expectation is from him." [Psalm lxii. 5.] They only are blessed, who trust in God; and all others are cursed. "Thus saith the Lord, Cursed be the man that trusteth in man. Blessed is the man that trusteth in the Lord, and whose hope the Lord is." [Jer. xvii. 5, 7.] They are blessed, who trust in the Son of God. Therefore he is the Lord.

385. John iii. 16.
386. 1 John iv. 9, 10.
387. Gal. iv. 4.
388. John i. 18.
389. 1 Tim. iii. 26.
390. 1 John iii. 8.
391. Acts xiii. 33.
392. Rom. i. 4.
393. Isaiah vii. 14. ix. 6.
394. Heb. vii. 3.
395. Job ii. 7, 8, 9.
396. Job xxxvii. 19, 20.

397. It has been observed, p. 377, that the denial of the eternal sonship of Christ seemed to have a tendency to a rejection of the doctrine of the Trinity; and in what way. But what is here observed, shews how the denial of the former tends, another way, to the rejection of the latter. For if the former be rejected, because it is incomprehensible, and appears inconsistent, it may be expected that when the doctrine of the Trinity is more particularly considered, it will appear equally unintelligible; and therefore be rejected, for the same reason. Is it not probable, that Sabellius, the ancient Antitrinitarian, was in this way led to give up the doctrine of the Trinity?

398. Matt. i. 18, 20.
399. Heb. ii. 14, 16.
400. Job xi. 12.
401. Psalm xxv. 9.
402. Heb. vii. 26.
403. 1 Cor. i. 30. Col. i. 19.
404. Isa. xlv. 24, 25.
405. 1 Pet. ii. 7, 8.
406. Eph. ii. 6.
407. John xvi. 28.
408. John v. 19. x. 30.
409. John iii. 35. xvi. 19.
410. John xiv. 13, 14.

CHAPTER III - CONCERNING THE DESIGN AND WORK OF THE REDEEMER

THIS is a subject upon which professing christians are far from being agreed. They differ in opinion respecting it, according to their different views of the moral state and character of man; from what he is to be redeemed; and of what is necessary to be done or suffered in order to his redemption. And this lays the foundation of their difference of opinion respecting the person and character of the Redeemer. For he must be answerable to the state of man, and to that which must be done or suffered in order to his being delivered from sin and misery, and made completely happy forever consistent with the divine law, and the wisdom and honour of the moral Governor of man.

There are not a few in the christian world who entertain such ideas of God, his law and moral government; of the character of man, and the nature and crime of sin, that they see no need of a Mediator and Redeemer, in order to the pardon and salvation of men: And therefore consider Jesus Christ as an impostor, and all who believe in him as deluded; and wholly discard divine revelation, and plunge into the darkness of Deism.

The Jews are so ignorant of the nature of the moral law, and their own state, that they think they stand in need of no Redeemer, but one who shall deliver them from the power and oppression of man, and bestow on them temporal, worldly dominion, prosperity and happiness. They therefore reject Jesus Christ, and hope for the deliverance they desire, by their expected Messiah.

There are many professing christians, who have much the same sentiments respecting God, law, sin, and the moral state of man, with Jews and deists; and consequently, though they profess to believe that Jesus Christ is the Saviour of men, they see no need of a Saviour that is more than a man, or a mere creature; and therefore do not believe in his divinity.

Others have such views of God, his law and moral government, of the character and state of man in his apostasy, and of what is necessary to be done and suffered in order to their redemption, that they feel the need of a divine Redeemer; whose person and character has been described in the foregoing chapter, and which they are prepared to see plainly exhibited in the Bible.

From this view, it appears that in order to understand the work of the Redeemer, the design of his undertaking, and what he does effect, mc must have right views of the law of God which man has transgressed; and of the state into which he is fallen by this rebellion.

The law of God points out the duty of man, and requires of him what is perfectly right, and no more, or less. It cannot therefore be altered in the least degree, so as to require more or less, without rendering it less perfect and good. It is therefore an eternal unalterable rule of righteousness, which cannot be abrogated or altered in the least iota, by an infinitely perfect, unchangeable legislator and governor, consistent with his character, his perfect rectitude and righteousness. This law necessarily implies, as essential to it, a sanction or penalty, consisting in evil, or a punishment, which is in exact proportion to the magnitude of the crime of transgressing it; or the desert of the transgressor, which is threatened to be executed on the offender. This penalty which is threatened must be no more, nor less, than the sinner deserves, or the demerit of the crime. The least deviation from this would render the law so far imperfect, and wrong. Every creature under this law is under infinite obligations to obey it without any deviation from it in the least possible instance, through the whole of his existence; and every instance of rebellion tends to infinite evil, to break up the divine government, and bring ruin and misery on all the moral world: Therefore every transgression of this law, or neglect to obey it, deserves infinite evil as the proper punishment of it. Consequently this evil, this punishment, must be the threatened penalty of the law; which has been shown in a former chapter.

Man by transgression has incurred the penalty of this law, and fallen under the curse of it; "For it is written, cursed is every one that continueth not in all the things which are written in the book of the law to do them." [411] This curse cannot be taken off, and man released, until it has its effect, and all the evil implied in it be suffered, which man can never do, so as to be delivered from it, or from suffering, because a finite creature is not capable of suffering the evil contained in the curse in any limited duration; and therefore his sufferings must be without end, or everlasting. And no future obedience, should man repent and live perfectly obedient after he had transgressed, would atone for his sin, or remove the curse in the least degree, according to law: for his obedience, though ever so perfect, and continued ever so long, would be no more than what he constantly owed, and therefore no more than his duty, had he never transgressed. Thus man by sin fell into an irrecoverably lost state, and brought the curse of the law of God upon him, from which it is impossible he should deliver himself, or be delivered, consistent with this law, either by all possible sufferings or obedience of his own.

This is the law of God, and is the voice of God to man, and is an unalterable expression of his heart, or moral character and perfection. It therefore cannot be altered or abated in the requirements of it, or in the threatening. It is as unchangeable as the divine character itself, being founded on the eternal, unchangeable reason and nature of things. And it is not consistent with the truth of God not to execute the threatening of his law: For this would not only be giving up and making void his law; but acting contrary to his own declaration. Divine threatenings are predictions, declaring what shall be, and what God will do in case of transgression of his law. And it is as inconsistent with truth not to execute his threatening, in the true meaning of it, as it is not to accomplish and bring to pass, what he has declared and promised shall take place. This law therefore must be maintained in the true meaning and spirit of it; as the grand and only perfect rule of rectoral justice, rectitude, or righteousness. And if it were possible that God should do any thing in his conduct towards moral agents, which should be inconsistent with this his law, or express the least disregard of it, it would be infinitely wrong, and contrary to truth, rectitude and righteousness, wisdom, and goodness. For this would be injurious to himself, and to his moral kingdom, and subversive of the greatest general good. Therefore if man could not be redeemed and saved consistent with maintaining this law, and showing the highest regard to it, God could not be true, just, wise or good, in saving them or showing them any favour.

But to pardon man and restore him to favour and happiness, in this situation, and remove the curse which the divine law fastens upon him, would be acting contrary to this law, repealing and renouncing it as a rule of righteousness, as not good and right: It would be joining with the sinner to disregard and dishonour the law; and favour, justify and encourage rebellion. This therefore would be inconsistent with rectitude, righteousness, wisdom and goodness, and infinitely contrary to these, and would put an eternal end to all perfect moral government. It would dethrone the Governor of the world, destroy his kingdom, and give full scope to the reign of rebellion, confusion and misery forever. Therefore it were better, infinitely better, that rebel man, even all mankind, should have the curse of the law fully executed on them, and they be totally miserable forever, than that this infinitely greater evil should take place by shewing favour to him, contrary to the dictates of the most perfect, righteous, and infinitely sacred law of God.

This otherwise insuperable difficulty, this mighty bar and obstacle in the way of shewing any favour to man, and escaping eternal destruction, is the ground of the necessity of a Mediator and Redeemer, by whom it maybe wholly removed, and man be delivered from die curse of the law; and saved, consistent with the divine character, with truth, infinite rectitude, wisdom and goodness; and so as not to set aside and dishonour, but support and maintain the divine law and government. This is the light in which the scripture very expressly sets this matter. St. Paul, speaking of the pardon and salvation of man by Christ the Redeemer, says, "Whom God hath set forth to be a propitiation, through faith in his blood, to declare his righteousness for the remission of sins that are past: To declare, I say, his righteousness: That he might be just, and the justifier of him which believeth in Jesus." [412] Here the design of the Redeemer is expressed, and the great thing he is to accomplish is to maintain and declare the righteousness, the rectitude, and unchangeable truth and perfection of God in opening a way by his blood, his sufferings unto death, for the free pardon of sinful man, consistent with his rectoral justice and truth, and doing that which is right and just both with respect to himself, his law and government, and all the subjects of his kingdom.

The work of the Redeemer therefore has a primary respect to the law of God, to maintain and honour that, so that sinners may be pardoned and saved consistent with that, without setting that aside, or showing the least disregard to it, in the requirements and threatenings of it; but that it may be perfectly fulfilled; and especially that the threatening might be properly and completely executed, without which God could not be true or just in pardoning and saving the sinner. It was therefore predicted that he should "Magnify the law, and make it honourable." [413] And Christ himself declares that he came into the world to fulfil the law. "Think not that I am come to destroy the law or the prophets: I am not come to destroy, but to fulfil. For verily I say unto you. Till heaven and earth pass, one jot or one tittle shall in no wise pass from the law, till all be fulfilled."[414] The law could not be fulfilled by Jesus Christ without his suffering the penalty of it, and obeying it perfectly. For to give up the penalty, and not execute the threatening of the law, when it is transgressed, is to dissolve and destroy the law: For a penalty is essential to a law, and where there is no penalty threatened there is no law, as has been shown. Therefore had the Redeemer undertaken to save man, without regard to the penalty of the law and suffering it himself, he would have come to make void the law and destroy it, to all intents and purposes. He could not "make

The System of Doctrines, contained in Divine Relation, Explained and Defended Volume I

reconciliation for sin, and bring in everlasting righteousness," which it was predicted he should, [415] without suffering the penalty of the law, the everlasting rule of righteousness. In doing this his love of righteousness and hatred of iniquity was exercised and displayed in the most signal manner, and to the highest degree. Therefore it is with respect to this regard which he paid to the divine law in suffering the penalty and obeying the precepts of it, that it is said to him, "Thou hast loved righteousness, and hated iniquity; therefore God, even thy God, hath anointed thee with the oil of gladness above thy fellows." [416] The same is expressed in other words by St. Paul. "And being found in fashion as a man, he humbled himself, and became obedient unto deaths even the death of the cross. Wherefore God hath highly exalted him, and given him a name which is above every name." [417] His being obedient unto death, strongly expresses his laying down his life for sinners, suffering and dying in their stead, agreeable to the particular command which he had received of his Father. [418] To this end he was "made under the law, to redeem them that were under the law." [419] Sinful men were under the curse of the law; and in order to redeem them, the Redeemer must take their place under the law, and suffer the penalty, bear the curse for them, and in their room, which is expressed yet more fully, and in the most plain and unequivocal words in the preceding chapter. "Christ hath redeemed us from the curse of the law, being made a curse for us." By being made a curse for us, can be nothing else but suffering the penalty, the curse of the law, under which we were, and which man must have suffered, had not the Redeemer suffered it for him, as he could not be redeemed in any other way, without destroying the law.

From this general view of the design and work of the Redeemer of man, taken from the holy scriptures, the way is prepared for a farther stating and explanation of this subject, under the following particulars.

I. One important and necessary part of the work of the Redeemer of man, was to make atonement for their sins, by suffering in his own person the penalty or curse of the law, under which, by transgression, they had fallen; so that sinners might be pardoned and saved, consistent with the divine law, and without the least respect to that, or in any degree making it void; but so as to establish and honour the law.

There is no truth in the Bible more clearly and abundantly revealed than this. This truth is evident from what has been above observed from the scriptures; but it is proper more particularly to attend to the scripture representation of this important subject.

The institution of sacrifices of beasts and other animals, after the apostasy of man, and the declaration, that redemption should take place by the seed of the woman; and those more expressly appointed under the Mosaic dispensation, do all, more or less, illustrate and confirm this truth, and point out vicarious sufferings as necessary and effectual to make atonement for sin. The guilty person was ordered to bring the beast to the altar, and lay his hands on the head of it, and confess his sin; and then it was put to death and sacrificed on the altar by the priest, instead of the sinner, and he was forgiven, an atonement being made for his sin by the death and blood of the beast. [420] These sacrifices were of various kinds, and offered on different occasions, as types of Christ, and those things which related to him, and the atonement he was to make. For all these sacrifices were designed types of Christ, and in this all their worth and efficacy consisted. The death and blood of a beast could not in any measure or degree make atonement for sin, and was of no avail any farther than it had respect to Christ, and was a type and figure of his death, of his blood which he shed, which was the only real atonement, and which alone avails to take away sin. "For it is impossible that the blood of bulls and of goats should take away sins." It was therefore in early times expressly declared, that sacrifices and offerings were not desirable, or of any worth, in themselves considered, and that God did not institute and require them for their own sake, as making any real atonement for sin; but that this should be made by an incarnate Redeemer, to whom they pointed as types and shadows of him. [421]

And he is particularly pointed out by Isaiah, as making atonement for sin by suffering the evil which it deserves in the room of sinners, and for them, that they might escape punishment, and be pardoned. He says, "He was wounded for our transgressions, he was bruised for our iniquities. The chastisement of our peace was upon him, and with his stripes we are healed. The Lord hath laid on him the iniquity of us all. He was cut off out of the land of the living: For the transgression of my people was he stricken. It pleased the Lord to bruise him. He hath put him to grief: When thou shalt make his soul an offering for sin, he shall see his seed. By his knowledge shall my righteous servant justify many; for he shall bear their iniquities. He poured out his soul unto death, and he bare the sin of many." [422] To bear sin, or iniquity, is to suffer the punishment of it, or the evil which it deserves, and with which it is threatened. This appears not only from the plain, natural import of the phrases, but from the use of it in the Bible, of which there are many instances. The following are a few of them. "The holy garments shall be upon Aaron and his sons, when they come near unto the altar to minister in the holy place, that they bear not iniquity and die." [423] "They shall therefore keep mine ordinance, lest they bear sin for it, and die therefor, if they profane it." [424] Neither must the children of Israel henceforth come nigh the tabernacle of the congregation, lest they bear sin, and die." [425] The apostles express the import of the sufferings and death of Christ by the same phrase. "So Christ was once offered to bear the sins of many." [426] "Who his own self bare our sins in his own body on the tree." [427]

In the epistle to the Hebrews, the typical meaning of sacrifices of beasts is explained, and declared to be designed to point out the sacrifice and atonement which Christ has made, when he offered himself once for all, as a sacrifice to put away sin, and bear the sins of many; the plain meaning of which is, that he, by his sufferings, took on him the penalty of sin, and bore the punishment of it, so as effectually to put it away from all who believe in him, that it may never be laid to their charge, to condemn them: he having made full atonement and reconciliation. In this sense he is said to be the propitiation for the sins of men. And men are said to obtain redemption and forgiveness of sins by or through his blood, in allusion to the blood of the sacrifices under the law, which was the most essential thing in them, and is said to make the atonement. "The life of the flesh is in the blood, and I have given it to you upon the altar, to make an atonement for your souls: For it is the blood that maketh atonement for the soul." [428] Our Saviour says of the sacramental cup, when he instituted the Lord's supper, "This is my blood of the New Testament, which is shed for many, for the remission of sins." [429] Agreeable to this, St. Paul says, "We are justified by his blood." [430] In whom we have redemption through his blood, the forgiveness of sins." [431] And St. John says, "the blood of Christ cleanseth us, (that is, christians) from all sins." [432] St. Peter tells believers that they were "redeemed by the precious blood of Christ, as of a lamb without blemish, and without spot." [433] In heaven the saved adore the Redeemer and say, "Thou art worthy, &c. For thou wast slain, and hast redeemed us to God by thy blood." [434]

There are a multitude of passages in the New Testament which set this point in this same light, and clearly import that what Christ suffered was in man's stead, and does avail to release all who believe in him, from suffering the penalty of the law; and that by this alone they are redeemed from the curse of the law, which is eternal destruction. These passages are too many to be particularly quoted. Only a few therefore will be mentioned. Christ says, "The Son of man came not to be ministered unto, but to minister, and to give his life a ransom for many." [435] He redeems or ransoms them by giving his life, his suffering unto death; this is the price, the ground of their deliverance. St. Paul says to believers, "Ye are bought with a price." [436] The word in the original, which is here translated bought, is the same with that in Rev. v. 9. which is translated redeemed. "Thou hast redeemed us to God by thy blood." The price by which men are bought, and redeemed from the curse of the law, from endless destruction, is the blood of Christ, which he shed for the remission of sins, that is, his suffering unto death. The death of Christ, and the blood of Christ, mean the same thing. In shedding his blood and dying, he was made a curse, by which he has bought, redeemed, and delivered his people from the curse of the law. His life was the ransom he gave, the price which he paid for our redemption. Therefore the death of Christ is mentioned as that by which alone believers are delivered from condemnation, the condemning sentence, the curse of the law. "Who is he that condemneth? It is Christ that died." [437] "For when we were without strength, in due time Christ died for the ungodly." [438] "I delivered unto you first of all, that which I also received, how that Christ died for our sins." [439] "For that he died, he died unto sin [or for sin] once." [440] "And for this cause he is the Mediator of the New Testament, that by means of death, for the redemption of the transgressions that were under the first Testament, &c." [441] In these passages, and other similar ones, the death of Christ is represented as having respect to the sins of men, and as redeeming them from the curse which sin deserves, by taking the curse on himself. When it is said "Christ died for our sins," the meaning must be that his death is the atonement and propitiation for sin; and that by it he suffered the evil with which sin is threatened in the law, or the penalty and curse of the law; or that which is equivalent. To suffer for sin and for the sinner, is so far to take place of the sinner, as to suffer the evil which he deserves, and which otherwise the sinner must have suffered. Or, which is the same, the sufferings of Christ answer the same end with respect to law, and divine government, that otherwise must be answered by the eternal destruction of the sinner. The same sentiment is strongly expressed by St. Peter. "For Christ also hath once suffered for sins, the just for the unjust, that he might bring us to God." [442] Here it is to be observed, that three things are asserted in this sentence.

   1. That the sufferings of Christ make atonement, and are the only ground or means of the sinner's reconciliation to God.

   2. That the sufferings of Christ were therefore for sin, and consequently must be the evil which sin deserves, and that to which the sinner was exposed, and which he must have suffered, had not Christ suffered it in his stead, or that which is equivalent.

   3. That the last clause, "That he might bring us to God," respects the pardon of sinners, their deliverance from the curse of the law, and restoration to favour, which could not take place consistent with the holy righteous law of God, had not Christ suffered for their sin.

The System of Doctrines, contained in Divine Relation, Explained and Defended Volume I

On the whole, The scripture represents the atonement which Christ has made, by which sinners are delivered from the curse of the law, the wrath to come, to consist wholly in his suffering unto death for their sins, by which he suffered the evil which the law threatens for sin, or a complete equivalent, so as fully to answer the end of the threatening of the law, and all the purposes of moral government, consistent with the pardon of the sinner, as much as if the curse had been executed on the transgressor: And that this was one great, and the most important, essential and difficult part of the work of the Redeemer, and really implies the whole.

Thus by the death, the blood of Christ, full atonement is made for sin; the curse of the law is executed on the Redeemer, by which he has bought, redeemed his people from the curse, and opened the way for their pardon and complete redemption. He has been made a curse that he might deliver all who believe in him from the curse; but not so as in the least degree to remove their unworthiness and ill desert, but this remains, and will remain forever, it being improper, undesirable, and impossible that this should be removed, or that they should ever cease to deserve eternal destruction. They remain, and must continue to be as criminal as ever they were; so long as it remains true that they have been guilty of crimes which are pardoned, and from which they are justified by the blood of Christ.

In order more fully to explain and establish the atonement of Christ, which he has made by his suffering unto death, as it has been represented from the holy scripture; and to obviate as far as possible, every difficulty and objection which may arise in the minds of any, it is proper and necessary to consider the following questions.

Question 1. Where is the justice of an innocent person suffering for the guilty, and, on that account, delivering the criminal from the sufferings which he deserves? How can such a procedure honour the law, and support government?

Answer 1. The scripture states the matter so, and abundantly asserts, that Christ, though perfectly innocent and holy himself, did die for sinners, and in their behalf; that he suffered, the just for the unjust; and that by this, all who believe in him are delivered from the evil, the suffering, which they deserve, and saved forever. Therefore every objection to this, is equally an objection to the Bible. Let deists object, and triumph in the imagination that it is unanswerable; but let christians believe, and with care and honest meekness consider, whether this supposed difficulty may not be easily removed.

Answer 2. Can it be reasonably asserted; is it true, that an innocent, worthy person may not justly, and with the utmost propriety, suffer in the room of a criminal, in order to save the latter from suffering, in any case whatsoever? Is not the contrary true, and agreeable to the common sense of mankind? Benevolus sustained the best and most worthy character of any man in the kingdom. His wife was publicly guilty of a crime, for which the law of the state denounced a punishment, which she could not suffer and survive it; but it must prove fatal to her, if inflicted on her. The law was so good and important, that if the penalty were not inflicted, and the law were disregarded in favour of the criminal, the consequence would be most fatal to the kingdom, and sap the foundation of all authority, law and government, and introduce endless confusion and misery. The husband saw all this, and had rather his wife should suffer the extremity of the law, than that good government should be dissolved, or the law disregarded, which he loved, and wished to have maintained. He loved his wife so much, that he was willing to suffer the penalty of the law himself, if she might by this means escape it. He knew that he was able to go through this suffering, however dreadful, and survive it; and that his doing this in the sight of the whole kingdom, would do more honour to the law, and government would be better established and maintained, than if his wife should suffer as she deserved. He therefore stepped forward, and offered, and desired to take the evil upon himself, and suffer the penalty of the law in the room of his wife, and for her crime. His offer was accepted, and he suffered the whole, without the least mitigation.

All the inhabitants and good subjects in the kingdom looked on and had not a thought of any injustice done to him, who offered to suffer for his wife; and did actually suffer the evil which she deserved. They saw and admired his benevolence and goodness to his wife, and his disposition and zeal to maintain the law and government. They beheld, and were highly pleased with the uprightness, rectitude and righteousness of their king, and his fixed determination to maintain his law, while he inflicted the penalty of it on a person whom he esteemed and loved above all others in his kingdom, when he stood in the place of the transgressor: And a greater discovery was made of this, and his high displeasure at rebellion, than if the criminal herself had been punished. They were struck with the propriety, righteousness, wisdom and goodness, exercised and manifested in the whole affair, and ever after had a more clear apprehension, and greater sense of the sacredness, importance, and excellence of the law, and of the unreasonableness and magnitude of the crime of transgressing it; and loved and revered their king, and his law and government, more than ever they had done before.

The husband and wife were unspeakably more happy in each other, than they were before, or than they could have been, had not all this taken place. Their mutual love was stronger and more sweet and happy. She saw more of his worthiness, excellence and love, than she could otherwise have done, and was most happy and swallowed up in the sweetest exercise of gratitude, and the most endearing affection, which knew no bounds or end.

There were some indeed, who never had been cordial friends to the king; and had no great esteem of his laws or government, or of the husband; who thought the transgression of the wife small and trivial; which might and ought to have been forgiven, without all this ado, and suffering of the husband. They were disaffected, and offended with the whole transaction, and made innumerable and endless objections.

This story may serve, in some measure, to illustrate this point, as well as some others, which will come into view hereafter; and to shew that an innocent, and most worthy person, may suffer for the crimes of the guilty, and yet no injustice be done to the sufferer; and the criminal may be by this, delivered from suffering what he deserves, and yet the law which he has transgressed, be well supported and honoured.

The Redeemer voluntarily took the place of sinners; he chose to suffer in their stead. His language was, "Then said I, Lo, I come. In the volume of the book it is written of me: I delight to do thy will, O my God; Yea, thy law is within my heart." [443] "I lay down my life for the sheep. No man taketh it from me; but I lay it down of myself." [444] "Being in the form of God, he thought it not robbery to be equal with God; yet made himself of no reputation; and took upon him the form of a servant, and was made in the likeness of men: And being found in fashion as a man, he humbled himself, and became obedient unto death, even the death of the cross." [445] He suffered in the sight of all the moral world, and the design of his suffering was, and still is publicly declared and known, and that it was his choice thus to bear the evil which sinners deserved, that he might by this redeem them from it. And this is so far from being unjust or improper, that the righteousness and wisdom of God are hereby manifested and declared.

Quest. 2. The curse of the law dooms the sinner to be given up to the dominion of sin, and spiritual death without end: How then could Christ suffer the curse of the law, who knew no sin?

Ans. The curse of the law is the evil, the punishment of sin, and not sin, which is the cause of suffering: the crime itself which is threatened and punished. What is threatened as the penalty of the law, is natural evil, or pain and suffering for transgression, or moral evil. Spiritual death is moral evil; sin, the transgression of the law; for this the penalty is threatened and inflicted, and is not the penalty itself. This consists wholly in natural evil, pain and suffering; and not in actually violating the law. It is true, that being dead in trespasses and sins, or endless continuance under the power and dominion of sin, is implied in the sinner's suffering the penalty of the law; but this is not the penalty, or any part of it, but the natural evil which attends it, and of which it is the occasion. The Mediator did not suffer precisely the same kind of pain, in all respects, which the sinner suffers when the curse is executed on him: He did not suffer that particular kind of pain which is the necessary attendant, or natural consequence of being a sinner, and which none but the sinner himself can suffer. But this is only a circumstance of the punishment of sin, and not of the essence of it. The whole penalty of the law may be suffered, and the evil suffered may be as much, and as great, without suffering that particular sort of pain. Therefore Christ, though with» out sin, might suffer the whole penalty, that is, as much and as great evil, as the law denounces against transgression. The evil which sinners may suffer, on whom the penalty of the law is inflicted, may, and doubtless will, differ in many circumstances, and not be precisely of the same kind, in all respects; and yet each one of them suffer the penalty of the same law.

Quest. 3. How can the sufferings of Christ be suffering the curse of the law, or the evil which the law threatens, or so great an evil as the eternal destruction of the sinner, and of millions of them, since his sufferings were of a short duration, and were not, perhaps, equal in degree, to those which some one of the damned suffers every hour?

Ans. The magnitude of the sufferings of Christ, or the evil of his suffering as he did, docs not wholly consist in the quantity or degree of pain which he endured, or in the duration or length of time in which he suffered. The degree of pain which he suffered was very great; unspeakably greater, no doubt, than ever was, or can be suffered by any mere creature. He did not suffer in the least in his divine nature; but altogether in his human nature, but this was capable of suffering an unspeakably greater degree of pain, than any mere creature, not only by reason of the superior greatness of the human nature, which has been mentioned; but from the perfect union with the divine nature. A consciousness of this, and of the dignity and worthiness implied in it, must aggravate his suffering far beyond conception. And by this union the human nature was sustained and made capable of enduring a degree of sufferings far beyond, and much more dreadful, than what any mere creature is capable of bearing. But, as has been observed, the greatness of the evil of the sufferings of Christ, does not wholly, or chiefly consist in the degree of pain which he suffered, or in the duration of his suffering: But in the greatness, dignity, and worthiness of the person who

The System of Doctrines, contained in Divine Relation, Explained and Defended Volume I
suffered.

The greatness of the evil, in the sufferings and reproach, and disgrace of any person, does not consist merely in the degree of pain which he suffers; but it is the greater or less, according to the excellence and worth of the person who suffers. This is so in the estimation of all, who attend to the matter, and is agreeable, to the common sense and feelings of mankind. It is a greater evil for the excellent head of a family to be condemned, reproached, and spit upon, tortured in the most cruel manner, and put to death, by the servants of the family, than it would be to have one of the servants treated so, and suffer all this. It would certainly be so to the children of the family, who esteemed and loved their father, being sensible of his excellence and worth; and it would be judged so by all. If the general of an army, who had supported his station and character with the greatest dignity and honour, and who is the life and support of his army, should be made the object of reproach and contempt by his soldiers, and dragged through the ranks in a most ignominious manner, to the place of execution, and there put to death for a coward and traitor: This would be an unspeakably greater evil, than it would be for a private sentinel to suffer all this pain and disgrace.

If a king who had long maintained a most righteous, wise and good government, and made a nation happy, being a person of the greatest excellence and true greatness and dignity, and sustaining the best character in the world, should be taken from his throne, by a number of banditti, and openly scourged through the streets of the city, and cast into prison; and then be taken from thence, and publicly put to a most cruel death; this would be a much greater evil, more undesirable and grievous, than for one of the lowest of his subjects to suffer all this reproach and pain. There is need only to mention these instances, in order to gain the assent of every one who will attend to the truth which is asserted, without any long train of reasoning upon it. It seems to be self evident; an irresistible dictate of common sense.

Should such a king have a son of a most amiable and excellent character, having the greatest natural abilities, and being endowed with great wisdom and benevolence, beloved and honoured by all the virtuous, and justly dearer to his father than any other person: And this son should fall into the hands of a number of ruffians, who after they had joined to reproach, ridicule, and mock him, should put him to the most ignominious and cruel death that they could invent: Would not this be with the highest reason, beyond expression, a greater evil, and more grievous to the father, and all the inhabitants of that kingdom, than if the worthless servant in his family were treated thus, and suffered all this contempt and pain? It is presumed every one to whom such a case is proposed, will answer in the affirmative. And this is granting what most certainly none can deny, viz. That the more excellent and honourable any person is, and the more he is justly esteemed and beloved, and the greater his worth and importance, the greater and more grievous is the evil, in his unjustly suffering reproach and pain; and that the evil of such suffering, is great, in proportion to the excellence, dignity, worth and importance of the person who suffers.

From this truth, which is so evident and certain, it follows, as an undeniable consequence, that for the Redeemer to suffer as he did, is an infinite evil. For, as has been shewn, he is a person of infinite greatness, dignity, excellence, worth and importance; and infinitely beloved and dear to the Father. To the Father who sees all things as they are, and most perfectly comprehends the infinite excellence, dignity and worth of his infinitely well beloved and only begotten Son, it must appear an infinite evil for him to suffer what he did for the redemption of sinners. And in the sight of the Son, he undertook to suffer infinite evil, when he came into the world. And to the redeemed, as they grow in a view and sense of the greatness, dignity and worth of their Redeemer, and know more and better who he is, who died on the cross to redeem them, the greater will the evil of his sufferings appear; and consequently, the more clearly will they see the greatness of the price by which they were bought, and the sufficiency of his blood to cleanse from all sin, and how perfectly the threatening of the law is answered in the sufferings of Christ. [446]

The evil of the sufferings of Christ, being in the magnitude of it commensurate with the dignity and worth of his person, is equal to, is as great as the evil which is threatened to the transgressors of the law, and as great as the sinner deserves; yea, it is as great as the endless sufferings of all mankind; for that is no more than infinite; therefore Christ by his sufferings, paid a price, and made an atonement sufficient to redeem the whole world from the wrath to come: And it is not owing to any want or defect in this, that all are not saved; for it is boundless; but this is owing to something else, which will be considered in the sequel.

Thus it appears that though sin be an infinite evil, and deserves infinite natural evil, which is the penalty of the law of God, and the threatened punishment of sin, yet it could be suffered by Christ in a limited duration, a short time, since the evil of his suffering as he did must be great in proportion to the greatness, dignity, and worthiness of the sufferer, which are infinite.

If it should be asked, how the sufferings of Christ can be considered as an infinite evil, since he is not less, but more happy and glorious, and will be so forever, than if he had not suffered; and the good which comes to his church and kingdom by his suffering, is, and will be so great, as to overbalance and swallow up all the evil? This may be answered by observing,

1. If there be any thing in this argument, and the evil of suffering be not so great, but less, in proportion to the greatness of good of which it is the occasion; then it will follow, that there is no evil at all in the suffering of Christ; because it is the occasion of overbalancing good, and of much more good, on the whole, than if he had not suffered. If every degree of good which is the consequence of suffering, and of which suffering is the occasion, does cancel one degree of the evil of suffering, and render it no evil; then the overbalancing good, occasioned by suffering, cancels all the evil of the suffering, and renders it no evil: Which it is supposed none will admit; for all will grant there is some degree of evil, at least, in the sufferings of Christ.

2. The evil of suffering is not the less, in itself considered, however great be the good of which the pain and suffering is the occasion. Therefore the evil of the sufferings of Christ is as great, as if they had been the occasion of no good, but of evil. We must determine what evil there was in the suffering of Christ, not by taking into view the consequences of his suffering, but by considering the suffering itself, and the person suffering; and if the evil appears to be infinitely great, thus considered, as it has been proved it does, then, whatever be the consequence of the evil suffered, and however great the good be of which it is the occasion, it alters not the magnitude of the evil suffered; but it must remain eternally the same, in itself considered.

It is granted, and has been proved, in a former chapter, that no evil has taken place in the universe, or ever will, that is not the occasion of an overbalancing good; so that, on the whole, there is more good than if there had been no evil: And in this sense, all evil is turned into good, that is, it is on the whole, all things considered, not evil, but good. But it does not follow from this, that there is nothing of the nature of evil, or no evil, considered in and by itself: There is, notwithstanding, in this view of it, infinite evil.

If the overbalancing good, of which evil is the occasion, cancels the evil, in itself considered, then the damned suffer no evil; for all their sufferings are the occasion of an overbalancing good. The querist, therefore, may as well ask, how eternal damnation can be an infinite evil, or any evil at all, since it is the occasion of an overbalancing good? And he may with equal reason assert, that Joseph suffered no evil by being sold a slave into Egypt, and east into prison there, "whose feet they hurt with fetters, and he was laid in iron," and say there was no evil in all this, since God meant it for good; and it was the occasion of so much good to Joseph himself, and to his father's house. Ask Joseph. Ask his father. Ask common sense.

Quest. 4. If Christ suffered as great, and as much evil, yea, more than the redeemed would have suffered, had they not been redeemed, but been miserable forever; then there is no less evil in the universe, than there would be, if they had not been redeemed; but really much more. Where is the advantage then of redemption, and what is gained by it?

Ans. The advantage gained by redemption, to the universe, is the overbalancing good which is produced by it. All natural evil is, in itself considered, undesirable, and cannot be desired for its own sake; but may be desired and chosen, for the sake of the good of which it is the occasion, and which cannot take place in any other way. It would have been undesirable that there should be evil in the universe, and therefore there would have been none, had it not been necessary in order to a greater, overbalancing good: But it is desirable that every instance and degree of evil, which is necessary to promote the greatest good, should take place, however much and great this be. The suffering and death of the Redeemer is in itself an infinite evil; but as this was necessary in order to effect a proportionably greater, overbalancing, superabounding good, it was desirable it should take place; for the sake of "the glory that should follow." This event is of infinite advantage to the universe. God is glorified more by the redemption of man than by all his other works, and there will be an eternal, bright, and most happifying display of the divine perfections, which could not have taken place, had not Christ thus suffered. Had he not suffered as he did, he would not have entered into his glory, that glory and felicity which he will enjoy forever as the fruit of his suffering. And an eternal, glorious and most happy kingdom exists in consequence of this. Thus not only the salvation of the redeemed from eternal destruction is effected by the suffering of the Redeemer, but they are eternally happy; and not only so, but they and all holy beings will be unspeakably more happy forever, than they could otherwise have been; and God and the Redeemer are beyond all conception more glorified; so that there will be infinitely more good in the universe, both moral and natural, than could have been, had not Christ suffered and entered into his glory. And all the other evil that has been, or will take place, is, by the sufferings of Christ, made the occasion of much greater good, than it could otherwise have been. Surely no one, who well considers all this, will ask, "Where is the advantage of redemption, and what is gained by it?"

Question 5. To suffer the penalty of the law is to be accursed, the subjects of God's displeasure and wrath; but God the Father was not displeased with his Son Jesus Christ; for he was always his beloved Son, and even in his sufferings the Father was pleased with him, and loved him because he gave his life for the redeemed. How then could Jesus Christ suffer the penalty of the law?

Ans. St. Paul says, "Christ hath redeemed us. from the curse of the law, being made a curse for us: as it is written, cursed is every one that hangeth on a tree." [447] In the place to which the apostle refers, the words are, "He that is hanged, is accursed of God." And there is indeed no real curse but the curse of God. Christ therefore was made such, even the curse of the law, in order to deliver believers in him from this curse. The curse of the law consists in the infinite evil, pain and suffering which sin deserves, as has been shown. He who suffers this for sin, suffers the curse of the law, is accursed, or made a curse. Jesus Christ suffered this curse, the infinite natural evil in which the penalty or the curse of the law consists; and in suffering it for sinners, and in their stead, was made a curse. This might be consistent with his having the approbation of the Father, and his favour and love to the highest degree. The displeasure of God, which was the cause of his sufferings, and which was manifested and expressed in his sufferings when he voluntarily took, and stood In the place of sinners, was displeasure with sin, and the sinner, and not with him who suffered; the state of the case being fully understood by the spectators. Great displeasure and wrath was indeed discovered and expressed in the sufferings of Christ. For all natural evil, wherever it takes place, is an expression of the divine displeasure with sin; and could not have been inflicted, in any case, had no moral evil existed; and the greater the natural evil is, which is inflicted, the more or the greater degree of displeasure is expressed. And for the Son of God to suffer all this, the whole curse, without any mitigation or abatement, when he so far espoused the cause of sinners, as to take their place, and suffer for them, when he was not only innocent, but infinitely beloved by the Father, and most honourable and worthy in his sight, was a much greater manifestation and expression of the divine hatred of rebellion, and his unalterable disposition to inflict the penalty of his law, and maintain his moral government, than if every sinner had been punished, and the penalty of the law were inflicted on all transgressors without exception. The Father's not sparing his own Son, but giving him up to suffer the whole curse of the law, when he espoused the cause of sinners, is a most striking evidence of rectitude and righteousness, and regard to his law, and fixed determination to support it, and inflict the penalty, even though his own well beloved Son must suffer it. And that must be great displeasure and wrath which is expressed by the suffering and death of the Son of God, a person so infinitely worthy, and so beloved by the Father.

When the Son of God is beheld thus suffering, expiring on the cross in the sight of the whole universe, and crying out, "My God, my God, why hast thou forsaken me?" it is natural to inquire and consider, "Wherefore hath the Lord done thus unto his only begotten, dearly beloved Son: What meaneth the heat of this great anger?" The answer will be easy to all the discerning: They will understand the reason and design of the whole, and the instruction will dwell on their minds with increasing clearness and energy forever. It will be forever known and kept in view in the kingdom of God, that mankind rose in rebellion, and fell under the curse of the law of God, and his high displeasure: And that a way might be opened for a reconciliation, and favour to man, consistent with the divine law which cursed him, and with the righteousness and wisdom of Governor of the world, the Son of God took the place of man, was made under the law, and took the curse upon himself; which therefore was inflicted on him without the least mitigation. This is the reason of these dreadful sufferings of this infinitely great and worthy personage. "It pleased the Lord thus to bruise him, and put him to grief," as the strongest expression of his great displeasure, and the heat of his anger with the sinners whose cause he espoused, so as to take their place, and answer for them. This wrath is not against the Son of his love; but against the rebellion of those sinners for whom he suffers. [448]

The Redeemer being united to those sinners for whom he had undertaken to suffer by the most strong, ardent, benevolent affection, and by thus taking their place as their head and Saviour, was prepared in and by his human nature to be impressed with a clear apprehension and awful sense of the dreadful displeasure of God with them, and with sin, and to have the most painful sensation, of their infinitely miserable situation as deserving and justly exposed to the effects of the heat of his anger and wrath. And thus this anger and wrath, in this sense, fell on him, and his soul, in this situation, and thus united to them, was necessarily filled with the greatest pain and distress. And all things were so ordered, when the time of his most dreadful sufferings came on, as to raise this view and sensation to the highest degree. The comfortable and happifying sense of the love and favour of God was withdrawn, and the human soul was filled with the most dreadful gloom, distress and horror in a most keen sense of the anger and wrath of God, net against himself personally, bur with those whom he loved, and were, in a sense, one with him; so that their evil was his evil, and it even necessarily came on him. In this sense he suffered the displeasure and wrath of God. He felt it as insupportably dreadful, and had an overwhelming sense of it. And the displeasure and wrath of God against sinners was the cause of all his sufferings.

This appears to have been the chief source of the sufferings of Christ. What he suffered by his body, by the cruelty and rage of men, who could only torture him in his body, though great, was as nothing, compared with what he suffered in his mind, by the circumstances just mentioned. Many martyrs have suffered, as great bodily pain as was inflicted on the Redeemer; and they have endured it with great comfort and joy. Their minds have appeared to be out of the reach of the bodily tortures which were inflicted on them, so that they hardly felt them; but rejoiced in God, and the light of his countenance. Why then was the soul of the Redeemer troubled, and sorrowful even unto death? Why were there no expressions of comfort and joy even on the cross? Why did he cry out "My God, my God, why hast thou forsaken me?" The view of the case as stated above, will fully account for it, and appears to be the only satisfactory account of the matter.

Thus we see how Christ suffered for sin, was made a curse, that is, suffered the curse of the law, the curse of God: and in his sufferings, he, in a sense, suffered and felt the displeasure and wrath of God; and the anger of God against sin and the sinner was in a high and eminent degree manifested and expressed in the sufferings and death of Christ, consistent with his not being displeased, but well pleased with Christ himself, and loving him because he laid down his life for his people.

The instance mentioned above, of the husband suffering for the crime of his wife, and in her stead, serves in some measure to illustrate this point. The displeasure of government, or of the king, with the criminal, and the great offence she had given, and his fixed determination to manifest and express this by inflicting the penalty threatened to such offences, were as fully exhibited, and made known by the suffering of the husband in her stead, as if she had suffered, and, in some respects, much more, as the king would not, in this case, spare him, though he was a person so greatly esteemed and beloved. And he might with truth be said to suffer the displeasure and wrath of the king, as this was the cause of his sufferings, and was expressed in them; of which he was not personally the object, but the criminal.

Question 6. How is the threatening of the law in truth and reality executed by the sufferings of another, and not of him who is threatened? The transgressor only is threatened; and if it be not executed on him, it is not really executed at all. How can the sufferings of another, who is not the transgressor, and is not threatened, answer any end with respect to the threatening?

Ans. 1. It has been shown, and it is abundantly evident from scripture, that the sufferings of Christ had respect to the threatening of the law. Were there no such threatening, or were it not to be regarded, there could be no occasion for any suffering, and there would be no reason why Christ should suffer in order to the redemption of man. It has also been made evident that Christ did suffer the curse of the law, or the threatened penalty.

He suffered the evil threatened, or as great evil, a complete equivalent, if not precisely the same evil in every circumstance, which the sinner must have suffered, had the threatening been executed on him. It has, moreover, been shewn that all the ends of die threatening, and of a penalty, are as fully answered by the sufferings of Christ, as they could be by the execution of it on the sinner: As much respect is paid to the divine law; government is as well supported; the rectitude and righteousness of God, is as much declared; and his displeasure with the sinner and hatred of rebellion, and determination to punish it, as much manifested; and in some respects much more, and to greater advantage. If there be any difficulty still remaining in the case, it is, whether a substitute may suffer the penalty in the room of the sinner, and the latter, by this means, escape punishment, consistent with the threatening, and so that it shall be truly and properly executed, and the truth of the legislator in the threatening be maintained. Or whether the threatening can be really executed by vicarious sufferings.

This leads to

Ans. II. It is evident from scripture, that the law of God does admit of a substitute, both in obeying the precepts, and suffering the penalty of it; and that this is consistent with the true spirit and meaning of it.

When man was first created, and placed under the law of God, and moral government, Adam, the Father of the human race, was constituted their public head and representative, to obey the law for them, so that they should have the benefit of his obedience, and obtain eternal life by it, if he persevered in obedience through the appointed time of trial. Thus Adam was made a substitute, to obey the divine law for all mankind, in their room and stead. And it was hereby publicly declared by God, the Legislator, that his law admitted of a substitute. And if the law admitted of a substitute to obey for all the rest, of whom he was made the natural and constituted head; and by his single act of disobedience to bring sin and ruin on ail his posterity; and God had declared that this was the best and most wise way of administering his moral government in this world: then a substitute might suffer the penalty of the law for man, and redeem him from that sin and ruin which was brought upon him by the disobedience of a substitute, if a proper person, sufficient to suffer this, and survive the suffering, can be found. Had Adam, after he transgressed and incurred the penalty of the law, been able to suffer it, and survive and perfect the obedience which was required, this would have answered the law, according- to the declared meaning of it: He would have retrieved

The System of Doctrines, contained in Divine Relation, Explained and Defended Volume I
himself, and saved his posterity from sin and ruin. Adam was infinitely unequal to this: But a "second Adam" was found; a second public head and representative, of whom the first Adam was a type, figure or model, who was able to suffer the penalty of the law for man, and in his stead, and survive the dreadful scene; and by it redeem man, even all who are united to him by believing in him, from the curse of the law. [449]

Therefore, this being the declared meaning of the law, that it admitted a substitute, both to obey the precepts of it, and to suffer the penalty, and that the threatening of it was to be so understood; a second public head and substitute, who was revealed and promised when the first Adam had ruined himself and his posterity, has risen and suffered the penalty, in the room of sinners. Thus the threatening has been fully executed according to the true and declared meaning of it, when it was given; and as it has been fully explained in the divine conduct, in constituting a second man, the last Adam, and inflicting the threatened penalty on him. And in this way, "mercy and truth are met together: Righteousness and peace have kissed each other." [450] God has, agreeable to the strictest truth, executed the threatening of his law, according to the true intent and meaning of it; and by this has opened a way for reconciliation and peace with man, while his truth and righteousness are maintained, and gloriously manifested.

Quest. 7. Do not the sufferings of Christ remove the ill desert of those who believe in him? Christ has suffered all the evil that sin deserves, all that to which the sinner is liable, from the threatening and his ill desert, as great, and as much as could justly be inflicted on the sinner. If the sinner could have suffered all this evil himself, and survive such sufferings, he would then have no ill desert, it would not be just to inflict any more evil upon him. And if Christ has suffered it all for him, and in his stead, how can he deserve any punishment? And what grace is there then in pardoning the sinner who believes in Christ; or rather, What need has he of pardon?

Ans. The sufferings of Christ do not alter the character of the sinner, in the least. His ill desert is according to his whole moral character, according to what he is, and has done, as a moral agent; he may justly be treated according to this. And to treat him thus, would be doing him no injury. Therefore not to treat him according to his moral character, but to treat him better and more favourably, is mere grace and undeserved favour. The sufferings of Christ, therefore, do not make the least alteration, or any abatement of his ill desert, as the sinner's own character is not hereby made better.

If the sinner were to suffer the penalty himself, in his own person; and were able to do this, and survive his suffering; this would alter his moral character, as he would then have completely compensated for his crime, it being extinguished by his suffering all the evil which it deserves; no more could be required, or justly inflicted upon him. His whole character being considered, his crimes and sufferings, he would stand right in law, and have no need of a pardon, and there would be no grace in not punishing him yet more. The vicarious sufferings of a substitute are quite different, and opposite, in this respect, to the sufferings of the sinner, which have been supposed, though really impossible. For in the case of vicarious sufferings, the sinner's character remains the same, and he continues as ill deserving as ever, and must feel so, if his discerning and feeling be according to truth. Had Adam persevered in obedience, to the end of the time of his trial, by his vicarious obedience, all his children would have been admitted to the enjoyment of the favour of God, and eternal life; but this vicarious obedience of their substitute would not have rendered them in the least degree more deserving of such favour, than if there had been no such obedience. For Adam's obedience was not their own personal obedience, and never could be; and therefore could not be considered as such. So the sufferings of Christ, not being the sufferings of the sinner, but of a substitute, cannot render the sinner less ill deserving in himself, or personally considered, more than the vicarious obedience of a substitute can render those for whom he obeys more worthy of reward.

The husband's suffering for his wife, the punishment which she deserved, may serve to illustrate this point. His suffering did not render her in the least less deserving of punishment, as it did not alter her character; and it was as much an act of mere grace to pardon her, as if her husband had not suffered. The end that his suffering answered, was to open the way for her pardon, consistent with public justice, and the general good; and not to reader her the less ill deserving.

Ques. 8. Would it not have been a higher exercise of mercy and grace to save sinners without an atonement; without buying and redeeming them at so great a price? Many have thought that the doctrine of an atonement stated above, as necessary m order to the exercise of divine grace, in pardoning and saving sinners, gives a dishonourable notion of the goodness of God, and represents his mercy unspeakably less, than it would appear to be, if sinners were forgiven and saved, without any price paid for their redemption, or atonement made for their sins.

Ans. If the nature and design of an atonement be well understood, and kept in mind, as it has been stated and represented in the beginning of this chapter, it will appear that the benevolence and grace of God, in saving sinners without an atonement, were this consistent with rectitude and wisdom, would have been unspeakably less, than that which is now exercised in the redemption of sinners by the atonement of Christ; this being necessary to render their salvation possible, consistent with righteousness, truth, and goodness itself. Indeed, as the case was, there would have been no grace in pardoning sinners, and saving them without an atonement, for this would have been contrary to infinite goodness. A full answer to this question is found in the first chapter of this part.

Having considered the atonement which it was necessary for the Redeemer to make by his own sufferings, in order to redeem man; and which he has actually made by suffering the penalty of the law, which was the greatest, and most difficult part of his work, as the Redeemer of men, it must in the next place be observed,

II. The work of the Redeemer consists, in part, in his perfect obedience to the law of God. This is an essential part of the character and work of the Redeemer of man; for he could not directly honour the precepts of the law in any way, or by any thing, but by obeying them; and the least instance of disobedience or disregard to any one of them would have ruined his character as the Redeemer of man.

The Son of God, united to the human nature, and considered as God and man in one person, was not under any original obligation to that obedience which he voluntarily took upon himself to perform. This divine person was above any obligation to obedience, as a subject and servant. He was, in the human nature, perfectly holy, as God is holy; but this he might be, and continue so forever, and yet not be under obligation to yield the obedience to which he submitted. The Son of God did not take upon him the form of a servant, merely by becoming man, by being made flesh, and taking the human nature into a personal union; but as he became flesh, and was made in the likeness of men, that hereby he might be capable of obeying and suffering in the human nature, he voluntarily took upon himself the form of a servant, and being found in fashion as a man, he humbled himself, and became obedient unto death. [451] "When the fulness of time was come, God sent forth his Son, made of a woman, made under the law." [452] The Son of God being made of a woman, that is, being made flesh, and becoming man, uniting himself to the human nature, did not necessarily put him under the law, or lay him under obligation to obey it, as a subject, or servant, or to suffer the penalty of it. Therefore, the apostle, in these words, distinguishes between these; he was not only made of a woman, took the human nature into a personal union with himself; but was also made under the law. When he was originally above law, or any obligation to obedience, he voluntarily took the place of sinners, and was made under the law, and became obliged to suffer the penalty, and obey the precepts of it, "to redeem them that were under the law, and under the curse of it, and that they might receive the adoption of sons." It was necessary that he should suffer the curse of the law, to redeem men from the curse of it; and it was equally necessary that he should obey the precepts of the law, in man's stead, that believers in him might receive the adoption of sons, and obtain complete deliverance from sin, and become heirs of eternal life.

The atonement made by Christ, in his suffering the penalty of the law, has respect only to the threatening of the law, that by suffering what was threatened, and what sin deserves, sinners who believe in him might be delivered from the curse. Thus Christ died for sin; was sacrificed or offered to bear the sins of many; and he shed his blood for the remission of sins, as the scripture asserts. This atonement therefore only delivers from the curse of the law, and procures the remission of their sins who believe in him; but does not procure for them any positive good: It leaves them under the power of sin, and without any title to eternal life, or any positive favour, or actual fitness or capacity to enjoy positive happiness. This would be but a very partial redemption, had the Redeemer done no more than merely to make atonement for sin, by suffering the penalty of the law for sinners, and in their stead. It was therefore necessary that he should obey the precepts of the law for man, and in his stead, that by his perfect and meritorious obedience, he might honour the law in the preceptive part of it, and obtain all the positive favour and benefits which man needed, be they ever so many and great.

It has been observed, that when man was first created, it was made known by the Legislator, that his law admitted of vicarious obedience; that the obedience of one might be the proper ground of granting the greatest favours to all whom he represented, and for whom, and in whose stead he acted. This he did by constituting Adam a public and federal head of his posterity, and substituting him to act for them all, so that by his obedience through the time of his trial, his children should obtain eternal life. If this were proper and wise, and consistent with the exercise of the most perfect moral government, and with the true design and spirit of the moral law, as it most certainly was; then there is equal propriety and wisdom in substituting the second public head, the Redeemer of men, to act, to obey, for all the redeemed, who shall believe in him, so that they shall have as much favour, at least, as if they had performed perfect obedience in their own persons. The obedience of the second Adam, the Son of God, must be infinitely more worthy of regard, and meritorious, than the obedience of the first Adam, for two reasons.

The System of Doctrines, contained in Divine Relation, Explained and Defended Volume I

1. He was infinitely greater and more excellent, and worthy, than Adam was. Therefore his obedience was proportionally more excellent, meritorious and pleasing to God. And it was proportionally more honourable to the law, which he obeyed, and to the Legislator and divine government. It may be truly said, that the obedience of Christ to the divine law had more excellence and worth in it, than the highest, most perfect and all possible obedience of all the mere creatures in the universe; and the law of God is unspeakably more dignified and honoured in the precepts of it, by the former, than it can be by the latter.

2dly. The obedience of Adam, the first public head, was but a just debt which he owed to God, for himself, in his own person. The law required perfect obedience of him; he was under indispensable obligation to this every moment of his existence: Therefore it was impossible for him to merit any thing by doing more than his duty, while he gave himself wholly to God, in the strongest love of which he was capable, and in the highest and most difficult acts of obedience; he gave no more than he owed, as an original and just debt, arising from his existence and capacity, as a creature of God. But the Son of God, as has been observed, was under no obligation to obey as he did, as a subject and servant: he owed nothing of this nature for himself, he being above all law, in this respect, until he voluntarily took upon him the form of a servant, and put himself under the law, not only to suffer the penalty of it, not for himself, but for others; but to obey it, not for himself, as if he owed such obedience, but for others, that they might have the benefit of it. In this respect, the obedience of the Redeemer was in the highest sense and degree worthy of reward, and meritorious for himself and those for whom he obeyed. All the glory, which is the consequence of his obedience and sufferings, and all the positive good to himself, and his church, is the reward of the Redeemer, and of the redeemed with him. Because he took upon him the form of a servant, and was obedient unto death: Therefore God hath highly exalted him, and given him a name, which is above every name." [453] The Lord is well pleased for his righteousness sake, and hath delivered all things into his hands, and made him head over all things to the church, to complete the redemption of it, and give eternal life to as many as were given to him.

In this view it may be said that the reward of the obedience of the Son of God is infinitely greater than that which the first Adam would have obtained, had he obeyed. The Redeemer has by his obedience obtained unspeakably greater good, happiness and glory, for his church, the redeemed, than the obedience of Adam would have procured for his posterity. Speaking of the redeemed, he says, "I am come that they might have life, and that they might have it more abundantly." [454] They are raised up to sit with him, even on his throne, to reign with him, as kings and priests, sharing with him in his felicity and glory. All this is the fruit and reward of the obedience of the Mediator. The redeemed enjoy the benefit of his obedience as much as if they themselves had performed it, or it were their own obedience, though they, in themselves, in their own persons, are as unworthy as if Christ had not obeyed the law for them.

The obedience of Christ, though most excellent and meritorious, is not an atonement for the sins of men, or really any part of it. It is impossible that any mere obedience, however excellent and meritorious, should make atonement for the least sin. This can be done by nothing but suffering the penalty of the law, the evil with which transgression is threatened, as has been shown, while attending to the sufferings of Christ.

Christ did, indeed, obey in suffering; and this was, perhaps, the highest act or instance of his obedience. As a servant he received a commandment from the Father to lay down his life to make atonement for the sins of men. This was the most difficult part, and the greatest trial of his obedience. He set his face as a flint, and went through the whole with a persevering steadiness and resolution; and in this was the strongest exercise and expression of his love to God and man, and regard for the law of God, and the divine government. And this was therefore the most pleasing to God, and the most meritorious part of his obedience, when he "became obedient unto death, even the death of the cross;" as it was also the greatest instance of his suffering, in which the atonement which he made by suffering, chiefly consisted. And it was necessary that his suffering should be voluntary, and so an act of obedience, as far as he was active, in order to his suffering justly, and making any atonement thereby. But though the Redeemer obeyed in sufferings, and suffered in obeying; and his highest and most meritorious obedience was acted out in his voluntary suffering unto death, and in this greatest instance of his suffering, the atonement which he made for sin chiefly consisted; yet his obedience and suffering are two perfectly distinct things, and answered different ends; and must be considered so, and the distinction and difference carefully, and with clearness kept up in the mind, in order to have a proper understanding of this very important subject. The sufferings of Christ, as such, made atonement for sin, as he suffered the penalty of the law, or the curse of it, the evil threatened to transgression, and which is the desert of it, in the sinner's stead; by which he opened the way for sinners being delivered from the curse, and laid the foundation for reconciliation between God, and the transgressors, by his not imputing, but pardoning their sins, who believe in the Redeemer, and approve of his character and conduct. By the obedience of Christ all the positive good, all those favours and blessings are merited and obtained, which sinners need, in order to enjoy complete and eternal redemption, or everlasting life in the kingdom of God. By this he has purchased and obtained the Holy Spirit, by whom sinners are so far recovered from total depravity, and renewed, as to be prepared and disposed to believe on Christ and receive him, being offered to them: And he carries on a work of sanctification in their hearts, until they are perfectly holy. Therefore Christ says, he will send and give the Holy Spirit, and he Father will send him in his name: and he is called the Spirit of Christ, "If I go not away, the Comforter will not come unto you; but if I depart, I will send him unto you. And when he is -come, he will reprove the world of sin, and of righteousness, and of judgment. The Comforter, the Holy Ghost, whom the Father will send in my name, he shall teach you all things. When the Comforter is come, whom I will send unto you from the Father, even the Spirit of Truth, which proceedeth from the Father, he shall testify of me." [455] "If any man have not the Spirit of Christ, he is none of his." [456] This gift of the Holy Ghost really comprises all positive good which Christ has by his obedience purchased for the redeemed. And as "Christ is the end of the law for righteousness to every one that believeth," [457] all such being interested in his righteousness, and having the benefit of it as much as if they had in their own persons perfectly obeyed the law, have eternal life made sure to them; the Holy Spirit is given to them to abide with them forever, as the earnest of their eternal inheritance; and they have a divine promise that they shall never perish, but shall persevere in holiness, until they are made perfect, "being kept by the power of God, through faith unto salvation." All which favours they receive by the obedience and merit or righteousness of Christ, which is imputed to them, or avails to procure all these benefits for them, in consequence of their union to him by faith. But these matters will be more fully considered in some of the following chapters.

Before this head is dismissed, it may be useful to observe the following things. Though there be a real distinction between the atonement which is made by Christ for sin by suffering; and his obedience, by which sinners who believe in him are recommended to all the positive blessings, which they want, and are bestowed on them; yet both these are generally included and meant by the righteousness of Christ; but a principal respect seems to be had to the latter, and sometimes perhaps that only is intended. He who reads the Bible with care will take notice of this. The righteousness of Christ does most properly consist in his obedience, by which believers in him obtain eternal life, and all positive blessings; yet as his obedience implies his sufferings, and his sufferings imply his obedience, and one is as necessary for the salvation of men as the other, they are both included in his righteousness; as they are both necessarily included in his obedience unto death. [458]

It maybe farther observed, that to be justified by Christ, sometimes means only a being pardoned, or deliverance from the curse of the law by the sufferings and atonement of Christ, or has a principal respect to that; though it includes positive favour, and a title to eternal life, which are given to believers, for the sake of the obedience and worthiness of Christ. Pardon of sin, or deliverance from the evil which sin deserves, is distinguishable from what is called "justification of life," [459] which implies a tide to eternal life, though these are never separated; for he who is pardoned, is by one and the same act of God, also made heir of eternal life, including all the favours which the believer receives for the sake of the worthiness and obedience of Christ; and is treated as well as if he were perfectly righteous, out of respect to the obedience and righteousness of the Redeemer. The following seem to be instances in which to justify, or be justified, intends only forgiveness of sins on account of the sufferings or atonement of Christ; or, at least, to have a primary and chief respect to that--"Be it known unto you, men and brethren, that through this man is preached unto you the forgiveness of sins: And by him all that believe are justified from all things, from which ye could not be justified by the law of Moses." [460] "Much more then being now justified by his blood, we shall be saved from wrath through him." [461] Here justification seems to mean no more than pardon of sin, or rather opening the way to pardon by the suffering and death of Christ in their stead, Christ having died for them.

Redemption seems also to be sometimes used in a more restrained sense, and primarily, if not wholly respects deliverance from the curse of the law by the sufferings of Christ, or forgiveness of sins through the atonement he has made by suffering the curse of the law. The following appear to be instances of this: "In whom we have redemption through his blood, the forgiveness of sins."[462] "Christ hath redeemed us from the curse of the law, being made a curse for us." [463] Yet this includes, and is connected with deliverance from sin and all evil, and the bestowment of eternal life, and comprehends the whole work of the Redeemer.

III. Another part of the work of the Redeemer, is to complete the salvation of those whom he redeems, and to finish and perfect the work of redemption. This has been in some measure brought into view under the former head, but requires a more particular consideration. In consequence of the suffering and obedience of Christ, and as a reward of the latter, he is exalted, to give repentance and remission of sins, and complete salvation to those who shall be actually redeemed. All things are given into his hands, and all power in heaven and earth: And he is made head over all things to the church; that he might sanctify and cleanse it, and present it to himself a glorious church, not having spot or wrinkle, or any such thing; but that it should be holy, and without blemish. As all men are naturally in a state of total depravity, enemies to God, his law and government; and therefore enemies to the Redeemer, and all his designs and works; not one of them can be persuaded to come to him, and accept of the offered salvation, unless he be made willing by his mighty power, renewing his heart, taking away the heart of stone, the rebellious heart, and giving a discerning, obedient heart. This is represented in the scripture by a variety of phrases, and abundantly asserted, which may be more fully considered in a following chapter. The Redeemer having renewed by the spirit, those whom he designs to save, so far as to bring them to a union with himself by faith, and to become his real friends, carries on this work through life, until they are brought at death to perfection in holiness; and he will raise their bodies at the last day, and give them eternal life. All this he has declared he will do. He has said, "All that the Father giveth me, shall come to me, and him that cometh to me, I will in no wise cast out. This is the will of the Father, which hath sent me, that of all which he hath given me, I should lose nothing, but should raise it up again at the last day. And this is the will of him that sent me, that every one which seeth the Son and believeth on him, may have everlasting life, and I will raise him up at the last day."[464]

He is exalted to the right hand of God, and sits on the throne of the universe, having all things in his hands, and governing the whole world, so as in the best manner to save the redeemed, and fulfil the good pleasure of his goodness towards them, and totally to disappoint, overthrow and destroy all his and their enemies, putting them under his feet, when he will come to judge the world in righteousness.

The Redeemer, in prosecuting his work, sustains the character, and performs the offices of prophet, priest and king. He is, in the moral world, especially in his church and kingdom, what the sun is in the natural world, the light thereof. He is therefore called "the Sun of righteousness." He said, "I am the light of the world: He that followeth me, shall not walk in darkness, but shall have the light of life. I am come a light into the world, that whosoever believeth on me, should not abide in darkness." [465]

The Redeemer is the author of all the moral light and instruction afforded to men. He has given the divine revelation which we enjoy. He inspired men by his Spirit to write that part of scripture which the church enjoyed before his incarnation. [466] He taught and instructed men when in the flesh on earth; and inspired the apostles and others to write what is contained in the New Testament, in which, among other things, all the future, grand events, that relate to his church and kingdom, and to the world of mankind in general, which are to take place to the end of the world, are foretold; and by all which life and immortality are brought to light. And he opens the eyes of blind sinners, and turns them from darkness to marvellous light, causing the light of truth contained in divine revelation to shine in their hearts. And he forms the hearts of his disciples more and more to true discerning, till they are cured of all their mistakes and darkness, and brought into perfect light and day. In order to this he has instituted and maintains all the external means of instruction and knowledge; with reference to which St. Paul says, "When he ascended up on high, he led captivity captive, and gave gifts unto men. And he gave some Apostles, and some Prophets, and some Evangelists, and some Pastors and Teachers, for the perfecting of the saints, for the work of the ministry, for the edifying of the body of Christ; till we all come in the unity of the faith, and of the knowledge of the Son of God, unto a perfect man, unto the measure of the stature of the fulness of Christ." [467]

And he not only exerciseth the office of a prophet till he has brought his church to a state of perfect light and knowledge, but he will sustain this character in heaven forever: For the Lamb shall be the everlasting light of it. [468] He will make new discoveries, and give increasing light and knowledge without any end. The Redeemer therefore is promised in the character of a prophet, when his incarnation is foretold. "For Moses truly said unto the fathers, a prophet shall the Lord your God raise up unto you, of your brethren, like unto me." [469]

Christ is also a priest in his church. The great high priest, of whom all the priests, constituted by the laws of God given to Moses, were types. He has offered the only sacrifice, by which full atonement is made for sin. And in this transaction, he is both the priest, the sacrifice, and the altar. And though by his once offering himself a sacrifice for the sins of his people, he has made complete atonement for sin; yet he continues to exercise the office of the priest, and u ill do so forever. "He is made an high priest forever, after the order of Melchisedec. Because he ever liveth, he hath an unchangeable priesthood. Wherefore he is able also to save them to the uttermost, that come unto God by him, seeing he ever liveth to make intercession for them." [470] Therefore he appears on the throne in heaven, as a Lamb that had been slain, and is represented as entering and remaining there with his own blood. The atonement of Christ, which he has made by his blood, for the sins of the redeemed, and his meritorious obedience, and the consequent intercession which he will forever make for them, will be their everlasting security from wrath and destruction, and for their enjoyment of the divine favour, and eternal life, as their ill desert, in their own persons, and in themselves considered, will remain without the least diminution forever. Therefore the Redeemer continues a high priest forever, and because he ever lives to make intercession for his people, they shall live also, eternally dependent on his atonement, merit, and worthiness, for safety from evil, and for all the good which they enjoy. "Behold the man whose name is the branch, and he shall grow up out of his place, and he shall build the temple of the Lord: (that is, the church.) Even he shall build the temple of the Lord, and he shall bear the glory, and shall sit and rule upon his throne, and he shall be a Priest upon his throne." [471] He will continue in the office of a priest, as long as he shall sit upon his throne, and his kingdom lasts, which shall be forever. This leads farther to observe,

Jesus Christ, in the work of redemption, acts in the character of ruler and king. He is a prophet, and a priest upon his throne. He exerciseth the authority of a king. This is abundantly asserted in scripture. "I have set my king upon my holy hill of Zion." [472] "My heart is inditing a good matter: I speak of the things which I have made touching the king." [473] He is the king, by way of eminence. He ib King of kings, and Lord of lords. He has supreme authority as legislator in his church. He has made institutions and laws which are binding on his people, they being obliged implicitly to obey his commands in all things. And he is the only lawgiver. And as all men are naturally in a state of rebellion, and enemies to God, he not only commands them to repent and submit to him; but he effectually conquers and subdues all those who become his willing subjects, by a powerful operation on their hearts, changing a; id renewing them, and bringing them to a cordial obedience to him. Thus his people are all made willing in the day of his power. He protects his church and people from all their enemies, and from all harm; and gradually removes all the disaffection to him in their hearts, until they are all brought to a most cheerful, perfect obedience to him, and his throne is established in their hearts, and he rules there without a competitor. And he rules in the midst of his enemies. They are all under his powder and control, and he restrains, guides and governs them, so that they cannot cross and impede his designs, or do the least hurt to his interest and kingdom, however much they may desire and attempt it; but he uses them all to promote and answer his own ends. The wrath of man shall praise him: and the remainder of wrath he will restrain. [474] And he will finally subdue all his enemies, and put them under his feet.

The Redeemer now reigns over all. All things are delivered into his hands; both angels, men, and devils are in his hand, and under his direction and control: Yea, all creatures and things, visible and invisible, in the whole created universe, both greater and less, are sustained and guided by him, in all their various circumstances and motions; and he is ordering and using them to answer his own ends, as King of Zion, and head over all things to the church. In the mean time he is forming his church, and will not cease working till he has made it the most perfect, beautiful, happy and glorious society and kingdom, that infinite power, wisdom and goodness can produce; which shall stand and flourish forever, as a monument to display all these: and in which his boundless, wonderful love and grace, in the redemption of man, and his unchangeable truth and faithfulness, shall be celebrated without end, and with increasing admiration and praise.

In the exercise of his kingly office, when all the redeemed are brought into his kingdom, and the number of his church is completed, he will appear and sit as judge of all moral agents; will raise the dead; and cause all the angels and devils, and all mankind to stand before his tribunal; and when the moral character of every one shall be properly examined and displayed, he will, as king and the final judge of all, pronounce the blessed sentence on the redeemed, admitting them as the happy members of his eternal kingdom: And he will sentence all those of mankind u ho shall then appear not to have been his friends in this world, to endless punishment, with the devil and his angels.[475] And having thus completed the work of redemption, by gathering the redeemed into his kingdom; and putting all his enemies under his feet, consigning them to deserved, endless punishment, he will reign forever in his church, his mediatorial kingdom, which shall have no end. That his kingdom is an everlasting kingdom, and the Redeemer shall reign in it forever, is abundantly declared in the Scripture. It is needless to cite now more than the words of the angel to the virgin Mary. "He shall be great, and shall be called the Son of the Highest: And the Lord God shall give unto him the throne of his father David. And he shall reign over the house of Jacob forever, and of his kingdom there shall be no end." [476]

What St. Paul says may be thought, at the first view, to be inconsistent with this. His words are, "Then cometh the end, when he shall have delivered up the kingdom to God, even the Father; when he shall have put down all rule, and all authority and power. And when all things shall be subdued unto him, then shall the Son also himself be subject unto him that put all things under him, that God may be all in all." [477] In order to understand this passage, and see that it is consistent with other parts of scripture, where the Redeemer is said to reign in his kingdom forever, the following things must be observed.

    1. In consequence of the Son of God, or second Person in the Trinity, undertaking the work of

redemption, by becoming the Son of Man, and taking upon himself the form of a servant, and doing and suffering all that was necessary in order to effect this, and having actually gone through all this; he was exalted, in and by his human nature, and rewarded by having all power, and all things put into his hands, and being made head over all things to the church; and is appointed the supreme and universal king and governor of the universe, to use and dispose of all, so as in the best manner to accomplish and perfect the work of redemption, and complete the salvation of the redeemed, and vanquish and totally overthrow all his and their enemies, by putting them under his footstool. This must be considered as a peculiar kind and degree of power and authority with which he is invested, by which he sits on the throne of the universe, and is sole ruler, in the natural and moral world, until the ends of this investiture shall be answered; and he has finished the work, to accomplish which, he is thus exalted. He will then, when an end to this is come, deliver up to the Father this delegated power and kingdom; and no longer, as God and man, sit at the right hand of the Father, as supreme ruler in the universal kingdom. This leads to observe,

2. When all this is accomplished, the Son of God, being God and man, and considered in the character and capacity of Mediator and Redeemer of his church, will take his proper place which is assigned to him in the economy of redemption, or covenant between the Father and Son; which is not that of supreme ruler and legislator in the universal kingdom of God; but in this respect, and in his human nature he will be subject to the Father. And then God, the Deity, will be all in all, in a higher sense, and more perspicuously, than when the supreme rule was in the hand of a person who is a man, and the Son of man. And who made use of the agency and offices of angels and men in carrying on his designs, which will then all be put down: And who is opposed, and his power and authority disputed by his enemies, devils and men, which will then all be subdued, and put out of the way.

3. The Redeemer will still remain the head of his church, and reign forever as king in his mediatorial kingdom; crowned with everlasting honour, happiness and glory, of which he will lose nothing by delivering up the kingdom to the Father, and being subject to him, in the sense abovementioned. He will be admired, praised and glorified by angels and the redeemed forever; and he will be their everlasting, unchangeable prophet, priest and king.

As the covenant between the Father and the Son has been now mentioned, it will be proper here to give a brief explanation of that. It is evident from scripture, as well as from the nature of the case, that there was a mutual agreement and engagement between the Father and the second person of the Trinity respecting the redemption of man, by which the distinct part which each person in the Trinity was to act, was fixed, and undertaken. This mutual agreement is of the nature of a covenant and engagement with each other, to perform the different parts of this great work which were assigned to them. This is an eternal covenant, without beginning, as is the existence of the triune God, and as are all the divine purposes and decrees. The second person was engaged to become incarnate, to do and suffer all that was necessary for the salvation of men. The Father promised that on his consenting to take upon him the character and work of a Mediator and Redeemer, he should be every way furnished and assisted to go through with the work; that he should have power to save an elect number of mankind, and form a church and kingdom, most perfect and glorious': In order to accomplish this, all things, all power in heaven and earth, should be given to him, until Redemption was completed: And then he should reign in the exercise of all his offices, as Mediator, in his church and kingdom forever.

All this is expressed or implied in the representation the Bible gives of this affair, in the following passages, as well as others which might be mentioned. "I have set my king upon my holy hill of Zion. I will declare the decree: The Lord hath said unto me, Thou art my Son, this day have I begotten thee. Ask of me, and I will give thee the heathen for thine inheritance, and the uttermost parts of the earth for thy possession, &c." [478] Here the Father makes promises, and enters into engagements with the Son, which is here called the decree, or covenant. To the same purpose are the following words: "The Lord said unto my Lord, Sit thou at my right hand, until I make thine enemies thy footstool. The Lord shall send the rod of thy strength out of Zion; rule thou in the midst of thine enemies." [479] "Behold my servant whom I uphold, mine elect in whom my soul delighteth: I have put my Spirit upon him, he shall bring forth judgment to the Gentiles. I the Lord have called thee in righteousness, and I will hold thine hand, and will keep thee, and give thee for a covenant of the people, for a light of the Gentiles." [480] The consent and engagement of the second person is expressed in the following words: "Sacrifice and offering thou didst not desire, mine ears hast thou opened, (or a body hast thou prepared me.) Burnt offering, and sin offering, hast thou not required. Then said I, lo, I come. In the volume of the book it is written of me, I delight to do thy will, O my God; yea, thy law is within my heart." [481] Upon this engagement of the Son, "the Father saith unto the Son, thy throne, O God, is forever and ever. A sceptre of righteousness is the sceptre of thy kingdom. Thou hast loved righteousness, and hated iniquity; therefore God, even thy God, hath anointed thee with the oil of gladness above thy fellows." [482] The whole of this is comprehended and implied in the following words of our Saviour when on earth. "All that the Father hath given me, shall come unto me; and him that cometh to me, I will in no wise cast out; for I came down from heaven, not to do mine own will, bat the will of him that sent me. And this is the Father's will who hath sent me, that of all which he hath given me, I should lose nothing; but should raise it up again at the last day." [483] To this covenant Jesus Christ refers when he said to his disciples, after his resurrection, "Behold I send the promise of my Father upon you:" but tarry ye in Jerusalem, until ye be endued with power from on high. And being assembled together with them, he commanded them that they should not depart from Jerusalem, but wait for the promise of the Father, which, saith he, ye have heard of me. [484] By the promise of the Father, he meant the gift of the Holy Ghost, to furnish them for their work as his apostles. And this promise must be the promise made to him in the covenant of redemption, that upon his obedience unto death, the Holy Spirit should be sent, effectually to apply the redemption hereby obtained, to those who were; given to him.

The blessed Trinity in the one God may be considered as a most exalted, happy and glorious society, or family, uniting in the plan of divine operations; especially in accomplishing the work of redemption, which really comprehends all things, and is the grand design and end of all. In this each one has his part to perform according to a most wise, mutual regulation and agreement, which may be called a covenant. In performing these several parts of this work, one acts as superior, and another as inferior; or one acts under another; and by his authority, as appointed and sent by him. This is by divines called the economy of the work of redemption; or the economical agreement or covenant between the persons of the adorable Trinity respecting the redemption of man. [485] According to this economy, the Son, the Redeemer, acts under the Father, and by his will and appointment; and in this respect takes an inferior part; and in this sense he is supposed to speak, when he says, "The Father is greater than I." [486]

Though in the passages of scripture which have been mentioned, and others of the same kind, the third person in the Trinity, the Holy Spirit, is not expressly mentioned as covenanting, or engaging to perform any part of this work; yet he is necessarily understood as concerned and included in this covenant, as he is m the holy scripture every where represented as acting an equal part in the redemption of man; and therefore must be considered as taking that particular part by consent and agreement. This covenant is called by most divines now, the covenant of redemption, to distinguish it from what is called the covenant of grace, which takes place between God, or the Redeemer, and believers in him, which will be particularly considered hereafter.

The work of the Redeemer, which has been in some measure described above, consists in his actually performing the part assigned to him, and undertaken by him, in the covenant of redemption; and in his sustaining the character and executing the offices which he inherits as a reward for his humiliation; in which he will continue forever, even when he has delivered up the delegated rule and kingdom which he now has, to the Father, and is, in the sense above explained, subject to the Father.

IMPROVEMENT

I. WE learn from the view which has been now given from the scriptures, of the work of the Mediator and Redeemer, how important and essential the doctrine of his divinity is: As he must be God as well as man, in order to perform this work. A mere creature would be infinitely unequal to this.

It is necessary that this should be believed; that his infinitely high and glorious person and character, as the true God, should be kept in view, in order to trust in him as the Redeemer of man from the infinite evil which he deserves; from a state of total moral depravity, to the favour of God, to perfect holiness and eternal life, by his suffering and obedience, and by his power, wisdom and goodness.

It is necessary that he should be a person of infinite dignity, excellence and worthiness, in order to make atonement for sin by suffering the penalty of the law, as it has been explained above from the scriptures. The sufferings of a mere creature could do nothing towards this; and had such an one offered to undertake this, it would have been so far from pleasing the governor of the world, that it must be considered as an affront offered to him, most dishonourable to his character, law, and government. And the obedience of a mere creature, or of all creatures, could not so honour the law, and the divine authority expressed by it, which sinners had reproached and trampled under foot by their rebellion, as to obtain favour, recovery from a state of sin, and eternal life for them, out of respect to the merit and worthiness of such obedience. This could be done by none but a person of infinite greatness and worth; and one who was under no obligation to obey antecedent to his voluntarily taking upon him the form of a servant. And it requires infinite power, skill and wisdom to recover a rebel from total depravity and enmity against God and his law, to obedience and holiness; and infinite condescension and goodness. All this is ascribed to the Redeemer in the holy scripture, as has been shown. And surely none can believe all this, and rely with confidence on the

Redeemer for such redemption, who does not believe him to be truly God, infinitely great, honourable, powerful, wise and good.

They who have such a low and dishonourable idea of the divine character, his law and moral government, as to believe sin to be infinitely less criminal than it really is, that it is not infinitely odious and criminal, and does not deserve infinite natural evil as the just punishment of it; That it is not necessary that the threatening of the law should be in any sense executed, in order to the maintenance of public truth and righteousness: That man is not so depraved but that he may recover himself from sin to holiness when proper methods are taken with him, and motives set before him to induce him to repent, and renounce his rebellion, without any supernatural renovation by the Spirit of God; and that in this way he may obtain forgiveness, and recommend himself to the divine favour, so as to obtain eternal life: They who have such wrong notions of God, and his law, of sin and of themselves, do not, and cannot see the need of a divine person, of one that is really the true God united to the human nature, to be the Redeemer of men: Therefore they cannot believe that Jesus Christ is such an one. Consequently they read the Bible under this prejudice, and find things there which appear to them contrary to the real divinity of Christ. They greedily catch at them, and make the best use of them they can, in their opposition to that doctrine; at the same time, exerting all their abilities to show the unreasonableness and absurdity of such a doctrine, and in the most plausible manner possible to explain away those passages of scripture, which are understood by those who believe in the divinity of the Redeemer of man, plainly to assert this doctrine; and to make them consistent with his being a mere creature. This appears to be the case with the Arians and Socinians, both in former ages, and in this, who join in the denial of the divinity of Christ, though they differ in other things respecting him; the former holding that he is the first and greatest creature that God has made, who after he had existed thousands of years a mere spirit, took a body in the womb of the Virgin Mary, and was born of her, &c. The latter suppose he had no existence before he was conceived and brought forth by the virgin, his mother.

But others, who view the divine character, and the law of God, the nature and desert of sin, the depravity, and lost, undone state of man, in the scriptural light in which they have been set in the preceding part of this system, are prepared to see their need of such a Redeemer as the Bible reveals; they consult that, and find that he is there declared to be "God with us," God, who created, and upholds all things, manifest in the flesh; that he has given his life a ransom for sinners; has been made a curse to deliver men from the curse, dying for their sins; that he has obeyed the divine law in its requirements; that he is risen from the dead, and exalted to the right hand of the Father, able effectually to draw men unto him, and to save to the uttermost all them who come to God by him. They believe and are sure, and address him as Nathaniel did, "thou art the Son of God, thou art the King of Israel." And as Thomas, "My Lord; and my God." And say with the beloved disciple, "We know that the Son of God is come, and hath given us an understanding that we may know him that is true; and we are in him that is true, in his Son Jesus Christ. This is the true God and eternal life." And they rest satisfied in the natural and plain sense of the words of this same John, "In the beginning was the Word, and the Word was with God, and the Word was God. And the Word was made flesh, and dwelt among us; and we beheld his glory, as of the only begotten of the Father, full of grace and truth."

II. From the view we have had, by attending to the Bible, of the atonement for sin made by Christ, we learn, that they have made a great mistake, who think that this consists wholly in the obedience of the Redeemer; and that his sufferings, as such, and as distinguished from his obedience, are no part of the atonement: And therefore that he did not in any sense suffer the penalty of the law, in whole or in part; nor had his sufferings any direct reference to this; and answered no end, except that hereby his love to God and man, was exercised in a higher degree, and his obedience was more tried and conspicuous by obeying unto death, than if he had not been obliged thus to suffer.

This notion of the atonement entirely excludes and denies the real atonement, clearly and abundantly stated and taught in the scriptures; and places it in that in which it does not consist. Therefore as this error wholly subverts the true scripture doctrine of the atonement of Christ, it is great, dangerous, and hurtful, in proportion to the importance and necessity of an atonement, and of believing and confiding in that atonement, which, according to divine revelation, is the only foundation of the hope of a christian.

If the threatening and penalty of the law may be disregarded, and set aside, so as to pass wholly unexecuted, in order to pardon and favour the transgressor, without any vicarious sufferings of another in his stead, it will be difficult, and doubtless impossible, to show or see why a vicarious obedience to the precepts of the law is necessary in order to the sinner's salvation. And why the obedience only of the Redeemer should be a sufficient ground, or any reason at all, why man should be delivered from the curse of the law, it is presumed no one can tell; or why it was necessary that a substitute should obey the law in man's stead, if there was no need of his suffering the penalty also. Upon this plan there appears to be no need of a Redeemer, unless it be to reveal the mercy of God to sinners, and his readiness to pardon and save all who repent and return to obedience, and persevere therein: And to set an example of holy obedience, and to lay down his life in confirmation of the truths which he had taught: And what need there is that the Redeemer should be more than a mere man, in order to do all this, it is believed, none can tell. The Socinian's Redeemer is therefore equal to the whole of this work.

III. We farther learn what a great delusion they embrace, who think they, in their own persons, are become innocent and worthy, by the atonement and obedience of Christ: That his sufferings and obedience are so imputed to them, that they are really become their own sufferings and obedience; that his righteousness and holiness is in such a sense and degree, their own righteousness and holiness, that they themselves are, in the sight of God, perfectly innocent and holy. And some go so far as to say they have no ill desert or sin; nor can they sin, let them do what they will. This is to a dreadful degree, perverting the doctrine of the atonement of Christ, and his work, as the Redeemer of sinners, and of pardon and justification through him.

It has been shewn, that the sinner who is interested in the atonement of Christ, and is delivered from the curse of the law, is left as ill deserving as he ever was, in his own person; and this his ill desert, never will, or can be removed. And it is equally true, that the sinner who is interested in all the merit and worthiness of Christ, and is for the sake of that, justified, and made heir of eternal life, is still as unworthy as ever in himself, in his own person, of the least favour: as unworthy as he could be, if the Redeemer had merited nothing for him, or he had no interest in his righteousness; and must remain so, and know that he is so, forever; And the least thought to the contrary would be infinitely criminal, and a most ungrateful and horrid abuse of the atonement and righteousness of Christ.

Every thing contrary to the divine law, in the believer, is his own sin, and as criminal, as if he had no interest in the righteousness of Christ; and much more so. What the Redeemer has done and suffered is imputed to him; that is, is reckoned in his favour, so that he has the benefit of it, as much as if it were his own; and it avails to obtain deliverance, from the curse of the law, for him, and eternal life: But it leaves him as unworthy of any favour, as deserving of eternal destruction, and as great a criminal as he ever was.

IV. The work of the Mediator, and his design in it, as it has been now considered, brings into view his wonderful love and grace, which is exercised towards man.

In order to have an adequate view of this, we must rise in our conceptions to the height from which he descended; and comprehend his greatness, worthiness and glory; and then take a full and comprehensive view of the depth to which he descended in his humiliation; and the magnitude of the evil which he suffered, in order to redeem man. But this is absolutely impossible to men or angels; therefore, the love of Christ never will be fully known by angels, or the redeemed: For it "passeth knowledge," as inspiration has declared. This, therefore, must be an endless theme, and has laid a foundation for endless progression in knowledge, love and happiness. The more the redeemed shall know of Christ, the greater view they will have of the evil which he suffered for their redemption. This infinitely exceeds all instances of love among creatures. This will be exhibited forever, as infinitely the greatest instance of love and grace in the universe, except the love of the Father, in giving his Son; which will be celebrated by the redeemed, and all the friends of God, without end. St. Paul dwelt on this theme, when on earth. "I live, said he, by the faith of the Son of God, who loved me, and gave himself for me." [487] "Walk in love, as Christ also hath loved us, and hath given himself for us." [488] "Ye know the grace of our Lord Jesus Christ, that though he was rich, yet for your sakes he became poor, that ye through his poverty might be rich."[489]

The love of Christ, exercised towards sinners, is great in proportion to the greatness of the evil he suffered for their redemption. The latter is infinite, so therefore is the former. And though he sought the glory of God, and the general good, in what he did and suffered, yet his love to sinners is not in the least diminished, or the less, by reason of this: For he gave himself for them. "Unto him that loved us, and washed us from our sins, in his own blood. And hath made us kings and priests unto God and his Father; to Him be glory and dominion, forever and ever, Amen." [490]

Footnotes:

411. Gal. iii. 10.
412. Rom. iii. 25, 26.
413. Isaiah xlii. 21.
414. Matt. v. 17, 18.

415. Dan. ix. 24.
416. Heb. i. 9. Psal xlv. 7.
417. Phil. ii. 8, 9.
418. John x. 18.
419. Gal. iv. 4, 5.

420. The paschal lamb was an eminent type of Christ, with a principal reference to which he is so often called "The Lamb, the Lamb of God." Therefore he is called the christian's passover. "For even Christ our passover is sacrificed for us." [1 Cor. v. 7.] This lamb was slain, and roasted with fire, as an emblem of the sufferings and death of Christ. There was a particular direction and command respecting the blood of this lamb. "And they shall take of the blood, and strike it on the two side posts, and on the upper door post of the houses, wherein they shall eat it.--And the blood shall be to you for a token upon the houses where you are: And when I see the blood, I will pass over you, and the plague shall not be upon you to destroy you, when I smite the land of Egypt." [Exod. xii. 7, 13.] As the blood of this slain lamb, when applied according to divine direction, secured the Israelites from the destruction which fell on the Egyptians; so Christ was slain and sacrificed, that they to whom his blood is applied by their believing in him, may have their sins forgiven, and be secured from that destruction which they deserve, being delivered from the wrath to come. [Eph. i. 7. 1 Thess. i. 10.]

421. Psalm xl. 6, 7, 8. Heb. x. 4-9.
422. Isaiah liii. chap, throughout.
423. Exod. xxviii. 43.
424. Levit. xxii. 9.
425. Numb. xviii. 22.
426. Heb. ix. 28.
427. 1 Pet. ii. 24.
428. Levit. xvii. 11.
429. Matt. xxvi. 28.
430. Rom. v. 9.
431. Eph. i. 7.
432. 1 John i. 7.
433. 1 Pet. i. 19.
434. Rev. v. 9.
435. Matt. xx. 28.
436. 1 Cor. vi. 20. vii. 23.
437. Rom. viii. 34.
438. Rom. v. 6.
439. 1 Cor. xv. 3.
440. Rom. vi, 10.
441. Heb. ix. 15.
442. 1 Pet. iii, 18.
443. Psalm lxvii. 8.
444. John v. 15, 18.
445. Phil. ii. 6, 7, 8.

446. In the view of the infinite natural evil there is in the sufferings and death of the Son of God, may be seen the magnitude of the crime of which the Jews and all who joined with them, were guilty, who were active in bringing this evil upon him; who condemned, reviled and mocked him, inflicted pain and distress upon him, and put him to an ignominious and most cruel death. The crime of all sin is great in some proportion to the magnitude of the natural evil which is effected by it, or which it tends to produce. In this instance, the natural evil which they effected is infinite; therefore their crime in doing this was infinite, that is, they hereby rendered themselves infinitely guilty and ill deserving. It was just, that they should suffer as great and as much natural evil, as their volitions did actually produce, or tended to produce. And all who have reproached and slighted the Redeemer, all who have opposed and rejected him, from that time to this day, have really joined with those who put him to death, and in their hearts say, "Let him be crucified," and are guilty of that which is infinitely criminal, and deserve to have infinite evil inflicted upon them. And in this instance of the sin of men, actually producing infinite natural evil, is to be seen the infinitely evil and malignant nature of all sin It tends to produce infinite natural evil; and therefore the sinner deserves to have this evil inflicted upon him, which has been before observed.

447. Gal. iii. 13.
448. See Deut. xxix. 22-28.
449. See Rom. v. 14. 1 Cor. xv. 45, 47. Gal. iii. 13. Ps. lxxxix. 19, 20.
450. Psalm lxxxv. 10.

451. Phil. ii. 7, 8. The words in our translation are, "He took upon him the form of a servant, and was found in the likeness of men." But it is more agreeable to the original, to render it thus: Being made in the likeness of man; (or as Dr. Doddridge translates it, "When made in the likeness of men") he took upon him the form of a servant.

452. Gal. iv. 4.
453. Phil. ii. 7, 8, 9.
454. John x. 10.
455. John xiv. 26. xv. 26. xvi. 7, 8.
456. Rom. viii. 19.
457. Rom. x. 4.
458. Phil. ii. 8.
459. Rom. v. 18.
460. Acts xiii. 38, 39.
461. Rom. v. 9.
462. Eph. i. 7.
463. Gal. iii. 13.
464. John vi. 37, 39, 40.

465. John viii. 12. xii. 46. These words of Christ serve to explain what is said by this Evangelist, [Chap. i. 5.] "Who was the true light, which lighteth every man that cometh into the world." The words of Christ suppose, and implicitly assert, that he who believeth not, is in darkness, and abideth in darkness. And this Apostle asserts the same thing. He says, "He that hateth his brother (which is true of every unbeliever) is in darkness, and walketh in darkness, because that darkness hath blinded his eyes." [1 John 2.] Therefore Christ's lightening every man that cometh into the world, cannot mean that he actually illuminates the mind of every man in the world, for the words of Christ, and of his beloved disciple, assert the contrary. The meaning therefore must be, either that he lightens every man in the world without exception, who has any true light; that is, all who believe, and come to the light: Or that he is the only objective light in the world; there being no other light to be seen, but that which he affords objectively: which objective light is set before all men, and is offered to all, in a greater or less degree. It nevertheless remains true that all who are not christians, and do not follow Christ, have no light within them, but walk in total darkness, from which they are turned when they believe. Therefore Christ says, "I am the light of the world. He that followeth me, shall not walk in darkness, but shall have the light of life." [John viii. 12] This implies that all who do not follow him, have no degree of that light of which he speaks, when he says, "I am the light of the world;" but are wholly involved in that darkness which is opposed to this light; and live and walk in it.

466. 1 Pet. i. 11.
467. Eph. iv. 9, 12, 13.
468. Rev. xxi. 22. Isai. x. 19.
469. Acts iii. 22. Deut. xviii. 15.
470. Heb. vi. 20, vii. 24, 25.
471. Zech. vi. 12, 13.
472. Ps. ii. 6.
473. Ps. xlv. 1.
474. Ps. lxxvi. 10.
475. Matthew xxv. 31-46.
476. Luke i. 32, 33.
477. 1 Cor. xv. 24, 28.
478. Psalm ii. 6, 7, 8.
479. Psalm cx. 1, 2.
480. Isaiah xlii. 1, 6.
481. Ps. xl. 6, 7, 8.
482. Heb. i. 8, 9. from Ps. xlv. 6, 7.
483. John vi. 27, 38, 39.
484. Luke xxiv. 49. Acts i. 4.
485. Economy is derived from a compound Greek work, and signifies the regulations and rules of a household or family, by which each member is to act his proper part.
486. John xiv. 28.
487. Gal. ii. 20.
488. Eph. v. 2.
489. 2 Cor. viii. 9.
490. Rev. i.

CHAPTER IV - ON THE APPLICATION OF REDEMPTION

Section I - On the Application of Redemption in general

THE first Adam was united to all his posterity as their father, head, and constituted representative and substitute; and all mankind were united to him, as such. This may be considered, both as a natural and constituted union; by which all his children were to have the benefit of his obedience, as much as if it were their own personal obedience, should he obey through the time of his trial; so that his holiness should insure perfect, everlasting holiness and happiness to them: And, on the other hand, his disobedience should descend to them, and make them sinners, and entail sin and ruin on all his posterity; so that their sin, guilt and ruin, were connected with his rebellion, and, in this sense, his sin, was their sin.

The second Adam has no such natural union with mankind, as their natural father and head, and they have no union to him in this way: But they must, in some way and manner, be united to him, and he to them, in order to his becoming their head and representative, so as to share in the saving benefits of his atonement and righteousness. He is constituted by God a public head and representative, as the first Adam was, and is substituted to obey and suffer for man; but in order to their being actually interested in the benefit of his atonement and righteousness, they must be united to him, and he to them, so as to be in a sense one, as the head and members of the natural body are one. This union, by divine constitution and appointment, is to take place and consist in a mutual voluntary consent; the Redeemer offering himself to them, and they consenting and complying with his proposal and offer, and accepting of him, and trusting in him as their Redeemer. This lays the foundation for a treaty with mankind; in the prosecution of which, redemption is actually applied; not to all mankind, but to those who cordially embrace the offer, and accept of Christ, and salvation by him. This is particularly stated in the scripture. Christ says, "God so loved the world, that he gave his only begotten Son, that whosoever believeth in him, should not perish, but have everlasting life." [491] These words suppose, and implicitly assert, that none but believers are to be saved by the Redeemer, as no others have that relation to him, and union with him, which is necessary, in order to give them an interest in redemption by him. This Christ expressly asserted, when he commissioned the apostles to go forth and treat with men, in order to effect the application of his redemption; without which no man could be saved. "And he said unto them, Go ye into all the world, and preach the gospel to every creature. He that believeth, and is baptised, shall be saved; but he that believeth not, shall be damned." [492]

As all mankind are united to Adam, as his posterity, his seed; so Christ has a seed, a posterity, who are by their union to him, made the children of God, and joint heirs with him, to whom the promise of salvation is made. These are not all mankind, but believers in him. For thus saith the scripture. "The children of the promise are counted for the seed. Know ye, therefore, that they which are of faith, the same are the children of Abraham. For ye are all the children of God, by faith in Christ Jesus. For as many of you as have been baptized into Christ, have put on Christ. And if ye be Christ's, then ye are Abraham's seed, and heirs according to the promise; heirs of God, and joint heirs with Jesus Christ. Now we, brethren, as Isaac was, are the children of the promise."[493]

The Redeemer has made an atonement sufficient to expiate for the sins of the whole world; and, in this sense, has tasted death for every man, has taken away the sin of the world, has given himself a ransom for all, and is the propitiation for the sins of the whole world, so that whosoever believeth in him may be saved, and God can now be just, and the justifier of him that believeth in Jesus. Therefore, the gospel is ordered to be preached to the whole world, to all nations, to every human creature: And the offer of salvation by Christ is to be made to every one, with this declaration, that whosoever believeth, is willing to accept of it, shall be delivered from the curse of the law, and have eternal life.

But as all mankind are totally depraved, and are become enemies to God, his law and government, and consequently equal enemies to the Redeemer, and salvation by him, they are all prepared and disposed to refuse to accept of the offered salvation, and reject it with their whole hearts, whatever motives are set before them, and methods taken to persuade them to comply. This lays the foundation of the necessity of the renovation of the hearts of men by the holy Spirit, in order to their believing and embracing the gospel; of which the scripture speaks abundantly. Christ taught, that except a man be born of the spirit, he cannot enter into the kingdom of God, or so much as see it. St. Paul says, that all believers are the subjects of the mighty power of God, operating upon them, by which they have been brought to believe: That they, being naturally dead in trespasses and sins, have been made alive by God; and that faith is the gift of God; that they are saved not by any works of righteousness which they have done, but by the washing of regeneration, and renewing of the Holy Ghost; so that it is not of him that willeth, nor of him that runneth, but of God who sheweth mercy, and worketh in them by his Spirit, to will and to run, &c. &c.

By this renovation, men are said in scripture to be made new creatures, and to be created in Christ, unto good works; and believers are said to be in Christ, and to put on Christ. This union of the believer to Christ may be considered as consisting in two things, viz. 1. In Christ's uniting himself to him by his Spirit, by which he takes possession of him, is formed in him, and dwells in him: And by the Spirit of God, the believer is drawn to him. "No man cometh unto me, says Christ, except the Father, which hath sent me, draw him." 2. In the believer's uniting himself to Christ, by actually cleaving to him, trusting in him, and loving him; all which is implied in saying faith, or believing on Christ; and which is also implied in Christ's uniting himself to the believer, mentioned in the foregoing particular. This union is begun in regeneration and conversion, by which Christ, by his Spirit, takes possession of the heart, produces faith and christian holiness; in the exercise of which, the believer cleaves to Christ in holy love. But of these it is proposed to treat more particularly in some following sections.

This union between Christ and believers in him, is represented by a variety of similitudes in scripture. It is represented by a building composed of stones, all resting on a chief corner stone, which bears up the whole. By the natural body, consisting of head and members, all united to the head; the life and every function of the body, and each of the members depending upon their union with the head, and being derived from that: It is compared to the union of the food and drink, to the stomach and body, being taken into that, and digested, and thereby spreading life and spirit through the whole, for its constant support. "Except ye eat the flesh of the Son of man, and drink his blood, ye have no life in you. Whosoever eateth my flesh, and drinketh my blood, hath eternal life." [494] It is illustrated by the union of the branch with the vine, by which the former derives life, sap and nourishment from the latter. "I am the vine, ye are the branches." [495] To mention no more, it is frequently represented by the union between the husband and the wife, which is a voluntary or a moral union, and by which the wife shares in the dignity, goods and possessions of her husband, and receives protection and support from him. The church is therefore called "the bride, the Lamb's wife." Believers, by their union to Christ, receive the benefit of his sufferings and obedience, and are made rich, partaking in all his fulness; and become joint heirs with him of eternal inheritance.

The union between Christ and believers is a moral and spiritual union: In this respect, "He who is joined to the Lord, is one spirit." [496] It is an imperfect union in the beginning of it: It is therefore a growing union, until it shall be made perfect; it being a lasting union, which shall continue forever. And when this becomes perfect, which it will not, in its most complete state, till the resurrection, there will be a full and perfect participation of redemption by Christ; and that prayer of Christ will then be completely answered. "Neither pray I for these alone, but for them also which shall believe on me through their word: That they all may be one, as thou, Father, art in me, and I in thee; that they also may be one in us. And the glory which thou gavest me, I have given unto them; that they may be one, even as we are one. I in them, and thou in me, that they may be made perfect in one. That the love wherewith thou hast loved me, may be in them, and I in them."[497]

Section II - On Regeneration

IT has been observed, that mankind being naturally under the power of sin and total depravity, it is necessary that they should be the subjects of a renovation by the Spirit of God, in order to their union to Christ, and being redeemed by him. It is proposed now to attend more particularly to this renovation, as it is represented in the holy scriptures.

Regeneration and conversion are often used only as two words, meaning the same thing; and it is certain that all that can be properly understood by them, is that change and renovation which is expressed in scripture, by being born again, born of the Spirit of God, and born of God, created in Christ Jesus, unto good works, &c. Yet, as there are two distinct things included in this change, which it is necessary should be distinguished, in order to understand this subject, these words may be properly used, to make and keep up this distinction, as many divines have done. In this renovation, there is the operation of the cause, which is the work done by the Spirit of God; and there is the effect, which consists in the exercises of the regenerate, in which they are active, and agents. Though these imply each other, and cannot be separated, more than the cause can be separated from the effect; yet they must be distinguished, and the former may properly be called regeneration. In order to explain this, and prevent mistakes concerning it, the following things must be observed.

1. The Spirit of God is the only agent and cause by whose energy the effect takes place; and so far as the Spirit of God, is the cause and agent, the subject, the heart of man, is passive, being the subject on which, or in which, the effect is wrought. Though the effect be activity, or the exercise of the new heart, in which the renewed person is the agent; yet, in the operation which causes the effect to exist, and therefore in the order of nature, is antecedent to the effect, the Spirit of God is the only agent, and man is the passive subject.

2. This change, of which the Spirit of God is the cause, and in which he is the only agent, is instantaneous; wrought not gradually, but at once. The human heart is either a heart of stone, a rebellious heart, or a new heart. The man is either under the dominion of sin, as obstinate and vile as ever, dead in trespasses and sins; or his heart is humble and penitent; he is a new creature, and spiritually alive. There can be no instant of time, in which the heart is neither a hard heart, nor a new heart, and the man is neither dead in trespasses and sins, nor spiritually alive. The Spirit of God finds the heart of man wholly corrupt, and desperately wicked, wholly and strongly, even with all the power he has, opposed to God and his law, and to that renovation which he produces. The enmity of the heart against God continues as strong as ever it was, till it is slain by the instantaneous energy of the divine Spirit, and from carnal it becomes spiritual, betwixt which there is no medium, according to scripture and reason. All the exercises of the hard, impenitent, unrenewed heart, are exercises of impenitence and rebellion, of enmity against God and his law; whatever the external conduct may be, they are the corrupt fruit of a corrupt, rebellious heart. The exercises and fruit of a heart, dead in trespasses and sins, are dead works. If this were not demonstrably certain from the nature of the case, it is abundantly asserted in the scripture, and our Saviour has decided it in the most express manner. His words are, "Either make the tree good, and his fruit good, or else make the tree corrupt, and his fruit corrupt. A good man, out of the good treasure of his heart, bringeth forth good things: And an evil man, out of the evil treasure, bringeth forth evil things." [498] St. Paul repeatedly asserts the same thing. By a number of quotations from the Old Testament, he proves that all men are by nature, altogether, and to a great degree, corrupt; that there is nothing morally good in them, or done by them. [499] He asserts that antecedent to regeneration, man does nothing morally good; that all of this kind is the consequence of it. "We are his workmanship, created in Christ Jesus unto good works." [500] And again he says, "We ourselves also were sometimes foolish, disobedient, deceived, serving divers lusts and pleasures, living in malice and envy, hateful, and hating one another. But after that the kindness and love of God our Saviour appeared, not by works of righteousness, which we have done, but according to his mercy, he saved us by the washing of regeneration, and renewing of the Holy Ghost." [501] Here he describes their state and moral character, which is the character of all men, antecedent to regeneration. He denies their having done any good works; but, on the contrary, says, all their works were evil, and gives them a very bad character. He then ascribes all their reformation, and the alteration of their character for the better, to their regeneration, by which alone they were washed from their moral pollutions.

3. The subject of this operation, in which this change and effect is wrought, is the will or the heart; that is, the moral and not the natural powers and faculties of the soul. As moral depravity is wholly in the will or heart, the source and seat of all moral actions, the divine operation directly respects the heart, and consists in changing and renewing that. The understanding or intellect, considered as distinct from the will, is a natural Faculty, and is not capable of moral depravity. It may be hurt and weakened, and improved to bad purposes, as other natural faculties may, by the moral corruption or sinfulness of the heart: But nothing is necessary, in order to remove the disorders of the intellect, and all the natural powers of the soul, but the renovation of the heart; so far as the will is right, the understanding, considered as a natural faculty, will be rectified, and do its office well. Therefore regeneration is in scripture represented as consisting in giving a new heart, a heart to know the Lord, &c. The scripture indeed speaks of the understanding being enlightened; and of its being darkened; and of being without understanding, as criminal; and represents a good understanding, as comprehending all virtue or holiness. But the understanding in these instances is not considered and spoken of as mere intellect, distinct from the will or heart; but as comprehending and principally intending the heart, which is the seat of all moral perception and exercise. In scripture the distinction between the understanding and the heart is not often made; but the former is generally spoken of as implying the latter, and consisting in that discerning, which is implied in right exercises of heart; and cannot take place any farther than the heart is renewed, and the will is right. Therefore we read of "a wise and understanding heart." And wisdom and understanding are words frequently used in scripture as nearly synonymous, and denoting die same

thing: But wisdom belongs to the heart, and is of a moral nature; and that in which, according to the scripture, true holiness consists.

All moral, criminal darkness, has its seat in the heart, as all sin has, and the former cannot be distinguished from the latter; and selfishness is the essence of both. And on the contrary, all true light and understanding, which is of a moral nature, belongs to the heart, and implies real holiness, and cannot be separated, and even distinguished from it, as one necessarily implies and involves the other. This is asserted by our divine teacher in the following words: "The light of the body is the eye: If therefore thine eye be single, thy whole body shall be full of light. But if thine eye be evil, thy whole body shall be full of darkness." [502] The single and evil eye are opposites, and belong to the heart, and consist in the exercises of that. This is said by Christ of the evil eye. "For from within, out of the heart of men, proceed evil thoughts, adulteries, fornications, murders, thefts, covetousness, wickedness, deceit, lasciviousness, an evil eye, blasphemy, pride, foolishness. All these evil things come from within, and defile the man." [503] Here an evil eye, which fills the mind with darkness, and is darkness itself, is numbered among the evil things which belong to the corrupt heart, and of which that is the source, and is altogether criminal. And, consequently, the single eye, which is opposite to the evil eye, must also belong to the heart, and consists in that which is real holiness, or which implies it. Where this is, the man is full of light.

Therefore, in regeneration, the heart being changed and renewed, light and understanding take place; and there is no need of any operation on the understanding, or intellectual faculty of the mind, as distinguished from the heart, or any change in that, which does not necessarily take place, upon the renovation of the will or heart.

As the moral disorder and depravity of man lies wholly in his heart, the cure and renovation must begin and end there; and when the heart is perfectly right, the man will be wholly recovered to perfect holiness.

This point is particularly observed and stated, to expose and rectify a mistake which has been too often made, representing regeneration as consisting: chiefly, if not wholly, in renewing the understanding, as distinguished from the will, and letting light into that, antecedent to any change of the heart, and in order to it; and by which light in the understanding, the will is inclined and turned from sin to holiness. This is turning this matter upside down, and has a dangerous and bad tendency. It supposes that human depravity lies in the understanding, and not in the will; or, at least, that it has its foundation and beginning in the former; and that when that comes right, the will or heart acts right, of course. The consequence is, that there is little or no moral depravity in the heart, that being ready to do its office well, when the understanding is set right: Therefore, man is not blameable for his depravity, and not being holy, since his blindness, which alone, is in the way of his acting right, is not dependent on his will, or owing to any disorders in that. It is, indeed, imposable to give true moral light and understanding to the depraved mind of man, by any operation whatsoever on the intellect, antecedent to the renovation of the will; for the darkness is in the latter, and consists in the wrong inclination of that; and therefore cannot be removed, but by renewing the heart.

Others have supposed, that there is in regeneration, an operation on the understanding, or intellect first, in order to enlighten the mind; and then by divine energy, the will is renewed, and brought to comply with the light let into the understanding. But this is unscriptural and contrary to the nature and order of things; and tends to lead to hurtful mistakes, as has been observed. Nothing is necessary but the renovation of the will, in order to set every thing right in the human soul: And if the will be not renewed, or a new heart be not given, by an immediate operation, no operation on any other faculty of the soul, and no supposable or possible change can set the heart right, or renew it in the least degree. The scripture makes no such distinction between the faculties of the soul in treating of this matter; but represents the renovation of the will, or giving a new heart, as setting the whole soul right in all the powers and faculties of it.

4. The divine operation in regeneration, of which the new heart is the effect, is immediate, or it is not wrought by the energy of any means as the cause of it; but by the immediate power and energy of the Holy Spirit. It is called a creation, and the divine agency in it is as much without any medium, as in creating something from nothing. Men are not regenerated in the sense in which we are now considering regeneration, by light or the word of God. This is evident from what has been observed under the last particular. If the evil eye, which is total darkness, and shuts all the light out, be the evil, corrupt heart of man; then this corrupt heart must be renewed, in order to there being any true light in the mind, and previous to it. There must be a discerning heart, which is the same with a new heart, in order to see the light; and therefore this cannot be produced by light. The evil eye, which shuts out all the light, cannot be cured, and made a single eye, by seeing the light: And the light cannot have any effect, or answer any end, till they are so far made single, as to admit the light: Therefore, that operation which changes the evil eye to a single eye, cannot be by means of light; but must take place antecedent to any light, or any influence or effect that can be produced by

The System of Doctrines, contained in Divine Relation, Explained and Defended Volume I

it. It is said the Lord opened the heart of Lydia, that she attended unto the things that were spoken by Paul. It would be a contradiction, and very absurd, to say, that the word spoken by Paul, was that by which her heart was opened; for she knew not what he did speak, until her heart was opened to attend to his words, and understand them. Her heart was first opened, in order to his words having any effect, or giving any light to her. And this must be done by an immediate operation of the Spirit of God on her heart. This was the regeneration now under consideration, by which her heart was renewed, and formed to true discerning, like the single eye.

St. James says, "Of his own will begat he us, with the word of truth." [504] But here in regeneration he includes the effect wrought, or conversion, and does not mean only the act by which the effect is produced, as distinguished from the effect, which is intended by the regeneration now under consideration. The effect produced by the regenerating energy of the Spirit of God, in the adult, is active conversion, which supposes light and truth in the discerning mind, and exercises answerable to it; which is to be particularly considered, under the next general head.

5. The divine operation in the regeneration of which we are speaking, though very great and powerful, is altogether imperceptible by the subject on whom the work is wrought, and by which he is regenerated. Nothing is perceived but the effect, which in the adult consists in perception of truth, and answerable exercises. The cause is to be learned and known only by the effect. When Adam was created, he perceived nothing, and was conscious of nothing, but his own existence, perceptions and exercises. The divine operation, which was the cause of his existence, was over and finished, before he began to perceive any thing. Every creature is constantly supported by God, and divine energy attends and is exerted in all our motions and actions; "For in him we live and move, (or which is more agreeable to the original, are moved) and have our being." "And the inspiration of the Almighty giveth us understanding." Yet we perceive nothing but the effect, and argue the cause from the effect. So it is in this case. "The wind bloweth where it listeth, and thou hearest the sound thereof, but canst not tell whence it cometh, and whither it goeth: So is every one that is born of the Spirit." [505]

6. The grace granted in regeneration is a sovereign, undeserved and unpromised favour.

The sinner, who is the chosen subject of this operation, and object of this favour, is infinitely ill deserving; and is disposed to go on in rebellion, till this change is wrought. He is obstinate, and refuses to hearken to the divine command, to repent and embrace the gospel, and the offer of mercy, whatever methods have been taken with him to reclaim him. However much he may be terrified with the fears of threatened destruction, and the evil, dangerous state in which he is; and though he may have earnest desires to escape misery, and be happy forever; and may make many prayers, and do many things, he has not the least inclination to repent, submit to God and accept of offered mercy; but directly contrary to all this, he with his whole heart abuses every favour granted to him, rejects the offer of mercy, opposes God, slights Christ, and resists the Holy Ghost, in all his prayers, and in all he does; for still his heart is ii heart of stone, an impenitent, rebellious heart, and is full of enmity against God. This character is given of all the unregenerate, in the scripture. Therefore he is not only undeserving of any favour, and especially of this, and infinitely ill deserving; but is constantly provoking God to give him up to utter destruction. When the sinner is in this situation, God has mercy on him, and by his Spirit gives him a new heart. Surely this is, in the highest sense, sovereign mercy; God is infinitely far from being under obligation to any sinner to do this for him: "Therefore hath he mercy on whom he will have mercy, and whom he will he hardeneth."

And God has not obliged himself by any promise to grant this mercy to any individual person, antecedent to his actually doing it. He has made no promise, in his word, to those who do not accept nor desire the mercy and salvation which he offers, but reject it with their whole heart; which is true of all the unregenerate, as has been observed. There are indeed promises made to the church, that God will pour out his Spirit, and regenerate sinners; but no individual, unconverted sinner can claim this promise, as it is not made to him in particular. There are promises made to those who repent and believe the gospel, that they shall be saved, that the Spirit of God shall dwell in them forever, &c. but the regenerating influences of the Spirit, which are antecedent to faith, and the first act of faith, which is the gift of God, are unpromised gifts and favours; and God cannot be under any obligation to those who receive them by promise, or any other way.

7. The divine operation, by which men are regenerated, and a new heart is given, is not in the least degree inconsistent with human liberty; nor does it impede or obstruct it, in any respect: But finds and leaves men in the free exercise of all desirable or possible freedom, and wholly blameable for all the exercises of their heart, not conformable to the law of God; and commendable for all right exercises of the new heart; which are as much their own, and as free, as if they had taken place without any divine influences, were this possible.

This is evident and certain, if liberty consists in voluntary action, or in the choice and exercises of the will, and in nothing else. No compulsion can be offered to the will, or the freedom of it be any way affected by any operation or influence on the mind which takes place antecedent to the exercise of the will, and in order to the choice that is made. Man is active only in willing; and in this only consists his moral freedom. And in this he is not capable of compulsion; and no impression that is made upon him, nor any operation whatsoever can take away his liberty in the least degree, unless it obstructs and is inconsistent with his acting voluntarily: For so far, and so long, as he does this, and puts forth acts of will, they are his own acts, and he is free; and enjoys and exercises all the freedom of which there can be any consistent conception, or that is possible in the nature of things. [See Part I. Chap. 4, page 174, &c.] Antecedent to regeneration man acts freely. With great strength of inclination and choice his heart opposes the law of God, and rejects the gospel, seeking himself wholly. And when the instantaneous, immediate energy of the holy Spirit renews his heart, he turns about, and loves and chooses what he hated before; and exercises as real freedom in his choice and pursuit of that which he had opposed and rejected.

8. Regeneration is but the beginning of a divine operation which does not wholly renew the heart at once; but from this small beginning the operation continues and goes on to perfection, that is, till the heart is made perfectly clean and holy; which will not be accomplished till death. For God continues to work in the regenerate to will and to do, and they are as dependant on divine influence for every after right exercise of will, as for the first. And God who begins this' good work in them will perform it, and go on with it, until the day of Jesus Christ. [506]

Section III - On Conversion

THE effect of the regenerating influence of the Spirit of God, which consists in conversion, is next to be more particularly considered.

Regeneration, in the sense in which it has now been considered, is the cause of voluntary action in him who is the subject of the operation, or issues in it; which consists in turning from sin to God, or in holy exercise, which is true love to God, and loving our neighbour as ourselves; which implies a sight and belief of the truth, repentance, faith in Christ, and submission and devotedness to him, his interest and service, &c. As the law of God requires love, and nothing but love, considered as comprehending all the proper and genuine fruits and expressions of it; so the new creature, or that which is born of God, consists wholly in love, as it is conformity to the law of God, which is all comprehended in these two commands, "Thou shalt love the Lord thy God with all thy heart, and with all thy soul, and with all thy mind. And thou shalt love thy neighbour as thyself." Therefore St. John says, "He that loveth is born of God. God is love, and he that dwelleth in love, dwelleth in God, and God in him. "As God is love, and this comprehends the whole of his moral character; so love in creatures, is the moral image of God, and it consists altogether in this. This love, of which God and the creature are the objects, is, in the nature of it, one and the same undivided affection, differing only as it is exercised towards different objects, on various occasions, and in diverse circumstances. It consists in universal benevolence; or benevolence to being in general capable of happiness, and all that affection and exercise of heart which is necessarily included in this. Universal benevolence, or goodness, is necessarily pleased with good and happiness wherever it takes place; for it seeks the general good, and that to the greatest possible degree; it must therefore be gratified, wherever happiness takes place, and that in proportion to the degree of it. And, of consequence, it must be pleased with every benevolent being, who wishes the greatest general good, and promotes it, according to his capacity, and the opportunity he has to do it. Therefore benevolence must have the greatest degree of pleasure in that being who has the greatest degree of benevolence, and does the most good. And this is the love of complacence, and is necessarily implied in benevolence, and really an exercise of it, and can take place no where but in the benevolent heart. Benevolence esteems benevolent affection, as the greatest excellence and worth; and therefore exercises the highest love of esteem towards him who has the greatest degree of benevolence, and does the most good. And the benevolent person exercises true gratitude towards every being who is doing good to individuals, and promoting the greatest general or public good. Thus complacential love, the love of esteem and the love of gratitude, are included in benevolence, and essential to it; and are really nothing more than benevolent affection. He who has universal benevolence has all virtuous, holy love, as all is necessarily implied and comprehended in this. The new, benevolent heart, is an illuminated heart. The eye is now become single, and all is full of light. The person is now turned from darkness to marvellous light, and being spiritual, discerneth and knoweth all things. He sees and believes the great truths contained in divine revelation; and cordially embraces them as true and excellent.

This holy affection, in which the new creature consists, discerns the being and perfections of God, as realities and glorious, as they were never seen before. And this holy love is fixed, in the first place, on this sum and fountain of all being, benevolence and perfection, as the supreme object of benevolent affection. Here the benevolent heart finds an object every way, and in all respects,

The System of Doctrines, contained in Divine Relation, Explained and Defended Volume I
suited to draw forth the strongest exercises of benevolent, friendly affection, in rejoicing in his infinite, eternal, independent existence, felicity and glory; exercising and enjoying supreme delight, and complacential love in his infinite perfection and benevolence; and sweet gratitude to him for the glorious exercise and display of his love; devoting himself to his service and honour, and exerting cordial and strong benevolence and friendship, in ardently desiring that God may be glorified to the highest degree forever; and wishing to be the active instrument of this, as the greatest happiness he can desire, or imagine.

The new heart sees and approves of the divine law in the extent and spirituality of it, requiring perfect love to God and man; and threatening disobedience with infinite evil; and it is agreeable to him that this law should be maintained and honoured forever. And in this light he sees his own total depravity, and the unsearchable wickedness of his heart. He beholds the exceeding sinfulness of sin, and its desert of infinite evil, as a proper punishment. He hence sees his own infinite odiousness and ill desert, and condemns and abhors himself for all his transgressions, and contrariety to God and his law: And confesses his sins, repenting as in dust and ashes. The new heart is therefore a broken, contrite, humble, penitent heart. True repentance is necessarily implied in real conversion; and therefore the whole of conversion is often in scripture expressed by it, and called repentance. And this continues and increases through the whole life of a real convert. [507]

The new man discerns the character of Christ, and the way of salvation by him, with entire approbation, and great pleasure, and believes the gospel with all his heart, and flies to the Redeemer, as the only hope for sinners; trusting in him alone for pardon, righteousness, strength and redemption. And his benevolent love to God and man is in the highest degree pleased with the gospel, which establishes, magnifies and honours the law, and brings honour to God in the pardon and salvation of sinful, lost men, who believe on the Saviour. Conversion is turning from a state of obstinacy and disobedience, to a cordial submission and obedience to Christ. The real convert says as Saul did when he was renewed, "Lord, what wilt thou have me to do?" This is necessarily implied in repentance and faith. A new heart is an obedient heart; therefore obedience cannot be separated from a new heart; and they are indeed one and the same thing. Consequently they are put together as implying each other, and being really the same in the words of inspiration. "A new heart will I give you, and I will put my Spirit within you, and cause you to walk in my statutes, and ye shall keep my judgments, and do them." [508] The new heart consists in love, as has been shown, and all holy obedience consists in this. It is love expressed and acted out in all proper ways.

This leads to observe farther, that this love, which is the new creation, or the new creature, has not only the supreme Being for its object; but creatures also, who are capable of happiness. It wishes well to every such creature, so far as their good and happiness is consistent with the greatest public, general good, and no farther; for universal benevolence seeks the greatest good of the whole; and therefore is ready to give up, not to desire, but to renounce the good and happiness of individuals, when, and as far as it is inconsistent with the greatest good of the whole, all beings and all things taken into view. And as the good man is not capable of determining with any certainty that it is inconsistent with the greatest good of the whole that any who are on the stage of life with him should be happy, his benevolence will extend to all, and will wish them well, and pray for all men, even his enemies, if he have any. But his benevolence will be more particularly, and in a stronger degree exercised towards those who are most in his view, with whom he is most acquainted, whose wants, dangers and miseries, and whose capacity of happiness are most in his sight; and those who are more especially under his care, and to whom he is under advantage, and has more opportunity to do good. And he will feel himself united, in a peculiar degree, and with a more fervent love, to those who appear to him to be benevolent and engaged in desiring and promoting the greatest general good, in the exercise of true love to God and man. As such who are friends to God and his kingdom, to Jesus Christ, and the greatest public good, appear to the benevolent to have more real existence than others, and to be of much more importance in the scale of being, and are objects of the peculiar benevolence of the Deity; they are in this view peculiarly dear to them, and excellent in their eyes; and they embrace them with a distinguishing, strong and sweet, benevolent and complacential love.

Having given a more general view of conversion, which is the effect of the regenerating influences of the Holy Spirit, and which consists in the volitions and actions of the regenerate, it is of importance that what has been mentioned, should be more particularly explained; which will be attempted in the following sections.

Samuel Hopkins

Section IV - On Disinterested Affection

IT has been already shown that moral depravity, or sin, consists in self love; and that holiness consists in disinterested benevolence, which is, in the nature of it, and in all its exercises, wholly contrary and opposed to self love. [See Part I. Chap. VIII. page 277, &c. to which the reader is referred.] But as this is a subject so very important, and necessary to be well understood, in order properly to distinguish true religion, and real conversion, from that which is not so, but false religion, and mere delusion, it is thought proper to bring it again into view here, in order farther to explain and confirm this truth, which is overlooked by too many, and opposed by others.

Not a few have believed and asserted, that there is no such thing in nature as disinterested affections; and that all the actions of men flow from self love, as their foundation and source. Others allow that disinterested affection may take place in the human heart; but that it either springs from self love, and is grafted upon it; or so coincides with it, and regulates it, that both these sorts of affection, if they do really differ in their nature, are included in the exercises of true holiness; and that self love is the real foundation of all true religion.

These sentiments and pleas in favour of self love, it is believed, are owing, in many instances, to wrong or confused ideas, and not properly distinguishing between self love, and that which is of a different nature and kind.

First. Many do not appear to distinguish between self love, and a desire or love of happiness; or a capacity of pleasure and enjoyment, and of being pleased with and choosing one object, rather than another. These are quite distinct and different things: The latter is really nothing but a capacity or power of will and choice, for without this there could be no such thing as preferring one object to another, or exercise of choice. This therefore is essential to the existence of a moral agent, or to any act of will whatever, and is neither self love, nor disinterested affection, but necessary to both. Self love consists in a moral agent's placing his happiness in what he views as his own private personal interest, and in nothing else, in distinction from the interest or happiness of any other being, and in contradiction to it. This only pleases him, for its own sake, and is the ultimated object of all his desires and exertions.

Disinterested benevolence is pleased with the public interest, the greatest good and happiness of the whole. This is the highest good to the benevolent person. In this he places his happiness, and not in the interest and happiness of any individual, or of himself, any farther than it is consistent with the greatest interest and happiness of the whole, and really included in it, and serves to promote it. in this state of the case, is it not easy to see the distinction between a capacity of pleasure and choice, or being pleased, and enjoying happiness; and placing our happiness in our own personal good and interest only; or in the public good for its own sake? And who docs not see the difference and opposition between the two latter?

Secondly. By many there is not a proper distinction made, and kept in view, between self-love, and that regard which the benevolent person must have for himself and his interest and happiness, which is necessarily included in disinterested affection. Disinterested, impartial benevolence, to being in general that is capable of good and happiness, regards and wishes well to every being and creature in the system, according to the degree of his existence, worth and capacity of happiness, so far as all this comes into the view of the benevolent person, and so far as the good and happiness of each is, or appears to be, consistent with the greatest good of the whole. And as he himself is one individual part of the whole, he must of necessity be the object of this disinterested, impartial benevolence, and his own interest and happiness must be regarded and desired, as much as that of his neighbour, or any individual of the whole society; not because it is himself, but because he is included in the whole, and his happiness is worth as much, and as desirable as that of his neighbour, other circumstances being equal. This is not self love; but the same universal, disinterested, impartial, public benevolence, which wishes well to being in general, and therefore to himself, because he has an existence, and is one among the rest, and equal to his neighbour. This is loving his neighbour as himself; not with the least degree of self love; but with the same disinterested, public affection, with which he loves being in general. The least spark of self love will interrupt this reasonable and beautiful moral order and harmony, and render him partial and interested in his affection, and so far detach him from the whole and make him set up a selfish, private interest of his own, in distinction from that of the rest, and in opposition to it.

By not making this distinction, and not attending to the nature of disinterested benevolence, as it regards the interest of the benevolent person himself; and therefore taking it for granted, that all the regard a person has for himself and desire of his own happiness is self love, in distinction from disinterested benevolence, they have concluded with great assurance, that self love is essential to man, and even his duty. But when the distinction is properly made, and the matter plainly stated, the mistake is discovered, and it appears that disinterested benevolence will take all proper and sufficient care of every individual in the system, and will desire and seek the best interest and happiness of all, and of the benevolent person himself, so far as is consistent with the greatest good of the whole: And that this is not self love, but the same disinterested, impartial benevolence, when it takes into view his own happiness, and values and seeks it as much as that of his neighbour. The self love which can be distinguished from this universal, disinterested benevolence, and is not of this kind, cannot be distinguished from selfishness; but is the very same affection, and is directly and wholly opposed to disinterested, holy love: And is, as has been observed, the root and essence of all sin.

To distinguish between self love and selfishness is to attempt to make a distinction where there is no difference; unless by self love be meant disinterested benevolence. Disinterested affection and self love are very distinct and opposite affections, and the latter, in every degree of it, cannot be distinguished from selfishness: For these are two words, for one and the same thing. Some would distinguish between inordinate and well regulated self love; and suppose the former is selfishness and sinful; but the latter innocent, and even good and virtuous. But unless by well regulated self love be meant disinterested affection, the distinction is groundless and vain. And to suppose a certain degree of self love, subordinated to a contrary affection, love to God, and to our neighbour, is virtuous, or even innocent; and that the same self love in a higher degree of it, and not subordinated by a different and contrary affection, is sinful, is very unreasonable and absurd, and a supposition which is utterly impossible. For if holiness and sin do not consist in the nature of moral affection and exercise, there can be no such thing as either sin or holiness. And to suppose these opposites to consist in the degree of the same affection exercised, and not in different kinds of affection, is really to make them not opposites, or not to differ in nature and kind; but to be one and the same thing, under different modifications. For the nature and kind of moral exercise and affection is not changed by their being more or less of it, or by being under restraints or not. If the lowest degree of such affection be innocent and good, the highest possible degree of it must be so much better, and have a proportionably greater degree of moral goodness. And if the highest possible degree of such affection be sinful and wrong, the least possible degree of the same kind of affection must in the nature of it be sinful, though less in degree. If ten or a hundred degrees of self love be enmity against God, and contrary to uprightness and disinterested benevolence to men, and a disposition of mind to injure them; then one degree of this same self love is enmity against God, and opposite to benevolence to men in its nature, and in proportion to the degree of it. And though it may be under restraints, and counteracted by opposite affection, it is yet of the same nature, and the same kind of affection, and as really opposes the general good, which disinterested benevolence seeks, as that same self love, when it is under no restraint, and reigns as the only moral affection of the heart.

Therefore in the scriptures we find no such distinction between self love and selfishness; or between well regulated self love, and that which is inordinate, or between a less and greater degree of this same affection, representing one as innocent and good, and the other sinful: But self love is condemned in every degree of it, in all its exercises and fruits. No worse character is given of men than this, that they are lovers of their own selves. And men are commanded not to seek their own wealth, and mind their own things, in distinction from those of others, and of Jesus Christ, and condemned for doing it. And that love, which seeketh not her own, is recommended as that only in which true religion or real holiness does consist: And surely there can be no self love in that love which seeketh not her own.

This leads to what is chiefly designed in this section, viz. to prove from scripture that disinterested affection, or benevolence to being in general, and all the affection which this implies, as it has been now explained, is that in which true religion, or the new creature does summarily consist.

1. It has been observed and shewn in the chapter to which reference is made in the beginning of this section, that this may be proved from what is said by the apostle John. [509] He says "God is love;" in which he evidently designs to comprehend his whole moral character. He mentions the highest exercise, and greatest manifestation of this love. This, he says, is in giving the Son of God to die for the redemption of sinners. This, all will grant, is, in the highest sense and degree, disinterested benevolence, as it is exercised towards those who are not only unworthy and ill deserving, but unreasonable and abusive enemies. This disinterested benevolence he urges christians to imitate; and represents it as that in which Christianity summarily consists; for he says, he that loveth is born of God, and this love being perfect, casteth out fear; and he who exercises this disinterested benevolence, (for he is speaking of no other love but this) he who dwelleth in this love, dwelleth in God, and God in him. That is, the moral image and character of God is formed in him, he partakes of the divine nature, and he is united to God, and God to him. This leads to observe, that as the new creature is a conformity to the moral character and image of God, by which Christ is said to dwell in believers; it must consist in disinterested benevolent affection; for in this only can christians be like God.

2. Jesus Christ is a remarkable and striking instance of disinterested benevolence, in which christians are to imitate him; and do so, as far as they are christians.

The love which he exercised, in taking man's place, and dying for him, is in the highest sense disinterested, as he suffered this for men, when they were his enemies. "God commandeth his love toward us, in that while we were yet sinners, Christ died for us." His love to the Father, and to sinners, expressed in what he did and suffered, is represented as wholly disinterested, to set forth the nature and excellency of it, and recommend it as a pattern to be followed by his disciples. "We then that are strong ought to bear the infirmities of the weak, and not to please ourselves: For even Christ pleased not himself; but as it is written, "The reproaches of them that reproached thee, fell on me." [510] By his not pleasing himself, is meant his not seeking himself, or acting from self love: The same that is intended by his not seeking and doing his own will, but the will of his Father; and saying, "Not my will, but thine be done." [511] That he did not please himself, but acted from a disinterested regard to the glory of God, is proved by the quotation the apostle here makes, "The reproaches of them that reproached thee, fell on me." He had such a disinterested regard to the honour of God, that if he were reproached, It was the same to him, as if he himself were reproached. This St. Paul mentions as an example for christians, which they are to imitate by feeling for their brethren in all the unhappiness that attends them, so as to bear their infirmities and burdens.

Again, in order to excite the Corinthians to show the sincerity, or genuineness of their love to the saints, that is, their disinterested benevolence, he mentions to them the example of Christ, and his love. "For ye know the grace of our Lord Jesus Christ, that though he was rich, yet for your sakes, he became poor, that you, through his poverty, might be rich." [512] He recommends the example of Christ, in this same view of it, to the Philippians. [513]

There are indeed, but few, if any christians, who do not consider the Saviour as acting a most disinterested part, in doing and suffering what he did for the salvation of sinners, as he could not have undertaken, and gone through it, from any other principle but disinterested benevolence: And this is considered as the highest excellency and perfection of his love. If any of those admit at the same time, that the love of christians, in whom is the same spirit that was in Christ, is not disinterested, they must be very inconsistent with themselves, as well as with the scripture.

3. That disinterested affection is essential to a disciple of Christ appears from the words of our Saviour, recorded by Matthew. [514] He there tells his disciples, that loving their relations, and those who loved them, did not difference them from other men, even the worst of them; because self love would do this. That therefore they could not be the children of God, or have the least degree of likeness to his moral character, unless they had, and exercised that disinterested benevolence, which would extend to their enemies, even the worst of them, and whatever injuries they had done to them; which would wish them well, and pray for them, while they were doing them all the harm they could do. That by this alone, they would be like their Father in heaven; and by being perfect in this, they would be perfect, even as he is perfect. The love here recommended, as so essential to a christian, and by which alone he is distinguished from other men, is disinterested, universal benevolence, as opposed to self love; for no other affection is opposed to self love, or will love our enemies, with cordial friendly desires of their good and happiness, leading us to do them all the good we can.

4. Our Saviour has enjoined disinterested affection, as that by which alone, men can follow him, and be his disciples, in the following words, "If any man will come after me, let him deny himself, and take up his cross, and follow me." [515] It will be difficult for any one to tell how a man can deny himself, in the exercise of self love; for this is in every degree of it self gratification. Therefore to deny ourselves, is to remove all self love, and to exercise that disinterested, universal love to being in general, which opposes self love, and renounces all selfish, private interest, and knows no self, as such; it being an impartial affection, it respects him who exercises it only as belonging to being in general, and included in universal existence. As the excellency of Christ consists in this disinterested love, no one will come to him, and cordially follow him, unless it be in the exercise of this same disinterested affection; for without this, none can approve of his character, which self love opposes.

5. St. Paul decides this matter in the most express terms, and asserts that all the exercises of true religion consist in disinterested affection, in that love which seeketh not her own. [516] He represents love as containing the whole of christian affection, without which there is nothing of any moral worth, or of real Christianity. And in describing this love, he says, "It seeketh not her own." Q.D. It is not self love which seeketh her own, and nothing else; but is directly opposed to this, and consists in that affection which is perfectly disinterested, which is universal benevolence to being in general, and has not the least partiality in favour of self. This is the wisdom that is from above, which is "Pure, peaceable, gentle, easy to be entreated, full of mercy and good fruits, without partiality and hypocrisy." [517]

6. That all true religion, or holy exercises of heart, consist in disinterested affection, is evident to a certainty, from the summary of the law of God, given by Christ himself, in the following words. "Thou shalt love the Lord thy God with all thy heart, and with all thy soul, and with all thy mind. This is the first and great commandment. And the second is like unto it. Thou shalt love thy neighbour as thyself. On these two commandments hang all the law and the prophets." [518]

The law of God is a transcript of his moral perfection; for by the creature's obeying it, he partakes of the divine nature, and puts on the moral image of God. But the moral character of God consists in disinterested love, as has been shown; therefore the love required in the law of God, is disinterested affection: It is not self love, but that which is entirely contrary to selfishness. He who loves God with all his heart, strength and mind, can have no self love, nor any love to himself, or any creature, but that which is implied in this, which certainly must be disinterested, as his love to God is. For disinterested love to God cannot imply interested and selfish affection to any other being, even our own, but necessarily excludes it. And it has been shown that the command to love our neighbour as ourselves, is so far from approving, or supposing self love, that it necessarily excludes every thing of this kind; as it requires that impartiality, and uprightness, which is contrary to every degree of self love, and can exist in nothing but disinterested affection. Men are no farther converted, than they are conformed in the exercise and affection of their hearts to the law of God, which requires disinterested love, and nothing else, and excludes and forbids all selfishness, or self love, which is the same. Therefore the new heart, and all truly christian exercises, consist in disinterested affection.

Before this subject of disinterested affection is dismissed, to prevent mistakes, and that the nature of it may be farther explained, the following particulars are to be observed and kept in view.

1. This disinterested benevolence regards the interest and happiness of those who are nearest and most in sight, more strongly and tenderly, than of those who are farther off, and more out of sight; and is more affected with the happiness or misery, and the good or bad character of the former, than of the latter.

The mind of man is not omniscient, and cannot have a full, comprehensive view of all men, and their circumstances at the same time; therefore those who are nearest to him, and most in his sight, must be more the objects of his benevolence, than others: And it is reasonable, and therefore his duty to regard these more than others, as they are more in his view, and he has a special care of them, and is under greater advantage to think of them, and do them good. And impartial, disinterested affection, will naturally, and even necessarily, operate thus.

He who has universal benevolence will have a greater regard for the inhabitants of the nation to which he belongs, and be more concerned for their interest, than for those of other nations. He will have a greater regard still for the inhabitants of the town and neighbourhood in which he lives, other things being equal. Consequently his benevolent care of the members of the family to which be belongs, will be exercised in a higher degree, and more constantly, and with greater sensibility, than towards those of other families; especially if he be the head of it. And as every person is nearest to himself, and is most in his own view, has opportunity to be better acquainted with his own circumstances, and to know his own wants, his mercies and enjoyments, &:c. and has a more particular care of his own interest, than of that of others; and is under greater advantage to promote his own happiness, than others; his disinterested, universal benevolence, will attend more to his own interest, and he will have more and stronger exercises of it, respecting his own circumstances and happiness, than those of others, all other things being equal; not because it is his own interest, but for the reason just given. And were the case reversed, and the circumstances, wants and interests of others, were more in his view, and more under his care, than his own, he would pay more regard to them, and have greater concern for them, and their interest and happiness, than for his own, all other circumstances being alike.

It hence appears that universal benevolence to being in general, not only includes a regard for the interest of every individual, and therefore an equal regard for our own interest; but a special and peculiar regard for the latter, and for that of the family, neighbourhood and town, and all those with whom we have any special connection. And this regard for ourselves, our own interest and happiness, which is necessarily included in universal benevolence, is not only a proper and reasonable regard, but is discerning, wise and judicious, and seeks our true interest. Whereas self love is partial and unreasonable in its own nature, and in every degree of it; and blinds men to their own true interest and happiness, and seeks happiness where it is not to be found; and as certainly and effectually renders them miserable, as if it were ill will to themselves.

2. As the great object of disinterested affection, or benevolence to being in general, is the greatest good of the whole, and it devotes all to this, it will give up any less good for the greater good, and the interest of individuals, for the sake of the greater public interest, and greatest good of the whole, when, and so far as the former is inconsistent with the latter. And the benevolent person is disposed and willing to give up and relinquish his own interest and happiness, when inconsistent

with the public good, or the greatest good of the whole; or when this may be necessary to promote a greater good, or more happiness, on the whole, than that of which he deprives himself. Yea, he will be willing to suffer positive evil, to save others, or the public from greater evil, or when necessary to promote and procure a greater and overbalancing good, on the whole. This is the nature of disinterested affection, and essential to it, which appears from what has been said of it above. In this the opposition and contrariety between holy love, and self love appears. He who has the former devotes, all to the greatest good of the whole; and gives up the interest of individuals, and his own interest, when necessary, to promote the good of the whole; and desires not his own happiness, or that of any other particular person, if inconsistent with a greater good to others, or with the greatest public good: And is willing to suffer, and that other particular persons should suffer, any deserved evil, which is necessary to prevent a greater public evil; or to promote the greater good of others, and of the whole. On the contrary, he who is under the government of self love, and so far as he is influenced by this, seeks, and is wholly devoted to his own personal, private interest, as the supreme good, placing all good and happiness in this; and therefore will not give up and relinquish his own supposed interest, or any part or degree of it, for the sake of the interest and happiness of any other being in the universe; their good and interest being nothing to him, no object of his desires and wishes, any farther than he thinks his own selfish good is connected with theirs, and promoted by it. Consequently, he, in the feelings and exercises of his heart, subordinates the whole interest of the universe, and of every other being, to his own little, personal, selfish interest, and wishes no good to any one, or to the whole any farther than it may promote his own selfish ends, and turn to his own advantage. And were self love under no restraints, but were acted out fully agreeable to the nature of it, it would give up and destroy all the good and happiness of the universe, and of ever) other being but the selfish person, and bring universal evil and misery on all, were this possible, in order to gain die least supposed advantage to himself. This is the true character of them who are, "lovers of their own selves."

 This view of disinterested affection will give in some measure, the distinguishing character and properties of the new creature. It consists in the love of benevolence, which implies all that disinterested affection, m the exercise of which the true convert loves God with all his heart, and his neighbour as himself. It implies repentance, faith in Jesus Christ, joy in God, in the Redeemer, humility, resignation to the divine will: A cheerful and pleasing dedication of himself, and of every thing with which he has any concern, to Christ, his interest and honour, and to be disposed of and used by him, in the way which he sees best, to answer his own infinitely wise designs; which shall in the highest degree possible promote the divine glory, and the greatest happiness of his kingdom. It is true wisdom, which discerns and pursues the only objects worthy to be desired and sought. It is goodness and truth, putting on bowels of mercies, kindness, humbleness of mind, meekness, temperance and sobriety. It is heavenly minded, setting the affection on things above, not on things on the earth, &c. &c.

IMPROVEMENT

 1. From this scriptural and rational view of disinterested affection, in which all true virtue, piety and charity consist, may be seen what a great and dangerous mistake they have made, who suppose that there is no virtue or true religion, but that which consists in self love, or originates from it; and that no man ever acts or can act from any higher or other principle, whatever he may think or pretend. Surely these "call evil good, and good evil; put darkness for light, and light for darkness; bitter for sweet, and sweet for bitter." [519] They call that virtue and goodness, which is directly opposed to all true virtue and goodness; and in which all moral evil consists. They call the only moral good, evil. They say there is no such thing as disinterested affection, and if there were, it must be evil. And all appearance of it, or pretension to it, is nothing but hypocrisy or delusion. They put that for light and wisdom, which is darkness itself, in which all moral darkness consists. They recommend and delight in that, as the source of all happiness, which is the most odious thing in nature, and is the source of all the mischief and misery among creatures.

 It is true, that mankind in general appear to act from no higher or better principle than self love. But this affords not the least evidence that man is not capable of disinterested affection, or that self love is not the essence and substance of all sin. It is indeed an evidence that the account the scripture gives of man is true, that he is naturally totally depraved, and wholly corrupt: And that he must be renewed by the Spirit of God, in order to his becoming in the least degree virtuous and holy.

 II. We hence learn how false and pernicious that doctrine is, which too many have held and asserted, viz. that true love to God originates from a knowledge or belief that he loves us, and designs to make us happy: Or that a man cannot love God, unless he first has evidence that God loves him with a design to save him. This is excluding disinterested affection entirely, and making all religious affection to consist in self love; for that love to any being which is wholly owing to a

The System of Doctrines, contained in Divine Relation, Explained and Defended Volume I
knowledge or belief that he loves us, is nothing but self love. Our Saviour therefore condemns this, as not true christian love; but a love which may be found in the most selfish, wicked man. He says, "If ye love them which love you, what thanks have ye? For sinners also love those that love them."[520] There is no need that a man should be regenerated and born of the Spirit of God, in order to his loving God, so far as he is persuaded that God loves him, with a design to save him from eternal destruction, and make him happy forever. This is consistent with being a real enemy to the divine character: And the greatest enemy to God will do this, without any change of heart for the better. And if any person has no other love to God but this, it is certain he has not a new heart, is not converted, and has not the Spirit of God; but all his religious affection and devotion is nothing but wickedness, and enmity against God and his law.

He who has a new heart, and universal disinterested benevolence, will be a friend to God, and must be pleased with his infinitely benevolent character, though he see not the least evidence, and has not a thought that God loves him, and designs to save him. And if he could know that God designed, for his own glory and the general good, to cast him into endless destruction; this would not make him cease to approve of his character; he would continue to be a friend of God, and to be pleased with his moral perfection. And he would, even on this supposition, and in this case, exercise true gratitude to God for all the good he had received or did now enjoy, and for his great and wonderful love to the world, in providing salvation for man. For benevolence exercised and manifested in doing good is the object of gratitude, and will excite it in him who has disinterested benevolent affection, though he receives no personal benefit by it.

Therefore they who cannot love God, unless he first manifest to them that he is their friend, and designs to save them, are the unregenerate, who have no disinterested affection; but are wholly selfish in all their religious exercises and affections; and their religion, whatever appearance it may put on, is false and destructive.

But if such love to God as this were true love, and real piety, it is impossible it should ever take place. For God has not discovered, and never will discover to any man, that he loves him, and will save him, who has no love to God: It is impossible therefore that he who does not now love God should have any real good evidence from any quarter that God loves him, or that he shall be saved. He must first love God in order to have any evidence that God will not destroy him forever. He therefore who cannot love God until he has evidence, and God discovers to him that he shall be saved, never can be brought to love him; because this discovery never will be made to him, so long as he does not love God; and if he thinks he has had such a discovery, it is mere delusion, and he is made to believe a lie: Consequently all his love to God is built on a falsehood and delusion. So that they who can have no love to God, unless he first discovers to them that he intends to save them, and think they have had such a discovery, and from this they began, and continue to love him, are deluded two ways, and in two respects. Their supposed discovery that God loves them, and will save them, and their belief of this, is altogether a delusion, and they only believe a lie. But if this were a true and real discovery, and this were possible, yet their love and religious affection which is wholly founded on this discovery, and they love God only because he loves them, and for no other reason, has no moral goodness in it; it is nothing but self love, and therefore nothing but sin: And such cannot be saved, or enjoy God, nor can God love them unless they have new hearts given them, by which this same self love will be destroyed, in a degree at least, and disinterested affection takes place, which will be friendly to God, and love him, whether he be friendly to them, or not.

An expression of St. John has been often produced to confront what has been now advanced; and to prove that the only ground and reason of christians loving God, is a belief of his love to them. This is in the following words, "We love him because he first loved us." [521] It is of importance carefully to consider what is the real meaning of these words of inspiration, lest by inattention or prejudice we should put a wrong sense upon them, and overlook the truth which is designed to be communicated by them. It has been observed, that in this context the apostle is considering and recommending the love of God in giving his Son to die for the redemption of sinners, and urging christians to imitate this love, which is certainly disinterested love; love to men while they hated God, and not love to them because they loved him. Christians therefore could not imitate the love of God here recommended, by loving him purely because he loved them; for this would be so far from imitating the love of God, that it would be only an exercise of self love, which is in nature and kind directly opposed to the disinterested love of God. Therefore the apostle cannot here mean to recommend self love, or interested affection; and assert that the only ground and reason of their love to God, was the manifestation and evidence given to them that God loved them; and that they had good evidence that God loved them, and designed to save them, before they began to love him, and as necessary in order to their loving him: Not only because this would be inconsistent with the whole context, and make all his reasoning contradictory, futile and absurd; but to suppose this, is to make him assert that which is utterly impossible, as has been just now observed. Besides, by putting this sense upon these words, they are made inconsistent with the other parts of the Bible, which represent the holy love of christians to consist in disinterested affection, in opposition to self love; which, it is presumed, has been made evident in this section. Moreover, by understanding these words in this sense, they stand in direct contradiction to the assertion of our Saviour, viz. That to love those who love us, and that purely because they love us, is not a virtuous, holy love, but that which the worst of men may have. "For if ye love them which love you, what thank have ye? For sinners also love those that love them." [522] It is therefore certain, that those words of the Apostle cannot be understood in this sense, without making him contradict himself, and to assert that which is inconsistent with all the rest of the Bible, and with the plainest dictates of reason and common sense.

And if another meaning offers itself, which is consistent with all those, and which the context points out, and which is a natural and easy sense, who will hesitate to embrace it? The Apostle is in this passage celebrating the love of God in giving his Son to be a propitiation for the sins of men, as the pattern of all holy love. He says, "Herein is love: Not that we loved God; but that he loved us, and sent his Son to be a propitiation for our sins." He refers to the love of God as the original ground and cause of all the good which came to them; he loved them first, while men were sinners and had no love to him, but were his enemies. His love laid the foundation of all good, moral and natural, in man. Therefore, "We love him because he first loved us." That is, had he not been first in his love, before we loved him, and opened a way for our reconciliation, by sending his Son to be a propitiation for our sins, and by his Spirit regenerated us unto holy disinterested love, to which the unrenewed heart is an utter stranger: Had he not thus first loved us and done all this for us, we should never have known what true disinterested love is. Therefore we are certain that the cause of our loving God is his love to us, which has opened the way for it, and actually wrought it in us. "We love him, because he loved us," and gave us the spirit of love in our regeneration; for none but those who are born of God do love him. Thus it appears that these words perfectly coincide with the whole context, when understood in the sense now put upon them; and are very far from asserting that we cannot love God, unless we have evidence or believe that he loves us, and designs to save us; or that a christian's love to God originates wholly from a belief that God loves him. It does originate from the love of God to him, in the sense now given: It is wholly owing to the love and kindness of God, in giving his Son to die for him; and then saving him by the washing of regeneration, and renewing of the Holy Ghost. So that it is not of him that willeth, nor of him that runneth, but of God who sheweth mercy. Had not God first loved him, and done all this for him, he never would have had any true love to God.

III. From this subject may be inferred the propriety and importance of public teachers constantly and with clearness distinguishing between self love, and disinterested affection, and showing that true religion, and all holy exercise consists in the latter, and not at all in the former. If this be not done, and a clear distinction between these two opposites be not constantly made and kept up, true religion cannot be set in a proper light, and distinguished from all counterfeits, and they may leave their hearers in ignorance, and lead them into deception, in this important matter, and to rest in a religion that is nothing more than mere selfishness, and opposition to true holiness. If that religion be not taught and inculcated which is opposed to self love: but on the contrary, selfish affections are recommended as true holiness, the blind lead the blind, and they both are like to fall into the ditch. Mankind, when they turn their thoughts to religion, being naturally wholly selfish, are strongly inclined to approve and take up with a selfish religion; as this only is agreeable to their hearts. They are therefore disposed to like that preaching best which gratifies and flatters their self love and pride. And if they are taught that they may be converted and be good christians, without denying themselves and crossing their self love; but in the full gratification of this; and disinterested affection, or that wherein it consists, be spoken of with disapprobation, and condemned as wrong or impossible, or is kept wholly out of sight: This tends to confirm them in a delusion, which doubtless proves fatal to thousands. The more men are inclined to embrace and be satisfied with a selfish religion, the more careful and zealous should public teachers be, to oppose it, and detect the delusion, and preach up that pure and undefiled religion, which consists in renouncing self, and in the exercise of disinterested affection. This would be striking at the root of self love, pride and human depravity, and setting holiness in a true and beautiful light. And though such preaching, when it is understood, may not please, but offend those who have nothing but self love; yet it ought to be inculcated, whether they will hear, or whether they will forbear.

And it is of importance to keep it in view, that universal benevolence, and impartial disinterested goodness is the sum and source of all holy affection, as it is all implied and contained in this, by whatever different names it may be called, as has been shown. It tends to confuse and mislead the mind on this subject of love, if when love to God is spoken of and described, it is represented as consisting wholly in the love of complacency, and benevolent affection is implicitly excluded: Whereas this is the essence of the whole; and the love of complacency and of gratitude ought to be considered as the exercise of universal, disinterested benevolence, in order to set the subject in the clearest light, and to prevent mistakes. Too many who hold the truth on this point in theory, or will assent to it, at least, when it is proposed and explained to them, yet, when they treat on love to God, do either by the influence of habit and custom, or through inattention, leave out all idea of benevolence, as if the love of complacency and gratitude were distinct and stood alone, independent of universal benevolence. And this is too often the case, when love to our neighbour is mentioned. Disinterested benevolence, which is the sum, and comprehends all, is overlooked, as if no such affection existed. This is a misrepresentation of love, and has an evil tendency.

IV. This subject exhibits a rule by which all who suppose themselves to be converted, and real christians, may try their conversion, and religious exercises and conduct, in order to determine of what kind their religion is, whether true or false.

Many have asserted, as has been observed above, that it is impossible to love God unless we first believe that he designs to save us; and that such belief is the necessary foundation of all friendly affection to him. If their hearts agree with their theory, and all their love to God originates from a persuasion that he loves them, it is certain, that all their supposed piety is mere delusion; and that they are not friends, but enemies to the true God; which has been shown above.

There have been, and now are many, who, when they have given a relation of their conversion, have represented that they were first brought to love God, from a persuasion that he first loved them, and designed to save them, that Christ died for them, &c. And that all their after religious exercises and love are founded on this persuasion, and sink or rise, as that is stronger or weaker. If this account which they give of themselves, of their conversion and religious exercises, be in fact true, all their religion, from beginning to end, falls short of real Christianity; and is of a contrary nature. It was impossible they could have such a persuasion on good ground antecedent to their loving God; therefore they believed without any evidence, and all their religion was founded on delusion and falsehood. But if it were miraculously revealed to them, that God designed to save them, and all their love to him originated from such a revelation, and they could not love him, on any other supposition, all their religious exercise has its foundation in selfishness, and is nothing but self love, and consistent with enmity against God.

Others give a different account of their first conversion and after religious exercise, which may consist in disinterested affection, and has that appearance; yet ought to be carefully considered and examined, lest some fatal deception should lurk at bottom. They may reasonably inquire, whether old things are passed away, and all things are become new, in this respect; that whereas they were naturally wholly selfish in their views, exercises and desires, they now have disinterested affection, and new views and desires, which appear to be of this kind. Whether they have that benevolent regard to God and the Redeemer, as to lead them to desire, above all things, that he may be glorified, and his will be done, whatever it may be; that his interest and kingdom may be promoted, and come to perfection, so as to comprise the greatest possible happiness and glory of the universe: And whether they thus "seek first the kingdom of God," and devote all they have, and themselves, to his glory, and the greatest good of the whole; having no other interest but this, and what is comprehended in it; not desiring their own happiness, or that of any other individual, unless it be consistent with the glory of God, and the greatest general good: And whether they are sincerely desiring and seeking the good of all men now living, and wishing every one to be happy, so far as may be consistent with the w ill of God, and the greatest general good; and actually endeavouring to do good to all men, as they have opportunity; and careful not to injure their character, persons or interest, in any respect, by word or action; at the same time, being liberal and bountiful to the poor and distressed to the utmost of their ability; and expressing their benevolence to all, by praying for them: And whether they love their enemies with benevolent affection, whatever injuries they may have done them: and are disposed to do good to them; and do wish them well, and pray for them: Whether those who appear to them to be the benevolent friends of God and man, are peculiarly dear to them, to whom their hearts are united in strong benevolent affection, and complacential love. If they find their religious affection is of this nature, and implies all this, and their words and actions are in some good measure answerable, they may reasonably conclude that they are born of the Spirit of God, and that their religion consists in disinterested affection.

It must be added, that this disinterested benevolence will farther evidence itself in religious, holy joy in God, his works and revealed designs, in which there is no selfishness, but the contrary. It will rejoice in the infinite, independent, unchangeable, and eternal felicity of the triune God, Father, Son and Holy Ghost; and that he is able, and will glorify himself to the highest possible degree forever. It rejoices in the hope and assurance of the glory of God, and that nothing has, or shall take place, which shall not turn to his glory: That the wrath of man shall praise him, and the remainder of wrath he will restrain. It will also rejoice, that the greatest good, and highest happiness of the creation, will be promoted, and take place. That all the evil that does, or shall exist, cannot prevent this; but is all ordered, and will be overruled by infinite wisdom and goodness, to answer this end; so as to issue in the greatest good of the whole. Thus the felicity and glory of God, and the greatest good and happiness of the creation, as one united whole, is the great object of the desire, hope and joy of the truly benevolent. They rejoice in the divine character and perfection; in the independent supremacy, and infinitely wise and good government of God, under which nothing can take place, but what is, all things considered, wisest and best, and necessary in the best manner to promote the greatest good of the whole. They acquiesce and rejoice in his infinitely wise and holy will, that it is done in heaven, and on earth, and will be done forever; And that his counsel and designs, which have fixed all events, from the greatest to the least, are established forever, and cannot be obstructed, or altered.

In all this the benevolent christian does rejoice, independent of his own personal interest; and whatever may be the will of God concerning that, and whatever may become of him, and other individuals, whether his or their particular personal interest and happiness be consistent with the glory of God and the general good, and included in these, or not. Yet he who exercises this disinterested affection, views his own personal interest as great and important; yea, he feels it to be much greater and more important, than when he was wholly selfish; and has a proper regard for it. But as the public interest now appears to him to be infinitely greater, and of more worth, than the happiness of any individual, he is disposed to give up and renounce all the latter, so far as it is inconsistent with the public interest, and as is necessary to promote the greatest common good. And that self love which is contrary to this, is enmity to the greatest good of the public, and to the good of society; and therefore enmity against God.

The true christian, who, so far as he is such, exercises this disinterested affection, may consider all this, and examine himself by it; and yet be left in doubt, whether he has any degree of such affection, or not; and sometimes may even conclude against himself, that he is an utter stranger to it. This may, in some instances, be owing to not attending to, and understanding the distinction and difference between a proper and great regard to their own interest, which is included in disinterested affection, as it has been stated above, and that self love, which seeks a selfish interest only: And they are ready to look upon all regard to their personal interest and desire of happiness to be self love; and hence are led to doubt whether they have any other affection; and sometimes to conclude they are wholly selfish. This also may arise from a view and sense of the great degree and strength of self love, which yet continues with them. He who has any degree of disinterested affection has a proportionable greater discerning of the nature and exercise of selfishness, which is in his own heart. His disinterested love may be said to be the eye which discerns his self love, in all its secret workings, and the real odiousness of it. His attention is therefore turned to this; he looks upon it so much, and watches it so constantly, and sees so much of it, that sometimes he sees nothing else, and is ready to conclude he is wholly selfish in all he does; and is a stranger to disinterested affection. It is hoped that what has been said on this subject, in this section, will be some help to all honest inquirers, who have some degree of disinterested affection, to discern their own character, and to make proper distinction between the love of a true christian and self love; and thus obtain evidence that they are born of the Spirit of God. And that those who have never been renewed to holiness, but are wholly selfish in all their exercises, will, by attending to these things, if they will attend, be convinced that they are far from having any true religion.

These latter are in great danger of continuing in their deception, and holding fast their delusion. They find religion so frequently, and so much represented as a selfish thing, both in public preaching, in books, and in conversation; and disinterested affection so much spoken against, as a mere chimera, and impossible; and so much said in favour of self love; that they may be disposed to treat what is the subject of this section, as erroneous and whimsical, and not worthy of their attention.

And if they be convinced that true religion does consist in disinterested affection, as described above, they are in danger of considering the exercises of their self love, as being disinterested benevolence; since, by the supposition, they know not what the latter is, experimentally; and their self love, in so many ways, puts on the garb of disinterested benevolence, and makes a plausible appearance: And they are so partial in favour of themselves, and their own affections, that they are easily deceived into a favourable opinion of them. Even from self love and pride, they may exert themselves for the public good, either because they consider their own interest as connected with that of the public, and dependent upon it; or because this is the way to escape infamy, and get the applause of their fellow men. And they may be kind and generous to others, either because others love them, or from a selfish desire to have the name of generous, charitable persons. And they think they do these things from a disinterested regard to the public, and to others, because it has such an appearance. Besides, the most selfish person has some affections which are not self love, nor disinterested benevolence, but have some resemblance to the latter. What is called natural affection, the affection of parents to children, and of children to parents, &c. is not, of itself, and in the nature of it, moral affection; but what is called mere instinct. This is called love, by which parents and children are inclined to desire the welfare of each other, and looks like disinterested benevolence:

But is really nothing but instinct, which falls below moral agency; accompanied and strengthened by self love, in selfish persons; and therefore is no evidence that they who have this in the highest degree, have the least degree of disinterested affection under consideration, or universal benevolence, which is essential to holy love.

And what is called natural pity or compassion, is not self love, nor is it universal benevolence, but an instinct, which God, for wise reasons, and for the good of mankind, has implanted in all men. This being a sort of benevolence, is by many mistaken for disinterested holy love, and so are deceiving themselves and others. Would men know their own moral character, they must distinguish these from universal benevolence, and that disinterested affection, in which all true religion consists. [523]

V. This subject teaches us the excellency of real Christianity; and that it is suited to promote the happiness of individuals who partake of the true spirit of it, and of society, where it prevails.

Self love tends to natural evil, and always produces it, unless it be restrained and counteracted. It contracts the mind of him who is under the power of this selfish affection. It sinks it down to a sordid littleness and lowness of spirit, and prevents his proper enjoyment of the good and happiness of others; and subjects him to innumerable, painful feelings and miseries, which are the necessary attendants of pride, envy, covetousness, &c. And this same self love is the source of all the evils that take place in society. All instances of unrighteousness, oppression and cruelty, of contention and war, and of every injury done by one to another, or to the public; and all deceit, falsehood and hypocrisy, incontinency, and every unruly lust; and every thing which worketh evil to others, and to society, are the fruit of self love. Take this away, and all these will cease. And this is removed as far as the spirit of true Christianity is imbibed.

But universal benevolence, christian love, spreads happiness, wherever it flourishes. It enlarges and ennobles the mind, and puts the benevolent person in possession of the good and happiness of others, so that he enjoys it all in a great degree, and rejoices with those who rejoice. By this he becomes a cordial and judicious friend to every one, and more especially to those with whom he has the most connection; and is disposed to do good to all, as he has ability and opportunity: And is devoted to the good of the public, and of the society to which he belongs, being ready to give up his private, personal interest, in any part or the whole of it, when the public interest demands it, and this is necessary for the good of the whole. This disinterested benevolence will lead every one to take his proper place, and to be industrious, active, prudent and faithful in his own business, and honest, upright, sincere and true in all his concerns and dealings with his fellow men. This love is kind, it is mercy, humility, condescension, meekness, peaceableness, temperance, long suffering, and brotherly kindness. This will form rules by which they may fill their station with honour and usefulness; to use their influence for the public good, and the happiness of every individual, so far as is consistent with the greatest public happiness. And this will induce those in more private stations, to acquiesce in, and support good government; to live in peace with all men, if possible. And this will unite all the particular members of the society to each other, and form them into a band of brothers, all engaged to promote the general good, and the best interest of each other, so far as it may be consistent with, and subserve the greatest good of the whole.

Whenever Christianity shall spread over the whole world, and the distinguishing spirit and power of it take place universally, forming men to a high degree of universal benevolence, and disinterested affection, it will unite mankind into one happy society, teaching them to love each other as brethren, each one seeking and rejoicing in the public good, and in the happiness of individuals: This will form the most happy state of public society that can be enjoyed on earth. And when we take into view their love to the Redeemer, their devotedness to his honour and service, and obedience to his laws, in the practice of piety, devotion and mercy; their joy in his character, exaltation and honour; their gratitude to him for their redemption from infinite evil, and making them heirs of unspeakable felicity; their unshaken trust in him for the fulfilment of all his promises; and their clear and sure prospects of their eternal happiness, and the endless and increasing glory of his kingdom:--This will be the greatest likeness of heaven of any thing that has taken place on earth, or ever will. And they will hereby be made meet for the eternal inheritance of the saints in light.

This leads to a view of the most perfect, happy, and glorious society in heaven, in the eternal kingdom of God. All the beauty, happiness, and glory of it, will consist in this disinterested love, made perfect, reigning, and having its proper and full effect, without impediment, both in God, and in every member of this kingdom.

Section V - Concerning Divine Illumination

THE divine oracles represent all the wicked, by which are meant all men who are not righteous, to be in a state of darkness; from which they only are recovered, who are born of God, and become real christians. "The way of the wicked is as darkness: They know not at what they stumble." [524] "The natural man receiveth not the things of the Spirit of God; for they are foolishness unto him: neither can he know them, because they are spiritually discerned." [525] "Ye were once darkness, but now are ye light in the Lord." [526] All unbelievers, ungodly and disobedient, are said in scripture to be blind, and not to know God, in places too many to mention here. St. Paul says, "If our gospel be hid, it is hid to them that are lost; in whom the god of this world hath blinded the minds of them which believe not, lest the light of the glorious gospel of Christ, who is the image of God, should shine unto them." [527] "The Lord Jesus shall be revealed from heaven, in flaming lire, taking vengeance on them that know not God, and that obey not the gospel." [528] Agreeable to this, men are said by conversion, by which they become true christians, to have their eyes opened, and to be turned from darkness to light. To be called out of darkness into marvellous light. To be delivered from the power of darkness, and translated into the kingdom of God's dear Son. [529] And conversion from sin to God is described by being enlightened. [530]

This ignorance and darkness, and the contrary light or knowledge, are, according to scripture, of a moral nature, and consequently consist not in intellectual ignorance, and knowledge, as distinct from any thing which belongs to the heart, and not implying any sensations and exercises of the latter: For that darkness or light which belongs to the intellect, or speculative understanding, as distinct from the heart, and in which the heart has no influence or concern, has nothing moral in it, and is neither virtuous nor vicious, sin or holiness. Therefore the scripture constantly speaks of this darkness and light, this ignorance or want of understanding, and the contrary understanding and knowledge, as having their seat in the heart, and belonging to that, and predicated of it, and as being, as that is, whether right or wrong, wholly corrupt or renewed. The following passages are sufficient to prove this. "Yet the Lord hath not given you an heart to perceive, and eyes to see, and ears to hear unto this day." [531] When the great ignorance and delusion, and stupidity of idolators, in worshipping an image, which they have formed out of a tree, is described, it is, in the conclusion, all ascribed to their hearts. "They have not known, nor understood; for he hath shut their eyes, that they cannot see; and their hearts, that they cannot understand. And none considereth in his heart, neither is there knowledge nor understanding, to say, I have burnt part of it in the fire, &:c. He feedeth on ashes. A deceived heart hath turned him aside, that he cannot deliver his soul, nor say, Is there not a He in my right hand?" [532]

St. Paul asserts the same of the Gentiles in general. They became vain in their imaginations, and their foolish heart was darkened. Having the understanding darkened, being alienated from the life of God, through the ignorance that is in them, because of the blindness of their heart." [533] And he asserts the same of the Jews. That their blindness, respecting Christ and the gospel, was wholly in their hearts, or owing to the vail drawn over them by their opposition to God, and turning away from him: And that this blindness could not be removed, unless their hearts were renewed, and turned to the Lord. "Their minds were blinded.--Even unto this day, when Moses is read, the vail is upon their heart. Nevertheless when it shall turn to the Lord, the vail shall be taken away."[534] The evangelist John says the same of the Jews, which Isaiah had long before said of them. "He hath blinded their eyes, and hardened their hearts; that they should not see with their eyes, nor understand with their heart, and be converted, and I should heal them." [535] So all their ignorance and errors are ascribed to their evil hearts in the following words, taken from the 95th Psalm. "Wherefore I was grieved with that generation, and said, They do always err in their heart; and they have not known my ways." [536] "He that saith he is in the light, and hateth his brother, is in darkness, even until now. He that hateth his brother, is in darkness, and walketh in darkness, and knoweth not whither he goeth, because that darkness hath blinded his eyes." [537] This darkness is here said to consist in the heart, in the evil disposition of that, in not loving but hating his brother, which is an exercise of the heart, and belongs to that only.

It hence appears why this darkness is always spoken of in divine revelation as criminal. It is sinful in every degree of it, as it consists in the moral depravity of the heart. This blindness of mind is not only connected with sinful depravity, but consists in the sinful exercises and lusts of the mind, and cannot be distinguished from sin in the heart. Sin is in every degree and in every exercise of it, delusion and blindness itself: And when the heart is totally corrupt or sinful, which is true of every unrenewed heart, as has been proved, this blindness, this moral darkness, is total, and wholly excludes every degree of the opposite, which is called light, understanding, knowledge and wisdom, in the scriptures. It is, according to scripture, a wilful blindness, being wholly owing to the opposition of the heart to the light of moral truth, or rather, consisting altogether in this. It is represented by closing the eyes to keep light out, however clearly it may shine, and can be kept out

The System of Doctrines, contained in Divine Relation, Explained and Defended Volume I

by nothing but by not making a right use of the eyes, by refusing to open them. Men are naturally totally blind to the things of the moral world, except it be only in mere speculation, because they are totally corrupt, and wholly abuse and pervert the natural powers and faculties of their mind, and their capacity of moral exercises and true discernment, by loving darkness and hating the light. Consequently, this blindness is nothing but sin, and consists wholly in the criminal, inexcusable exercise of the will or heart. Hence this darkness is condemned and forbidden by God in his word; and they who are in this sense blind, are commanded to open their mental eye, to renounce the darkness and delusions in which they are, and receive the knowledge of the truth, in the love of it. "Hear, ye deaf, and look, ye blind, that ye may see." [538] "Awake, thou that sleepest, and arise from the dead, and Christ shall give thee light." [539] And hence Christ, when he was on earth, and since his ascension to heaven, did so often say, "He that hath ears to hear, let him hear. He that hath an ear, let him hear."

And that the above representation of this matter is agreeable to truth and to scripture, is confirmed beyond all dispute, by the most plain and express statement of it, by our Saviour himself. His words are, "He that believeth not, is condemned already, because he hath not believed in the name of the only begotten Son of God. And this is the condemnation, that light is come into the world, and men loved darkness rather than light, because their deeds were evil. For every one that doth evil, hateth the light, neither cometh to the light." [540] Believing on Christ implies a discerning the truth respecting the character of the Redeemer, and redemption by him, and approving and loving it: and in this does faith consist. Unbelief is directly the opposite; it is blindness and darkness itself. St. Paul says, "If our gospel be hid, it is hid to them that are lost: In whom the god of this world hath blinded the minds of them which believe not." It consists in opposition to the most desirable, charming, glorious light and truth, and in hating it, and loving the opposite darkness. Therefore this is a voluntary, chosen darkness. It is altogether criminal, and is that for which they are justly condemned.

It hence follows, that the light and understanding which is opposed to this moral darkness does also belong to the heart, and implies a virtuous character, and does consist in true holiness, or moral excellence. And in this light it is represented in the sacred writings. What Solomon asks, and God promises to give him, is called wisdom and knowledge, in one place, [541] and in another place, is called a wise and understanding heart. [542] Indeed, true wisdom has its seat in the heart or will, and consists essentially in the right moral disposition of the mind, as has been shewn: And it is abundantly evident, that the word is generally used in this sense in the scripture. And this in scripture is the same with true light, or discerning, understanding and knowledge. The virtuous, holy heart, is an enlightened, wise and understanding heart. And the totally depraved, vicious heart, is darkness itself, blind, foolish, and without understanding. That true light and knowledge, the knowledge of God, does not consist in mere speculation, but depends upon the heart, and consists in the moral disposition and exercises of that, is evident from the following words of God by Jeremiah: "I will give them an heart to know me." [543] Therefore our Saviour placed all holiness of heart, and all true happiness, in the knowledge of the only true God, and the Redeemer, as the whole is comprehended in this. "This is life eternal, that they might know thee the only true God, and Jesus Christ whom thou has sent." [544] Agreeable to this the Psalmist says, "Give me understanding and I shall keep thy law: Yea, I shall observe it with my whole heart. Give me understanding, and I shall live." [545] That the illumination which takes place in the mind, in regeneration and conversion, respects the heart, and has its seat in that, is asserted by St. Paul in the following words: "God, who commanded the light to shine out of darkness, hath shined in our hearts, to give the light of the knowledge of the glory of God, in the face of Jesus Christ." [546] And that true light and knowledge implies renovation of heart, or true holiness, and is really the same thing, is evident from St. Paul's mentioning these as synonymous. In his epistle to the Colossians, he describes the new man, or renewed hearty in the following words: "And have put on the new man, which is renewed in knowledge, after the image of him that created him." [547] And in his epistle to the Ephesians, in describing the same new man, he uses these words; "And be renewed in the spirit of your mind; and put on the new man, which after God is created in righteousness and true holiness. " [548] From these two passages, compared together, it may be inferred with certainty, that knowledge comprehends righteousness and true holiness, and is the same thing.

That true light and knowledge, the knowledge of God, which is peculiar to them who are renewed and born of the Spirit of God, is seated in the heart, and implies voluntary exercise, even that love, in which all holiness consists, according to scripture, may be proved from the following passage: "Beloved, let us love one another: For love is of God: and every one that loveth is born of God, and knoweth God, He that loveth not, knoweth not God; for God is love." [549] In these words, love and knowing God, are asserted to be so connected, that where love is, there is the knowledge of God; and they who have no love, do not know God. Hence it may be inferred, that the knowledge of God is dependent on love; for he who does not love, does not know him: There must therefore be this love, in order to know God, as the latter cannot exist without the former; and does exist wherever the former exists. And it is farther inferred, that love, and the knowledge of God, cannot be distinguished, as the one implies the other, and are the same exercise of the heart. Loving God is knowing him, and knowing God is loving him. Love is the eye of the mind, by which the objects in the moral world are seen in a true light; and where this eye, this discerning, is not, the mind is in total darkness with respect to moral objects. The reason of this is here given, "For God is love." As love comprehends all moral excellence, and in this the moral character of God consists; therefore he who loveth not, cannot have any true idea or conception of love; he cannot know the divine moral character, which is love. Love is here to be understood in its general nature, "Every one that loveth. He that loveth not." That is, he whose heart is not formed to the exercise of universal, disinterested benevolence. This, as has been shown, comprehends all virtuous, holy love; and is the same affection, whether it be exercised towards God or our neighbour. All the difference is owing to the difference of the objects of this same love.

In this view it appears that the same thing is asserted by this apostle in the preceding part of this epistle. He says, "he that hateth his brother is in darkness, and walketh in darkness, even until now. But lie that loveth his brother, abideth in the light." [550] He that loveth is born of God, and is divinely illuminated, and knoweth God, and the objects of the moral world, and walketh in the light. He that loveth not is in total darkness with respect to these objects: he hath not seen God, nor known him; for the pure in heart only, that is, they who love, see God. [551] Love is the only light of the moral world. Could this be extinguished, all would be total darkness. And they who are fallen into the darkness of sin, or self love, in which all sin radically consists, as has been shown, can be recovered to light, by that renovation only, that purity of heart which consists in love, or disinterested affection. Hence it appears that when this apostle says, "God is light, " [552] and "God is love," [553] he does not mean any thing really different by light and love; for they cannot be distinguished; but are the same thing. Light is love, and love is light.

This same sentiment, which is inculcated by the apostle John in the passages just considered, is also asserted by St. Paul, in the following words. "Knowledge puffeth up, but love edifieth. If any man think that he knoweth any thing, he knoweth nothing yet as he ought to know." That is, if any man who does not love, think he has true knowledge by mere speculation, and that all light and knowledge consists in this, and desires and seeks no other, he does yet know nothing respecting moral, spiritual objects, as he ought to know, and must know, in order to have the true knowledge of God. "But if any man love God, he (that is, God) is known by him." [554] That is, if any man have love, he is illuminated, and has true light and knowledge, which does not consist in mere speculation, but in the sensations and taste of the heart, by which he discerns the divine character with approbation, and knows the only true God; which is the knowledge that all men ought to have, as they are commanded to love, and all their duty lies in this. All mere speculative knowledge that is possible to be attained without love, leaves men in total moral darkness, in the exercise of selfishness and pride, in opposition to every part and degree of their duty.

Agreeable to this, the same apostle says, "With the heart man believeth unto righteousness."[555] That light and discerning respecting the truths of the gospel, and the character of Christ, which is implied in true faith, is not mere speculation, but depends on the disposition and exercises of the heart. Therefore Christ says to the Jews, "how can ye believe, which receive honour one of another; and seek not the honour which cometh from God only?" [556] In these words it is declared that selfishness and pride, which are directly opposed to that love which consists in disinterested affection, do blind the mind to spiritual objects, and effectually shut out that light and discerning which is essential to faith in Christ; and that they only whose hearts are benevolent and humble, have the true light, and see spiritual objects as faith beholds them.

We are taught the same thing by Christ, when speaking expressly and particularly of illumination. His words are, "The light of the body is the eye: If therefore thine eye be single, thy whole body shall be full of light. But if thine eye be evil, thy whole body shall be full of darkness. If therefore the light that is in thee, be darkness, how great is that darkness." [557] Our divine teacher is here speaking of moral or spiritual light and darkness, and says, that these are as the eye of the mind is, and depend on the single or evil eye. If we attend to the scripture, we may learn what is meant by the single and evil eye. Jesus Christ says, "From within, out of the heart of men, proceed evil thoughts, adulteries, fornications, murders, thefts, covetousness, wickedness, deceit, lasciviousness, an evil eye, blasphemy, pride, foolishness: All these evil things come from within, and defile the man." [558] From these words we learn, that an evil eye belongs to the heart, and is an exercise of the heart, as it cometh out of the heart. Therefore it is of a moral nature, and is itself criminal, as it is called an evil thing, and is ranked among other things, which are moral evils or sins, and defile men. We may infer from this with great certainty, that moral darkness belongs to the heart, and not the intellect, as distinguished from that.--That it consists in the exercise of the heart, and is in itself criminal, in every degree of it.

The System of Doctrines, contained in Divine Relation, Explained and Defended Volume I

And it may with equal certainty be determined, from other passages of scripture, what is the particular nature of that disposition and exercise which is called an evil eye, and in what this evil eye consists. Our Lord represents the householder, who hired men to work in his vineyard, at different times in the day, and ordered his steward to give as much wages to those who had laboured but one hour, as to those who had laboured the whole day; as saying to one of the latter who complained of this, "Is thine eye evil, because I am good?" [559] Here a contracted, selfish, envious spirit, is called an evil eye; and is opposed to goodness of heart, of benevolence, which is here called a good eye; and must be the same with a single eye. An evil eye always means selfishness, and that affection of heart which is included in it, whenever it is mentioned in the scripture. There are the following instances of this. When God commands the Israelites to open their hand wide, and give liberally to their poor brethren, he adds the following words; "Beware that there be not a thought in thy wicked heart, saying, the seventh year, the year of release is at hand: And thine eye be evil against thy poor brother, and thou givest him nought, and he cry unto the Lord against thee, and it be sin unto thee." [560] Here again, an evil eye is a selfish disposition of heart, in opposition to goodness or benevolence of heart. The same thing is denoted by an evil eye in the following passages: "Eat thou not the bread of him that hath an evil eye; neither desire thou his dainty meat. For as he thinketh in his heart, so is he: Eat and drink, saith he to thee; but his heart is not with thee." [561] Here his evil eye consists in the thoughts and disposition of his heart, which are opposed to his generous benevolent expressions, and really against his guest, which can be nothing but a selfish, covetous disposition, "He that hasteth to be rich, hath an evil eye." [562] Nothing but a selfish, inordinate craving, and a covetous spirit, will prompt men to make haste to be rich.

Having found what an evil eye is, that it consists in that disposition and those exercises of heart which are evil and criminal, in that self love which is contrary to benevolence and true goodness of heart, and fills the mind with moral darkness; it is easy to determine what is meant by a single eye, viz. that disposition of heart, which is opposed to selfishness. It is an upright, good, benevolent heart, or true, disinterested, benevolent love. This is evident from the passages of scripture already mentioned. A liberal, benevolent disposition, and a good eye, which is the same, is set in opposition to an evil eye. The single eye is the same with a bountiful eye. "He that hath a bountiful eye shall be blessed: For he giveth of his bread to the poor." [563]

That the single eye consists in benevolence and goodness of heart, is evident, (if any farther evidence be needed) in that the word in the original απλους, translated single, when a substantive, απλοτης, is used for liberality, bountifulness, or benevolence. It is so used in the following passages of scripture. "He that giveth, let him do it with simplicity." [απλοτητι] That is, with a liberal, bountiful heart. [564]

"How that in a great trial of affliction, the abundance of their joy, and their deep poverty, abounded unto the riches of their liberality." [565] [απλοτητος] "Being enriched in every thing, to all bountifulness" [566] [εἰς πασαν απλοτητα] "While, by the experiment of this ministration, they glorify God for your professed subjection unto the gospel of Christ, and for your liberal distribution [απλοτητ της κοινωνίας unto them, and unto all men." [567] "Who giveth to all men liberally, [απλως] and upbraideth not." [568]

It is easy to see that this representation of a single and an evil eye agrees exactly with those passages of scripture which have been mentioned above, in which disinterested love, as opposed to selfishness, is spoken of as essential to true light and discerning, with respect to things of a moral nature; so that he who loveth, knoweth God, and he who loveth not, knoweth not God; and consequently has no true knowledge of the things of the moral world; but is in total darkness. And that self love, by which a man hateth his brother, is moral darkness itself, and causeth him to walk in darkness. Herein the apostles perfectly agree with Jesus Christ, when he says that a single eye, that is, love, or a benevolent disposition of heart, is that which illuminates the mind, and is moral light and discerning: And that the evil eye, that is, selfishness, is moral darkness, and holds die mind in this darkness, where it reigns. Love or universal, disinterested benevolence, which implies all moral goodness, or righteousness and holiness, is the single eye which illuminates the mind, and fills the heart with moral divine light. This single eye fixes on one grand object, the glory of God, which implies the greatest good of his eternal kingdom, and the best good of every individual creature, so far as it tends to promote the general good, or is consistent with it. The evil eye is selfishness, and all that is implied in this, in which all moral evil or sin consists. This is moral blindness, or spiritual darkness; and while the heart is under the dominion of this, all the light which is set before the man, and all his speculations, will not in the least remove this darkness, but all the light that is in him is darkness. And "how great is that darkness!"

The same thing is asserted by Jesus Christ in the following passages. "Every one that doeth evil," that is, is wholly selfish in all he does, "hateth the light, neither cometh to the light, lest his deeds should be reproved. But he that doth truth," he that loveth, "cometh to the light." [569] "If any man will do his will, he shall know of the doctrine, whether it be of God, or whether I speak of myself." [570] He only doth the will of God who loveth: He shall know God and Christ; he and he only has light and discerning to see and know the truth, and distinguish it from error.

St. Paul sets this point in the same light, when he says, "And this I pray, that your love may abound yet more and more, in knowledge, and in all judgment." [571] The word here translated judgment, signifies taste and sensibility of heart, which is true moral light and discerning. This knowledge and judgment is here represented as consisting in love, or the concomitant or fruit of it.

The above scriptural account of the moral darkness of the minds of depraved men, and of divine illumination or spiritual light and discerning, is agreeable to reason, and supported by it; and is implied in what has been generally granted by those who have attended to the subject. It has been generally, if not universally conceded, and seems to be a plain dictate of reason and common sense, that the inordinate lusts of men, when they prevail and govern, do blind their minds with respect to moral objects: so that those lusts and evil inclinations of men must be suppressed, and mortified, in some degree, at least, in order to their discerning these objects, and seeing them in a true and proper light. The man who gives himself up to covetousness and worldly pursuits, to unrighteousness or sensuality, must, by the reigning of any or all of these lusts, be blind to the beauty and excellence of spiritual, moral objects, and truths, and those exercises of mind in which true virtue and holiness consists. And there is no other way to recover such an one to a true and proper discerning of the reality, importance, the beauty and excellence of the truths and objects of the moral world, including God, his law, Jesus Christ, the gospel, the nature and excellence of true religion, but by an alteration in the taste, disposition and desires of his heart, and recovering him to a contrary taste and disposition of mind.

And it is equally reasonable and certain that the more inward lusts of the heart, selfishness and pride, which are the essence, root, strength and support of these lusts which have been mentioned, and of all others, should be attended with moral blindness, where they reign, and are blindness, and moral darkness itself: And that true illumination and moral light consist in an opposite disposition and taste of mind. Things of a moral nature have relation to the exercises of the heart; and sin and holiness consist in self love and benevolence, as has been shown. He whose heart is destitute of benevolent affection can have no true idea of it, because ideas of exercises of heart are obtained by having exercises of that kind, and no other way. Therefore he who exercises no true love, knows not the true moral character of God; for this consists in love. And when this affection takes place in his heart, he has spiritual discerning, moral light breaks in upon his mind, he is turned from darkness to light, and sees and knows God, in his true moral character, and has some right view of things of the moral world. Agreeable to this, Solomon says, "Evil men understand not judgment: But they that seek the Lord, understand all things." [572]

This light and discerning, by which the true beauty and excellence of moral objects is seen, is not attainable by any kind or degree of mere intellectual speculation, as distinguished from relish and exercise of the heart. Moral beauty, amiableness and excellence is not the object of mere intellect or understanding, as distinguished from the will or heart; it is the object of taste, which belongs to the heart, and implies inclination and exercise of heart, and consists in it. Beauty and amiableness is discerned by taste; and seeing beauty implies inclination to it, or love of it. Benevolent, disinterested affection, which, as has been observed, is the single eye, is that in which true moral taste consists. This belongs to the heart, and where this exists, things of the moral world appear in their true beauty and amiableness, and are relished and loved. On the contrary, self love, which implies every sinful affection and lust, is that in which a wrong bias and taste of heart consists. It is blind to moral beauty; and those moral objects and affections, in which all the true beauty, amiableness and excellence in the universe consist, appear disagreeable and odious, so far as they are seen, which is real aversion, and hatred of them. This is blindness indeed! The only moral blindness, and the greatest darkness and delusion that can be in nature. It calls evil good, and good evil; it puts darkness for light, and light for darkness; bitter for sweet, and sweet for bitter.[573]

This will appear more evident and clear, perhaps, by considering the nature and tendency of self love, which comprehends every vice and lust of the mind, and is exercised in all sin; and the opposite nature of universal disinterested benevolence, in which all true virtue is implied.

Self love is an evil eye, which will not admit the light that discovers and brings into clear view, all the grand, beautiful and glorious objects in the moral world. It is fast shut against all those, and excludes them wholly from sight. It sees and regards but one infinitely little, diminutive object, self; it sinks the mind down and contracts it to this, and will not look at any other object, or interest, but this contracted selfish one. It feels as if this was the great and only interest, and subordinates every other being and interest, and every possible public good, to a private personal interest, seeing no other good but that which is suited to promote a personal, selfish good. This self love is therefore, in the nature of it, total blindness to the infinite importance of the being of God, and the amiableness and excellence of his character; and to the worth and glory of his kingdom, and desirableness of the greatest public good. And consequently, does not see the amiableness and worth of that disinterested, universal benevolence, which seeks the greatest good of the whole, and fixes on this, as the grand and most desirable object, and subordinates the interest of individuals to the common interest, and greatest good of the whole; and cannot have any relish or taste for this; but must be displeased with it and hate it, and all the beings who are of this character, as they are disposed to sacrifice and give up all his personal interest, which he holds as the only good, when necessary to promote the general good. This self love therefore is enmity against God, and the general good; and that affection must be hateful to the selfish person, which seeks the glory of God, and the greatest good of his kingdom, and does not regard, but gives up the interest of individuals, so far as the latter is inconsistent with the former. Thus self love is totally blind to the only great and real good in the universe, and to all the true beauty and excellence in it: This is the blindness, the darkness and deception of every one who loves his own self only. This darkness, as it has its foundation in the heart, and consists in the reigning affection of it, cannot be removed by any merely intellectual light, knowledge and reasoning, but remains in its greatness and full strength, whatever the understanding, considered as distinct from the will, may dictate, as there is no connection between mere intellectual knowledge, and the taste and inclination of the heart, and the former cannot alter the latter. This is verified by experience, in the innumerable instances of the taste and inclination of the heart contradicting and counteracting the conviction and dictates of the understanding, the former choosing that as good and best, and pursuing it, while the latter pronounces it to be wrong and evil. [574]

Disinterested, universal benevolence, or that disposition of heart which implies this, which is "an honest and good, or benevolent heart," is the single eye. This gives that light to the mind, in which it discerns the grand objects comprised in universal being; and sees what is the true, the greatest and only good of the universe; and fixes on this as the first object of choice and pursuit. This brings into view the first cause of all, the infinite source, and the sum of all being, as really existing, and sees him to be the first and great object of regard and benevolence. This discerns, tastes and relishes the true moral beauty and excellence of universal benevolence; approves of it and delights in it as the supreme moral good, and as comprehending the whole of it. It sees God as infinitely great, and infinitely benevolent or good, rejoices in his felicity and glory, and says, "Let him reign supreme, and be glorified to the highest degree forever," as involving the greatest good, the highest happiness and glory of his kingdom: It is pleased with the divine moral character, comprehended in his infinite benevolence or goodness, and delights in it above all things else. Thus he who loveth, knoweth God, for God is love.

And he who has this honest and good heart, this dis. interested, benevolent affection, sees the beauty, importance, righteousness and goodness of the law of God, which requires perfect love, universal benevolence, with all that affection which is involved in it, of every moral agent, on pain of his highest displeasure. He consequently sees all opposition to this law to be infinitely odious and detestable; and therefore views his own character, as a sinner, as unspeakably hateful, and, abhors himself, and sees the reason why God does hate all sin, and the propriety and desirableness that he should express and manifest his high displeasure at it, and infinite opposition to it, in threatening it with a just, deserved, endless punishment. And by all this, he is prepared to behold and understand the gospel, and see the truth, wisdom and glory of it, which exhibits infinite benevolence in the most advantageous and striking light, and is suited in the best manner to promote the honour of God, and the greatest happiness of his kingdom. And the character of Christ will come into view as infinitely amiable, worthy and important; and the benevolent heart will approve, love and rejoice. This is that knowledge of the only true God, and Jesus Christ whom he has sent, which is eternal life: It is the light of life, which is the attainment of all the followers of Christ. He who hath this love, "abideth in the light, and there is no occasion of stumbling in him."[575]

From all that has been now observed on this subject, it is easy to see, that divine illumination is effected by the renovation of the heart of man, by the Spirit of God, by which it is no longer wholly selfish, and under the dominion of pride and lust; but is formed to universal, disinterested benevolence, or true love. Nothing is wanting but such a change of heart, in order to the true light of the moral world shining into it. By this renovation the single eye is formed, and the mind is full of light. This is that change, and illumination which is ascribed in scripture to the Spirit of God. This is that change of heart which Jesus calls a being born again of the Spirit, without which men cannot see the kingdom of God. [576] And by which their eyes are opened, and they are turned from darkness to marvellous light, and know the only true God, and Jesus Christ whom he hath sent. By this renovation a wise and understanding heart is given, and God gives a heart to know him. And he shines in the heart, by giving this single eye, to give the light of the knowledge of the glory of God, in the face of Jesus Christ. [577] This is the same with giving a new heart, and a new spirit. [578] And is expressed in the following words: "I will put my laws into their minds, and write them in their hearts. And they shall not teach every man his neighbour, and every man his brother, saying, know the Lord; for all shall know me, from the least to the greatest." [579] Jesus Christ speaks of this illumination when he says, "It is written in the prophets, and they shall all be taught of God. Every one therefore that hath heard, and hath learned of the Father, cometh unto me." [580] And when he says to Peter, upon his professing his faith in him as the Christ, the Son of the living God, "Blessed art thou, Simon Barjona, for flesh and blood hath not revealed it unto thee, but my Father which is in heaven." [581] St. Paul speaks of this renovation of heart as necessary in order to true light and knowledge, and that the latter is implied in the former. "Be not conformed to this world: But be ye transformed, by the renewing of your mind, that ye may prove what is that good, and acceptable, and perfect will of God." [582]

This illumination, therefore, does not consist in discovering, or revealing to men any new truth not already made known and contained in divine revelation; but in forming the heart to true discerning, and hereby opening the eye of the mind, to see the truths revealed in the scriptures; or in forming the single eye, which will receive the light, which before shined; but was not admitted, and could not shine in the heart, because the eye was evil, and shut against the truth. This is expressed by the Psalmist in the following words: "Open thou mine eyes, that I may behold wondrous things out of thy law." [583] The scriptures contain a fulness of moral light and instruction; they will make him wise unto salvation, who understands and believes; who discerns the truths there revealed. There is therefore no need that any new truth should be immediately suggested to the mind which is not contained in the Bible. All that is wanting, is to have the mind disposed and prepared to receive the light which is extant, and shines in the word of God: This is to have a single eye, a new, benevolent heart. He who has such an heart, is hereby brought into a new moral world; sees the things revealed in the scriptures in a new light; they now appear in their reality and divinity, beautiful, consistent, harmonious, important, and affecting, as they never did before, infinitely above any thing else that can be imagined. Thus the light shines in the heart to give the light of the knowledge of the glory of God, in the face of Jesus Christ. [584] This establishes the heart in a belief and assurance of the truth of the gospel and of divine revelation, as no degree of mere speculation can do. This is expressed by St. John in the following words: "We know that the Son of God is come, and hath given us an understanding that we may know him that is true. This is the true God, and eternal life." [585]

As the renovation of the heart is but in a small degree at first, and the eye of the mind is not fully opened at once; but this work is begun in an imperfect degree, and carried on to perfection: So this light is comparatively small and imperfect in the beginning, and gradually increases, and the christian grows in grace, in holiness, and in the knowledge of Jesus Christ, which implies the knowledge of all divine things. "The path of the just is as the shining light, which shineth more and more to the perfect day." And as the enlightened mind sees but in part, in this world, and is never omniscient, some truths and objects are more particularly and clearly in view at one time, and others at another: which may be owing to particular divine internal influence, or the agency of other invisible beings, or to external circumstances, and occurrences; all which are under the immediate influence and guidance of the omnipotent, omnipresent, all-wise Being, who worketh all in all.[586]

It is proper to observe here, that though the heart or will be the seat of this illumination, and moral light and darkness are as the disposition of the heart is, yet the whole mind, in all the faculties of it, is concerned, and some way included and affected in this affair. Intellectual light and conviction, considered as distinct from the heart, is included in this illumination. Ideas are conveyed to the heart by this medium. Where there are no speculative ideas, which are in some measure agreeable to the truth, and no right judgment and conviction respecting intellectual objects; the benevolent heart will not be properly illuminated, or be under advantage to exercise itself properly towards external objects. When the single eye is formed, it will receive light and view the objects of moral sight, by the medium of the intellect. Therefore there appears to be a propriety, that there should be some degree of speculative light and conviction in the minds of the adult, before a new heart or single eye is given, in order to prepare them to discern the truth properly, and to have exercises agreeable to it.

And when a new heart, a single eye is given, it will help to rectify the mistakes which may have been made by the intellectual judgment, as the latter is influenced and biassed in judging of things by the taste and inclination of the heart. So far as the heart is honest and good, the prejudices which bias the speculative judgment will be removed, and the mind will speculate more clearly, and a conviction of the truth will be more clear, strong and steady; and the attention of the mind to moral divine subjects will be more fixed and engaged, and a foundation is laid for the enlargement of the mind in intellectual knowledge of these things, and the rational powers of the soul; for the taste and benevolent exercises of the new heart, are perfectly rational, and will be approved by right reason, and a rectified judgment. Thus, by the renovation of the heart, forming it to a right taste, a disposition to disinterested benevolence, all the powers of the soul are sanctified; the ignorance and mistakes of reason and judgment, which originated from an evil eye, or self love, are removed; the whole mind is enlightened, and all the faculties of the soul harmonize, and do their office well.

When the heart is perfectly right, in the exercise of benevolent, disinterested affection, the soul is full of light, and the man is perfectly holy, in all his faculties and powers.

The sum of what has been said above on the subject of divine illumination is this. As all mankind are, while in their natural state, totally depraved and sinful, and this depravity is in the nature of it moral darkness, they are wholly blind to the things of the Spirit of God. This blindness has its foundation in the heart, and consists in the wrong taste and sinful inclination of that, and not in any natural defect in the intellectual and reasoning faculties of the soul, as distinguished from the inclination of the heart. This blindness is therefore a wilful blindness, as it consists in the disposition, and exercise of the heart or will. They have eyes, they have all the natural mental faculties, which are necessary to discern spiritual things, as well as any other objects: But they see them not, because they voluntarily shut their eyes, and refuse to open them, and admit the light which shines around them, as this light of divine truth is above all things disagreeable to them; they hate it, and will not come unto it, lest their deeds should be reproved. This blindness is therefore wholly the fault of man, and criminal in every degree of it, being moral depravity itself. It consists in self love, which implies the whole of moral depravity, of every thing in the heart that is or can be contrary to the law of God. This is the evil eye, which fills the whole mind with moral darkness. This is blindness to invisible spiritual things; does not see the beauty, consistence and harmony of moral truth; and therefore has no sense and cordial belief of their reality, or that they do indeed exist, whatever reason and speculative judgment may dictate. Therefore, "The fool," every man in his natural state, who is in this moral darkness, "saith in his heart, there is no God." [587] This is the feeling and language of a heart wholly depraved and under the power of self love: Which cannot be removed by any mere speculations and reasoning on the subject, so long as the heart is thus wholly corrupt. And this selfishness and pride, with all the lusts implied in this, tend to weaken and pervert the reasoning powers of the mind, and bribe and bias the reason and speculative judgment, so as to reject the truth, and embrace error in speculation, respecting things of a moral nature. And this is the ground and source of all the false, unreasonable reasoning, and errors in judgment upon subjects of a moral nature, which do take place among mankind. And therefore all false reasoning, and every error and delusion in speculation and judgment, is blameable and sinful, as all these have their foundation in the corrupt biasses of the heart, and are altogether governed and produced by them.

The real christian is, in becoming such, turned from this darkness to marvellous light, which is effected by the omnipotent influences of the Spirit of God, in the renovation of the heart, which was before totally corrupt, forming it to disinterested, universal benevolence, and so making it an honest and good heart; and forming the single eye, by which the truths revealed in the scriptures, relating to the being and perfections of God, his law and moral government; the state and character of man; the character and works of the Mediator; the way of salvation by him; the nature of duty and true holiness, &c. are seen in their true light, as realities, beautiful, divine, important, excellent, harmonious, glorious, and above all things else interesting and affecting; and the mind is filled with this spiritual, marvellous, glorious light. By this all the powers of the mind are enlarged and strengthened. Reason and judgment, being no longer biassed by an evil heart, are rectified,, and the reasoning, speculative faculty, is exerted in an honest, attentive pursuit, in the investigation of truth.

Though the blindness of man in his natural, totally depraved state, be of a moral nature, and voluntary, and therefore wholly criminal; yet it is as great, and is as much beyond the power of means to remove it; and the man is as far from recovering himself to light, as if the blindness was owing to an essential defect in the natural powers of the soul: And the immediate, almighty energy of the divine Spirit is as necessary to remove this darkness, and illuminate the mind, as if natural faculties were wanting. Therefore this illumination is constantly ascribed in the scripture to God, as the agent and cause in producing this effect. It is a common observation, in which all agree, that none are blinder than they who will not see. They have eyes, but see not. He who has eyes, and shuts them fast, and will not open them to admit the light, from an obstinate aversion from the light, is as much in the dark, as he who has no eyes; and the former can be no more made to see, than the latter, so long as his will is obstinately set against opening his eyes. And it may require the same power and agent to alter his disposition, and give him a contrary one, that is necessary to give eyes to him who has none. Yea, in the case before us, a greater exertion of power is necessary to form the single eye, than to create the natural faculties of the soul; for the former is effected in opposition to the whole strength of the will, and of Satan, who possesses the corrupt heart, and blinds the mind of them who do not believe; whereas there can be no opposition to the latter. Therefore this illumination is said in the scripture to be the effect of the exceeding great and mighty power of God. [588]

IMPROVEMENT

I. From the view we have now had of divine illumination, we are led particularly to reflect on the mistake many have made, in supposing that this saving light is communicated to the understanding, independent of the will or heart, and considered as a power distinct from it; that this light has its seat in the understanding, and belongs to that, and not to the will, the former, and not the latter, being the leading, governing power of the mind. This is not agreeable to the representation of the matter in the scripture, as has been shown. And this is not only unscriptural, but leads to dangerous and hurtful consequences.

It has not been uncommon to represent the moral depravity of man, to consist in the understanding being darkened, as a distinct thing from the moral disorders and corruption of the heart; and to speak of enlightening the understanding, and subduing the will, or renewing the heart, as two distinct and different operations. This tends to darken and confuse the subject of divine illumination, and places it in that, in which it does not consist, according to the scriptures. And it represents the blindness of men to things of the Spirit of God, as a natural defect, and not in the least criminal, since the understanding, as distinguished from the will or heart, is not capable of virtue or vice, or of any thing that is criminal. For whatever darkness there be in the understanding, which is independent of the will, and does not originate from that, it is not a moral disorder, but purely natural; and therefore cannot be blameable. This way of representing this matter has therefore, doubtless, led many to consider the darkness in which all unrenewed men are, with respect to the things of the Spirit of God, as being in no degree criminal: And many, if not most, who have considered themselves in this state of darkness, have viewed it only as an unhappiness, and not as their sin.

Others have supposed that nothing is necessary in order to enlighten men, and their becoming virtuous and holy, but to have light take place in the understanding, that the proper illumination of this, will influence and gain the will to a compliance with that which reason dictates to be truth, to be right and best. Of these, some suppose that nothing is done, in order to enlighten the understanding, and lead men to reason and judge right, but to set light before them by external application, in a way suited to excite the attention, &c. Others suppose a powerful divine operation is necessary to let that light and conviction into the understanding, which will effectually move the will to choose that which is right, and persuade the heart to love God, and embrace the gospel, &c. Both these really deny the moral depravity of man, either expressly or implicitly; at least, that the heart is totally corrupt. For if the will be always disposed and ready to comply with the truth whenever the understanding is convinced of it, and sees it; then the will is not depraved, there is no obstinacy and rebellion in the heart. All the defect is in the understanding, in not dictating the truth to the heart. But this defect in the understanding, however great it may be, is not a moral, but a natural defect: For, as has been shown, the understanding, considered as not including the will or heart, or the mere speculative faculty of the soul, is not a moral faculty, and is not capable of virtue or vice. According to this, the heart cannot be faulty, while it acts according to the dictates of the understanding, whatever they may be, which it is supposed always to do, and therefore never can be guilty of any moral evil: And the understanding, as such, and as distinguished from the will, is incapable of fault. Therefore there can be no such thing as moral evil, or sin; to be sure, man is not capable of any such thing.

It appears from what has been said on this subject, that all these suppositions are contrary to the representation which the scripture gives of this matter, and not agreeable to reason, or to fact and experience. They who thus set the understanding or intellect, considered as a faculty distinct from the will, first, as the leading faculty of the soul, by which the will is in all cases directed and governed, do certainly make a great mistake, and turn things upside down. The will is the only active faculty of the soul. The understanding, so far as it can be considered as a distinct faculty, and not implying any degree of will, is wholly passive, and not capable of action. Every motion and action of the mind of man is voluntary; and therefore is the motion or action of the will. All mental exercise originates in the will, which is the seat of all moral action.

Besides, they suppose what is in the nature of things absolutely impossible, and build their whole theory upon it, viz. That the understanding, independent of the heart, is capable of receiving or having a true idea of moral exercise, or of the real beauty and excellence of the things of the Spirit of God. Such ideas suppose taste and affection of heart, without which they cannot be perceived, or take place in the mind. This is as impossible, as that a blind man should have a true idea of the beauty of light and colours; or that a man may perceive the sweetness of honey, and be pleased with it, by mere reasoning upon it, or touching it with his finger, while he has not the least degree of taste or relish for it, as has been before observed.

II. From what has been said on this subject, other mistakes which have been made about divine illumination, are detected, and appear to be delusive and dangerous. Some have thought they were savingly enlightened, by their being led to see, in an unaccountable manner to them, an extraordinary external light and brightness; either by their bodily eyes, or in their imagination, which has affected them much. Or they have had their eyes opened, as they suppose, clearly to see

Christ on the cross, or seated in heaven; and heaven, and the inhabitants of it, have been seen by them, &c. All things of this kind, are as far from spiritual discoveries, as darkness is from light, and are mere imaginary conceptions, of which he who has the most depraved heart is as capable as any other person. And as they do not suppose a renewed heart, so they have no tendency to make it better.

Others have thought themselves divinely taught and illuminated, by having some new thing, which they call truth, suggested to their minds, by a voice from heaven, or some immediate impulse, which is not contained in the Bible. And not a few, instead of learning their duty from the Bible, have expected, and thought they have had light, and direction given to them immediately from heaven, to make known what they were to say and do: and have thought themselves directed, in all their actions, by some invisible, divine impulse. All these are not only entirely different from divine illumination; but are dangerous delusions; and have proved fatal to many who have depended upon them.

Imaginary ideas may attend divine illumination, and often do, in this very imperfect state: That is, a person may have a discerning heart given to him, by which he sees the saving truth; yet by the influence of his imagination, he may have many ideas imposed on his mind, which accompany the true light which shines in his heart But these mere imaginary ideas, are no part of the truth, which the enlightened mind sees; and therefore ought not to be regarded as such.

III. We are led by this subject, more particularly to reflect upon the total and very great criminality of moral blindness, which is opposed to divine illumination. This has been brought into view, in considering this subject; and it is of importance that it should be always remembered, believed and realized by every person. Since this darkness consists wholly in the sinful inclinations of the heart, it must be wholly sinful. And the greater, the more strong and fixed it is, the more criminal it must be. The necessity of divine influence and power, in order to remove this darkness, is so far from proving it no crime, that it is a demonstrative evidence that it is a very great crime; as it is so strongly fixed in the heart. We are, and must be, under obligation to understand and approve all that moral truth, of which our natural capacities are capable, and which we have opportunity and are under advantage to see. All that blindness and error which is contrary to this, and prevents our seeing it, is contrary to our obligation, a violation of it; and therefore altogether criminal. There is a great difference between a person who has no eyes, and therefore cannot see the light, it being naturally impossible; and another who has good eyes, but from an aversion from seeing, shuts them fast, and will not open them to admit the light. The former cannot be under obligation to see, or blamed for not seeing; the latter may, and it is wholly his own fault, that he does not see. The scripture represents moral blindness by this, and says, men have eyes, and see not, because they hate the light, and shut their eyes.

We are wholly blameable, and have no excuse for all our blindness respecting the things of the Spirit of God, and for every error and mistake into which we fall, concerning things of a moral nature; and the greater our blindness is, and the more gross and numerous are our errors and mistakes in these things, and the more clear the light is, which is set before us, the more inexcusable and guilty we are. Our Saviour says, "If the light which is in thee, be darkness, how great is that darkness!" And we are prepared now to say, if all this great darkness be wholly criminal, and that in proportion to the greatness of it, how great is our guilt!

IV. How reasonable is it that men should be called upon and commanded to open their eyes, and see, in a moral sense! It has been observed, that God does so, in the scripture. He says, "O ye simple, understand wisdom, and, ye fools, be ye of an understanding heart." [589] If men be wholly blameable for not seeing when God has given them capacity to see, and sets light before them, and their blindness be wholly wilful; no reason can be given why they should not be exhorted and commanded to do what they ought to do, and can have no excuse for not doing it, however fixed and obstinate they are in their blindness, and however far they are from a disposition, or moral power or possibility to come to the light, from their fixed and strong hatred of it; so that they never will obey, if left to themselves. It is of great importance that this should be well understood and believed, as it is necessary in order to our understanding the scripture, and our own character and blameableness.

END OF VOL. I.

Footnotes:

491. John iii. 16.
492. Mark xvi. 15, 16.
493. Rom. viii. 17. ix. 8. Gal. iii. 7, 26, 27, 29. iv. 28.
494. John vi. 53, 54.

495. John xv. 5.
496. 1 Cor. vi. 17.
497. John xvii.
498. Matth. xii. 33, 35.
499. Rom. iii. 9, &c.
500. Eph. ii. 10.
501. Tit. iii. 3, 4, 5.
502. Matt. vi. 22, 23.
503. Mark vii. 21, 22, 23.
504. James i. 18.
505. John iii. 8.
506. Phil. i. 6. ii. 13.

507. The total depravity of man, and the infinite odiousness and criminality of all sin, are so implied in all the leading truths in the Bible, that a thorough conversion, and a cordial acknowledgment of them, in the light of the divine character and law, is essential to belief and hearty reception of the most important doctrines of the gospel. And it will doubtless be found, on proper examination, that all the gross errors respecting the gospel, which are, or have been embraced, and propagated, have originated from ignorance of the law of God, and the nature and ill desert of sin, and an express or implicit denial of these.

508. Ezek. xxxvi. 26, 27.
509. 1 John iv.
510. Rom. xv. 1, 3.
511. John v. 30. vi. 38.
512. 2 Cor. viii. 8, 9.
513. Phil. ii. 4, 5, 6, 7, 8.
514. Chap. v. 43, &c.
515. Matt. xvi. 24.
516. 1 Cor. xiii.
517. James iii. 17.
518. Matt. xxii. 37, 58, 39, 40.
519. Isaiah v. 20.
520. Luke vi. 32.
521. 1 John iv. 9.
522. Luke vi. 32.
523. See Edwards on the Nature of true Virtue, Chap. vi.
524. Prov. iv. 19.
525. 1 Cor. ii. 14.
526. Eph. v. 8.
527. 2 Cor. iv. 3, 4.
528. 2 Thess. i. 7, 8.
529. Acts xxvi. 18. Col. i. 13. 1 Peter ii. 9
530. Heb. x. 32.
531. Deut. xxix. 4.
532. Isai. xliv. 9-18, 19, 20.
533. Rom. i 21. Eph. iv. 18.
534. 2 Cor. iii. l4, 15, 16.
535. John xii. 40.
536. Heb iii. 10.
537. 1 John ii. 9, 11.
538. Isaiah xlii. 18.
539. Eph. v. 14.
540. John iii. 18, 19, 20.
541. 2 Chron. i. 10, 11.
542. 1 Kings iii. 9, 12.
543. Jer. xxiv. 7.
544. John xvii. 3.
545. Psalm cxix. 34, 144.
546. 2 Cor. iv. 6.
547. Col. iii. 10.
548. Eph. iv. 23, 24.
549. 1 John iv. 7, 8.
550. 1 John ii. 9, 10, 11.

551. Matt. v. 8.
552. 1 John i. 5.
553. Chap. iv. 8.
554. 1 Cor. viii. 1, 2, 3.
555. Rom. x. 10.
556. John v. 44.
557. Matt. vi. 22, 23.
558. Mark vii. 21, 22, 23.
559. Matt. xx. 15.
560. Deut. xv. 9.
561. Prov. xxiii. 6, 7.
562. Prov. xxviii. 22.
563. Prov. xxii. 9.
564. Rom. xii. 8.
565. 2 Cor. viii. 2.
566. Chap. ix. 11.
567. Verse 13.
568. James i. 5.
569. John iii. 20, 21.
570. John vii. 17.
571. Philip. i. 9.
572. Prov. xxviii. 5.
573. Isa. v. 20.--All this is implied in what Hierocles, a heathen, has observed and asserted, viz. "The mind, destitute of virtue, cannot see the beauty of truth." "Spiritual understanding consists primarily In a sense of heart of spiritual beauty; I say, a sense of heart; for it is not speculation merely that is concerned in this kind of understanding: Nor can there be a clear distinction made between the two faculties of understanding and will, as: acting distinctly and separately, in this matter. When the mind is sensible of the sweet beauty and amiableness of a thing, that implies a sensibleness of sweetness and delight in the presence of the idea of it. And this sensibleness of the amiableness or delightfulness of beauty, carries in the very nature of it the sense of the heart; or an effect and impression the soul is the subject of, as a subject possessed of taste, inclination and will." Edwards on Gracious Affections. Page 163, 164. First edition.

574. This was perceived by a heathen poet, and expressed in the following words: Sed trahit invitam nova vis, aliudque cupido; Mens aliud suadet. Video meliora proboque: Deteriora sequor.-- Translated thus. "My reason this, my passion that, persuades; "I see the right, and I approve it too, "Condemn the wrong, and yet the wrong pursue."

575. John viii. 12. xvii. 3. 1 John ii. 10.
576. John iii. 3, 5.
577. Jer. xxiv. 7. 2 Cor. iv. 6.
578. Ezek. xxxvi. 26.
579. Heb. viii. 10, 11.
580. John vi. 45.
581. Matt. xvi. 17.
582. Rom. xii. 2.
583. Psalm cxix. 18.
584. 2 Cor. iv. 6.
585. 1 John v. 20.
586. 1 Cor. xii. 6.
587. Psalm xiv. 1.
588. Eph. ii. 19. 2 Thess. i. 11.
589. Prov. viii. 5.

www.ingramcontent.com/pod-product-compliance
Lightning Source LLC
Chambersburg PA
CBHW032042150426
43194CB00006B/396